PRINCIPLED SENTENCING

Books are to be returned on or before
the last date below.

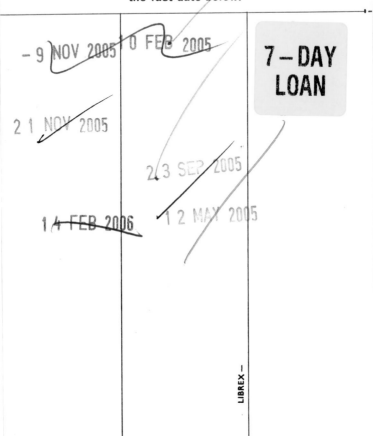

PRINCIPLED
SENTENCING

READINGS ON THEORY AND POLICY

Second Edition

Edited by

Andrew von Hirsch

and

Andrew Ashworth

·HART·
PUBLISHING
OXFORD

Hart Publishing
Oxford and Portland, Oregon

Published in North America (US and Canada) by
Hart Publishing c/o
International Specialized Book Services
5804 NE Hassalo Street
Portland, Oregon
97213-3644
USA

First published 1998; reprinted 1999, 2001, 2004

Hart Publishing is a specialist legal publisher based in Oxford, England.
To order further copies of this book or to request a list of other
publications please write to:

Hart Publishing, Salter's Boatyard, Folly Bridge
Abingdon Road, Oxford OX1 4LB
Telephone: +44 (0)1865 245533 or Fax: +44 (0)1865 794882
e-mail: mail@hartpub.co.uk
WEBSITE: http//www.hartpub.co.uk

British Library Cataloguing in Publication Data
Data Available
ISBN 1–901362–13–2 (paperback)

Typeset by Hope Services (Abingdon) Ltd.
Printed and bound in Great Britain on acid-free paper by
Biddles Ltd, King's Lynn, Norfolk

Preface

That the imposition of sentence is a decision of critical importance can scarcely be doubted. It determines how much the offender must suffer for his or her offence, and that suffering may include deprivation of liberty. When the facts of the offence are undisputed, as is often the case, the sentence is the primary decision to be made.

Before the 1970s in most English-speaking countries, however, the choice of sentence was little regulated. The law merely prescribed an (often-high) maximum for the permissible sentence, and occasionally a minimum. Within these broad bounds, little further guidance was provided, either in principle or detail. The determination of the sanction in the individual case was left to the discretion of the judge. In Britain (but not the U.S.), an appellate court could review the sentence; but its decisions attracted little attention.

The objectives of sentencing also received scant exploration. In the U.S., rehabilitation was supposed to be the paramount aim—but how treatment was to determine the sanction was usually left undetermined. In Britain, the idea of deterrence was also supposed to be important—but without much exploration of the *how*.

In the 1970s, sentencing theory and practice began to receive serious attention—and ideas changed. Faith in rehabilitation (at least, as the guide to choice of sanction) suffered a decline. Deterrence theory enjoyed a renaissance, but only a brief one. The "just deserts" philosophy, according to which the sentence is to be proportionate to the gravity of the crime, gained considerable influence. Some U.S. jurisdictions began experimenting with standards for guiding sentencing decisions. At the end of the decade, in 1980, Hyman Gross and one of the present editors put together an anthology of readings concerning these developments.[1]

In the 1980s, interest in sentencing theory continued to grow, with further elaboration of desert theory and renewed interest in prediction and in incapacitative rationales. Sentencing guidelines of different kinds were introduced in some American jurisdictions, while at the end of that decade two European countries—Sweden and England—enacted statutes enunciating principles for choosing sentence. At the beginning of the 1990s we put together the first edition of this work, which addressed some of these developments.

The 1990s have seen, in many jurisdictions, movement towards a populist "law and order" ethos favouring tough penalties. At the same time, by way of considerable contrast, there has been a renaissance of interest in reparative and restorative approaches to criminal justice. In the present volume, therefore, we have included not only up-to-date selections of readings on established areas of theory and policy, but also three new chapters to reflect more novel developments of the decade (notably restorative justice, critical sentencing theory, and "law and order" approaches). Each chapter opens with an introduction by one of the editors, designed to put the issues in perspective; then there is a selection of materials that we believe to be of particular interest; and, in conclusion, a bibliography of suggested further readings. We have included both American and British writings. In the interest of keeping the book within reasonable bounds, most of the selections have been edited, and some footnotes have been omitted.

We have made one significant but intentional omission: the death penalty. A civilized state, we feel, should not have this vile sanction at all, so there should be no occasion for the courts to have to decide when and why it should be imposed.[2]

We are indebted to Karen Shepherd and Amanda Savage for their assistance in preparing this edition, and to Richard Hart for his encouragement and guidance. Thanks are due to Kathleen Daly and to Nicola Lacey for advice on chapters 7 and 8 respectively. We are particularly grateful to Sue Rex for preparing an essay for inclusion in the volume, and to Antony Duff, Judith Greene and Michael Tonry for adapting pieces of work specially for the volume. Indeed, we are grateful to all the authors whose work appears here.

A.v.H.
Cambridge

A.A.
Oxford

January 1998

Notes

1. Hyman Gross and Andrew von Hirsch, eds., *Sentencing* (New York: Oxford University Press, 1981).

2. See, e.g., Jeffrie G. Murphy, "Cruel and Unusual Punishments", in his *Retribution, Justice, and Therapy* (Dordrecht: D. Riedel, 1979). See also Hugo Adam Bedau, *Death Is Different* (Boston: Northeastern University Press, 1987). For a survey of the use of the death penalty, see Roger Hood, *The Death Penalty* (Oxford: Oxford University Press, revised ed., 1996).

   The discussion of the death penalty in selection 2.2 is included only to suggest certain problems of deterrence theory.

Contents

1

Rehabilitation

Rehabilitation is the idea of "curing" an offender of his or her criminal tendencies. It consists, more precisely, of changing an offender's personality, outlook, habits, or opportunities so as to make him or her less inclined to commit crimes.[1] Often, rehabilitation is said to involve "helping" the offender, but a benefit to the offender is not necessarily presupposed: those who benefit are other persons, ourselves, who become less likely to be victimized by the offender. Traditionally, rehabilitation has consisted in offering counselling, psychological assistance, training, or support—but a variety of other techniques might be used. Some of these, such as aversive therapies, may be less than pleasant.

Success in rehabilitation is measured by recidivism rates: whether the offender has been induced to desist. It is thus linked, but not wholly correlated, with the aggregate incidence of crime—which depends also on how many *new* entrants to criminal activity there are.

Success in rehabilitation involves *changing* offenders—which is why it is not easy to achieve. The treatment is applied at time 1, in hope that the offender will desist after the treatment has been completed, at time 2. A difficulty is that at time 2, the offender faces renewed temptations and pressures that may eradicate any effects of the treatment.

During the first six decades or so of this century, rehabilitation was supposed to be an important aim of sentencing. Sometimes, it was said to be the *primary* aim.[2] The Model Penal Code, an influential piece of draft legislation written by the American Law Institute in the early 1960s, illustrates the significance given to treatment in sentencing. Relevant portions of the Code are excerpted in Selection 1.1. The sentence, according to the Code, is to be directed chiefly toward preventing further crimes by the defendant. Two themes are thus stressed: resocializing the offender, and separating him from the community if he is likely to offend again.

These two themes are apparent in § 7.01 of the Code, dealing with the grounds for imprisonment. According to that section, a sanction in the community—usually probation—is preferred.[3] Prison is warranted in two main circumstances, however. One (§ 7.01(1)(b)) is where treatment can more effectively be administered in a prison setting. The other (§ 7.01(1)(a)) is where the offender is thought likely to reoffend, is deemed unresponsive to treatment, and requires incapacitation. (This latter theme will be addressed more fully in Chapter 3 below.)

According to the Code—and this was typical of the traditional rehabilitative ideology—the gravity of the actor's criminal conduct was relatively unimportant. Someone convicted of a comparatively serious crime could be given a sentence in the community if that appeared to promote his or her reintegration into society. Conversely, someone convicted of a lesser offence could be imprisoned if he or she could better be treated in confinement. Proportionality—the notion that punishment should bear a fair proportion to the blameworthiness of the offender's criminal conduct—was deemed no ideal. One saw such "retributive" thinking as impractical and unprogressive, because it meant that some offenders would continue to be punished long after they had been successfully rehabilitated, whereas others would have to be released (having completed their "deserved" sentences) before they were cured. Some rehabilitationists took this view to its logical extreme, and held that the gravity of the offence should scarcely be considered at all.[4]

What also is noteworthy is the wide discretion granted to the sentencing judge in pursuing these aims. Within the (quite high) statutory maxima, the judge in the individual case is free to decide the severity of the sentence. The Code's provisions in § 7.01 are meant only to be principles the judge should consider. That discretion is linked also with notions of rehabilitation. Individual offenders are assumed to have differing treatment needs. The optimum sentence thus should best be decided in the particular case, not fixed in advance.

The Code, like other pre-1970s sources, is quite optimistic about treatment. It is assumed that there are known and effective therapies, both inside the institution and in the community, that can be applied to a wide variety of offenders. In the 1970s, that optimism began to fade.

How does one determine whether a treatment programme works? It is no proof of success that significant numbers of treated offenders later lead law-abiding lives—because they might have done so spontaneously (e.g., by virtue merely of having become older). One needs controlled experiments, in which recidivism rates for offenders who participated in a treatment programme are compared with those for similar offenders who have not participated.[5] Such experiments began to be made in earnest after the Second World War, and surveys of the results of numerous studies became available by the end of the 1960s.[6] The results were disappointing: few programmes appeared to succeed, and those that did so succeeded only for carefully selected subgroups of offenders.

Selection 1.2, by Stephen Brody, examines these findings. It has not been shown, he notes, that *nothing* works. Certain types of programmes have shown success—but only when applied to specified subtypes of offenders having certain identifiable problems or characteristics. Since treatment research was done on a limited range of treatment modalities, different methods might also succeed somewhat better. But programmes do not exist, he concludes, that can routinely and successfully be applied to the majority of offenders coming before sentencing courts. This raises serious questions about whether rehabilitation can serve as the primary aim of sentencing.

The decline of faith in rehabilitation, and its causes, is the subject of the next extract, Selection 1.3 by Francis Allen. This author, writing in 1981, attributes the growing scepticism about the rehabilitative penal ethic to three main sources: first, a general decline in belief in the malleability of human nature; second, growing awareness of the vulnerability of the treatment ethic to various forms of debasement; and third, disclosures of how little is actually known about the means to rehabilitation. Allen concludes that although experimentation with treatments is likely to continue, rehabilitation cannot now or in the foreseeable future maintain its earlier supposed role as a central aim of punishment or of sentencing policy.

Rehabilitationism, however, has by no means lost all its defenders. Some authors suggest that a revival of the treatment ethic would make punishments more humane and help combat "law and order" sentiment. Francis Cullen and Karen Gilbert advance such arguments in their 1982 book, *Reaffirming Rehabilitation*, a portion of which appears as Selection 1.4. The authors' essential argument is that rehabilitation carries a humanizing message better than other penal theories. While the aim of treatment admittedly is to prevent offenders from committing new crimes, the message is that such prevention can best be accomplished "if society is willing to punish its captives humanely and to compensate offenders for the social disadvantages that have constrained them to undertake a life in crime". Merely affirming the rights of convicted persons is a much weaker incentive to their decent treatment, the authors argue, because most people are concerned with crime prevention and not with justice or rights for offenders *per se*. Rehabilitation conveys the idea that crime prevention can best be achieved by responding to offenders' needs and treating them properly.

Selection 1.5, by Andrew von Hirsch and Lisa Maher, is a reply to arguments such as Cullen and Gilbert's. Whether and to what extent treatment is a suitable basis for punishment decisions, von Hirsch and Maher argue, cannot be resolved by sweeping assertions about the supposed humaneness of rehabilitation. One needs to take a look at the not so easy particulars, concerning *how* treatment considerations could decide sentences. The question of effectiveness still needs to be faced: while certain treatments may work for certain carefully selected subgroups of offenders, rehabilitative cures do not exist for the bulk of cases that appear before courts for sentence. If no known treatment exists for the run-of-the-mill car thief, burglar, or robber, how can rehabilitation possibly serve as the main basis for sentence?

The alleged humaneness of rehabilitation also needs closer examination, the authors suggest. Just why, and under what conditions, is a treatment-based sentence less onerous? The more promising treatments for drug offenders, for example, require quite intensive and protracted interventions. A treatment perspective may (and certainly did in the past) legitimise substantial intrusions into the lives of offenders.

Finally, von Hirsch and Maher suggest, the consistency of treatment-based sentencing with the requirements of justice—particularly, of proportionality—needs to be considered. Traditional rehabilitative schemes—most notably, the indeterminate sentence—flouted proportionality blatantly, and this was one reason for those schemes' demise. How are such problems to be avoided today? A possibility is to permit rehabilitative interventions only within certain bounds fixed by the blameworthiness of the criminal conduct.[7] If so, how are these bounds to be determined, and to what extent will they interfere with effective therapies? A more drastic solution would be to discard proportionality requirements entirely. But if so, how will manifestly unjust responses be avoided? Merely extolling rehabilitation, as Cullen and Gilbert do, will not make such uncomfortable questions go away.

During the 1990s, there has been a considerable revival of interest in rehabilitative techniques—especially those concentrating on improving offenders' reasoning skills; and some commentators have described these efforts quite optimistically.[8] These recent efforts are the subject of the final Selection 1.6 by Sue Rex. She does note a degree of progress in methods of rehabilitation. Her analysis contrasts strikingly, however, with Cullen and Gilbert's approach in Selection 1.4. Dr. Rex maintains that rehabilitative approaches must be capable of working if they are to be justifiable: that is, they must actually be capable of reducing the rate at which "treated" offenders return to crime. Appeals to the supposed humaneness or caring character of the treatment are not enough.

While Rex maintains that some interventions can succeed, the successful programmes tend to work only on selected offender subgroups. (In this regard, she echoes Brody's caution in Selection 1.2—regarding programmes' *selective* potential for success.) Rehabilitative efforts, she thus concedes, may not have much overall impact on crime rates. This cautious optimism is more likely to be sustainable than the sweeping claims, made by some rehabilitation advocates in the past, for treatments' potential for reducing crime.

The programmes which Rex discusses aim at building up the offender's capacity for moral reasoning and moral choice. This makes them more congruent with choice-based conceptions of sanctioning, such as those discussed in Chapter 4 below. Finally, Rex—unlike Cullen and Gilbert—does not feel that using rehabilitative approaches requires a rejection of notions of proportionality. Indeed, she favours fashioning rehabilitative interventions that can be accommodated within a sentencing framework that makes the seriousness of the criminal offence the central criterion for deciding the sentence's severity. Her rehabilitative model, then, is one designed to try to reconcile interests in "offender reform" and "justice"— while at the same time recognizing the potential tensions between these objectives.

A.v.H.

Notes

1. Or, possibly, to commit crimes of a less serious nature than the offender would have perpetrated in the absence of treatment.
2. See e.g., National Congress on Penitentiary and Reformatory Discipline, "Statement of Principles", 1871, reprinted in H. Gross and A. von Hirsch, eds., *Sentencing* (New York: Oxford University Press, 1981), 52–6.
3. When the person is put on probation, the court is to impose such conditions "as it deems necessary to insure that he will lead a law-abiding life or [as are] likely to assist him to do so". Model Penal Code § 301.1(1). The section then lists a number of permissible conditions of probation, the last of which is "any other condition reasonably related to the rehabilitation of the defendant and not unduly restrictive of his liberty or incompatible with his freedom of conscience": § 301.1(2)(1). The rehabilitative flavour of these provisions is evident.
4. See, e.g., the 1972 edition of the Model Sentencing Act, reproduced in Selection 3.1 below. The Act gives little or no weight to the gravity of the offence in normal sentences and states in § 1 that "sentences should not be based upon revenge and retribution".

5. For a summary of experimental techniques, see, e.g., Roger Hood and Richard Sparks, *Key Issues in Criminology* (London: Weidenfeld and Nicolson, 1970), ch. 7.

6. The most noted of these is Douglas Lipton, Robert Martinson, and Judith Wilks, *The Effectiveness of Correctional Treatment* (New York: Praeger, 1975). For other analyses, see Suggestions for Further Reading, below.

7. For the "pros" and "cons" of such an approach, see Selections 4.4, 4.5, 6.4, 6.5 below.

8. See, e.g., J. McGuire, *What Works: Reducing Reoffending* (Chichester: Wiley, 1995). For more on newer rehabilitative techniques, see Suggestions for Further Reading, and also the notes to Selection 1.6.

1.1

The Model Penal Code

Section 7.01. Criteria for Withholding Sentence of Imprisonment and for Placing Defendant on Probation.

(1) The Court shall deal with a person who has been convicted of a crime without imposing sentence of imprisonment unless, having regard to the nature and circumstances of the crime and the history, character, and condition of the defendant, it is of the opinion that his imprisonment is necessary for protection of the public because:

(a)   there is undue risk that during the period of a suspended sentence or probation the defendant will commit another crime; or
(b)   the defendant is in need of correctional treatment that can be provided most effectively by his commitment to an institution; or
(c)   a lesser sentence will depreciate the seriousness of the defendant's crime.

(2) The following grounds, while not controlling the discretion of the Court, shall be accorded weight in favour of withholding sentence of imprisonment:

(a)   the defendant's criminal conduct neither caused nor threatened serious harm;
(b)   the defendant did not contemplate that his criminal conduct would cause or threaten serious harm;
(c)   the defendant acted under a strong provocation;
(d)   there were substantial grounds tending to excuse or justify the defendant's criminal conduct, though failing to establish a defense;
(e)   the victim of the defendant's criminal conduct induced or facilitated its commission;
(f)   the defendant has compensated or will compensate the victim of his criminal conduct for the damage or injury that he sustained;

From the American Law Institute, *Model Penal Code* (Philadelphia: American Law Institute, 1962). Copyright © 1962 by The American Law Institute. Reprinted by permission.

(g)   the defendant has no history of prior delinquency or criminal activity or has led a law-abiding life for a substantial period of time before the commission of the present crime;

(h)   the defendant's criminal conduct was the result of circumstances unlikely to recur;

(i)   the character and attitudes of the defendant indicate that he is unlikely to commit another crime;

(j)   the defendant is particularly likely to respond affirmatively to probationary treatment;

(k)   the imprisonment of the defendant would entail excessive hardship to himself or his dependents.

(3) When a person who has been convicted of a crime is not sentenced to imprisonment, the Court shall place him on probation if he is in need of the supervision, guidance, assistance, or direction that the probation service can provide.

Comment

1. The draft is based upon the view that suspension of sentence or probation may be appropriate dispositions on conviction of any offense, unless of course a mandatory sentence . . . is prescribed. Vesting such large discretion in the Court invites the effort, however, to formulate criteria to guide its exercise. Such guides, if properly defined, should serve to promote both the thoughtfulness and the consistency of dispositions, while distributing responsibility between the legislature and the court. . . .

2. Rather than attempt to state considerations making for and against a sentence of imprisonment, the draft enumerates the types of factors that may justify the Court in withholding a prison sentence, with or without probation. . . .

The factors enumerated in paragraphs (a) to (h) relate primarily to the question whether the defendant is a source of future danger to the public, but they have some bearing also on the relative necessity of a strong sanction for deterrent purposes.

1.2

How Effective Are Penal Treatments?

STEPHEN BRODY

Until quite recently, a belief that a solution to crime would eventually be found in better and more effective ways of improving, reforming, or treating criminals was solidly entrenched in the "liberal" tradition. But over the last few years a penological *volte-face* seems to have taken place, with rather astonishing ease and speed. To put it briefly, rehabilitation has come to be seen not only as an unrealistic and unrealizable aim, but one which is positively threatening to prisoners' rights and humanitarian principles and ultimately even harmful to offenders' chances of going straight. The ramifications of such a revised attitude, of course, extend very widely into all aspects of criminology and penology, and particularly into matters of sentencing and the disposal of convicted persons. The aim of this paper is to condense what is known from existing research into a few statements—to look at it through the wrong end of a telescope, as it were, rather than through a microscope, which is the customary viewpoint—and thus to consider what sorts of research programmes are needed from now on.

Is Sentencing Policy Ineffective?

A major contribution to the research literature on sentencing is Lipton, Martinson, and Wilks's (1975) encyclopedic survey of evaluative research into the effectiveness of correctional treatment. However, they missed out most English research, which has been included subsequently in a more modest review for the Home Office (Brody 1976). Along with earlier reviews, both these publications presented similar evidence which has encouraged a widespread conviction that no one type of sentence works any better—that is, is no more effective in preventing recidivism—than any other.

From Stephen Brody, "Research into the Aims and Effectiveness of Sentencing", (1978) 17 *Howard Journal of Criminal Justice* 133. Excerpted and reprinted by permission.

It has to be emphasized that even if it is true, research results have actually provided little evidence for such a belief. This is because, with one or two exceptions, only a very limited range of sentencing alternatives have ever been studied, and consequently only a relatively small proportion of the offender population has ever been considered. Most of the major North American evaluative studies have set out to establish the superiority of institutions or programmes, custodial or non-custodial, which attempt by psychological means to correct or cure offenders over traditional institutions in which repression and punishment are supposed to be the authorities' prime concern, and in which context even the divisions between custody and community care tend to become blurred.

There has been a concentration on innovative and experimental schemes and on the selected offenders—most of them young—who are involved in them. The bulk of ordinary criminals, who take up most of the courts' time, have aroused little interest.

Does Treatment Really Not Work?

One good reason for not completely abandoning a faith in rehabilitation is that a number of studies have shown that improvements *can* be effected in failure rates. What is strikingly consistent about these studies is that in all of them the treatment (whatever form it took) was effective only when it was applied to certain types of offenders, or when it was aimed at modifying such specific aspects of behaviour as addiction or aggressiveness. What is more surprising is that researchers have so rarely allowed for individual variations, or "interaction effects", in their experimental designs, but have expected one particular programme to work equally for all offenders and to provide a universal remedy. Martinson and his colleagues (Lipton, Martinson, and Wilks 1975) can fairly be criticized for underplaying results which pointed to individual variations (Palmer 1975).

There is an even better reason why treatment has so often been shown to have no effect, which is simply that none has been given. It is very often the case, if they are submitted to detached observation, that contrasted institutions or programmes are not very different in practice or in their impact on offenders, regardless of what facilities, staff–inmate ratio, or professional services one may claim against the other. At worst, the language of therapy is employed only in the service of good public relations or to disguise, wittingly or unwittingly, the true state of affairs that pervades correctional institutions and processes.

Even where treatment programmes may reasonably be said to have been properly instigated, there is a lot of confusion about what they are likely to achieve, and how. Much of this confusion can only be explained as springing from an unrealistic understanding of human nature, contaminated no doubt by a lingering equation between crime and psychopathology.

Research so far has on the whole confirmed what one would expect: that individual successes may sometimes be claimed by routine psychotherapy or counselling with intelligent, articulate neurotic offenders; by guidance in personal, social, and domestic matters among those hampered by incompetence in these spheres; by sympathy and encouragement for those unsure of their limits and capabilities; and by direct assistance and support for those weighed down by practical difficulties. But none of these approaches is appropriate for other than a minority of the offender population, whose misdemeanours reflect some real psychological maladjustment and not just their social "deviance".

Are Measures of Effectiveness Good Enough?

The generally disappointing results of research into the relative effectiveness of different sentences is sometimes blamed on the insensitivity of reconviction as a criterion for success. There is, certainly, some truth in this claim, and to try to overcome it, many researchers have looked also for qualitative differences in patterns of reoffending—that is, to see whether offenders given differential treatment differ in the number of times they are subsequently arrested, in the types of offense they commit, the types of sentences they get, in the time between release and the next conviction, and so on. By and large, none of these indices has been shown to discriminate any more tellingly than simple reconviction.

Much less frequently, rehabilitative effectiveness has been judged either by changes in behaviour and attitudes during the course of a sentence or by longer-term changes in personality and personal adjustment after release or termination. Although indices of behaviour during a sentence—such as absconding rates, number of disciplinary infractions, "unit-management problems", and so on—*have* generally been able to demonstrate differences between different institutions, variations may partly be accounted for by differences in standards of control and supervision. In any case, offenders' compliance with a regime tells us little more than that it is being operated efficiently. Measured changes in offenders' attitudes during their sentences can be more informative, if one accepts the validity of the measuring instruments. Such changes are by no means inevitable, partly for the same reasons that reconviction rates are so often unaffected by treatment.

Studies using post-sentence changes in social and vocational adjustment as criteria for evaluation have been least satisfactory, and the results are difficult to interpret. Studies of the long-term effects of probation on non-criminal behaviour, such as Lohman's in California (1967) and in the IMPACT Experiment in England (Folkard *et al.* 1976), have been unable to claim success.

Research into changes in attitudes, personality, and adjustment has done little more than to complicate the uncertainties already mentioned with regard to the effects of different sentences on reconviction rates. There is no obvious correlation between changes in attitudes and recidivism: in some studies improvements take place in one sense but not in the other, and if occasionally both improve, more often neither do.

On the other hand, measures of long-term adjustment have often been found to relate quite well to reductions in recidivism rates. For instance, there is a reasonable negative correlation between work adjustment and reconviction among young offenders, and it is offenders who are released to settled homes, sound marriages, and stable jobs who always have the best prognoses. Unfortunately, measures of both adjustment and reconviction often bear little relation to type of sentence or type of treatment, from which it may be concluded that favourable circumstances and incentives in his ordinary life play a much more important part in determining success than what happens to an offender in the course of his sentence. But more probably, what usually happens is that adverse outside circumstances or influences rapidly counteract any small psychological gains which might have been accomplished during a sentence, and former habits soon overpower what little extra stamina might have been built up. No follow-up measure, of criminal or any other sort of behaviour, has yet been able to overcome this difficulty and to indicate the relative *potential* advantages of different institutions, regimes, or sentences.

References

Brody, S. R. (1976) *The Effectiveness of Sentencing* (Home Office Research Study No. 35, London: H.M.S.O.).

Folkard, S. *et al.* (1976) *IMPACT Vol. II* (Home Office Research Study No. 36, London: H.M.S.O.).

Lipton, D., Martinson, R., and Wilks, J. (1975) *Effectiveness of Correctional Treatment* (Springfield, Mass.: Praeger).

Lohman, J.D., *et al.* (1967) *The San Francisco Project* (Research Report No. 11, Berkeley: School of Criminology, University of California).

Palmer, T. D. (1975) "Martinson revisited", 12 *Journal of Research in Crime and Delinquency*, 133–52.

1.3

The Decline of the Rehabilitative Ideal

FRANCIS A. ALLEN

The modern decline of penal rehabilitationism cannot be fully explained by the persuasiveness of the logical cases arrayed against it. Yet the criticisms are important, for in them may be found the assumptions on which contemporary efforts to recast criminal justice are based. Some modern reactions present very little of intellectual interest; they comprise essentially irritated responses to the prevalence of crime and offer only an all-encompassing faith in the efficacy of coercion and repression. Such a characterization, however, is in no way descriptive of the views of many who today oppose the rehabilitative ideal. The latter are troubled by the political implications of penal rehabilitationism and are sensitive to the conflicts built into a system of criminal justice that seeks to express simultaneously the values of human responsibility and the reform of offenders. Accordingly, attention needs to be given to the modern critique of the rehabilitative ideal.

The modern case against the rehabilitative ideal has been in the making at least since the years immediately preceding World War II. It derives from a variety of sources and was largely formulated before political movements in the late 1960s appropriated it for their own purposes. Although these critics share no common fund of assumptions, the modern critique of the rehabilitative ideal appears to rest on three principal propositions. First, the rehabilitative ideal constitutes a threat to the political values of free societies. Second—a distinct but closely related point—the rehabilitative ideal has revealed itself in practice to be peculiarly vulnerable to debasement and the serving of unintended and unexpressed social ends. Third, either because of scientific ignorance or institutional incapacities, a rehabilitative technique is lacking; we do not know how to

From Francis A. Allen, *The Decline of the Rehabilitative Ideal: Penal Policy and Social Purpose* (New Haven: Yale University Press, 1981). Copyright © 1981, Yale University Press. Reprinted by permission.

prevent criminal recidivism by changing the characters and behaviour of offenders.

The liberal political stance and penal rehabilitationism coexist in a continuing state of tension, even though the resulting unease is more acutely sensed in some periods than in others. From the liberal perspective, any system of penal regulation, however oriented, is at best a necessary evil—the necessity stemming from the presence in the community of those who unjustifiably subvert the interests and volition of other persons. The movement from penal incapacitation of offenders to their reform, however, introduces a new order of concerns; for efforts to influence by coercive means the very thoughts, feelings, and aspirations of offenders threaten trespass by the state upon areas of dignity and choice posited as immune by the liberal creed. One reason the tension between liberalism and the rehabilitative ideal has not always been seen as critical is that the means often employed in rehabilitative efforts have been such that, if at all successful, they require a considerable voluntary cooperative effort on the part of the subject. When, however, the rehabilitative effort moves from the use of devices like those of traditional psychotherapy to what have been called the extreme therapies—psychosurgery, aversive conditioning, and certain other forms of behavioural modification—the state employs rehabilitative techniques that typically impose feelings and perceptions on the subject that in a meaningful sense are not of his own making, techniques that one observer describes as "manipulating people inside the perimeter of their conscious defenses".[1] The liberal unease with such forms of rehabilitation reflects, not a Luddite rejection of scientific "advance", but rather an awareness that they constitute incursions by the state into areas of human freedom and autonomy believed to lie outside the proper province of state action.

The principles of consent and voluntarism derived from liberal political values suggest certain limitations on the methods that may legitimately be employed in rehabilitative efforts. The widespread disregard of these limitations, both in this country and around the world, constitutes one of the serious modern complaints about penal rehabilitationism.

The political implications of the rehabilitative ideal, however, encompass far more than the kinds of rehabilitative techniques employed. Regardless of the means applied, a range of problems emerge involving control of the discretion of public agencies, and these problems have proved persistent and disturbing. The issues are among the most frequently discussed in the recent legal literature on corrections.

Therapeutic theories of penal treatment have often conceived of crime as symptomatic of an affliction, but the nature of the disease and how it differs from other pathologies are generally obscure. Vagueness in the conception of the disorder is communicated, in turn, to thought about its cure. Much of the political unease engendered by this version of the rehabilitative ideal stems from its central conception. One immediate consequence of a rehabilitative regime is a drastic enlargement of state concerns. The state's interests now embrace not only the offender's conduct but, as Michel Foucault has put it, his "soul"; his motives, his history, his social environment.[2] A traditional restraint on governmental authority is the notion of relevance: the state is limited in its inquiries and actions to that which is pertinent to its legitimate purposes. But when there are no clear limits on what may be relevant to the treatment process and when the goals of treatment have not been clearly defined, the idea of relevance as a regulator of public authority is destroyed or impaired.

The assumption of the benevolent purpose of the rehabilitative regime and the highly subjective and ill-defined notions of how rehabilitation is to be achieved and of what it consists, generate other problems. One of these is the tendency of those engaged in rehabilitative efforts to define as therapy anything that a therapist does. Because such disabilities as loss of liberty and other privileges are defined as therapeutic, the officer's sense of self-restraint may be weakened. One consequence, frequently remarked, is the tendency of rehabilitative regimes to inflict larger deprivations of liberty and volition on its subjects than is sometimes exacted from prisoners in more overtly punitive programmes.

These, then, constitute part of the catalogue of political concerns that have been engendered by the rehabilitative ideal. Whether they or any part of them counsel the total abandonment of penal rehabilitationism or whether it is prudent to persist in rehabilitative efforts if forewarned of their perils, requires further consideration. For the moment, however, it is sufficient to say that the political concerns just discussed take on even greater seriousness when a second broad tendency of the rehabilitative ideal is considered: its tendency in practical application to become debased and to serve other social ends far removed from and sometimes inconsistent with the reform of offenders.

Understanding the phenomena of debasement is advanced if attention is first directed to the ways in which language has been employed by those initiating and administering programmes of penal rehabilitation. What is involved is more than the usual insistence on a technical vocabulary, but rather a marked tendency toward euphemism and obfuscation. What distinguishes the language of rehabilitation is the degree of faith reflected in the efficacy of label changes, the extraordinary gaps between the epithets employed and the commonsense realities that the words are intended to describe, the amorphousness of concepts central to the system of thought. In one place or another solitary confinement has been called "constructive mediation" and a cell for such confinement "the quiet room". Incarceration without treatment of any kind is seen as "milieu therapy" and a detention facility is labelled "Cloud Nine". The catalogue is almost endless. Some of the euphemisms are conscious distortions of reality and are employed sardonically or with deliberate purpose to deceive. The more serious distortions, however, are those that reflect the self-deception of correctional functionaries. The burgeoning of euphemisms and the insecure grasp on reality that their use often reveals, signal a system of thought and action under extreme pressure. They are symptomatic of factors contributing to the debasement of rehabilitative objectives in practical application.

Central among the causes of debasement is the conceptual weakness of the rehabilitative ideal. Vagueness and ambiguity shroud its most basic suppositions. The ambitious scope and complexity of its agenda make these characteristics comprehensible and perhaps inevitable. Ambiguities afflict the very notion of what rehabilitation consists. A consensus on the ends of rehabilitation sufficient to spark movements of penal reform may, however, camouflage wide diversities of orientation that became critical when institutional programmes are attempted.

Equally serious is the vagueness that surrounds the means to effect rehabilitation. Much that is most bizarre in the history of penal rehabilitationism stems from scientific ignorance about how changes in the behaviour of offenders are to be achieved. In general, scientific ignorance has not inspired caution in the devotees of the rehabilitative ideal. On the contrary, the very absence of knowledge has encouraged confident assertions and dogmatic claims. One consequence is the creation of expectations that are inevitably disappointed. As programmes fail, euphemisms and pretext burgeon. Among the groups most seriously disenchanted by this cycle are the inmates themselves. A profound obstacle to penal rehabilitation in the contemporary world is the cynicism of the prisoners engendered, at least in part, by such institutional charades.

This leads naturally to the third and final proposition in the critique of the rehabilitative ideal. The proposition is that there is no evidence that an effective rehabilitative technique exists, that we do not know how to prevent criminal recidivism through rehabilitative effort. The statement of the proposition that has received widest attention was that of Robert Martinson. "With few isolated exceptions", he wrote in 1974, "the rehabilitative efforts that have been reported so far have had no appreciable effect on recidivism".[3] One of the most important aspects of the

Martinson study may well be that its immediate and widespread impact constitutes a demonstration of public attitudes in the 1970s receptive to the conclusions stated.

In a remarkably short time a new orthodoxy has been established asserting that rehabilitative objectives are largely unattainable and that rehabilitative programmes and research are dubious or misdirected. The new attitudes resemble in their dominance and pervasiveness those of the old orthodoxy, prevailing only a few years ago, that mandated rehabilitative efforts and exuded optimism about rehabilitative capabilities. Those who resist the hegemony of the new orthodoxy have challenged the criteria of success imposed by the critics on rehabilitative programmes and research and have argued that the critics' own studies provide basis for at least moderate optimism about future prospects of rehabilitative attempts.[4] Some have suggested that the methods employed in the modern attack on the rehabilitative ideal are often more polemic and ideological in their nature than scientific.[5] Even though these controversies continue, it is not too soon for certain general observations to be made. Proponents of rehabilitative research have argued with considerable force that to the extent the modern critique of the rehabilitative ideal rests on scientific ignorance of many matters vital to rehabilitative programmes, the indicated response is not the abandonment of those efforts but, rather, the production of new knowledge. Yet the proponents share with the critics a profound dissatisfaction with most past examples of rehabilitative research and practice. They express an awareness of the complexities inherent in such endeavours that was typically lacking in the enthusiasm for penal rehabilitation even in the recent past. A new spirit of caution pervades claims about the rehabilitative potential of correctional programmes; and the era when penal rehabilitationism can be accepted as the dominant mode of crime control seems more remote today than at many times in the past.

What role is likely to be accorded the rehabilitative ideal in the emerging modern synthesis? One point seems clear: whatever functions are assigned to penal rehabilitationism in the remaining years of the twentieth century, they are likely to be peripheral rather than central to the administration of criminal justice. This is true not only because of the new awareness of the limited efficacy of rehabilitative programmes and the other factors making up the modern critique of the rehabilitative ideal, but also because even an effective programme of inmate reform contributes only tangentially to the strategy of public order. In that strategy the deterrence of the great majority of the population from serious criminal activity is always the consideration of first importance, not the rehabilitation or incapacitation of the much smaller number of persons convicted of criminal offences.

Notes

1. Neville, *Ethical and Philosophical Issues of Behavior Control* (Am. Assn. for the Advancement of Science, 27 December 1972) 4.
2. M. Foucault, *Discipline and Punish* (New York: Pantheon Books, 1977), at 19.
3. "What Works? Questions and Answers about Prison Reform", *Pub. Interest* 24, 25 (Spring 1974). See also Martinson, "New Findings, New Views: A Note of Caution Regarding Sentencing Reform", (1979) 7 *Hofstra I., Rev.* 243.
4. See, e.g., Palmer, "Martinson Revisited", 12 *J. Research in Crime and Delin.* 133 (1975). Cf. Martinson, "California Research at the Crossroads", (1976) 22 *Crime and Delin.* 180.
5. Gottfredson, "Treatment Destruction Techniques", 16 *J. Research in Crime and Delin.* 39 (January 1979).

1.4

Reaffirming Rehabilitation

FRANCIS T. CULLEN AND KAREN E. GILBERT

There can be little dispute that the rehabilitative ideal has been conveniently employed as a mask for inequities in the administration of criminal penalties and for brutality behind the walls of our penal institutions. However, the existence of inhumanity and injustice in the arena of crime control does not depend on the vitality of rehabilitation. Indeed, a punitive "just deserts" philosophy would serve the purposes of repressive forces equally well, if not with greater facility. It would thus seem prudent to exercise caution before concluding that the failure of the criminal justice system to sanction effectively and benevolently is intimately linked to the rehabilitative ideal and that the ills of the system will vanish as the influence of rehabilitation diminishes.

This line of reasoning is liberating in the sense that it prompts us to consider that the state's machinery of justice might well have been *more* and not less repressive had history not encouraged the evolution of the rehabilitative ideal. This suggests in turn that preoccupation with the misuses and limitations of treatment programmes has perhaps blinded many current-day liberals to the important benefits that have been or can be derived from popular belief in the notion that offenders should be saved and not simply punished. In this respect, the persistence of a strong rehabilitative ideology can be seen to function as a valuable resource for those seeking to move toward the liberal goal of introducing greater benevolence into the criminal justice system. Alternatively, we can begin to question whether the reform movement sponsored by the left will not be undermined should liberal faith in rehabilitation reach a complete demise. In this context, several major reasons are offered below for why we believe that liberals should reaffirm and not reject the correctional ideology of rehabilitation.

Admittedly, rehabilitation promises a payoff to society in the form of offenders transformed into law-abiding, productive citizens who no longer desire to victimize the public. Yet treatment ideology also conveys the strong message that this utilitarian outcome can only be achieved if society is willing to punish its captives humanely and to compensate offenders for the social disadvantages that have constrained them to undertake a life in crime. In contrast, the three competing justifications of criminal sanctioning—deterrence, incapacitation, and retribution (or just deserts)—contain not even the pretense that the state has an obligation to do good for its charges. The only responsibility of the state is to inflict the pains that accompany the deprivation of liberty or of material resources (e.g., fines); whatever utility such practices engender flows only to society and not to its captives. It is difficult to imagine that reform efforts will be more humanizing if liberals willingly accept the premise that the state has no responsibility to do good, only to inflict pain.

Now it might be objected by liberal critics of rehabilitation that favouring desert as the rationale for criminal sanctioning does not mean adopting an uncaring orientation toward the welfare of offenders. The reform agenda of the justice model not only suggests that punishment be fitted to the crime and not the criminal, but also that those sent to prison be accorded an array of rights that will humanize their existence. The rehabilitative ideal, it is countered, justifies the benevolent treatment of the incarcerated but only as a means to achieving another end—the transformation of the criminal into the conforming. In contrast, the justice perspective argues for humanity as an end in and of itself, something that should not in any way be made to seem conditional on accomplishing the difficult task of changing the deep-seated criminogenic inclinations of offenders. As such, liberals should not rely on state-enforced rehabilitation to somehow lessen the rigours of imprisonment, but instead should campaign to win legal rights for convicts that directly bind the state to provide its captives with decent living conditions.

However, we must stand firm against efforts to promote the position that the justice model with its emphasis on rights should replace the rehabilitative ideal with its emphasis on caring as the major avenue of liberal reform. Support for the principles of just deserts and determinacy has only exacerbated the plight of offenders both before and after their incarceration. But there are additional dangers to undertaking a reform programme that abandons rehabilitation and seeks *exclusively* to broaden prisoner rights. More importantly, the realities of the day furnish little optimism that such a campaign would enjoy success. The promise of the rights perspective is based on the shaky assumption that more benevolence will occur if the relationship of the state to its deviants is fully adversarial and purged of its paternalistic dimensions. Instead of the government being entrusted to reform its charges through care, now offenders will have the comfort of being equipped with a new weapon—"rights"—that will serve them well in their battle against the state for a humane and justly administered correctional system.

The rights perspective is a two-edged sword. While rights ideally bind the state to abide by standards insuring a certain level of due process protection and acceptable penal living conditions, rights also establish the limits of the good that the state can be expected or obligated to provide. A rehabilitative ideology, in contrast, constantly pricks the conscience of the state with its assertion that the useful and moral goal of offender reformation can only be effected in a truly humane environment. Should treatment ideology be stripped away by liberal activists and the ascendancy of the rights model secured, it would thus create a situation in which criminal justice officials would remain largely immune from criticism as long as they "gave inmates their rights"—however few they may be at the time.

Those embracing the conservatives' call for "law and order" place immense faith in the premise that tough rather than humane justice is the answer to society's crime problem. In the political right's view, unlawful acts occur only when individuals have calculated that they are advantageous, and thus the public's victimization will only subside if criminal choices are made more costly. This can be best accomplished by sending more offenders away to prison for more extended and uncomfortable stays.

Liberals have traditionally attacked this logic on the grounds that repressive tactics do not touch upon the real social roots of crime and hence rarely succeed in even marginally reducing criminal involvement. Campaigns to heighten the harshness of existing criminal penalties— already notable for their severity—will only serve to fuel the problem of burgeoning prison populations and result in a further deterioration of penal living standards. The strategy of "getting tough" thus promises to have substantial costs, both in terms of the money wasted on the excessive use of incarceration and in terms of the inhumanity it shamefully introduces.

It is clear that proponents of the justice model share these intense liberal concerns over the appealing but illusory claims of those preaching law and order. However, their opposition to repressive crime control policies encounters difficulties because core assumptions of the justice model converge closely with those found in the paradigm for crime control espoused by conservatives. Both perspectives, for instance, argue that (1) offenders are responsible beings who freely choose to engage in crime; (2) regardless of the social injustices that may have prompted an individual to breach the law, the nature of the crime and not the nature of the circumstances surrounding a crime should regulate the severity of the sanction meted out; and (3) the punishment of offenders is deserved—that is, the state's infliction of pain for pain's sake is a positive good to be encouraged and not a likely evil to be discouraged. Admittedly, those wishing to "do justice" would contend that current sanctions are too harsh and that prison conditions should be made less rigorous. But having already agreed with conservatives that punishing criminals is the fully legitimate purpose of the criminal justice system, they are left with little basis on which to challenge the logic or moral justification of proposals to get tough [but see Chapter 9, below—eds.].

In contrast, the ideology of rehabilitation disputes every facet of the conclusion that the constant escalation of punishment will mitigate the spectre of crime. To say that offenders are in need of rehabilitation is to reject the conservatives' notion that individuals, regardless of their position in the social order—whether black or white, rich or poor—exercise equal freedom in deciding whether to commit a crime. Instead, it is to reason that social and personal circumstances often constrain, if not compel, people to violate the law and unless efforts are made to enable offenders to escape these criminogenic constraints, little relief in the crime rate can be anticipated. Policies that insist on ignoring these realities by assuming a vengeful posture toward offenders promise to succeed only in fostering hardships that will, if anything, deepen the resentment that many inmates find difficult to suppress upon their release back into society.

Existing survey data suggest that rehabilitation persists as a prevailing ideology within the arena of criminal justice. This does not mean that treatment programmes in our prisons are flourishing and remain unthreatened by the pragmatics and punitiveness of our day. But it is to assert that the rehabilitative ideal and the benevolent potential it holds are deeply anchored within our correctional and broader cultural heritage. That is, rehabilitation constitutes an ongoing rationale that is accepted by or "makes sense to" the electorate as well as to criminal justice interest groups and policymakers. Consequently, it provides reformers with a valuable vocabulary with which to justify changes in policy and practice aimed at mitigating the harshness of criminal sanctions—such as the diversion of offenders into the community for "treatment" or the humanization of the prison to develop a more effective "therapeutic environment". Unlike direct appeals for inmate rights to humane and just living conditions that can be quickly dismissed as the mere coddling of the dangerous, liberal reforms undertaken in the name of rehabilitation have the advantage of resonating with accepted ideology and hence of retaining an air of legitimacy.

Liberal critics have supplied ample evidence to confirm their suspicions that state-enforced therapy has too frequently encouraged the unconscionable exploitation of society's captives. However, while the damages permitted by the corruption of the rehabilitative ideal should neither be denied nor casually swept aside, it would be misleading to idealize the "curious" but brutal punishments of "bygone days" and to ignore that reforms undertaken in the name of rehabilitation have been a crucial humanizing influence in the darker regions of the sanctioning process.

We have argued that rehabilitation is an ideology of benevolence that not only has precipitated reform movements that have tempered the harshness of punishments but also, as a persisting rationale for criminal sanctioning, retains the potential to be mobilized to justify future ameliorations of the correctional system. However, we are not insensitive to the abuse inherent in a system that links liberty to self-improvement but furnishes few means to secure this end. Under the practice of enforced therapy, the state ideally institutes comprehensive treatment programmes and in return demands that offenders take advantage of these opportunities and show signs of their willingness to conform. Liberal advocates of the justice model have argued that this link between being cured and being set free is coercive and must be broken. In place of enforced therapy which compels offenders to seek reform on the threat of longer stays behind bars, they assert that rehabilitation must become "voluntary".

We do not mean to imply that liberals should simply become resigned to accept state-enforced therapy as it is currently practiced—however despairing this alternative might seem—because it is the lesser of two evils. While we have argued for the advantages of trumpeting treatment ideology, we believe that it is equally important that liberal reform seeks to reaffirm rehabilitation in ways that negate its more abusive features. In this regard, a crucial flaw of state-enforced therapy is that it is imbalanced: the inmate has the obligation to be reformed in order to win release, but in the absence of sufficient pressure, the state has no real obligation to rehabilitate. It is thus incumbent upon liberals to attack this imbalance by exerting pressure on the state to fulfil more adequately its half of the bargain. This would involve undertaking a persistent campaign to expose the state's failure to meet its responsibilities and to institute policies that obligate correctional officials to supply inmates with the educational, occupational, and psychological services as well as the community programmes it has so long promised to deliver.

In short, we are proposing that liberals discard state-enforced therapy and embrace *state-obligated therapy* as an avenue of criminal justice reform. Since it has been tragically and repeatedly demonstrated that the state cannot be trusted through appeals to its good will to create uniformly meaningful treatment programmes, reforms aimed at obligating the state to rehabilitate must be sensitive to the need to restructure the prevailing interests in the correctional system that have long undermined the provision of treatment services to offenders.

1.5

Should Penal Rehabilitationism Be Revived?

ANDREW VON HIRSCH AND LISA MAHER

Penal rehabilitationism was in eclipse from the early 1970s to the middle of the 1980s. Treatment efforts seemed to offer only limited hope for success. Relying on treatment seemed also to lead to unjust results—for example, to excessive intrusion into offenders' lives in the name of cure.

Recently, however, there have been attempts at revival. Some researchers claim striking new successes in treatment techniques. These successes, Ted Palmer concludes in a 1991 survey of treatment methods, suggest that rehabilitative intervention has gained "increased moral and philosophical legitimacy", and that it is no longer the case that rehabilitation "should be secondary to punishment . . . whether for short- or long-term goals".[1] Some penologists—for example, Francis Cullen and Karen Gilbert—argue that a revival of the penal treatment ethic could help lead to a gentler and more caring penal system (see Selection 1.4 above). Interestingly, such arguments sometimes come from the ideological and political left—which had once been so critical of treatment-based punishments.

Reinstatement of a treatment ethic would raise a number of questions, however. How much more is known about the treatment of offenders now than was a few years ago? How often can treatment give us answers about how severely to sentence convicted offenders? Is treatment really as humane as it is made out to be? How fair is it to base the sentence on an offender's supposed rehabilitative needs? Rehabilitationism went into eclipse some years ago partly because it could not answer these questions satisfactorily. To what extent are better answers available today?

We approach these issues from heterogeneous viewpoints. One of us (von Hirsch) is a philosophical liberal and has long been an advocate of the desert model (see Selection 4.4 below). The other (Maher) has a fem-

This is an abbreviated and somewhat revised version of an essay that appeared in (1992) 11 *Criminal Justice Ethics* No. 1 and also in the 1st edition of this volume. Reprinted by permission.

inist orientation and is sceptical of a retributive penal ethic. In our present discussion of the new rehabilitationism, we will not be assuming another articulated sentencing philosophy. What we agree on are the questions, not the answers.

Questions of Effectiveness

During the late 1960s and the 1970s, critics of penal treatment were sometimes tempted to assert that "nothing works". The phrase now haunts them and confuses analysis. It assumes that the main problem of treatment is that of establishing its effectiveness, and that treatment can be declared a "success" once *some* programmes are shown to work. Both assumptions are erroneous. Even when treatments succeed, their use to decide sentencing questions raises important normative questions. And occasional successes are not enough.

The last large-scale survey and analysis of treatments, undertaken by a panel of the National Academy of Sciences,[2] is two decades old. It was distinctly pessimistic in its conclusions: when subjected to close scrutiny, few programmes seemed to succeed in reducing offender recidivism. Since then, there has been continued experimentation, and successes have been reported.[3] Some treatment advocates have suggested that such findings show that rehabilitation has been "revivified".[4]

Perhaps, however, caution is in order. The extent of recent treatment successes remains very much in dispute.[5] A source of continuing difficulty is that the "whys" of treatment (that is, the processes by which successes are achieved) are seldom understood. Without understanding the processes by which experimental programmes produce given outcomes, it is difficult to tell which features "work", and will continue to work, when programmes are extended beyond experimental groups and implemented more widely.

Programmes appear to have better prospects for success when they focus on selected subgroups of offenders, carefully screened for amenability.[6] Such a screening approach, however, necessarily limits treatments' scope. Perhaps this or that type of programme can be shown to succeed with this or that subgroup of offenders. Treatments do not (and are not likely to) exist, however, that can be relied upon to decide sentences routinely—that can inform the judge, when confronted with the run-of-the-mill robbery, burglary, or drug offence, what the appropriate sanction should be, and provide even a modicum of assurance that the sanction will contribute to the offender's desistance from crime. Even Palmer concedes

that recent treatment surveys do not "indicate that generic *types* of programmes have been found that consistently produce *major* recidivism
reductions", and that programmes that have positive effects for selected
offender subgroups "may have limited relevance to the remaining
[offender] subtypes—those which might comprise much of the sample".[7]
If treatment lacks such routine, predictable applicability, how can it serve
as a principal sentencing rationale?

Success depends, also, on the resources available for implementation.
The programmes that succeed tend to be well funded, well staffed, and
vigorously implemented. These features are easiest to achieve when the
programme is tried in an experimental setting. When the same programmes are carried out more widely, programme quality tends to deteri-
orate. Gendreau and Ross admit that "[we are] still . . . absolutely
amateurish at implementing . . . experimentally demonstrated programmes
within . . . systems provided *routinely* by government".[8]

Questions of Humaneness

Some new advocates of penal rehabilitationism, such as Cullen and
Gilbert, stress its humaneness. Reemphasizing treatment, they assert, is
humane because it is more caring: it looks to the needs of the offender,
rather than seeking merely to punish or prevent (see Selection 1.4 above).
Is it true that rehabilitation is concerned chiefly with the offender's own
needs? That depends on whether one is speaking of social service or of
measures aimed at recidivism prevention.

Social service is benevolent in intent, if not always in actual application:
the aim is to help the offender lead a less deprived life. It can sometimes
be achieved by fairly modest interventions: the unskilled offender, for
example, might be taught skills that make him better able to cope.
Providing these services is, we agree, desirable, although it is far from clear
to what extent they reduce recidivism. The offender who is taught to read
will not necessarily desist from crime as a result.

Treatment programmes, however, seldom aim merely at social service.
The objective, instead, is recidivism prevention: protecting *us* against
future depredations on the offender's part. To accomplish that crime-preventive aim, the intervention may well have to be more drastic. It will take
more to get the drug-abusing robber to stop committing further robberies
than to teach him or her a skill. (A review of current research suggests
that the best indicator of successful drug treatment outcomes is length of
time in treatment.)[9] To describe such strategies as intrinsically humane or

caring is misleading: it confuses humanitarian concerns with treatment-as-crime-prevention.

Cullen and Gilbert admit this last point—that rehabilitation is aimed at recidivism prevention. They argue, however, that few people care much about being humane or benevolent to convicted criminals as an end in itself. Rehabilitationism, they argue, offers a more attractive reason—a crime-preventive one—for decent penal policies. There is something circular about this argument. It assumes that rehabilitative punishments *are* capable of reducing crime significantly, or at least that people will believe they are. And it assumes that treatment-oriented punishments are inherently gentle.

Are rehabilitative responses intrinsically less onerous? Not necessarily. Consider offenders convicted of crimes of intermediate or lesser gravity. A proportionate sanction for such offenses should be of no more than moderate severity (see Selection 6.4). What of a rehabilitative response? That would depend on how much intervention, and how long, is required to alter the offender's criminal propensities—and to succeed, the intervention may have to be quite substantial (as in the just-noted case of drug treatments).

A rehabilitative ethic also tends to shift attention from the offender's actual criminal conduct to his or her lifestyle or personal characteristics. For example, the cultural presumption that women are less "rational" often results in their lawbreaking being perceived as symptomatic of social (or biological) pathology. Women found guilty of relatively minor offenses thus are readily subjected to substantial treatment interventions.[10] Concerns about offenders' attitudes may elicit intrusive responses aimed at "correcting" individual ways of thinking and feeling.

Cullen and Gilbert, and some other new rehabilitationists, argue for a return to a treatment model, on grounds that other models (e.g., desert) have led to harsh results. How supportable are such claims? The severity or leniency with which a given sentencing philosophy is implemented will vary with the manner of its implementation and the criminal justice politics of the jurisdiction involved. That legislatively mandated "deserved" penalties were harsh in California seems attributable mostly to the character of criminal justice politics in that state, and to the legislature's having set the specific penalties. A similar philosophy led to different (and less harsh) results in Minnesota and Oregon, where both the form of guidance and the criminal justice politics were different.[11] Similar considerations apply also to rehabilitationism. Were California to return to a rehabilitative ethos, it is far from certain—given California's politics—how "humane" or benevolent the results would be.

Some new rehabilitationists' rejection of other models, such as desert, is based on a socially critical perspective: how the rationale is likely to be implemented in a society characterized by race, class, and gender inequalities. Such a critique, however, cuts both ways: one would need also to consider how rehabilitationism might be implemented in such an unpropitious social setting. It is fallacious to reject desert, for example, because of how "they" might carry it out, and then urge a treatment ethic on the basis of how "we" might implement it—that is, on the assumption of a much more supportive social system and legal culture than exists today. If rehabilitation is kinder, gentler, or better because that is how good people would implement it, then please tell us when and how, in a society such as our own, the good people take over.

While the new rehabilitationists are taking such a critical stance, they might also apply it to the rehabilitative ethic itself. Historically, the treatment ethos supported (as Michel Foucault has pointed out)[12] expansion of official and expert power/knowledge. If penal rehabilitationism is revived, what checks are there against a further proliferation of these powers?

Questions of Fairness

Criminal punishment, by its nature, condemns. The sanction not only visits deprivation but also conveys that the conduct is wrong and the offender to blame for having committed it. This holds whatever purpose is adopted for deciding sentences. Whether the sentence is based on the seriousness of the offender's crime or on his or her need for treatment, it will still imply something about the impropriety of the behaviour.

The basis for the principle of proportionality of sentence is the criminal sanction's censuring implications. Conduct that is more blameworthy—in the sense of involving greater harm and culpability—is to be punished (and thereby condemned) more severely; conduct that is less reprehensible is to be punished (and hence censured) more mildly (see Selection 4.4 below). Treatment, however, can seldom rely on criteria relating to the blame-worthiness of the conduct; whether the offender is amenable to a particular treatment depends, instead, on his or her social and personal characteristics. This creates the potential problem of fairness: one is using criminal punishment, a blame-conveying response, and yet deciding the intervention on the basis of those personal and social variables that have little to do with how reprehensible the behaviour is.

How serious is this problem? The answer depends, of course, on how much emphasis proportionality receives. A thoroughgoing desert conception would require the severity of the penal response to depend heavily on the degree of reprehensibleness of the conduct—thus limiting the scope for rehabilitative considerations to deciding among responses of comparable severity (see Selection 1.6 below). Not everyone supports a desert model, and some new rehabilitationists say they reject it. But then, it needs to be explained what role, if any, the degree of blameworthiness of the conduct should play.

One possibility would be to give proportionality a limiting role: the seriousness of the criminal conduct would set upper and lower bounds on the quantum of punishment—within which rehabilitation could be invoked to fix the sentence (see Selection 4.5 below). That kind of solution requires one to specify how much weight its desert elements should have—that is, how narrow or broad the offence-based limits on the sentence should be. Here, one faces the familiar dilemma: the narrower that one sets those limits, the less room there would be for treatment considerations; whereas the wider one sets the limits, the more one needs to worry about seemingly disparate or disproportionate responses.

Another possibility would be to try to dispense with notions of proportionality altogether.[13] Such a strategy, however, would pose its own difficulties. It would, first, have to be explained how it is justifiable to employ punishment—a blaming institution—without regard to the blameworthiness of the conduct. Or, if one proposes to eliminate the censuring element in punishment, it needs to be explained how this possibly may be accomplished. (The juvenile justice system, for example, long purported to convey no blame, but who was fooled?) Second, the absence of significant proportionality constraints could open the way for abuses of the kind that discredited the old rehabilitation—for example, long-term, open-ended intervention against those deemed to be in special need of treatment. (One thinks of the young car thief who was confined for sixteen years at Patuxent Institution in Maryland, because he refused to talk to the therapists.) One might hope that we are more sophisticated now about the therapeutic value of such interventions—but are such hopes enough without some *principled* restraint upon rehabilitative responses?

Finally, one could be more ambitious and think of replacing the criminal sanction with a wholly different set of measures. Nils Christie has argued that state punishment be supplanted by communitarian responses aimed at resolution of conflicts (see Selection 7.1 below). Some feminist writers have been exploring alternative conceptions of justice. This, however, would involve not just a change in sentencing philosophy, but a completely new set of institutions for responding to what is now termed criminal behaviour. One would have to consider whether, and how, these new institutions could afford protection against excessive, or seemingly unfair, intrusions. Whatever one thinks of such suggestions (and one of us has been sceptical of Christie's),[14] they constitute a different level of argument: one that concerns basic social and institutional change. These writers are not speaking, as the new rehabilitationists are, about retaining the criminal sanction and merely giving sentencing more of a treatment emphasis.

Concluding Thoughts

In offering the foregoing criticisms of the new rehabilitationists, we are not denying that treatment can have a legitimate role in a fair system of sanctions. How large that role should be depends not only on how much is known about treatment but also on what normative assumptions one makes—including those regarding proportionality.[15] Rehabilitation, however, cannot be the primary basis for deciding the sentence, nor can it be the rationale for supporting less harsh sanctions than we have today. If we want sanctions scaled down, as they surely should be, the main and explicitly stated reason for so doing should concern equity and the diminution of suffering.

The most dangerous temptation is to treat the treatment ethic as a kind of edifying fiction,[16] that if we only act as though we cared—and minister treatment to offenders as a sign of our caring—a more humane penal system will emerge. No serious inquiry would be needed, on this view, about the criteria for deciding what constitutes a humane penal system or about how a renewed treatment emphasis could achieve its intended effects or lead to reasonably just outcomes.

Such thinking is a recipe for failure. It is likely to cause the new treatment ethos to be rejected, once its specifics (or lack of them) are subject to critical scrutiny. And it could do no more good than the old, largely hortatory treatment ethic: create a facade of treatment behind which decision-makers act as they choose. Those who wish to revive penal rehabilitationism need to address the hard questions, including the ones we have tried to raise here.

Notes

1. Palmer, "The Effectiveness of Intervention: Recent Trends and Current Issues", (1991) 37 *Crime & Delinq.* 330, 342.

2. Panel on Research on Rehabilitative Effects, "Report", in *The Rehabilitation of Criminal Offenders* (L. Sechrest, S White, and E. Brown, eds., 1979).

3. See, e.g., Fagan, "Social and Legal Policy Dimensions of Violent Juvenile Crime", (1990) 17 *Crim. Justice & Behavior* 93.

4. Gendreau and Ross, "The Revivification of Rehabilitation: Evidence from the 1980s", (1988), 4 *Justice Quar.* 349.

5. Compare Lab and Whitehead, "An Analysis of Juvenile Treatment", (1988) 34 *Crime & Delinq.* 60, and Lab and Whitehead, "From 'Nothing Works' to 'The Appropriate works' ", (1990), 28 *Criminology* 405, with Andrews, Zinger, *et al.*, "Does Correctional Treatment Work?" (1990) 28 *Criminology* 369, and Andrews, Zinger, *et al.*, "A Human Science Approach or More Pessimism", (1990) 28 *Criminology* 419.

6. Palmer, "Treatment and the Role of Classification", (1984) 30 *Crime & Delinq.* 245; Sechrest, "Classification for Treatment", in *Prediction and Classification* (D. Gottfredson and M. Tonry, eds., 1987); see also, Palmer, above n. 1; and Selection 1.2 above.

7. Palmer, above n. 1, at 389.

8. Gendreau and Ross, above n. 4, at 345.

9. Anglin and Hser, "The Treatment of Drug Offenders", in *Drugs and Crime* (J. Wilson and M. Tonry, eds., 1990).

10. See, e.g., Pearson, "Women Defendants in Magistrates' Courts", (1976) 3 *British J. L. & Society* 265; Phillips and De Fleur, "Gender Ascription and the Stereotyping of Deviants", (1982) 20 *Criminology* 431.

11. A. von Hirsch, *Censure and Sanctions* (1993), ch. 10; see also Selection 5.2 below.

12. M. Foucault, *Discipline and Punish* (1977).

13. An attempt to develop an alternative penal theory that dispenses with desert principles is set forth in J. Braithwaite and P. Pettit, *Not Just Deserts* (1990), at 124–5. That theory, however, relies primarily on deterrence and incapacitation rather than treatment. In our view, the theory has manifold difficulties, discussed in von Hirsch and Ashworth, "Not Not Just Deserts: A Critique of Braithwaite and Pettit", (1992) 12 *Oxford J. Legal Studies* 83.

14. von Hirsch, "Review of N. Christie", (1982) 28 *Crime & Delinq.* 315. See also Selection 7.2 below.

15. For a limited suggested role of treatment considerations under a desert model, see Selection 1.6 below. For a somewhat expanded role under a "mixed" model, see N. Morris and M. Tonry, *Between Prison and Probation* (1990), ch. 7; see also Selection 6.5 below.

16. See Rothman, "Decarcerating Prisoners and Patients", (1973) 1 *Civil Liberties Rev.* 8.

1.6

A New Form of Rehabilitation?

SUE REX

Interest in rehabilitation has been rekindled since the decline in the 1970s which had led Francis Allen (see Selection 1.3 above) to conclude that it was likely to play only a peripheral role in the administration of criminal justice. This essay considers the factors which contributed to that renewed interest, and, in the light of it, the prospects for reconciling rehabilitation with the requirements of proportionality. To illustrate the new developments, I shall draw on examples from British probation.

New Interest in Rehabilitation

By the late 1970s, the "decline of the rehabilitative ideal" was having a profound effect on British probation practice, casting doubt on its "transcendent justification" of providing a scientific cure for crime.[1] In 1978, the head of the Home Office Research Unit challenged the Probation Service to show that its activities—described 20 years before as "the most significant contribution made by this country to the new penological theory and practice"—should not "simply be abandoned on the basis of the new accumulated research evidence".[2]

Probation's supporters sought for a time to preserve its activities, without relying on the idea of treatment: what they proposed retaining from the treatment era was the aim of keeping offenders out of prison.[3] But by the late 1980s, it was becoming clear that—in the perceived absence of effective treatments—the strategy of merely offering sentencers "alternatives to custody" was failing to restrain the continued growth in the prison population.[4] In these circumstances, it was not surprising that the Probation Service should, as it did, "rediscover" rehabilitation; this aim

This essay is published here for the first time. The author thanks Anthony Bottoms, whose ideas contributed to this essay.

received official endorsement in the Government's "Tackling Offending" initiative of 1988.[5]

As Stephen Brody's analysis (see Selection 1.2 above) suggests, rehabilitation research did not unequivocally support the "nothing works" conclusion.[6] More recently, the application of meta-analysis (allowing the findings of a number of different evaluations to be aggregated and evaluated as a group) has suggested that some forms of rehabilitative programmes can be effective in reducing recidivism, at least amongst certain types of offenders. Research into effectiveness has, nevertheless, been dogged both by methodological limitations and by the inherent difficulty of establishing consistent associations between particular types of intervention and subsequent behaviour, official knowledge of which is influenced by police and prosecution practice. McIvor rightly summarizes "our understanding . . . of what works, with which offenders and under what conditions, in reducing offending behaviour" as being "still embryonic".[7] Although some programmes have been found to reduce recidivism rates by up to 10–12 per cent, these tend to apply to relatively small subgroups of offenders; thus it would be premature to justify rehabilitative programmes on the basis of their impact on overall rates of crime.

It must be with an appropriate note of caution, then, that I attempt to draw from the research literature so far available four features which appear to offer some hope for rehabilitation (and which incidentally bear some relation to what is known about what causes and stops people from offending). I shall be suggesting that efforts to reduce offenders' impulsivity need to be combined with attempts to strengthen their community ties and help them resolve the social and personal problems which have contributed to their offending. These interventions can be reinforced by the development of probation practices that actively encourage "prosocial" behaviour.

Components of Successful Rehabilitation

Reducing impulsivity

What the literature on criminal careers tells us about the characteristics of persistent offenders—specifically, their impulsivity and poor abstract reasoning[8]—suggests that the "maturing" process by which they eventually abandon crime may be accelerated by improving their reasoning skills. This perspective has informed such programmes as "Reasoning and Rehabilitation", developed by Ross in Canada and described by McGuire as one of the most thoroughly developed cognitive-behavioural pro-grammes.[9] The aim of these techniques is to teach offenders to stop and think before acting, to consider the consequences of their actions for themselves and others, and to consider alternative ways of behaving. Evaluation of the STOP programme in Mid-Glamorgan suggests that reasoning-based approaches can be effective in reducing recidivism, though the effects may wear off over a period of time if this kind of work is not "complemented by attempts to assist [offenders] with the problems that they encounter in their everyday lives in the real world".[10] This brings me to the second matter which rehabilitative programmes need to address: offenders' social environments.

Strengthening community ties

The importance of people's social networks is a consistent theme in explanations of crime and desisting from offending. Reviewing the literature on after-care provision for released prisoners, Haines draws on control theory's notion of an attachment to societal bonds, to suggest that what matters in offenders' resettlement is the social environment to which they return: the support of family and friends, and a situation which fosters law-abiding attitudes and behaviour.[11] He argues that after-care services should focus on maintaining and strengthening the community networks which can help meet prisoners' employment and accommodation needs. But here, of course, lies a potential vulnerability: if a neighbourhood has undergone serious deterioration in employment opportunities and social structure, supportive community networks may not be available.

Research on criminal careers has also investigated the connections between social bonds and criminality. According to Sampson and Laub, attachments formed through marriage and employment during adulthood can help to reverse earlier involvement in deliquency.[12] Other studies suggest that the links between social development and a cessation of offending is complex: an offender might not necessarily form a relationship with someone who encourages social conformity; paternity might well be symptomatic of a chaotic, risk-taking lifestyle, rather than of "settling down".[13] Reporting ex-offenders' explanations in interviews that certain transitional events had exerted their effect by bringing about changes in their self-identity and sense of maturity and responsibility, Graham and Bowling suggest that a "moral dimension" needs to be added to the development of cognitive skills.[14] Evidence is emerging that probation officers can promote moral development by consciously adopting a particular supervisory style—a style which has become known as "pro-social modelling".

Pro-social modelling

"Pro-social modelling" is concerned with the process and manner of super-vision, and involves a departure from former non-directive approaches. The supervisor, working together with the supervised offender, develops a set of goals designed to promote desisting from crime. This involves identifying an offender's specific crime-related problems (such as heavy involvement with alcohol), and agreeing on steps by which these can be overcome. This strategy is, perhaps, most thoroughly explored in Christopher Trotter's Australian study—which found that breach and reconviction rates of groups supervised by Community Corrections Officers assessed as using "pro-social" methods (including reflective lis-tening and problem-solving) were significantly lower than those of similar groups of offenders.[15] The approach involves having the supervisor act as a positive role model, encouraging probationers in similar behaviour, and using praise and support to reward it. There is some evidence from research into British probation practice in support of pro-social modelling, though it is an approach yet to be systematically developed.[16] That research suggests that probationers want probation to be a "purposeful" experience, appreciate probation officers who show respect and concern for them, and are more ready to accept encouragement and direction from supervisors who do so—though practitioners may not always realize that this is the case.[17]

Legitimacy

Why might their treatment at the hands of "pro-social" supervisors make offenders more ready to accept such supervisors as role models, to com-ply with relevant requirements and to allow themselves to be positively influenced? It may be helpful to turn to political philosophy in order to gain an understanding of the mechanisms involved, and to David Beetham's arguments about the circumstances in which people will co-operate with figures of authority.[18] According to Beetham, a willingness to co-operate depends upon the "moral authority" of those in positions of power. Empirical support for this proposition comes from a slightly dif-ferent standpoint, in Tyler's surveys of members of the American public about their experiences of and attitudes towards the law.[19] These suggest that people's belief that decisions are fair, particularly that they have been *reached* fairly, will influence their longer term relationship with authority and generate a moral commitment to lawful conduct. So far, the concept of legitimacy has not been related explicitly to rehabilitative programmes, though there are hints from research into community service about the importance of legitimate modes of authority in helping to induce compliance.[20]

Rehabilitation within a Justice Model?

The new evidence about effectiveness has undoubtedly helped to strengthen the case for rehabilitation. However, it still leaves open the question whether, and how, rehabilitation could be accommodated within a sentencing framework that emphasizes proportionate sentences. Certainly, the criticized excesses of traditional "treatment" has caused advocates of the "New Rehabilitation" to distinguish its techniques from those of that earlier model. This is evident both in how it is suggested that rehabilitative aims should be pursued in practice, and in how it is proposed that they should influence sentencing decisions.

Turning first to the content of rehabilitative techniques, it is clear from my discussion above that there has been a recent focus on offenders' rational and moral agency: their decision-making and the moral aspects of their behaviour. Bottoms characterizes the shift from treatment to rehabilitation as a conceptual shift from the training or expert treatment of obedient subjects to persuading rational agents to co-operate in their own longer-term interest.[21] Raynor and Vanstone have been prompted by the new research evidence to explore how rehabilitative programmes with the specific object of preventing further offending can respect people's moral agency.[22] This notion of offender reform—that "tasks" directed at an offender's crime-related problems should be collaboratively defined on the basis of negotiation between the probation officer and the offender—has some congruence with the wider contemporary emphasis on individual choice.

What also concerned the critics of the traditional treatment ideology was the excessive power over offenders that it seemed to justify—in North America, for example, the indeterminacy of sentences imposed for reasons of treatment. Such objections were encapsulated in Norval Morris's maxim that "power over a criminal's life should not be taken in excess of that which would be taken were reform not considered as one of our purposes".[23] Many contemporary proponents of rehabilitation maintain that rehabilitative goals should be pursued within a framework of sentences proportionate to the gravity of the offence.[24] Raynor suggests that "no proportional sentence should be artificially inflated simply to make even a possibly effective programme available, since this would conflict . . . with the moral principle of fairness of treating like cases alike".[25] Hudson's formula of "desert-determined *amounts* of punishment, but rehabilitation-determined *content*",[26] as applied to non-custodial sanctions, actually seems close to the principles suggested by Wasik and von Hirsch (see Selection 6.4 below): that the choice between two or more equally "deserved" sanctions can be based on preventive grounds, without offending desert. It is such a model that England's Criminal Justice Act 1991 seeks to apply, in requiring the sentencer to select an order which is both *most suitable* to the offender (e.g., probation, if the aim is rehabilitative), and which imposes *restrictions on liberty* that are commensurate with the seriousness of the offence.[27] Doubtless, however, there is a degree of inherent tension between such "suitability" concerns and concerns about proportionate restrictions on liberty.

Some commentators, such as Peter Raynor, perceive an essential incompatibility between the underlying goals of rehabilitation and justice: justice is retributive, and backward-looking to the seriousness of the offence; whilst rehabilitation is consequentialist, and forward-looking to the prevention of crime.[28] But this assumes that a desert model, such as von Hirsch's, is entirely retributive and backward-looking, whereas it clearly contains forward-looking elements. Not only does von Hirsch include crime prevention as a general justifying aim of punishment, but his notion of censure has a communicative function which expects "some kind of moral response" from the offender.[29] Raynor believes that social justice requires a more contextualized theory of justice which takes account of offenders' social and economic circumstances, and acknowledges that offenders' choices are constrained by those circumstances. Von Hirsch does address the question of social justice, however, suggesting that social deprivation could conceivably be treated as reducing the culpability of individual offenders or taken into account in setting the overall penalty scale.[30] Are their theoretical positions so far apart? Perhaps the only way to find out is to bring some practical focus to the debate, by developing proposals for how ideas of social justice could inform decisions and actions in criminal justice.

Notes

1. W. McWilliams, "Probation, Pragmatism and Policy" (1987) 26 *The Howard Journal,* 97–121.
2. Respectively, Radzinowicz, L. (1958) *The Results of Probation* (London:

Macmillan) and Croft, J. (1978) *Research in Criminal Justice* (London: H.M.S.O.)—both cited by A. E. Bottoms, and W. McWilliams, "A Non-Treatment Paradigm for the Probation Service" (1979) 9 *British Journal of Social Work*, 159–202.

3.   According to McWilliams, above n. 2, the Radical, Personalist and Managerial Schools of probation practice each had their own reasons for adopting diversion as the primary goal: the Managerial school in pursuit of the efficient use of resources; the Radical school in the name of the working class struggle; and the Personalist school to assist the work that could be done with that person in the community.

4.   See A. E. Bottoms "Limiting Prison Use in England and Wales" (1987) 26 *The Howard Journal*, 177–202.

5.   See Home Office, *Tackling Offending: An Action Plan* (London: Home Office, 1988) setting out the Government's short-term strategy for the diversion of serious young adult offenders from custody by the provision of intensive probation programmes which would tackle offending and offer sentencers a credible alternative to a custodial sentence.

6.   Martinson stated in 1974 that "the rehabilitative efforts that have been reported so far have had no appreciable effect on recidivism", a conclusion he was later partly to retract (see R. Martinson) "What Works? Questions and Answers about Prison Reform" (1974) 35 *Public Interest*, 25; and R. Martinson, "New Findings, New Views: A Note of Caution Regarding Sentencing Reform" (1979) *Hofstra Law Review*, 243–58).

7.   G. McIvor, *Sentenced to Serve: Evaluative Studies in Social Work* (Aldershot: Avebury, 1992), p. 13.

8.   D. P. Farrington, "Human Development and Criminal Careers", in M. Maguire, R. Morgan and R. Reiner, eds., *Oxford Handbook of Criminolog*, 2nd edn. (Oxford: Clarendon Press, 1997).

9.   R. R. Ross, E. A. Fabiano, and C. D. Ewles, "Reasoning and Rehabilitation" (1988) 32 *International Journal of Offender Therapy and Comparative Criminology*, 29–36; J. McGuire, *What Works: Reducing Reoffending* (Chichester: John Wiley, 1995).

10.   P. Raynor, and M. Vanstone, "Reasoning and Rehabilitation in Britain: the Results of the Straight Thinking on Probation (STOP) Programme" (1996) 40 *International Journal of Offender Therapy and Comparative Criminology*, 282.

11.   K. Haines, *After-Care Services for Released Prisoners: A Review of the Literature* (Cambridge: Institute of Criminology, 1990).

12.   R. J. Sampson, and J. H. Laub, *Crime in the Making: Pathways and Turning Points Through Life* (Cambridge, Mass: Harvard University Press, 1993).

13.   See D. J. West, *Delinquency: Its Roots, Careeers and Prospects* (Aldershot: Avebury, 1982); J. Graham and B. Bowling, *Young People and Crime* (Home Office Research Study No 145, London: Home Office, 1982).

14.   Graham and Bowling, above n. 13.

15.   C. Trotter, *The Supervision of Offenders; What Works* (Sydney: Victorian Office of Corrections, 1993).

16.   J. Ditton, and R. Ford, *The Reality of Probation: A Formal Ethnography of Process and Practice* (Aldershot: Avebury, 1994).

17. See the major quantitative study by E. Sainsbury, S. Nixon, and D. Phillips, *Social Work in Focus* (London: Routledge, 1982); this study found that probationers wanted supervisors to show greater rather than less firmness, which they interpreted as demonstrating concern, and that probation officers much underestimated the importance of their encouragement to probationers.

18. D. Beetham, *The Legitimation of Power* (London: MacMillan, 1991).

19. T.R. Tyler, *Why People Obey the Law* (New Haven: Yale University Press, 1990).

20. See A. A. Vass, *Sentenced to Labour: Close Encounters with a Prison Substitute* (St Ives: Venus Academica, 1984). Vass notes offenders' preference for, and greater willingness to co-operate with, authoritative (but not authoritarian) leadership; see also McIvor, above n. 7, a study of community service in Scotland, in which offenders' appreciation of certain types of placements was associated with higher rates of compliance and lower rates of subsequent recidivism—pointing to the possibility that a positive experience may influence long-term behaviour.

21. A. E. Bottoms, "The Philosophy and Politics of Punishment and Sentencing", in C. Clarkson and R. Morgan, eds., *The Politics of Sentencing Reform* (Oxford: Clarendon Press, 1995).

22. P. Raynor, and M. Vanstone, "Probation Practice, Effectiveness and the Non-Treatment Paradigm" (1994) 24 *British Journal of Social Work*, 387–404.

23. N. Morris, and C. Howard, *Studies in Criminal Law* (Oxford: Oxford University Press, 1964), p. 175.

24. For a comprehensive, but concise, account of the desert model see A. von Hirsch, *Censure and Sanctions* (Oxford: Clarendon Press, 1993). For summary of the principles involved, see Selections 4.4, 4.6, 4.7.

25. P. Raynor, "Some Observations on Rehabilitation and Justice" (1997) 36 *The Howard Journal*, 253.

26. B. Hudson, "Beyond Proportionate Punishment: Difficult Cases and the 1991 Criminal Justice Act" (1995) 22 *Crime, Law and Social Change*, 74. This article is excerpted in part as Selection 4.9.

27. For discussion of these requirements, see A. Ashworth, *Sentencing and Criminal Justice*, 2nd edn. (London: Butterworths, 1995), ch. 10.

28. Raynor, above n. 25.

29. von Hirsch, above n. 24, 10. See also Selection 4.4 below.

30. von Hirsch, above n. 24, 108.

Suggestions for Further Reading

1. The Ideological Background of the Rehabilitative Sentence

Wootton, B., *Crime and the Criminal Law*, 2nd edn. (1981); Grupp, S. E. (ed.), *The Positive School of Criminology: Three Lectures by Enrico Ferri* (1968); Menninger, K., *The Crime of Punishment* (1968); Rothman, D. J., *The Discovery of the Asylum* (1971); Rothman, D. J., *Conscience and Convenience* (1980): Garland, D., *Punishment and Welfare* (1985).

2. Critiques of the Broad Discretion Involved in Rehabilitation-Based Sentencing

American Friends Service Committee, *Struggle for Justice* (1971); Frankel, M. E., *Criminal Sentences* (1972); Gaylin, W., *Partial Justice* (1974); von Hirsch, A., *Doing Justice* (1976), ch. 4.

3. The Effectiveness of Rehabilitative Programmes

Bailey, W. G., "Correctional Outcome: An Evaluation of Reports", (1966) 57 *Journal of Criminal Law, Criminology and Police Science* 153; Hood, R. G. and Sparks, R. F., *Key Issues in Criminology* (1970), esp. chs. 6–8; Lerman, P., *Community Treatment and Social Control* (1975); Robison, J. and Smith, G., "The Effectiveness of Correctional Programs", (1971) 17 *Crime and Delinquency* 67; Martinson, R., "What Works?—Questions and Answers About Prison Reform" (Spring 1974) *Public Interest* 22; Lipton, D., Martinson, R. and Wilks, J., *The Effectiveness of Correctional Treatment* (1975); Palmer, T., "Martinson Revisited", (1975) 12 *Journal of Research in Crime and Delinquency* 133; Brody, S. R., *The Effectiveness of Sentencing* (1976); Martinson, R., "New Findings, New Views: A Note of Caution on Sentencing Reform", (1979) 7 *Hofstra Law Review* 243; Panel on Research on Rehabilitative Techniques, "Report" in L. Sechrest *et al.* (eds.), *The Rehabilitation of Criminal Offenders* (1979); Walker, N., Farrington, D. P. and Tucker, G., "Reconviction Rates of Adult Males after Different Sentences", (1981) 21 *British Journal of Criminology* 357; Palmer, T., "Treatment and the Role of Classification: A Review of Basics" (1984) 30 *Crime and Delinquency* 245; Greenwood, P. W. and Zimring, F. E., *One More Chance: The Pursuit of Promising Intervention Strategies for Chronic Juvenile Offenders* (1985); Gendreau, P. and Ross, R., "Revivification of Rehabilitation: Evidence from the 1980s", (1988) 4 *Justice*

Quarterly 349; Lab, S. P. and Whitehead, J. T., "An Analysis of Juvenile Correctional Treatment", (1988) 34 *Crime and Delinquency* 60; Whitehead, J. T. and Lab, S. P., "A Meta-Analysis of Juvenile Correctional Treatment" (1989) 26 *Journal of Research in Crime and Delinquency* 276; Andrews, D. A. *et al.*, "Does Correctional Treatment Work?" (1990) 28 *Criminology* 369; Lab, S. P. and Whitehead, J. T., "From 'Nothing Works' to 'The Appropriate Works'" (1990) 28 *Criminology* 405; Fagan, J. "Social and Legal Policy Dimensions of Violent Juvenile Crime", (1990) 17 *Criminal Justice and Behavior* 93; Anglin, M. D. and Hser, Y., "Treatment of Drug Abuse", in J. Q. Wilson and M. Tonry (eds.), *Drugs and Crime* (1990); Palmer, T., "The Effectiveness of Intervention: Recent Trends and Current Issues", (1991) 37 *Crime and Delinquency* 330; McGuire, J., *What Works: Reducing Reoffending* (1995); Ross, R. R. and Ross, R. D., *Thinking Straight* (1995); Harland, A. T., *Choosing Correctional Options That Work* (1996); Mair, G., *Evaluating the Effectiveness of Community Programmes* (1997).

4. The Ethics of Treatment-based Sentencing

Lewis, C. S., "The Humanitarian Theory of Punishment", (1953) 6 *Res Judicatae* 224 (1953); Morris, N. and Buckle, D., "The Humanitarian Theory of Punishment: A Reply to C. S. Lewis" (1953) 6 *Res Judicatae* 231; Lewis, C. S., "On Punishment: A Reply", (1954) 6 *Res Judicatae* 519; Smart, J. J. C., "Comment: The Humanitarian Theory of Punishment", (1954) 6 *Res Judicatae* 368; Kaufman, A. S., "The Reform Theory of Punishment", (1960) 71 *Ethics* 49; von Hirsch, A., *Doing Justice,* above, ch. 15; Murphy, J. G., *Retribution, Justice and Therapy* (1979), part 3; Bottoms, A. E. and McWilliams, W., "A Non-Treatment Paradigm for Probation Practice" (1979) 9 *British Journal of Social Work* 159; Raynor, P. and Vanstone, M., "Probation Practice, Effectiveness, and the Non-Treatment Paradigm", (1994) 24 *British Journal of Social Work* 387; Hudson, B., "Beyond Proportionate Punishment", (1995) 22 *Crime, Law and Social Change* 59; Raynor, P., "Some Observations on Rehabilitation and Justice", (1997) 36 *Howard Journal of Criminal Justice* 248.

5. The Politics of Penal Rehabilitationism

Allen, F. A., *The Borderland of Criminal Justice* (1964); Rothman, D. J., "Decarcerating Prisoners and Patients", (1973) 1 *Civil Liberties Review* 8; Orland, L., "From Vengeance to Vengeance: Sentencing Reform and the Demise of Rehabilitation", (1978) 7 *Hofstra Law Review* 29; Cohen, S., *Visions of Social Control* (1985); Garland, D., *Punishment and Welfare*, above; Hudson, B., *Justice Through Punishment: A Critique of the "Justice" Model of Corrections* (1987); Garland, D., "The Limits of the Sovereign State", (1996) 36 *British Journal of Criminology* 445.

2

Deterrence

Deterrence, as an aim of sentencing, is one of a cluster of forward-looking aims which may be termed preventive. Also within this cluster are rehabilitation and incapacitation. What they share is the idea that punishment is warranted by reference to its crime-preventive consequences. These aims are usually advanced within a utilitarian framework, the justification for punishment and the measure of punishment being found in a calculation of its utility compared with the attendant disutilities. Utilitarian theory has a range of complex and sophisticated principles, which are best exemplified still in Jeremy Bentham's ingenious and detailed writings on punishment, excerpts from which appear in Selection 2.1. On a broader consequentialist canvas, deterrence and the other forward-looking aims may be subsumed beneath the overall aim of the reduction or prevention of crime. This is, in turn, part of a set of social and political principles for government. Crime reduction or prevention is best regarded as an aim of the criminal justice system as a whole, including sentencing and extending to other aspects such as pre-trial detention, policing, community projects to foster non-criminal behaviour among teenagers, and so on. If we confine ourselves to sentencing, we find that the prevention of crime, as an aim, may be pursued by a number of different methods: rehabilitation, which seeks to alter offenders' attitudes so that they desist from crime (see Chapter 1 above); incapacitation, which seeks to restrain the offender from reoffending for a given period (see Chapter 3 below); and possibly "vindication", which aims for punishments sufficient to ensure that citizens aggrieved by offences accept the state's response and do not seek to "take the law into their own hands".[1]

That leaves special deterrence and general deterrence, which are the subject of the readings in this chapter. Special (or individual) deterrence seeks to further the aim of crime prevention by setting the sentence so that it is sufficient to deter this convicted offender from reoffending. General deterrence seeks to further the aim of crime prevention by setting it so as to induce other citizens who might be tempted to commit crime to desist out of fear of the penalty. Deterrent theories reached the height of their

supporter

influence in the first half of the nineteenth century, inspired by Bentham's many writings on penal policy. Doubts about those theories' practicality and, in particular, misgivings about the resulting severity of punishments grew in the second half of the century, although in England there were some who continued to advocate a strong policy of special deterrence toward persistent offenders. The growing interest in rehabilitation became evident toward the end of the nineteenth century and in the early twentieth century with the beginnings of probation, the American reformatory schools, and the English borstal.[2] However, deterrent assumptions continued to exert an influence on sentencing, and in the 1960s the Norwegian penologist Johannes Andenaes rekindled the theoretical debate on general deterrence.[3] Despite several reports sceptical of efforts to identify and assess the magnitude of deterrent effects of sentences,[4] deterrence philosophies retain some influence on both sides of the Atlantic in penal practice (e.g., mandatory minimum sentences in the US and England, and high sentencing ranges for some crimes in England) and in penal theory (e.g., the writings of James Q. Wilson[5] and of Nigel Walker[6]).

A sentencing system based on special deterrence would need to ensure that courts had detailed information on the character, circumstances, and previous record of the particular offender, and would then require courts to calculate what sentence would be necessary to deter the particular offender. Punishments might have to be increased substantially for persistent offenders,[7] even despite adherence to the limiting principle of frugality or parsimony (that the court should always impose the least punitive measure available, since punishment is an evil in itself). And such a system would give no appearance of consistency, since each sentence would be specially calculated so as to influence the individual offender involved. *Dis ddi.*

In the utilitarian philosophy of Bentham, the special or individual deterrent approach is placed second in order of priority to general deterrence, and relatively little is heard of individual deterrence as a specific aim of sentencing in the modern debate. As appears from Selection 2.1(a), Bentham regarded punishment as an evil because it involves the infliction of "pain". It can therefore be justified only if there are beneficial consequences to outweigh it, and these are to be found in the deterrence of persons from committing offences. It is assumed that citizens are rational persons and that a well-constructed sentencing system will in general present them with a sufficient disincentive to crime. A modern version of this, *Support* forming part of the economic theory of law, will be found in Selection 2.2 from the writings of Richard Posner.

The essence of the economic theory of criminal behaviour is that a person will commit a crime if the expected net benefit of doing so exceeds the expected net benefit of behaving lawfully. In calculating the expected net benefit of offending, account must be taken not only of the likely punishment but also of the probability of being detected.[8] Economic theorists are not purely deterrence theorists: their concern is to promote economically efficient penalties, and this optimizing approach leads them to take account of the costs of law enforcement as well as the probable benefits and disbenefits from the offender's point of view. It may also lead economic theorists to conclude that, because of the differing impact of deterrence and/or the differing costs of enforcement, certain serious crimes should be punished less severely than certain less serious offences. This is regarded as problematic by some economic theorists, including the British writer David Pyle, who recognizes that one consequence is that:

> "the criminal justice system might produce strange incentives, inducing individuals to switch from less serious to more serious crimes. It may be necessary to structure punishments so that such an incentive cannot exist. In other words, an element of marginal deterrence should be retained".[9]

How convincingly does Posner deal with this issue in Selection 2.2? Pyle goes on to argue that sentences for attempted crimes should generally be set at the same level as for completed crimes, except in cases where the offender voluntarily abandons the attempt before completion, and that punishments should be escalated for repeat offenders. But there remain general questions about both the theoretical reasoning on which the economic approach to punishment is based, and the empirical foundations that are claimed for it (cf. the rigorous examination of deterrence research by Beyleveld in Selection 2.3).

Returning to deterrence theory, it should be noticed that general deterrent punishments may exert their influence over differing time periods: long-term deterrence may come about through the perpetuation of fear of punishment for certain types of conduct, although this may be difficult to disentangle from the effects of moral education and social reinforcement through the law, as emphasized in certain strands of Scandinavian legal philosophy;[10] medium-term deterrence may be associated with legislative attempts to influence social behaviour by increasing certain maximum penalties or introducing some mandatory minimum penalties; and then there are "exemplary sentences" occasionally imposed in discretionary sentencing systems, visiting one or more offenders with a disproportionately high sentence in order to deter potential imitators.

What are the objections to general deterrence as a basis for penal policy? A major objection has been that since its distinctive aim and method is to create fear of the penalty in other persons, it may sometimes require the punishment of an innocent person or the excessive punishment of an offender in order to achieve this greater social effect. The calculation may be either (1) "punish someone now in order to prevent a number of probable future crimes", the sacrifice of an innocent person being regarded as justified by reference to the number of probable future victims who are thereby spared; or (2) "punish this offender with exceptional severity in order to prevent a number of probable future crimes", the excessive punishment being likewise regarded as justified by reference to the number of probable future victims who may be spared. In both instances the avoidance of a greater future harm (to victims of probable future offences) is taken to justify the infliction of present harm which the "punishment" represents.

Deterrence theorists may attempt to avoid the reproach that they accept the punishment of the innocent, as by arguing that such practices would not be permitted because they are not "punishment". This, however, is unconvincing, because utilitarian theories do not include a principle for the distribution of punishment which restricts it to those properly convicted of an offence (see the argument of Alan Goldman in Selection 2.4). The objection is often expressed by recalling Kant's injunction that a person should be treated as an end in himself, and never only as a means, and it is important to notice the two elements of this formulation. One is that to regard citizens merely as numbers to be aggregated in an overall social calculation is to show no respect for the moral worth and the autonomy of each individual. This, then, is the liberal objection based on respect for individual autonomy and the separateness of persons.[11] The other element is that citizens should not be used *merely* as a means to an end—the limitation "merely" draws attention to the fact that punishment is, to some extent, a means to a social end. It is justified insofar as modern societies seem incapable of responding adequately to harmful behaviour without resort to punishment. The point here is that the punishment of any given individual cannot be justified solely by reference to wider social benefits. A theory of punishment should include both a link with the general social justification for the institution of punishment[12] and principles of distribution which restrict its imposition to properly convicted offenders and which place limits on the amount of punishment.[13]

What of the justification for "exemplary sentences", imposing an unusually high sentence on an individual offender for a given type of offence, in the hope of deterring potential imitators? Bentham would consider the justification for such a sentence by reference to its wider social effects—for example, on public respect for the law—but it is by no means certain that he would rule out such sentences, especially in a situation where there is apparent public concern about a particular kind of criminal behaviour. The objection to exemplary sentences is that the quantum of a convicted offender's punishment is being determined entirely by the expected future behaviour of other persons, not by his own past behaviour. This objection reaches into the very foundations of deterrence theory, for it raises the question whether punishments should be in some way proportional to offences. It will be seen from Bentham's rules 2 and 3, in Selection 2.1(b), that the gravity of the type of offence is indeed relevant to the amount of punishment which may be justified to restrain it. This, however, does not sustain the claim that utilitarians can treat proportionality as a limiting principle on the amount of punishment. For one thing, Bentham is referring to proportionality between the punishment and probable future offences rather than the particular crime for which this offender is now being sentenced. And, for another thing, each of Bentham's "rules" is merely one of several factors relevant to the overall utilitarian calculation: the effect of the proportionality principle may be smothered by the influence of one or more of the other rules, and not restored by the principle of frugality. Thus, if the general deterrence theorist has reason to anticipate an upsurge in a particular type of offence, this would seem to justify the imposition of an unusually high sentence on a particular offender, as an "example" to potential offenders and in order to deter them.

Leaving aside the problems raised by "punishing" the innocent and by "exemplary" sentences, how effective might we expect a general deterrent strategy to be in achieving its goals? The logic of deterrence has an intuitive appeal, but close study of the requirements of general deterrence and of the available empirical evidence suggests that the simple logic cannot be translated easily into social situations. Three interconnected propositions may be used as a basis for discussion here. First, criminologists have found it difficult to gauge, even approximately, the extent of any general deterrent effects of penalties. Second, the effectiveness of general deterrent strategies may vary situationally. Third, it is wrong to assume that the probable penalty for an offence is always or often the most powerful influence on people's behaviour. Let us examine these propositions.

There are various explanations for the difficulties which criminologists have experienced in conducting and interpreting general deterrence research. One is that it is hard to discover how often the threat of legal punishment (rather than any other motivation) turns people away from offending, since its successful operation means that those concerned are not readily discoverable in most instances. Another is that it is hard to find out about *marginal deterrence,* that is, how much extra deterrence is gained or lost by varying the severity of sanctions. This is an issue of crucial importance if sentence levels are to be set on deterrence grounds. Moreover, in respect of both these points, a statistical association which appears to establish cause and effect, such as the decrease of an offence rate following an increase in the penalty, may have an entirely different explanation: a good research project would need to attempt to eliminate such possibilities.[14] Another difficulty is that criminological research has not always been designed to separate deterrent effects from the results of other influences such as situational factors. As Deryck Beyleveld argues in Selection 2.3, the first step is to formulate a proper definition of general deterrence. Surveys of the available research have shown that there are relatively few studies which have genuinely identified the existence and extent of general deterrent effects flowing from the legal penalty,[15] and that it would be unsafe to generalize from these specific studies to broad policy prescriptions. Yet this does not mean that general deterrent effects never occur; the difficulty has been in establishing in what situations and to what extent they do occur. Beyleveld makes the point that only the most drastic sanctions are likely to have deterrent effects which are easily recognizable. In less extreme situations the main contribution of criminological research has been to point out the pitfalls of simple-looking explanations and expectations of human behaviour.

The second proposition is that general deterrence may only be effective in certain situations. This is not simply a repetition of the point that few studies have located a general deterrent effect. Rather, it is an assertion that the conditions must be favourable if general deterrence is to operate. This refers, moreover, less to the actual or objective conditions in the world than to the conditions as potential offenders believe them to be: deterrence must work through the mind, and so the reasoning should always be in terms of what potential offenders believe. Thus, the risk of detection for the crime must not be thought so low as to make the threat of the penalty seem too remote and thus readily discounted. The penalty which is meant to constitute the deterrent must be publicized adequately, so that it catches the attention of potential offenders. That penalty must also be perceived as a deterrent—which may rarely be a problem, but there are some forms of sentence (such as the suspended sentence) which may be intended as a deterrent but regarded by some as a "soft option". Another point is that those who may commit the particular type of offence must be likely to consider the risks rationally: one study of English burglars found that they rarely thought they would be caught for the present offence, that they were not worried about the consequences of being caught (either because the expected sentence was accepted as an "occupational hazard" or because they refused to think about the consequences at all), and that the rewards of the burglary were rarely known in advance.[16] These findings do not exclude the possibility that others were deterred, although they do shed some light on the thought processes of those for whom deterrence appears not to have worked and therefore suggest limits to its efficacy.

One might expect that for impulsive crimes the likelihood of rational calculation is even lower, while for some organized fraud or drugs offences the likelihood might be high. One study of weapon choice for armed robbery claims to have identified the operation of marginal deterrence, in that higher penalties turn many robbers away from the carrying of firearms.[17] Thus, general deterrence might be expected to work selectively, and only where the conditions (as perceived by potential offenders) favour it. Some of the striking apparent failures of general deterrence, such as the continued rise in "muggings" for several weeks after the widespread reporting of a 20-year custodial sentence on a "mugger" in Birmingham, England, in 1973,[18] can only be explained by the absence of one or more of the necessary conditions.

The third proposition amounts to another attack upon, or qualification of, reasoning from "common experience" or "common sense". One of the most frequent fallacies in popular discussions of deterrence *is* to assume that the nature and magnitude of the probable penalty are the only or necessarily the most powerful influence on a person's behaviour. There is evidence that other indirect consequences of conviction, particularly what the offender's family would think and the probability of losing one's job, exert a more powerful effect.[19] This shows the fragility of assuming that the criminal justice system and its penalty scale will be the most powerful motivating force in people's behaviour (cf. Posner in Selection 2.2).

As a practical sentencing strategy, general deterrence requires the imposition (or at least the threatened or reputed imposition) of as much punishment as is necessary to reduce the frequency of offences of a given type, preferring less painful means of crime reduction where they are available, and in any event calling for no greater punishment than the offence is "worth" in terms of its degree of harmfulness. One problem of adopting this approach in practice is that Bentham's intricate "rules of proportion" for punishment would often conflict in their application to types of crime: how should one decide on sentence levels for a relatively minor type of offence which it is difficult to deter and for a relatively serious type of offence for which the prospects of deterrence seem good? Bentham's rules 2 and 5—see Selection 2.1(b)—appear to restrict the appropriate punishment for minor offences, and yet in explaining rule 1 Bentham warns that if the punishment is insufficient to outweigh the motivation to commit the offence, "the whole lot of punishment will be thrown away". Is proportionality or maximum deterrence to be the dominant consideration in such cases of conflict?

A second problem is that we lack sufficient empirical information on which to base the calculations of penalties. General deterrence theory refers to the beliefs of potential offenders. We know too little about these, and what we do know casts some doubt on "common sense" assumptions about the effect of criminal sentences on human behaviour. Moreover, Bentham's version of the theory urges restraint in the use and amount of punishment at all times, as well as maintaining that to inflict too small a punishment is to cause misery in waste: to satisfy both these injunctions would be a formidable task even if one did have perfect information.

On one point, however, there is strong empirical evidence of general deterrence. This is that the absence of a punishment structure (police, courts, and sentences) substantially reduces observance of the law. The police strikes in Melbourne, Australia, in 1918, and in Liverpool, England, in 1919, show that overall offence rates increase significantly in the absence of such a structure in practice; the imprisonment of the Danish police force in 1944 had similar consequences. Thus, one fundamental justification for the institution of state punishment is that it exerts this overall restraining effect: it deters many offences which would be committed if there were no such institution. Thus, an advocate of proportionate sanctions—who seeks fairer principles for the distribution of punishments and for the calculation of punishments than general deterrence can offer—may still accept general deterrence as an integral part of the justification for why the institution of legal punishment should exist.[20]

A.A.

Notes

1. On the little-discussed concept of "vindicative satisfaction", see Jeremy Bentham, *Introduction to the Principles of Morals and Legislation* (1789), ch. 13, para. 1, and Sir Rupert Cross, *The English Sentencing System*, 3rd edn. (London: Butterworth, 1981), 128–30 and 139–40. See also the discussion of "Montero's aim" by Nigel Walker, *Punishment, Danger, and Stigma* (Oxford: Blackwell, 1980), ch. 1.
2. For detailed analysis of trends in penal practice and theory in nineteenth century England, see Sir Leon Radzinowicz and Roger Hood, *History of English Criminal Law: volume 5, The Emergence of Penal Policy* (London: Stevens, 1985).

3. See, e.g., "The General Preventive Effects of Punishment", (1966) 114 *U. Pa. L. R.* 649 (1966), and 'The Morality of Deterrence," (1970) 37 *U. Chi. L. R.* 649 (1970).

4. See this chapter's Suggestions for Further Reading, section 2.

5. e.g., *Thinking about Crime*, 1st edn. (1975); 2nd edn. (1983).

6. e.g., *Punishment, Danger, and Stigma* (1980), ch. 4, and *Sentencing: Theory, Law, and Practice* 2nd edn. (London: Butterworth, 1996), ch. 7.

7. For a nineteenth-century English approach of this kind, see the discussion of Barwick Baker's ideas by Radzinowicz and Hood, above n. 2, ch. 23.

8 See G. S. Becker, "Crime and Punishment: an Economic Approach", (1968) 67 *Journal of Political Economy* 169.

9 D. J.Pyle, *Cutting the Costs of Crime* (Institute of Economic Affairs, 1995), p. 36.

10. e.g. Karl Olivecrona, *Law as Fact* (1939).

11. See H. Morris, "Persons and Punishment", (1968) 52 *The Monist* 475.

12. For elaboration of this point, see the final paragraph of this introduction and also the introduction to Chapter 4.

13. See H. L. A. Hart, *Punishment and Responsibility* (Oxford: Oxford University Press, 1968), ch. 1.

14. For a vivid example, see Appendix 6 to the Report of the Royal Commission on Capital Punishment (1953), excerpted in the first edition of this book at pp. 75–6.

15. See this chapter's Suggestions for Further Reading, section 2.

16. T. Bennett and R. Wright, *Burglars on Burglary* (1984), chs. 5 and 6.

17. Richard Harding, "Rational-Choice Gun Use in Armed Robbery: The Likely Deterrent Effect on Gun Use of Mandatory Additional Imprisonment", (1990) 1 *Criminal Law Forum* 427.

18. R. Baxter and C. Nuttall, "Severe Sentences: No Deterrent to Crime?" (1975) *New Society* 11–13.

19. For England, see H. D. Willcock and J. Stokes, *Deterrents and Incentives to Crime among Boys and Young Men Aged 15–21 Years* (London: H.M.S.O., 1968); for the USA, cf. H. G. Grasmick and D. Green, "Legal Punishment, Social Disapproval and Internalisation as Inhibitors of Illegal Behaviour", (1980) 71 *J. Crim. L. and Criminol.* 325.

20. See further von Hirsch, *Censure and Sanctions* (1993), ch. 2., and the introduction to Chapter 4, below.

2.1

Punishment and Deterrence

JEREMY BENTHAM

2.1(a) *The Aims of Punishment*

When any act has been committed which is followed, or threatens to be followed, by such effects as a provident legislator would be anxious to prevent, two wishes naturally and immediately suggest themselves to his mind: first, to obviate the danger of the like mischief in future: secondly, to compensate the mischief that has already been done.

The mischief likely to ensue from acts of the like kind may arise from either of two sources,—either the conduct of the party himself who has been the author of the mischief already done, or the conduct of such other persons as may have adequate motives and sufficient opportunities to do the like.

Hence the prevention of offences divides itself into two branches: *Particular prevention*, which applies to the delinquent himself; and *general prevention*, which is applicable to all the members of the community without exception.

Pain and pleasure are the great springs of human action. When a man perceives or supposes pain to be the consequence of an act, he is acted upon in such a manner as tends, with a certain force, to withdraw him, as it were, from the commission of that act. If the apparent magnitude of that pain be greater than the apparent magnitude of the pleasure or good he expects to be the consequence of the act, he will be absolutely prevented from performing it. The mischief which would have ensued from the act, if performed, will also by that means be prevented.

With respect to a given individual, the recurrence of an offence may be provided against in three ways:

From "The Principles of Penal Law", in *The Works of Jeremy Bentham* (J. Bowring ed. 1838–43), 396.

1. By taking from him the physical power of offending.
2. By taking away the desire of offending.
3. By making him afraid of offending.

In the first case, the individual can no more commit the offence; in the second, he no longer desires to commit it; in the third, he may still wish to commit it, but he no longer dares to do it. In the first case, there is a physical incapacity; in the second, a moral reformation; in the third, there is intimidation or terror of the law.

General prevention is effected by the denunciation of punishment, and by its application, which, according to the common expression, *serves for an example*. The punishment suffered by the offender presents to every one an example of what he himself will have to suffer, if he is guilty of the same offence.

General prevention ought to be the chief end of punishment, as it is its real justification. If we could consider an offence which has been committed as an isolated fact, the like of which would never recur, punishment would be useless. It would be only adding one evil to another. But when we consider that an unpunished crime leaves the path of crime open, not only to the same delinquent, but also to all those who may have the same motives and opportunities for entering upon it, we perceive that the punishment inflicted on the individual becomes a source of security to all. That punishment which, considered in itself, appeared base and repugnant to all generous sentiments, is elevated to the first rank of benefits, when it is regarded not as an act of wrath or of vengeance against a guilty or unfortunate individual who has given way to mischievous inclinations, but as an indispensable sacrifice to the common safety.

2.1(b) *The Quantum of Punishment*

Rule 1. The first object, it has been seen, is to prevent, in as far as it is worth while, all sorts of offences; therefore,

The value of the punishment must not be less in any case than what is sufficient to outweigh that of the profit of the offence.

If it be, the offence (unless some other considerations, independent of the punishment, should intervene and operate efficaciously in the charac-

From *An Introduction to the Principles of Morals and Legislation* (1789), ch. 14.

ter of tutelary motives) will be sure to be committed notwithstanding: the whole lot of punishment will be thrown away: it will be altogether *ineffi-cacious.*

The above rule has been often objected to, on account of its seeming harshness: but this can only have happened for want of its being properly understood. The strength of the temptation, *cæteris paribus,* is as the profit of the offence: the quantum of the punishment must rise with the profit of the offence: *cæteris paribus,* it must therefore rise with the strength of the temptation. This there is no disputing. True it is, that the stronger the temptation, the less conclusive is the indication which the act of delinquency affords of the depravity of the offender's disposition. So far then as the absence of any aggravation, arising from extraordinary depravity of disposition, may operate, or at the utmost, so far as the pres-ence of a ground of extenuation, resulting from the innocence or benefi-cence of the offender's disposition, can operate, the strength of the temptation may operate in abatement of the demand for punishment. But it can never operate so far as to indicate the propriety of making the pun-ishment ineffectual, which it is sure to be when brought below the level of the apparent profit of the offence.

The partial benevolence which should prevail for the reduction of it below this level, would counteract as well those purposes which such a motive would actually have in view, as those more extensive purposes which benevolence ought to have in view: it would be cruelty not only to the public, but to the very persons in whose behalf it pleads: in its effects, I mean, however opposite in its intention. Cruelty to the public, that is cruelty to the innocent, by suffering them, for want of an adequate pro-tection, to lie exposed to the mischief of the offence: cruelty even to the offender himself, by punishing him to no purpose, and without the chance of compassing that beneficial end, by which alone the introduction of the evil of punishment is to be justified.

Rule 2. But whether a given offence shall be prevented in a given degree by a given quantity of punishment, is never any thing better than a chance; for the purchasing of which, whatever punishment is employed, is so much expended in advance. However, for the sake of giving it the better chance of outweighing the profit of the offence,

The greater the mischief of the offence, the greater is the expense, which it may be worth while to be at, in the way of punishment.

Rule 3. The next object is, to induce a man to choose always the least mischievous of two offences; therefore

Where two offences come in competition, the punishment for the greater offence must be sufficient to induce a man to prefer the less.

Rule 4. When a man has resolved upon a particular offence, the next object is, to induce him to do no more mischief than what is necessary for his purpose: therefore

The punishment should be adjusted in such manner to each particular offence, that for every part of the mischief there may be a motive to restrain the offender from giving birth to it.

Rule 5. The last object is, whatever mischief is guarded against, to guard against it at as cheap a rate as possible: therefore

The punishment ought in no case to be more than what is necessary to bring it into conformity with the rules here given.

Rule 6. It is further to be observed, that owing to the different manners and degrees in which persons under different circumstances are affected by the same exciting cause, a punishment which is the same in name will not always either really produce, or even so much as appear to others to produce, in two different persons the same degree of pain: therefore

That the quantity actually inflicted on each individual offender may correspond to the quantity intended for similar offenders in general, the several circumstances influencing sensibility ought always to be taken into account.

Of the above rules of proportion, the four first, we may perceive, serve to mark out the limits on the side of diminution; the limits *below* which a punishment ought not to be *diminished*: the fifth, the limits on the side of increase; the limits *above* which it ought not to be *increased*. The five first are calculated to serve as guides to the legislator: the sixth is calculated,in some measure, indeed, for the same purpose; but principally for guiding the judge in his endeavours to conform, on both sides, to the intentions of the legislator.

2.1(c) Cases Where Punishment is Unjustified

All punishment is mischief: all punishment in itself is evil. Upon the principle of utility, if it ought at all to be admitted, it ought only to be admitted in as far as it promises to exclude some greater evil.

It is plain, therefore, that in the following cases punishment ought not to be inflicted.

1.   Where it is *groundless*: where there is no mischief for it to prevent: the act not being mischievous upon the whole.

From *An Introduction to the Principles of Morals and Legislation* (1789), ch. 13.

2. Where it must be *inefficacious*: where it cannot act so as to prevent the mischief.
3. Where it is *unprofitable*, or too *expensive*: where the mischief it would produce would be greater than what it prevented.
4. Where it is *needless*: where the mischief may be prevented, or cease of itself, without it: that is, at a cheaper rate.

2.2

Optimal Sanctions: Any Upper Limits?

RICHARD POSNER

[Posner's theory is based on the assumption that criminals in general behave as "national calculators" or, to be more precise, that a sentencing strategy which is based on this assumption will have the greatest preventive power. On this view, which is developed further in the sentencing context and more generally in Posner's *Economic Analysis of Law*, 2nd edn. (1977), ch. 7, and *passim*), crimes are committed because the expected benefits outweigh the expected costs; or, at least, significantly fewer crimes would be committed if the expected costs were known to exceed the expected benefits. In these calculations, benefits include any economic gain from the offence and other non-economic satisfactions (e.g., in crimes of passion or revenge); and costs include not only the expected punishment but also the opportunity costs of the criminal's time, expenses necessary to commit the crime, etc. These last points are important in Posner's theory because they suggest other possibilities of controlling crime apart from increasing punishments on convicted offenders (e.g., increasing the cost or scarcity of guns, or redistributing wealth). The extract below, however, concentrates on the potential of the criminal sanction for controlling crime—eds.]

We have seen that the main thing the criminal law punishes is the pure coercive transfer, or, as it might better be described in a case of tax evasion or price-fixing, the pure involuntary transfer, of wealth or utility. In discussing what criminal penalties are optimal to deter such transfers, I shall assume that most potential criminals are sufficiently rational to be deterrable—an assumption that has the support of an extensive literature. We saw earlier that the sanction for a pure coercive transfer should be designed so that the criminal is made worse off by his act, but now a series of qualifications must be introduced. First, some criminal acts actually are wealth-maximizing. Suppose I lose my way in the woods and, as an alternative to starving, enter an unoccupied cabin and "steal" some food. Should the punishment be death, on the theory that the crime saved my life, and therefore no lesser penalty would deter? Of course not. The problem is that while the law of theft generally punishes takings in settings of low transaction costs, in this example the costs of transacting with the absent owner of the cabin are prohibitive. One approach is to define theft so as to exclude such examples; the criminal law has a defense of necessity that probably would succeed in this example. But defenses make the law more complicated, and an alternative that sometimes will be superior is to employ a somewhat overinclusive definition of the crime but set the expected punishment cost at a level that will not deter the occasional crime that is value-maximizing.

There is a related but more important reason for putting a ceiling on criminal punishments such that not all crimes are deterred. If there is a risk either of accidental violation of the criminal law or of legal error, an expected penalty will induce innocent people to forgo socially desirable activities at the borderline of criminal activity. The effect is magnified if people are risk averse and penalties are severe. If for example, the penalty for carelessly injuring someone in an automobile accident were death, people would drive too slowly, or not at all, to avoid an accidental violation or an erroneous conviction.

1. "Afflictive" Punishment

The foregoing analysis shows that there is a place in the criminal justice system, and a big one, for imprisonment; and perhaps for other non-monetary criminal sanctions as well. Since the cost of murder to the victim approaches infinity, even very heavy fines will not provide sufficient deterrence of murder, and even life imprisonment may not impose costs on the murderer equal to those of the victim. It might seem, however, that the important thing is not that the punishment for murder equal the cost to the victim but that it be high enough to make the murder not pay—and surely imprisoning the murderer for the rest of his life or, if he is wealthy, confiscating his wealth would cost him more than the murder could possibly have gained him. But this analysis implicitly treats the probability of apprehension and conviction as one. If it is less than one, as of course it is, then the murderer will not be comparing the gain from the crime with the loss if he is caught and sentenced; he will be comparing it with the disutility of the sentence discounted by the probability that it will actually be imposed. Suppose, for example, that the loss to the murder victim is one hundred million dollars, the probability of punishing the murderer is .5, and the murderer's total wealth is one million dollars and will be confiscated upon conviction Then his expected punishment cost when he is deciding whether to commit the crime is only $500,000—much less than his total wealth.

This analysis suggests incidentally that the much heavier punishment of crimes of violence than seemingly more serious white-collar crimes is not, as so often thought, an example of class bias. Once it is recognized that most people would demand astronomical sums to assume a substantial risk of death, it becomes apparent that even very large financial crimes are less serious than most crimes of violence. The same people who would accept quite modest sums to run very small risks of death would demand extremely large sums to run the substantial risks that many crimes of violence create, even when death does not ensue. This point holds even if the white-collar crime (say, violating a pollution regulation) creates a safety hazard, provided that the probability that the hazard will result in the death of any given person is low. Even if it were a virtual certainty that some people would die as a result of the crime, the aggregate disutility of many small risks of death may be much smaller than a single large risk of death to a particular person. This is the nonlinear relationship between utility and risk of death that I have stressed.[1]

By the same token the argument sketched above for capital punishment is not conclusive. Because the penalty is so severe, and irreversible, the cost of mistaken imposition is very high; therefore greater resources are invested in the litigation of a capital case. Indeed, if I am right in suggesting that the cost of death inflicted with a high probability (a reasonable description of capital punishment) is not just a linear extrapolation from less severe injuries, it is not surprising that the resources invested in the litigation of a capital case may, as one observes, greatly exceed those invested in litigation in cases where the maximum punishment is life imprisonment, even if there is no possibility of parole. The additional resources expended on the litigation of capital cases may not be justified if the added deterrent effect of capital punishment over long prison terms is small. But there is scientific evidence to support the layman's intuition that it is great.[2]

Capital punishment is also supported by considerations of marginal deterrence, which require as big a spread as possible between the punishments for the least and most serious crimes. If the maximum punishment for murder is life imprisonment, we may not want to make armed robbery also punishable by life imprisonment, for then armed robbers would have no additional incentive not to murder their victims. But arguments based on marginal deterrence for a differentiated penalty structure are inconclusive, particularly when the greater offence is a complement of the lesser one, as is often the case with murder. Moreover, the argument does not lead inexorably to the conclusion that capital punishment should be the punishment for simple murder. For if it is, then we have the problem of marginally deterring the multiple murderer. Maybe capital punishment should be reserved for him, so that murderers have a disincentive to kill witnesses to the murder, though again the number of such complementary murders may be less if the initial murder is punished severely.

An important application of this principle is to prison murders. A prisoner who is serving a life sentence for murder and is not likely to be paroled has no disincentive not to kill in prison, unless prison murder is punishable by death. Considerations of complementarity might argue for making out-of-prison murders capital also, since reducing the number of murders and the fraction of murderers in prison would reduce the occasions for prison murder. What makes little sense is to have capital punishment for neither out-of-prison nor prison murders, so that the latter becomes close to a free good. This is the present situation in federal law. Notice that varying the probability of apprehension and conviction cannot preserve marginal deterrence in this situation. The probability of apprehension and conviction in the prison murder case is close to one; the problem is that for the murderer already fated to spend the rest of his life in prison, there is no incremental punishment from being convicted of murder again.

Of course there is no realistic method of preserving marginal deterrence for every crime, although medieval law tried. It is a reasonable conjecture (if no more than that) that because more medieval than modern people believed in an afterlife, because life was more brutal and painful, and because life expectancy was short, capital punishment was not so serious a punishment in those days as it is today. Furthermore, because society was poor, severe punishments were badly needed and law enforcement was inefficient, so that devoting much greater resources to catching criminals would not have been feasible or productive. In an effort to make capital punishment a more costly punishment to the criminal, especially gruesome methods of execution (for example, drawing and quartering)[3] were prescribed for especially heinous crimes, such as treason. Boiling in oil, considered more horrible than hanging or beheading, was used to punish murder by poisoning; since poisoners were especially difficult to apprehend in those times, a heavier punishment than that prescribed for ordinary murderers was (economically) indicated.

The hanging of horse thieves in the nineteenth-century American West is another example of a penalty whose great severity reflects the low probability of punishment more than the high social cost of the crime. But the most famous example is the punishment of all serious (and some not so serious) crimes by death in pre-nineteenth-century England,[4] when there was no organized police force and the probability of punishment was therefore very low for most crimes.[5]

Death is not the only modern form of "afflictive" punishment. Flogging is still used by many parents and, in attenuated form, in some schools. The economic objection to punishing by inflicting physical pain is not that it is disgusting or that people have different thresholds of pain that make it difficult to calibrate the severity of the punishment—imprisonment and death are subject to the same problem. The objection is that it may be a poor method of inflicting severe but not lethal punishment. Just to inflict a momentary excruciating pain with no aftereffects might be a trivial deterrent, especially for people who had never experienced such pain; while to inflict a level of pain that would be the equivalent of five years in prison would require measures so drastic that they might endanger the life, or destroy the physical or mental health, of the offender. For slight punishments, fines will do. Incidentally, I do not mean, by omission, to disparage non-economic objections to "afflictive punishment". But this is an article about economics.

The infliction of physical pain is not the only way in which the severity of punishment can be varied other than by varying the length of imprisonment. Size of prison cell, temperature, and quality of food could also be used as "amenity variables". It may seem very attractive from a cost-effectiveness standpoint to reduce the length of imprisonment but compensate by reducing the quality of the food served the prisoners; the costs of imprisonment to the state, but not to the prisoners, would be reduced. The problem is that this would make information about sanctions very costly, because there would be so many dimensions to evaluate. Time has the attractive characteristic of being one-dimensional, and differs from pain in that it has more variability. But as a matter of fact, society does vary the amenities of prison life for different criminals. Minimum security prisons are more comfortable than intermediate security prisons, and the latter are more comfortable than maximum security prisons. Assignments to these different tiers are related to the gravity of the crime, and in the direction one would predict.

2. Imprisonment

If society must continue to rely heavily on imprisonment as a criminal sanction, there is an argument—subject to caveats that should be familiar to the reader by now, based on risk aversion, overinclusion, avoidance and error costs, and (less clearly) marginal deterrence—for combining heavy prison terms for convicted criminals with low probabilities of apprehension and conviction. Consider the choice between combining a .1 probability of apprehension and conviction with a 10-year prison term and a .2 probability of apprehension and conviction with a five-year term. Under the second approach twice as many individuals are imprisoned but for only half as long, so the total costs of imprisonment to the government will be the same under the two approaches. But the costs of police, court officials, and the like will probably be lower under the first approach. The probability of apprehension and conviction, and hence the number of prosecutions, is only half as great. Although more resources will be devoted to a trial where the possible punishment is greater, these resources will be incurred in fewer trials because fewer people will be punished, and even if the total litigation resources are no lower, police and prosecution costs will clearly be much lower. And notice that this variant of our earlier model of high fines and trivial probabilities of apprehension and conviction corrects the most serious problem with that model—that is, solvency.

But isn't a system under which probabilities of punishment are low "unfair", because it creates ex post inequality among offenders? Many go scot-free; others serve longer prison sentences than they would if more offenders were caught. However, to object to this result is like saying that all lotteries are unfair because, ex post, they create wealth differences among the players. In an equally significant sense both the criminal justice system that creates low probabilities of apprehension and conviction and the lottery are fair so long as the ex ante costs and benefits are equalized among the participants. Nor is it correct that while real lotteries are voluntary the criminal justice "lottery" is not. The criminal justice system is voluntary: you keep out of it by not committing crimes. Maybe, though, such a system of punishment is not sustainable in practice, because judges and jurors underestimate the benefits of what would seem, viewed in isolation, savagely cruel sentences. The prisoner who is to receive the sentence will be there in the dock, in person; the victims of the crimes for which he has not been prosecuted (because the fraction of crimes prosecuted is very low) will not be present—they will be statistics. I hesitate, though, to call this an economic argument; it could be stated in economic terms by reference to costs of information, but more analysis would be needed before this could be regarded as anything better than relabelling.

There is, however, another and more clearly economic problem with combining very long prison sentences with very low probabilities of apprehension and conviction. A prison term is lengthened, of course, by adding time on to the end of it. If the criminal has a significant discount rate, the added years may not create a substantial added disutility At a discount rate of 10 per cent, a 10-year prison term imposes a disutility only 6.1 times the disutility of a one-year sentence, and a 20-year sentence increases this figure to only 8.5 times; the corresponding figures for a five per cent discount rate are 7.7 and 12.5 times.

Discount rates may seem out of place in a discussion of non-monetary utilities and disutilities, though imprisonment has a monetary dimension, because a prisoner will have a lower income in prison than on the outside. But the reason that interest (discount) rates are positive even when there is no risk of default and the expected rate of inflation is zero is that people prefer present to future consumption and so must be paid to defer consumption. A criminal, too, will value his future consumption, which imprisonment will reduce, less than his present consumption.

The discounting problem could be ameliorated by preventive detention, whereby the defendant in effect begins to serve his sentence before he is convicted, or sometimes before his appeal rights are exhausted. The pros and cons of preventive detention involve issues of criminal procedure that would carry us beyond the scope of this article, and here I merely note that the argument for preventive detention is stronger the graver the defendant's crime (and hence the longer the optimal length of imprisonment), regardless of whether the defendant is likely to commit a crime if he is released on bail pending trial.

The major lesson to be drawn from this is that criminal sanctions are costly. A tort sanction is close to a costless transfer payment. A criminal sanction, even when it takes the form of a fine, and patently when it takes the form of imprisonment or death, is not. And yet it appears to be the optimal method of deterring most pure coercive transfers—which are therefore the central concern of the criminal law.

Notes

1. This point is overlooked in "radical" critiques of criminal law. See, e.g., S. Box, *Power, Crime, and Mystification* (1983), 9.

2. See, e.g., D. Pyle, *The Economics of Crime and Law Enforcement* (London, 1983); Ehrlich, "The Deterrent Effect of Capital Punishment: A Question of Life and Death", (1975) 65 *Am. Econ. Rev.* 397; Ehrlich and Gibbons, "On the Measurement of the Deterrent Effect of Capital Punishment and the Theory of Deterrence", (1977) 6 *J. Legal Stud.* 35; Layson, "Homicide and Deterrence: A Re-examination of the U.S. Time-Series Evidence" (August 1984) (unpublished manuscript on file at the offices of the *Columbia Law Review*). The evidence has not gone unchallenged, of course. See D. Pyle, above, ch. 4, for discussion and references.

3. This punishment was still "on the books" in eighteenth-century England. For the grisly details, see W. Blackstone, *Commentaries* 92.

4. See, e.g., Langbein, "Shaping the Eighteenth-Century Criminal Trial: A View from the Ryder Sources", (1983) 50 *U. Chi. L Rev.* 1, 36–49.

5. Many capital sentences, however, were commuted to banishment to the colonies.

2.3

Deterrence Research and Deterrence Policies

DERYCK BEYLEVELD

For two or three decades ideals of rehabilitation and "treatment" of offenders have characterized the dominant control policy within the criminal justice systems of Britain and the United States. It is doubtful that this ideology ever held widespread favour among all groups of administrators and practitioners, social workers being a notable exception. Being the brainchild of "liberal" academics wedded to the positivist tradition in criminology, it has held sway largely by being imposed from above as an official or neo-official policy. At the present time, however, there is widespread disillusionment with the promise of rehabilitation, a disenchantment which affects even the ranks of those who originally fostered it. And there has been an increasingly vocal political constituency for a hard line with offenders. In Britain at least, urban terrorism, football violence, and the increasing use of guns in criminal offences are seen by many to threaten the fabric of society. "Treatment" is no way to deal with the evil forces within our midst and its practice should be abandoned. Political pressure to placate voters is considerable and increases the urgency of finding a new official strategy.

A general deterrence policy[1] has obvious attractions as an alternative. It is compatible with models of human action which assign actors a capacity for choice. Deterrence, if successful, does not depend upon any interference with the character structure of the individual. Unlike rehabilitation, it holds out a promise of being able to prevent persons entering the criminal justice system rather than merely dealing with them after they have done so. Because it threatens punishment it has some potential for placating the angels of vengeance. Of course, this image of being all things to all men may be an illusion once we spell out what we actually have to do in order to deter effectively. Successful deterrence may require punishment of the innocent; it may require curtailing some of the

From Deryck Beyleveld, "Deterrence Research as a Basis for Deterrence Policies", (1979) 18 *Howard Journal of Criminal Justice* 135. Excerpted and reprinted by permission.

requirements of due process; or it may involve too much interference in our private lives. On all counts it may be incompatible with human rights.

In this article, I review empirical evidence on the general deterrent effectiveness of legal sanctions.[2] I argue that there exists no scientific basis for expecting that a general deterrence policy, which does not involve an unacceptable interference with human rights, will do anything to control the crime rate. The sort of information needed to base a morally acceptable general policy is lacking. There is some convincing evidence in some limited areas that some legal sanctions have exerted deterrent effects. These findings are not, however, generalizable beyond the conditions which were investigated. Given the present state of knowledge, implementing an official deterrence policy can be no more than a shot in the dark, or a political decision to pacify "public sentiment".

Do Legal Sanctions Deter?

A deterrent effect of a sanction may be defined as a modification or prevention of a threatened behaviour brought about because the threatened audience considers that the sanction's presence creates too great a risk for the threatened behaviour to be performed as would otherwise have been intended.[3] Because the type and degree of modification or prevention, the threatened audience, the sanction, and the threatened behaviour may all vary, different types of deterrence are possible.[4] What they all share is a possible mechanism for producing compliance; modification of the intended behaviour (the offence) must have been produced by a calculation that the utility of modification outweighed the utility of offending as intended. To establish a deterrent effect of a sanction it is necessary to show that the sanction produced a modification or prevention of an intended offence, *and* that this effect was due to the sanction's influence upon the threatened audience's calculation of personal utility. A sanction can only exert such an influence if certain conditions are satisfied. For example, the potential offender must be capable of acting on the basis of personal utility, and must not be prevented from offending by other considerations, must be aware of the sanction and must have specific attitudes toward the sanction and beliefs about it (notably attitudes and beliefs relating to the subjective severity and probability of incurring the sanction). These conditions, varying from one type of deterrence to the next, may be adduced *a priori* from the definition of deterrence. The adequacy of a research design which attempts to evaluate the deterrent effectiveness of sanctions can be measured by its ability to establish that the necessary criteria describe the situation being investigated: that a modification of offence behaviour can be explained by the application to the situation of deterrence criteria.

Ecological comparisons

The majority of research reports attempting to evaluate deterrent effects use, in one way or another, what might be described as "Ecological Comparisons": that is, the offence rates of different jurisdictions over the same period, or the same jurisdiction at different times, are compared in cases where the jurisdictions vary according to the manner in which they deploy sanctions. Thus, jurisdictions without a sanction may be compared with those which have one, or jurisdictions which have relatively severe sanctions may be compared with those which have less severe sanctions, and so on. The general reasoning is that if a particular sanction deters a particular offence then jurisdictions with the sanctions will have lower offence rates than those without sanctions; those with relatively more severe sanctions (as measured, for example, by the length of imprisonment) will have lower offence rates than those with less severe sanctions; and those with relatively more probable sanctions (as measured, for example, by official arrest or conviction rates) will have lower offence rates than those with less probable sanctions.

The results of these studies are impressively uniform. Almost without exception regardless of variations in design, correlation technique, control or modelling procedure, the expected relations have been found between probability of sanctions and the offence rates, but have not been found between severity of sanctions and the offence rates. In the latter case, the only consistent exception is found with homicide, where severity is measured by the length of imprisonment for homicide.[5]

There are, however, at least three set of problems which must be solved before these results can be interpreted as evidence for *preventive* effects of sanctions. First, it has to be shown that the data are reliable, comparable, and in no way responsible themselves or in the way in which they are constructed for any artifactual relationships. Second, it has to be shown that the relationships are due to causal relations between the investigated vari- able sand not due to their independent causal relations with some third variable. Finally, it has to be shown that even if there is a causal rela- tionship between the investigated variables, it is changes in sanctions which produce changes in offence rates and not *vice versa* . . .

The investigation by Ross *et al*. (1970) of the effect of the introduction of the Breathalyzer in October 1967 (which was preceded by extensive publicity) on drunken driving avoids most of the above-mentioned difficulties. These researchers plotted road accident casualties monthly from January 1961 to December 1970 making corrections for the length of month, risk of accident (measured by vehicle miles), and seasonal variations in the casualty rate. This revealed a drop in all types of casualties immediately after the introduction of the Road Safety Act 1967 which could not be accounted for as a trend, regression to a mean, a mere random fluctuation, by more cautious driving being the effect of the Act, or by a number of other hypotheses (tested by independent data). The drop in casualties was much more significant for those times of the week when drivers could be expected to have been drinking than for other times. Ross (1973) argues that the evidence for a deterrent effect, due to an increased subjective probability of sanctions, is strong. If, instead of merely ruling out other explanations (since a possible alternative hypothesis may have been overlooked), independent evidence had been available that the subjective probability of sanctions did increase, then the inference would be more secure.

What is interesting about this study is that it attempts to do precisely what a study of deterrent effectiveness must do: establish a modifying or preventive effect, and then on the basis of properly constituted deterrence criteria show that the effect was due to the application of these criteria and not to other possible causes.

Questionnaires and interviews

Many researchers have realized that deterrence is a function of subjective attitudes and perceptions of potential offenders. Instead of correlating official data on severity and probability of sanctions with official offence rates, they have concentrated on self-reported offence rates and measures of subjective severity and probability of sanctions. The general reasoning here has been that if a sanction deters, then those with relatively higher estimates of severity/probability of sanctions will report lower offence rates than those with lower estimates. Another strategy has simply been to ask potential offenders what considerations inhibit persons when they consider offending, and to rank these considerations (fear of legal sanctions, fear of informal sanctions, moral inhibition, etc.) in order of importance . . .

The second strategy reveals that various population groups consider legal sanctions to be important controls of law violation (although none of the studies makes it clear whether this is a judgment about what controls others' behaviour or what controls the respondent's own behaviour).

Other controls, however, such as moral inhibitions, are generally reported to be more important. Significantly, those who display greater involvement in offending attach more importance to legal sanctions as controls than those with a lesser involvement.

A general significant finding is that knowledge of penalties is generally inaccurate, and probabilities of arrest, etc., are generally *over*estimated. In general, groups with specific offence involvements tend to have more accurate knowledge of associated penalties and probabilities of arrest (though still overestimated), etc., and this means *lower estimates of probabilities,* etc., than the general population. Findings of this nature counsel extreme caution about interpreting the results of these studies as evidence of deterrence. As with the ecological studies, there is a problem of causal direction. An inverse relationship between subjective probability of sanction and offence rates may be due to those with greater offence involvement having lower estimates of probabilities *because* of their involvement, and not to those with lower estimates being more willing to offend *because* of their lower estimates. There is also the possibility that the relationship between subjective probability and offence rates may be spurious. Those individuals who offend less frequently may also be those with greater moral inhibitions against offending. This group may also be prone to greater overestimation of probabilities of being sanctioned *because* of their moral inhibitions. It is possible that the estimates of those morally committed to the law are prone to a wish fulfilment that those not morally committed won't get away with it.

In general, we should question any results as relevant deterrence evidence which do not attend to subjective estimates by a respondent of severity/probability for himself. Few people regard themselves as "the average man". Whatever the statistical chances, objective or subjective, each person is likely to regard himself as an exception. He may think himself more or less gifted or lucky than average when it comes to his chances of "getting away with it". Estimates of general chances are simply not relevant. Once we are dealing with personal estimates, however, we need to consider that those who commit more offences may be inveterate optimists. Although the pessimists may be deterred, the optimists may always think they can "get away with it", no matter what the general objective chances against this are. The crucial thing to realize about these studies is that, *even if* they do show that some persons are being deterred *by their beliefs* about sanctions, this does not show that they are being deterred by actual legal sanctions, nor that changing sanctions will affect the beliefs of those who are most likely to offend. By failing to show how actual legal sanctions may or may not be productive of beliefs about them, these studies fail to say anything about the deterrent effectiveness of actual legal sanctions.

Field experiments

Field experiments are potentially an excellent means for evaluating deterrent effects. Unfortunately, their scope is limited by their cost and the need to secure co-operation from officials. A study by Schwartz and Orleans (1967) of tax evasion and the study by Buikhuisen (1974) of a campaign to deter driving with worn tyres are particularly fine examples of this kind of research. Although other studies report evidence for preventive effects of their sanctions, these are the only two which are immune from the usual caveats about the use of official statistics, adopt reasonably adequate control procedures, and provide plausible evidence that the prevention of their target behaviour is by deterrence.

Buikhuisen's study is worth describing in some detail: he investigated the potential deterrent effect of penalties for driving with worn tyres in The Netherlands (imprisonment for up to two months or a fine of up to three hundred Dutch guilders; driving licences could also be revoked for a period of up to two years). Groningen was chosen as the experimental city, and Leeuwarden as the control. The cities are similar in size, and a pilot investigation showed that in both cities 80 per cent of car owners parked their cars outside at night This enabled the tyres of samples of cars to be checked in both cities on two occasions, three months apart, before a police campaign against driving with worn tyres. Cars were investigated during the early hours of the morning and the car number and the position of worn tyres were noted. During the three months there was a "spontaneous" renewal rate of worn tyres of 46.3 per cent in Groningen and 43.5 per cent in Leeuwarden.

In Groningen, special patrol cars and newspapers conducted a two-week campaign warning drivers about the need to have legal tyres. In Leeuwarden, there was no publicity and no special patrols during the experimental weeks or for four months preceding the experiment. Immediately before the campaign samples of cars in both cities were inspected using the method of the pilot study. Immediately after the campaign these same cars were relocated to see if they had replaced worn tyres. Checks were made to ensure that none of the sample had been located by the police during the campaign.

During the two weeks of the experiment 54 per cent of the cars with worn tyres before the campaign had them replaced in Groningen; but the figure was only 27 per cent in Leeuwarden. Furthermore, during the campaign the Groningen police inspected 13,474 cars and found that only 189 had worn tyres: a much lower percentage than in The Netherlands generally. Eighty persons who had renewed their tyres during the campaign, and ninety-one who had not, were interviewed after the campaign. The majority of both groups knew about the campaign, but far more of the renewers than non-renewers did. More non-renewers than renewers claimed that they would risk driving with worn tyres if there was another campaign. Non-renewers tended to be younger, had less eduction, older cars, less need of a car for professional reasons, and paid less attention to their cars.

The particular merits of this study lie in the attempts to establish the "real" offence rate, to establish the spontaneous renewal rate, and to ascertain why the police succeeded or failed in terms of the characteristics and perceptions of the threatened audience. However, the renewal rate in Leeuwarden during the campaign was four times the spontaneous rate[6] (vs. six times in Groningen), and this is not explained. The interview questions were also not detailed enough to rule out the hypothesis that the renewals were prompted by the campaign raising safety consciousness rather than by drawing attention to legal penalties. Nevertheless, such faults are remediable within the general design.

Conclusion

Taking deterrence research as a whole, it must be concluded that, although there is some persuasive evidence for deterrent effect in some situations, most notably that reported by Ross *et al.* (1970) and Buikhuisen (1974), most studies are inconclusive, the main reasons being methodologically defective designs or procedures and inadequate deterrence criteria.

Can We Predict Deterrent Effects of Legal Sanctions?

Many studies which primarily attempt to identify deterrent effects, also attempt to draw policy conclusions from their results.

The inference most commonly drawn in ecological studies is that increasing the probability of arrest or conviction is likely to deter potential offenders, whereas increasing the severity of penalties is unlikely to have an effect. More specific statements are also made on occasion; for example, that the severity of sanctions can be decreased without affecting deterrence, sometimes even that severity should be decreased because high severity may militate against securing a high probability of conviction (as may happen if juries show reluctance to convict when very severe penalties are threatened); that certain types of offences are less deterrable than others (for example, violent crimes less than property crimes); that increasing, for example, police manpower (taken to index probability of arrest), by some exact amount, will deter an exactly specified number of offences.

Such inferences are of highly dubious validity. Even if we could assume, as we cannot, that the correlations upon which they are based are evidence about deterrence, a number of totally unwarranted assumptions must be made. These inferences are merely extrapolations from the magnitude and direction of empirically estimated correlation coefficients. Suppose, for example, that a particular set of studies does show that increasing severity of sanctions fails to deter. To draw a policy inference they must then *explain* why increasing the severity of sanctions does not deter. they can hardly claim that severity is not a deterrence criterion, so the likely explanation would be that severity levels are already above their upper thresholds (which is plausible when serious crimes are the topic of investigation). But if severity is decreased then it is possible that the upper threshold will be crossed. Below this threshold decreasing severity will then lead to decreasing deterrence.

It must also be assumed that the deterrence potential of the threatened audience (the ratio of those who need to be, and can be, deterred to those who need not or cannot be deterred) is not exhausted in the present situation by the existing values of probability/severity; that is, that all those who can *and* need to be deterred are not already deterred as much as possible.

In any case, this sort of discussion, as well as the policy proposals, are fanciful. In order to be discussing deterrence it must be assumed that changes in the objective probability/severity values will produce corresponding changes in the subjective values. The inferences, however, simply ignore the fact that deterrence involves people acting in a social setting. We really do not know how people come to have their attitudes towards, and perceptions of, laws and offences. People may simply not tolerate the sorts of things which may have to be done in order to increase the subjective probabilities of arrest and conviction. It may, for example, be necessary to alter police search and questioning procedures, to interfere with due process and to introduce identity cards and compulsory fingerprinting of the entire population. In any case, even if such "drastic" measures are not required, by not telling us what is required, the proposals are really empty as practical and practicable policy suggestions.

In general, these policy inferences rest upon a methodological error. They treat their correlations, not only as causal relationships, but as causal laws. Instead, they should be regarded as empirical relationships which are produced by hidden social processes and actions. It is from knowledge of these processes, not from the empirical generalizations which they explain, that scientific predictions can be drawn.

Questionnaires and interviews fare no better as a basis for policy proposals. They are sometimes used to generate policy predictions which correspond in all respects to those inferred in ecological investigations; the only difference being that subjective and self-report data are correlated rather than objective and official data. These inferences are subject to exactly corresponding objections relating to the possible operation of thresholds, the unknown deterrence potential, and the inutility of prescribing what it is not known how to accomplish.

The irony of the general run of policy inferences is that they provide information of little different order from what can quite legitimately be inferred *a priori* from an analysis of what it means to be deterred. "*If* someone views offending in terms of its utility; *if* the subjective probability/severity of sanctions is high enough, etc., then he will be deterred" is inferable from deterrence criteria. In order to implement a policy we need to know how to write out the hypotheticals. It is this very knowledge which is missing and which these studies circumvent by making unwarranted and often implausible assumptions.

One partial exception to these criticisms is Ross's (1973) discussion of the effect of the British Road Safety Act of 1967. Ross suggested that a reduction in the severity of penalties for drunken driving, the use of a more reliable Breathalyzer (which does not require blood- and urine-test back-ups), the introduction of random testing, and a lowering of the legal limit, would not only be adequate to deter drunken driving but would help ensure that any deterrent effect achieved by a publicity campaign would not quickly wear off. Ross's analysis shows that the initial deterrent effect of the 1967 campaign started to wear off as early as January 1968. He argues that the publicity for the campaign initially led to an increased subjective probability of incurring what were perceived to be rather severe penalties for drunken driving. However, examination of the ways in which alcohol tests were actually given, charges brought, and convictions secured, reveals that there was little objective basis for the supposed public belief that the sanctions were not easily avoided. The need to back up the Breathalyzer with blood and urine tests led to lowered charge and conviction rates because the delay allowed some "illegal" blood levels to become legal in the interim. The police were also reluctant to enforce the

Act because they feared worsening police–public relations. Ross postulates that the gap between the objective and subjective probabilities of sanctions led to an erosion of the initially high subjective probability. If this were so then the declining effect of the legislation would be explained. Ross's policy proposals are made on the basis of this explanation of the consequences of the 1967 Act in terms of the operation of social processes; and it should further be noted that he suggests that random testing may not be implementable because of public antagonism, despite the fact that, if implemented, it is likely to be an effective measure.

Ross's reasoning is by no means flawless; it rests on a number of plausible rather than tested assumptions, and he is rather cavalier and vague when he suggests that the severity of penalties can be decreased without lessening deterrence. In essence, however, the general design appears to be sound and his procedure is worth outlining in a schematic form.

1. Evaluate the deterrent effectiveness of a measure by assessing the likelihood that a preventive effect can be explained by the application of deterrence criteria. If no preventive effect is found (or if one declines) then assess how likely it is that this can be explained by the failure of application of a deterrence criterion.
2. Analyze the social situation attending the introduction of the measure and attempt to explain what social processes were responsible for the application or failure of application of the deterrence criteria (necessary attitudes, perceptions, etc., of potential offenders).
3. Evaluate the feasibility of actions which, if performed, would ensure that deterrence criteria will apply.

Such a procedure can be applied to field experiments as well as to the quasi-experimental design used by Ross. This has not, however, been the case when policy suggestions have been inferred from field experiments. For example, Kelling *et al.* (1975) conducted an experiment to determine the deterrent effectiveness of random patrol exercises in Kansas City. They failed to find such an effect and concluded that random patrols would be no more effective at deterring crime than a policy of only answering calls for service. This is unwarranted. Findings generated in particular experimental circumstances cannot form a basis for general policy predictions. The proper basis is an explanation of why the particular policy failed. This might identify some absent deterrence requirement in the original experimental situation which may be present in another situation . . .

Ross's procedure has its merits when it is possible to investigate a particular policy in detail. It can only base particular deterrence programmes relating to specific penalties, offences, and social circumstances. A different programme is required if it is desired to have a general basis for predicting the effects of policies in novel situations. A general theory for predicting deterrence is required. It may be thought that this can be generated by applying Ross's procedure to a wide range of penalties, offences, and social circumstances; but this is mistaken. How people react or act in specific situations is a function of the situations themselves, the principles which govern their behaviour, and their perceptions of the situations. The principles in question are not empirical generalizations of their behaviour in a wide variety of situations: it is doubtful that there can be such uniformities. When situations vary, behaviour will vary. Instead, the principles have to be abstracted from different situations, and must in no way be dependent upon them. In an adequate theory for predicting deterrence, principles will be stated which, in conjunction with statements about the social position of individuals or groups, will generate predictions about the attitudes and perceptions of these subjects. A theory for predicting deterrence is impossible without a theory of the generation of attitudes toward laws and offences and a theory of the communication of threats. Such theories are not available and so no scientific basis exists for a general policy of deterrence.

Can a General Policy of Deterrence Be Justified?

The concluding sentence of the last paragraph needs to be qualified. We do not know what difference doubling police manpower or increasing a fine from £10 to £100 would have on a potential offender's perceptions or calculation of the utility of an offence. But this does not mean that we don't know, with a fair degree of certainty, what would be the effect of a mandatory death penalty without trial administered in good science fiction style by robot parking meters on parking offenders. There are extreme policies which we can virtually guarantee will deterrently affect the perceptions and responses of all but those who are perfectly willing to suffer the penalty, cannot appreciate it, or do not act voluntarily. We could fingerprint the entire population, force everyone to carry identity cards, keep universal computer records, give the police unlimited powers of arrest, search, and questioning, dispense with due process, litter our cities and even the "privacy" of homes with spy cameras, and to cap it all we could institute extremely severe penalties for every offence. No doubt there are some who would be prepared to go to such lengths to eliminate any behaviour which offends them. It is to be hoped that they are and will remain the tiny minority. Such a policy would represent a gross violation of human rights, and fortunately, while this group remains a minority, such a policy will not be implementable.

It may also be stated as a general principle that the adequacy of our knowledge of deterrence for policy purposes varies inversely with the political morality and feasibility of the proposed deterrence policy. In general, we have good reason to believe that immoral, unimplementable policies would "work"; rarely reason to believe that more sane and realistic policies will achieve anything. This is quite simply because human behaviour is much more predictable in situations in which freedom of choice is severely limited. If the choice is a clear one between compliance and, for example, certain death, then it is a good bet that a deterrable individual will comply. But to make choices clear and restricted the social milieu must either be extremely repressive or else we require far more knowledge of human behaviour and institutions than we presently possess . . .

The airing of a general policy of deterrence is typical electioneering rhetoric. There are almost no specific policies which are scientifically grounded, and the idea as a general policy of control is appealing only while it is vague and unspecified. The rhetoric has attractions as a ploy to satisfy "public opinion"; "'Getting tough' with offenders or potential offenders by deterrence" is a slogan which may well attract votes. But would it continue to do so if it were generally realized that the slogan is empty, or else that implementation would involve social actions which would interfere with everybody's lives and not just with those whom the political constituency for deterrence views as the social enemy? The constituency will only be placated, except for short-term electioneering purposes, by results. When these results cannot be guaranteed, barring much unavailable knowledge, without alienating the constituency itself, then we do not have to look far for the motives behind the promises.

I do not want to suggest, however, that I am against any general policy of deterrence as a matter of principle. There would be a case for such a policy if it were scientifically grounded, and involved no violation of human rights in excess of the violations it could be expected to prevent by successful deterrence. I realize that there are some who may object to any deterrence policy on the grounds that it is "conservative". If this means that it is a policy which is directed at preserving whatever happens to be the present social and legal order, then it *is* conservative; but then the morality of conservatism depends upon the morality of that order. Then there are those who may suggest that a wholly moral order will not require deterrence: in Utopia all will obey the law by free choice; indeed, there may be no need for law. At most, however, this suggests that deterrence should not be the primary ideology of control. Our primary efforts should be directed at constructing Utopia, but until we succeed, deterrence may be necessary. In general, we must avoid a tendency to assume that alternative offence control and response policies are mutually exclusive options selected by different scientific theories and political ideologies. We should avoid thinking that if treatment doesn't work for all offenders then it should be replaced by deterrence *or* social change, etc., in a wholesale manner. People offend for different reasons and different responses are accordingly appropriate. Ideologies, furthermore, do not dictate treatment *or* deterrence, etc.: instead they dictate different hierarchical orderings of different sorts of responses; they dictate what should be the primary policy and what should be secondary policies according to a general theory of social goals and the desirable social order. Someone who approves of the existing social order may resist any radical social change; but room can be found for both treatment and deterrence within such an attitude. On the other hand, someone who disapproves of the existing order will primarily want to see it changed; but unless he disapproves of all existing laws and regards no-one as needing treatment, both deterrence and treatment can play subordinate roles.

"Deterrence" has for too long been associated with the sorts of policies which I regard as extreme. This has made the notion a politically loaded one. This is unfortunate, for deterrence is, in fact, a pervasive fact of human existence. When someone looks before crossing a road, that is probably because of deterrence; when he takes an umbrella to avoid getting wet, that too may manifest deterrence. We tend to associate deterrence with a legal context, but we need not do so, and doing so does not alter the phenomenon, only the context. For this reason it is important to understand its limits and operation, not only for purposes of control, but also for purposes of understanding social behaviour generally. If deterrence is not studied seriously or if deterrence policies are suggested and implemented without adequate grounding, we will achieve neither of these purposes, but merely add fuel to the flames of political passion.

Notes

1. This article concentrates on general deterrence: the deterrent effect of threats on potential offenders who have not as yet suffered the implementation of the threats. It is not concerned with the effects of implementing penalties on individuals.
2. This review draws upon Beyleveld (1978). It should be assumed that unreferenced remarks may be traced to this source.

3. For reasons for adopting such a narrow definition rather than equating deterrence with prevention, or allowing it to cover a number of mechanisms, see Beyleveld (1978), Introduction.
4. For a typology, see Beyleveld (1978), Introduction.
5. This should not be confused with the issue of the effectiveness of capital punishment.
6. That is to say, 27% in two weeks vs. 44% in three months.

References

Beyleveld, D. (1978), *The Effectiveness of General Deterrents Against Crime: An Annotated Bibliography of Evaluative Research* (Cambridge: University of Cambridge, Institute of Criminology Microfiche).

Buikhuisen, Q. (1974), "General deterrence: research and theory", 14 *Abstracts on Criminology and Penology*, 285–98.

Kelling, G. L., Pate, T., Dieckman, D., and Brown, C. E. (1975) *The Kansas City Preventive Patrol Experiment: A Technical Report* (Washington, D.C.: Police Foundation).

Ross, H. L. (1973), "Law, science, and accidents: the British Road Safety Act of 1967", 2 *The Journal of Legal Studies*, 1–78.

Ross, H. L., Campbell, D. T., and Glass, G. V. (1970), "Determining the social effects of a legal reform: the British 'Breathalyser' crackdown of 1967", 13 *American Behavioral Scientist*, 493–509.

Schwartz, R. D., and Orleans, S. (1967), "On legal sanctions", 34 *The University of Chicago Law Review*, 274–300.

Taylor, I., Walton, P., and Young, J. (1973), *The New Criminology* (London: Routledge and Kegan Paul).

2.4

Deterrence Theory: Its Moral Problems

ALAN H. GOLDMAN

[This essay was written as a reply to an article by Ernest van den Haag, "Punishment as a Device for Controlling the Crime Rate", (1981) 33 *Rutgers Law Review* 706. For present purposes the statement of van den Haag's views in the Goldman essay is sufficient—eds.]

Ernest van den Haag's initial defence of deterrence theory against an old objection to it, that deterrence justifies only the appearance of punishment, or the threat of punishment, and not its actual imposition, is sound. Van den Haag correctly points out that for threats to be plausible and effective, they must be carried out when their antecedent conditions are met. The deterrence theorist need only state his argument in two steps in order to avoid this objection: first, that threats of punishment are justified to reduce crime, and second, that the threats must be made good to achieve their purpose.

Van den Haag concludes from these premises that "every effort must be made to let no actually guilty persons escape punishment". Here this author begins to part company with him. The many procedural rights and safeguards of our legal system are founded on the premise that it is worse to punish an innocent person than to let a guilty one go free. This asymmetry is based on the certainty of harm in the former case, as opposed to its mere probability in the latter. The difference between imposing unjustified harm and simply not preventing it is recognized throughout our moral system: the bystander who fails to thwart the preventable crime is not as culpable as the criminal.

Van den Haag's emphasis on the duty to punish the guilty allows an internal criticism as well. The deterrence theory he advocates might not allow punishment of all those who deserve it. He points to the match between deterrence and other theories in requiring fault before punish-

From Alan H. Goldman, "Beyond the Deterrence theory", (1981) 33 *Rutgers Law Review* 721. Excerpted and reprinted by permission.

ment may be imposed. We cannot deter actions for which the agents are not responsible. Unfortunately there may be undeterrable crimes involving fault as well. Crimes without premeditation, so-called "crimes of passion", may fall into that class. If such crimes could be separated from others whose perpetrators attempt to make them appear unpremeditated, then the goal of deterrence would not justify punishing truly unpremeditated crimes. Yet surely the fact that a crime is unplanned, that the criminal does not contemplate the consequences to him of his action, should not entirely exempt it from punishment.

More serious than the failure of deterrence theory to justify deserved punishments are its excesses in the other direction, its seeming capacity to warrant punishments beyond those deserved. The well-known problem of justifying not punishing innocents when this would successfully deter a greater number of potential criminals is but one instance of this broader affliction of the theory. Van den Haag argues that the goal of deterrence does not necessarily require punishing innocent persons, even when officials can reduce crime and protect others by doing so. He asserts that only the utilitarian versions of deterrence theory authorize such punishment if it serves to minimize the sum of harm or misery. Deterrent threats are justified ultimately to prevent violations of certain fundamental moral rules. But these rules need not be utilitarian. They might themselves prohibit deceptive policies and practices. Van den Haag argues that because punishment of the innocent is deceptive, and because it is also a crime, non-utilitarian deterrence theories need not hold this practice justified, even when it might succeed in its aim.

The problem with this argument as a way of avoiding the standard objection is that it fails to capture what is seriously wrong in punishing the innocent. It is not the deception of third parties that is so wrong; and certainly the victim himself is not deceived, although it is he who is primarily and most seriously wronged. The injustice lies in the violation of the victim's right not to be harmed. Few moral theories would prohibit deception of parties not directly involved in particular cases if great gains in welfare could be achieved by it. Most would prohibit the more serious harm imposed by punishment of a person who does not deserve to be punished. But deterrence theory, utilitarian or not, in seeking to justify punishment, looks only to the future good to be gained by it. Looking instead to the past and to individual deserts arising from past conduct is the orientation of the rival retributive theory. It is this alternative view that appears necessary, not only to protect the innocent, but also to protect the guilty against excessive punishment. Both needs arise from the broader requirement to treat people as they deserve in relation to their past conduct. Neither seems capable of capture by future-looking deterrence theory.

Van den Haag sees retributive theory as telling us only that we punish because we feel we ought to. Of course it tells us much more. As he points out, Kantian retributive theory involves the notion of consent by the criminal to his own punishment. The idea is not that criminals actually consent, but that we must treat them as rational subjects who responsibly choose certain courses of conduct. According to Kant, rational subjects, in recognizing the moral equality of others, universalize their principles of action. They act only in ways they would will or approve for all other agents. In punishing criminals, we universalize the consequences of their actions in relation to them; we treat them as they treat their victims. Since they cannot find morally relevant differences between themselves and their victims, as rational subjects they would have to consent to equal treatment. Thus punishment within retributive limits treats them as rational moral beings and restores their moral status in the community.

While Kant's theory does provide a deeper moral justification for the retributive demand that the punishment equal the crime, the premise that the recognition of others as moral equals constitutes a requirement of rationality itself remains questionable. Hence the notion of hypothetical consent no longer figures prominently in modern retributive theory. Van den Haag himself suggests that the rational criminal at least consents to the rules under which he is punished, but this is equally doubtful and in any case not necessary to the justification of his punishment. What remains accepted of Kant's theory is his model of society as a community of equal subject (the "kingdom of ends"). Such citizens have equal rights, which they retain only as long as they continue to respect the same rights of others. When instead they violate certain rights of others, they forfeit those same or equivalent rights themselves. They may then be treated in a way equivalent to losing those rights, with the harm that results.

Hence the modern retributive theory, modelled not upon Kant's idea of rational consent, but upon his idea of a community of equal subjects all ends in themselves rather than means to communal welfare, continues to provide support for the equation of punishment with crime in determining degrees of harm imposed. This limit to justified punishment in relation to desert guarantees not only that innocents not be punished at all, but also that criminals not suffer more harm than they deserve. Certainly a criminal, in violating some rights of his victim, does not thereby forfeit all his own rights. We cannot slowly torture all criminals to death. If we ask which rights they do forfeit, the plausible answer appears to be the very ones they fail to respect. Forfeiture of rights is consequent upon and depends only upon the nature of the offending action, not upon how many more potential perpetrators remain to be deterred. This equation sets limits to justified punishments, limits necessary in the case of the guilty no less than in the case of the innocent. Only some form of retributive theory oriented toward past actions seems able to generate them.

Van den Haag is sensitive to this broader criticism of deterrence theory. He points out that the goal of deterrence itself tends to proportion penalties to the gravity of crimes. As Bentham argued, in order to discourage the escalation of minor crimes into major ones, in order to encourage the criminal to choose the lesser evil, deterrent threats must be more severe in relation to more serious potential crimes. If the penalty for rape or kidnapping is the same as for murder, for example, the rapist or kidnapper is encouraged to kill his victim and reduce his chances of apprehension. On utilitarian grounds, greater punishments for more serious crimes are further justified, first, to offset the greater gain to the potential criminal and so continue to deter him, and second, to protect the potential victim from greater harm.

Proportionality in deterrence is not equivalent, however, to the absolute limit on punishment entailed by retributive theories, nor is it sufficient to express our full moral sensibility. It is easy to provide examples in which all punishments are too severe. The state might, for example, impose penalties ranging from 10 to 30 years in prison for crimes from shoplifting to armed robbery. It would be possible to create such a range of penalties, excessive in the author's view, and still have punishments outside this range for greater and lesser crimes. Thus proportionality is insufficient. The charge can be levelled that even fully proportionate penalties use criminals unjustly as means to better protect the community against other potential criminals. If it is not permissible to use those innocent of crimes for such purposes, then it does not seem right to so use those convicted either, that is, to inflict on them a level of punishment beyond that called for by their actions.

Van den Haag denies that deterrence theories use criminals merely as means, in violation of the Kantian injunctions. He asserts that punishments are not imposed simply to deter others; rather, it is the threat of punishment that is intended to be sufficient to deter criminal activity. Once threats have been made, failure to carry them through against criminals would amount to reneging on a promise made to others. These others would then have been deceived into forgoing gains on the understanding that they would have been punished for seeking them.

This argument resembles the retributivist claim that, in the absence of punishment, criminals achieve an unfair advantage over non-criminals.

The difference is that van den Haag uses it only to justify the imposition of punishment once threatened. The threats themselves are strictly for deterrence purposes, and they must be adequate for those purposes. Perhaps his most important point here, however, is that criminals can avoid the punishment altogether because they are adequately forewarned. Therefore, when they assume the risks involved in criminal activity, despite the warnings, they must be seen as having done so voluntarily. Even given the risks, they must consider themselves as well off in relation to the rules as non-criminals, since they too could forgo the risks if they so chose. Thus van den Haag asserts that lesser threats would again give them an unfair advantage over others. Although they do not consent to their punishments, there is a sense in which they consent to taking the risk that they know may result in their being punished. In this sense van den Haag sees deterrence theory as meeting the Kantian requirement. Since criminals can avoid the harm imposed upon them while their victims cannot, the state is justified, according to this theory, in threatening criminals with whatever is necessary to protect their victims.

These points may be countered one at a time. First, representing the imposition of punishment as keeping a promise made to non-criminals does not show that criminals are not being unjustly used. Rather than used directly to deter others, they are used to maintain the plausibility of the threats and to honour the supposed promises. Promises, however, lack moral force when what is promised is itself morally impermissible. If A promises B that he will unjustly harm B's rival, his promise ought not to be kept. Similarly, if the promise to punish criminals beyond retributive limits lacks independent moral warrant, it cannot justify the imposition of the punishment. It is of course also questionable whether non-criminals understand threats of punishment as promises made to them. The normally moral person presumably forgoes commission of serious crimes on independent moral grounds, not solely because of legal threats. The non-criminal might regret that a criminal who goes free did not receive his just deserts, but he would hardly regret his own missed chance at getting away with murder.

Similar reasoning applies to the relevance of having warned criminals of the risks of punishment assumed in their activities. Warning that a certain reaction will follow a certain course of conduct does not suffice to justify the reaction if it lacks independent warrant. A's warning that he will assault B if B criticizes his argument does not warrant his doing so. Warning thieves that their hands will be cut off does not justify the punishment, even if, having been forewarned, they can avoid the penalty by refraining from further stealing. Advance announcements of penalties attached to various crimes may be a necessary condition for their just imposition; it is never sufficient. That punishment be within the limits set by retributive considerations of desert seems to be another necessary condition. Van den Haag does not succeed in showing that these considerations can be captured by deterrence theories alone.

Suggestions for Further Reading

1. The Concept of Deterrence

Zimring, F. E., *Perspectives on Deterrence* (1971); Zimring, F. E., and Hawkins, G., *Deterrence: The Legal Threat in Crime Control* (1973); Andenaes, J., *Punishment and Deterrence* (1974); Gibbs, J. P., *Crime, Punishment, and Deterrence* (1975); Posner, R., *Economic Analysis of Law*, 2nd edn. (1977); Beyleveld, D., "Identifying, Explaining, and Predicting Deterrence", (1979) *19 British Journal of Criminology 205*; Pyle, D., *The Economics of Crime and Law Enforcement* (1983); Quinn, W., "The Right to Threaten and the Right to Punish", (1985) 4 *Philosophy and Public Affairs 327*.

2. Empirical Evidence of Deterrent Effects

The two most systematic analyses, both including extensive bibliographies, are: Panel on Research on Deterrent and Incapacitative Effects, "Report", in Blumstein, A., Cohen, J., and Nagin, D. (eds.), *Deterrence and Incapacitation: Estimating the Effects of Criminal Sanctions on Crime Rates* (1978), and Beyleveld, D., *The Effectiveness of General Deterrents against Crime: An Annotated Bibliography of Evaluative Research* (1980).

For other empirical evidence, see Willcock, H. D., and Stokes, J., *Deterrents and Incentives to Crime among Boys and Young Men Aged 15–21 Years* (1968); Buikhuisen, W., "General Deterrence: Research and Theory", (1974) *14 Abstracts on Criminology and Penology 285*; Brody, S. R., *The Effectiveness of Sentencing* (1976); Grasmick, H. G., and Green, D., "Legal Punishment, Social Disapproval and Internalisation as Inhibitors of Illegal Behaviour", (1980) 71 *Journal of Criminal Law and Criminology* 325; Cook, Phillip J., "Research in Criminal Deterrence: Laying the Groundwork for the Second Decade", in Morris, N., and Tonry, M. (eds.), *Crime and justice: An Annual Review*, vol. 2 (1980); Ross, H., *Deterring the Drinking Driver* (1982); Thornton, R., *et al.*, *Tougher Regimes in Detention Centres* (1984), chs. 5 and 6; Bennett, T., and Wright, R., *Burglars on Burglary* (1984); Riley, D., "Drinking Drivers: The Limits to Deterrence?" (1985) 24 *Howard* J.C.J. 241; Cousineau, F. D., *Legal Sanctions and Deterrence* (1986); Williams, K. R., "Perceptual Research on General Deterrence: A Critical Review", (1986) 20 *Law and Society Review 545*; Grasmick, H. G., and Bursik, R. J., "Conscience, Significant Others and Rational Choice: Extending the Deterrence Model", (1990) 4 *Law and Society Review* 837; Schneider, A.L., *Deterrence and Juvenile Crime* (1990); Sherman, L., "Police Crackdowns and Residual Deterrence", in N. Morris and M. Tonry (eds.), *Crime and Justice*, vol.12 (1990); Harding, R., "Rational-Choice Gun Use in Armed Robbery: The Likely Effect on Gun Use of

Additional Imprisonment", (1991) 1 *Criminal Law Forum* 427; Riley, D., *DrunkDriving: The Effects of Enforcement* (1991); Nagin, D., and Paternoster, R., "The Preventive Effects of Perceived Risk of Arrest", (1991) 29 *Criminology* 561; McDowall, D., Loftus, C., and Wiersema, B., "A Comparative Study of the Preventive Effects of Mandatory Sentencing Laws for Gun Crimes", (1992) 83 *Journal of Criminal Law and Criminology* 378; Farrington, D., and Langan, P., "Changes in Crime and Punishment in England and America in the 1980s", (1992) 9 *Justice Quarterly* 5; Fagan, J. A., "Do Criminal Sanctions Deter Drug Crimes?", in D. MacKenzie and C. Uschida (eds.) *Drugs and the Criminal Justice System* (1994); Wright, R., and Decker, S., *Burglars on the Job* (1994); Farrington, D., Langan, P., and Wikstrom, P.O., "Changes in Crime and Punishment in America, England and Sweden between the 1980s and 1990s", (1994) 3 *Studies on Crime and Prevention* 104; Reilly, B., and Witt, R., "Crime, Deterrence and Unemployment in England and Wales", (1996) 48 *Bulletin of Economic Research* 137; Levitt, S.D., "The Effect of Prison Population Size on Crime Rates", (1996) 111 *Quarterly Journal of Economics* 319; Stolzenberg, L., and D'Alessio, S., "Three Strikes and You're Out: the Impact of California's New Mandatory Sentencing Law on Serious Crime Rates", (1997) 43 *Crime and Delinquency* 457; Paternoster, R., and Simpson, S., "Sanction Threats and Appeals to Morality: Testing a Rational Choice Theory of Corporate Crime", (1997) 30 *Law and Society Review* 549; Nagin, D., "Criminal Deterrence Research at the Outset of the Twenty-First Century", in (1998) *Crime and Justice*, vol. 23; von Hirsch, A., Bottoms, A. E., et al., *Criminal Deterrence and Penal Policy: A Literature Review of Recent Research* (Cambridge Institute of Criminology, 1998 forthcoming).

3. On the Pros and Cons of Deterrent Sentencing

De Tarde, G., *Penal Philosophy* (1912), esp. sec. 90; Becker, G. S., "Crime and Punishment: An Economic Approach," (1968) 76 *Journal of Political Economy* 169; Tullock, G., "Does Punishment Deter Crime?" (Summer 1974) *Public Interest* 103; Becker, G. S., and Landes, W. L., *Essays in the Economics of Crime and Punishment* (1974); von Hirsch, A., *Doing Justice: 'The Choice of Punishments* (1976), ch. 7; Walker, N. D., "The Efficacy and Morality of Deterrents", (1979) *Criminal Law Review* 129; van den Haag, E., "Punishment as a Device for Controlling the Crime Rate", (1981) 33 *Rutgers Law Journal* 706; Goldman, H., "The Paradox of Punishment", (1981) 9 *Philosophy and Public Affairs* 42; Smilansky, S., "Utilitarianism and the 'Punishment' of the Innocent", (1990) 50 *Analysis* 256; Simmons, A. J., "Locke and the Right to Punish", (1992) 20 *Philosophy and Public Affairs* 311; Farrel, D. M., "Deterrence and the Just Distribution of Harm", (1995) 12 *Social Philosophy and Policy* 220; Pyle, D., *Cutting the Costs of Crime: the Economics of Crime and Criminal Justice* (1995).

3

Incapacitation

Incapacitation is the idea of simple restraint: rendering the convicted offender incapable, for a period of time, of offending again. Whereas rehabilitation involves changing the person's habits or attitudes so he or she becomes less criminally inclined, incapacitation presupposes no such change. Instead, obstacles are interposed to impede the person from carrying out whatever criminal inclinations he or she may have. Usually, the obstacle is the walls of a prison, but other incapacitative techniques are possible—such as exile or house arrest.

Incapacitation has, usually, been sought through predicting the offender's likelihood of reoffending. Those deemed more likely to reoffend are to be restrained, for example, by imposition of a term of imprisonment—or of a prison term of longer duration than they otherwise would receive. This predictive approach is evident in the Model Penal Code, set out in part in Selection 1.1 above. The offender, according to §7.01(1)(a) of the Code, is to be imprisoned if "there is undue risk that [he or she] will commit another crime".

Who, then, is likely to reoffend? Prediction research in criminology has had a more than 60-year history, beginning with S. B. Warner's statistical studies of recidivism among Massachusetts parolees in the 1920s and the Gluecks' prediction studies among juvenile delinquents in the 1930s. The basic research technique has been straightforward enough. Various facts about convicted criminals are recorded: previous arrests and convictions, social and employment history, drug use, and so forth; and those factors that are, statistically, most strongly associated with recidivism are identified. A prediction instrument, based on these latter factors, is then constructed and tested. The studies suggest that a limited capacity to predict does exist. Certain facts about offenders—principally, their previous criminal histories, drug habits, and histories of unemployment—are (albeit only to a modest extent) indicative of increased likelihood of recidivism.[1]

Incapacitation was an important (although often less visible) element in the traditional rehabilitative penal ethic. Sentencing judges and correctional officials were supposed to gauge not only offenders' treatment needs but their likelihood of recidivism. "Curable" offenders were to be treated (in the community, if possible), but those judged bad risks were to be restrained. The traditional view had its appeal precisely because it thus offered both therapy and restraint. One did not have to assume that all criminals really were treatable, but merely that some might be. Therapy could be tried on the potentially responsive, but always with a fail-safe: the offender who seemed unsuitable for treatment could be separated from the community.

Illustrative of this dual approach—treatment in the community for seemingly treatable offenders, restraint for the bad risks—is the National Council on Crime and Delinquency's proposed Model Sentencing Act,[2] reproduced in part as Selection 3.1. The Act makes much of treatment: offenders, §1 asserts, "shall be dealt with in accordance with their potential for rehabilitation, considering their individual characteristics, circumstances, and needs". In their commentary to that section, the drafters also emphasize a preference for community sanctions and for reduced reliance on imprisonment. Nevertheless, the scope for predictive confinement is great. Section 1 states that whereas non-dangerous offenders are to be dealt with by non-custodial sentences, "dangerous offenders shall be identified [and] segregated . . . for long terms as needed". (During that custody, they are also to be "correctively treated".) Terms of up to five years are authorized for such individuals, with still longer maximum terms—of up to 30 years—authorized for those deemed especially dangerous.[3]

The Act prompts a number of questions. Under its provisions, the seriousness of the defendant's crime of conviction does not matter at all: a defendant convicted of *any* crime can be confined for up to five years if deemed a bad risk. (It is only for extended terms up to 30 years that the Act requires the current crime to be one involving violence.) Does this almost complete disregard of the gravity of the current crime pose questions of fairness—particularly, of proportionality? The drafters of the Act, in their comments, say not—because concern over the gravity of the current offence would fail to take the actor's personality, and hence his possible dangerousness, into account. Is this a sufficient reply? Another question is the degree of discretion the Act allows. For sentences up to five years, the judge has unfettered leeway to decide whether and how long to imprison any defendant. Even for the longer terms authorized for especially dangerous offenders, wide discretion remains: the judge merely "may" impose such extended terms. Is such broad leeway consistent with the idea of government by law? (This issue will be considered at length in Chapter 5 below.) Finally, how reliable are the predictions? For terms under five years, under the Act, the judge need consult only his or her own sense of how likely the defendant is to reoffend; for the longer terms, the judge is required to obtain a diagnostic report. But how trustworthy is a judge's (or even a diagnostician's) assessment of dangerousness?

The Model Sentencing Act is unusual in the very wide sweep of predictive power it allows. Actual sentencing statutes in most jurisdictions did not go quite so far. Usually, they imposed a maximum permitted sentence—and occasionally, a minimum sentence as well.[4] This meant that persons convicted of minor crimes could not receive sentences beyond the permitted maximum, on predictive grounds. For most felonies, however, the statutory maxima were high—giving wide scope to judges wishing to resort to incapacitative sentences.

Beginning in the 1970s, some penologists began raising doubts about predictive sentencing. One such discussion, by Andrew von Hirsch, is excerpted in Selection 3.2(a). The author points to the tendency of forecasts of criminality to overpredict. Although statistical forecasting methods can identify groups of offenders having higher than average probabilities of recidivism, these methods show a disturbing incidence of "false positives". Many of those classified as potential recidivists will, in fact, not be found to offend again. The rate of false positives is particularly high when forecasting serious criminality—for example, violence. The majority of those designated as dangerous turn out, when the predictions are followed up, to be persons who are not found to commit the predicted acts of violence when allowed to remain at large.

This tendency to overpredict is not easily remediable because it results from the comparative rarity of the conduct to be forecasted. Serious crimes, such as acts of violence, are, statistically speaking, rather infrequent events. When the conduct to be predicted occurs infrequently in the sample—and when the prediction method relies (as it must) on rough correlations between criminals' observed characteristics and their subsequent unlawful behaviour—the actual violators can be identified only if a large number of false positives are also included. It is like trying to shoot at a small, distant target with a blunderbuss: one can strike the target only if much of the discharge hits outside it.

False positives raises questions about the justice of predictive sentencing. Ostensibly, the offender classified as dangerous is confined to prevent him or her from infringing the rights of others. But to the extent the classification is mistaken, the offender would not have committed the infringement. The person's liberty is lost merely because people *like* him or her will offend again, and we cannot specify which of them will actually do so.

It should be noted, however, that the false positives argument is only a conditional challenge to predictive sentence: it questions not the propriety *per se* of confining a convicted offender to prevent injury to others in future, but only the propriety of doing so erroneously. Concern about false positives might thus conceivably diminish were it possible to predict future offending more accurately. Yet, as von Hirsch points out in a subsequently-written commentary excerpted as Selection 3.2(b), these more accurate predictions might have to rely even more on information concerning the defendant's social and personal history that would have still less to do with the degree of blameworthiness of his criminal choices. False positives, he concludes, may not be the central issue. Extending a person's punishment beyond his or her deserved term raises problems of proportionality (see Chapter 4), and would do so even if the predictions were quite accurate.

The question of dangerousness became the focus of debate in Great Britain, after the publication of the so-called Floud Report in 1981.[5] The report concedes the recalcitrance of the false positives problem: in predictions of dangerousness, at least half of those classified as risks will mistakenly be so classified. With such a high incidence of error, how then can sentencing on the basis of dangerousness be justified? The Report concludes that the protective sentence—defined as a term of confinement exceeding the deserved term for the past crime—should be limited to cases where the predicted harm from the offender is severe.

The Floud Report drew a number of replies—addressing the question of whether, to what extent and why the supposedly dangerous offender should be held beyond his or her deserved term. One reply was that of Nigel Walker, excerpted as Selection 3.3. In the interest of liberty, he argues, unconvicted persons should be presumed to be harmless, and thus need not fear losing their freedom on grounds of their supposed dangerousness. Any resulting risk to potential victims must be borne by those victims themselves. Once someone acts on his dangerous inclinations and is convicted of seriously harming others, however, he forfeits this presumption of harmlessness, so that he now may be held longer on grounds of the risk he presents to others. How persuasive is this argument? Punishing the offender as he deserves arguably does involve treating some of his rights as forfeited; but should dangerousness result in a greater forfeiture of his rights? And how is the forfeiture argument more than the restatement in other words of the conclusion which Walker wishes to draw, that dangerous offenders may be held longer?

Another response to the Floud Report is set forth in Selection 3.4, by A. E. Bottoms and Roger Brownswood. These authors reject the forefeiture thesis, and hold that being punished no more than one deserves is a requirement of fairness. Extending the sentence longer, then, sacrifices equity and the defendant's rights, and that sacrifice needs to be acknowledged. Rights, however, are only *prima facie* claims; and these may sometimes have to be overridden when the countervailing concerns are of sufficient urgency. Such urgency is present when an individual constitutes a "vivid danger" of seriously injuring others. Because a sacrifice of fairness is involved, however, a longer-than-deserved sentence should be invoked only when there is a substantial and immediate likelihood of serious injury occurring (see also, discussion of exceptional deviations from the deserved sentence in Selection 4.4 below). Is any response to this argument possible? Is the "vivid danger" situation really one involving conflicting rights—or is it a conflict between the defendant's right not to be held longer than he deserves and the public interest in crime prevention?

A different kind of defence of predictive sentencing is provided by Norval Morris, in Selection 3.5. Morris sees notions of desert as offering no more than broad limits on permissible punishment. (He defends this view of desert in a subsequent Selection, 4.5 below.) His point in the present selection is simply that prediction is justified within such bounds. If a fair reflection of the blameworthiness of a given offence consists of a term of imprisonment somewhere between x and y months, then a non-dangerous offender may legitimately receive a sentence closer to the lower bound, x, and the high-risk offender may legitimately receive one closer to the upper bound, y. Of course, this view is only as strong as its major premise, that desert offers only broad limits; and would require a theory about how those limits are to be identified. The justification of this premise—and the question of whether Morris can specify such limits adequately—is debated later (see, particularly, Selections 3.7, 3.8, 4.4 and 4.5 below).

If one accepts Morris' premise, the further question arises about whether—within his purported desert limits—there should be *any* requirement regarding the accuracy of the prediction. Could one offender get near the lower limit, x, and another near the upper limit, y, merely on the basis of a decision-maker's hunch that the latter person is more dangerous? Here, Morris adopts a fairly stringent criterion of what an adequate prediction should be: it needs to be *statistically* supported, and those statistics must show the person has a significantly higher likelihood of offending than other offenders of comparable crimes and criminal record. How drastically would this requirement restrict the use of prediction? How could the requirement be rationalized?

In the early 1980s, a number of studies, based mainly on interviews with incarcerated offenders, suggested that offence patterns are highly skewed, even among those individuals who recidivate after being convicted. While some recidivists reoffended only occasionally, others appeared to go on to frequent and serious reoffending. If incapacitative techniques could be targeted at the latter group—the frequent, serious violators—might these techniques not offer hope, after all, for reducing crime?

It was during this period that Peter Greenwood, a RAND Corporation researcher, published a report on a prediction technique which he termed "selective incapacitation". The technique, derived from interviews with confined offenders, made use of a few simple indicia of dangerousness, concerned mainly with offenders' criminal, unemployment, and drug-use histories. It was designed to identify "high-rate" predators—those who would commit violent offences (such as robbery) frequently. Because so many robberies were being committed by a small group of active robbers, he argued, identifying and isolating these persons could considerably reduce the incidence of such crimes. Greenwood devised a method of projecting the resulting crime reduction effect. He estimated that imposing substantially longer prison terms for the high-rate offenders could reduce the robbery rate by as much as 15 to 20 per cent, without even any significant increase in prison populations.

Greenwood's suggestions generated considerable interest among criminologists and policy-makers. Selective incapacitation is described with approval by James Q. Wilson, in a 1983 book from which Selection 3.6 is taken. It provides a useful summary of the technique and of the studies from which it is drawn.

Wilson, at the end of the extract, turns to the possible moral objections to selective incapacitation, and dismisses them. Selective incapacitation is not unfair or undeserved, he asserts, because desert sets merely broad outer limits on permissible punishments. Reliance on status factors such as employment is no serious problem, because such factors are used by the criminal justice system in other contexts. The possible inaccuracies of the prediction technique should be no bar to use, because the technique is superior to the informal predictive judgments that judges and prosecutors make today. How convincing are these arguments?

By the mid-1980s, however, objections to selective incapacitation were being raised, and these are summarized in Selection 3.7 by Andrew von Hirsch. Some of these objections concerned the empirical soundness of the prediction technique. It was pointed out that Greenwood's factors would no longer identify the high-rate offenders, if official data that courts must rely upon were utilized, instead of offenders' self-reports of their own criminal activities. The projections of large crime-reduction effects also were questioned. Those projections relied on doubtful extrapolations, from the criminal activity of *incarcerated* offenders to the activity of offenders generally. The projections also appeared to make unrealistic estimates of such important factors as the anticipated length of offenders' criminal careers. In 1986, a research panel of the National Academy of Sciences examined these issues, and concluded that selective incapacitation, at least as of the time the panel was writing, had a much more modest crime-reduction potential than Greenwood and Wilson had claimed.[6]

The ethical objection to selective incapacitation, also addressed in Selection 3.7, consists chiefly in the strategy's conflict with the requirements of proportionality. Selective incapacitation relies upon factors (e.g. early criminal history, drug use, and so forth) that have little bearing on the blameworthiness of the criminal conduct for which the offender stands convicted. The strategy can have significant crime prevention effects by its own proponents' reckoning, moreover, only if the differences in sentence length among those convicted of comparable offences are very large: the prison sentences visited on "high-risk" felons must be *much* longer than those visited on lower-risk felons convicted of the same offence. To sustain such large disparities, however, proportionality must either be disregarded entirely or be treated as only a marginal constraint.[7] How might a proponent of selective incapacitation respond to such an argument?

The final extract by Michael Tonry, Selection 3.8, takes a closer look at the debate over the ethics of predictive sentencing. He suggests how the force of the ethical objections to such strategies depends on the role and weight given to the idea of proportionality—a subject to be addressed in Chapter 4 below. The extract is particularly useful because it addresses specifically the views of several authors whose writings appear in previous excerpts.

A.v.H.

Notes

1. For a fuller description of such prediction techniques and their methodology and results, see Don M. Gottfredson, "Assessment and Prediction Methods in Crime and Delinquency", in President's National Commission for Law Enforcement and Administration of Justice, *Task Force Report: Juvenile Delinquency and Youth Crime* (U.S. Government Printing Office, 1967).

2. The Act was prepared by an advisory council of judges, sponsored by the National Council on Crime and Delinquency. The Act is model legislation only. This is the second edition, published in 1972. The first edition appeared in 1963.

3. The 5-year limit is set out in §9 of the Act, and the 30-year limit for dangerous offenders in §5.

4. See, e.g. Model Penal Code §§ 6.06 and 6.07.

5. The report is Floud J. and Young, W., *Dangerousness and Criminal Justice* (1981).

6. The report is set out in National Academy of Sciences, Panel on Research on Criminal Careers, "Report" in A. Blumstein, J. Cohen, J. Roth and C. Visher (eds.), *Criminal Careers and "Career Criminals"* (1986). For analysis of this report, see Andrew von Hirsch, "Selective Incapacitation Re-examined", (1988) 7(1) *Criminal Justice Ethics* 19.

7. For fuller discussion, see A. von Hirsch, *Past or Future Crimes* (1986), chs. 12, 15.

3.1

Sentencing on the Basis of Risk: The Model Sentencing Act

Purpose and Policy

The purpose of penal codes and sentencing is public protection. Sentences should not be based upon revenge and retribution. The policy of this Act is that dangerous offenders shall be identified, segregated, and correctively treated in custody for long terms as needed and that other offenders may be committed for a limited period. Non-dangerous offenders shall be dealt with by probation, suspended sentence, or fine wherever it appears that such disposition does not pose a danger of serious harm to public safety.

Persons convicted of crime shall be dealt with in accordance with their potential for rehabilitation, considering their individual characteristics, circumstances, and needs.

Although in general the nature of penal treatment is determined primarily by the quality of the custodial, supervisory, and administrative personnel, the philosophy and legal structure of sentencing are highly influential.

The legal structure controls the use of community treatment, suspended sentence, probation, and fines; specifies the length and place of confinement; and limits or facilitates a parole board's operation.

A model sentencing system must point the way to adequate protection of the public, as far as that can be obtained by the sentence. Sentencing on the basis of the offence does not satisfactorily provide public protection, because it does not sufficiently take into account the offender's personality.

A sentence that allows a defendant to remain in the community is preferred if it does not substantially compromise public safety—preferred because it entails lower cost to the taxpayer and less disruption to the life of the defendant and his family. The philosophy stated in this section supports non-institutional sentences wherever commitment is not clearly

From Council of Judges, National Council on Crime and Delinquency, "Model Sentencing Act, 2d Edition", (1972) 18 *Crime and Delinquency* 335. Copyright © 1972 by National Council on Crime and Delinquency. Reprinted by permission of Sage Publications, Inc.

needed for public protection Hence the statement at the outset that the purpose of penal codes and sentences is public protection.

In cases where the harm was slight or where the mere apprehension and prosecution are deemed sufficient for the purposes of deterrence, a suspended sentence may be the best alternative. Where greater control is required, probation or commitment is indicated, but not because the judge thinks it will do the defendant some good. Vengeance or punishment is not a proper motive for a sentence; so neither is treatment. The dominant purpose of the sentence—not only commitment but also suspended sentence, probation, and fine—is public protection.

[The Model Act then goes on to authorize up to five years' imprisonment for any offender whom the court deems likely to reoffend: and up to 30 years' imprisonment for offenders who have inflicted, or attempted to inflict, serious bodily harm, provided the court finds the offender is "suffering a severe mental or emotional disorder indicating a propensity toward continuing dangerous criminal activity"—eds.]

3.2

The Problem of False Positives

ANDREW VON HIRSCH

3.2(a) The False Positives Problem

Restraint of the potential recidivist—"predictive restraint", as we shall call it—has been an important theme in traditional sentencing theory. If the offender is thought likely to offend again, he should be incapacitated so that he cannot do so. The idea has been endorsed by the Model Penal Code, which states that an offender may be confined if the sentencing judge finds "there is undue risk that during the period of a suspended sentence or probation the defendant will commit another crime".[1] The Model Sentencing Act[2] relies still more heavily on prediction of future criminality in deciding which convicted offenders are to be confined. Predictive restraint is also very much part of sentencing practice in many jurisdictions. It is routine for sentencing judges and parole boards to try to gauge whether the convicted defendant is apt to revert to his criminal ways. If he is considered a potential recidivist, he is more likely to go to prison and stay there longer.

Restraining persons thought likely to return to crime seems sensible enough: whatever other disadvantages incarceration may have, it can prevent criminally inclined individuals from offending against persons outside—at least during their confinement. If incarceration serves this purpose, what more logical way is there of selecting which offenders are to be confined, and for how long, than by assessing their criminal propensities? But this assumes that one can, indeed, forecast recidivism accurately; and, not surprisingly, the proponents of preventive intervention claim much predictive acuity.

But the ability to predict dangerousness has not lived up to such hopes. One reason for error has been that predictors—be they judges, psychia-

From A. von Hirsch, *Doing Justice* (New York: Hill and Wang, 1976), ch. 3 with some textual changes.

trists, or correctional officials—seldom have taken the trouble to follow up their forecasts and check their accuracy, and thus learn from their mistakes. But even were forecasts verified systematically, that still would not yield the "reasonable accuracy" of which the Model Sentencing Act speaks so optimistically.[3] For a more fundamental problem is encountered: an inherent tendency to overpredict.

The forecasting of criminal behaviour has been a topic of interest to criminologists for nearly half a century—since E. W. Burgess at the University of Chicago published the first prediction table for parole recidivism in 1928.[4]

However, the forecasters' criterion of accuracy tended to be one-sided—looking only to success in identifying those persons who subsequently *do* offend. Overprediction, the other side of the coin, was seldom considered: in how many instances does the prediction yield what statisticians call "false positives"—persons mistakenly predicted to offend? When forecasting assaultive behaviour, for example, how many individuals predicted to commit assaults would have turned out subsequently *not* to attack anyone? When prediction is being relied upon to determine whether and for how long a convicted offender is to be confined, mistakenly classifying him as a potential recidivist has the gravest consequences—the extended loss of his liberty.

The tendency to overpredict derives from the comparative rarity of the conduct to be predicted. Serious crimes are, statistically speaking, infrequent events; and the rarer the event, the greater will be the incidence of false positives. Thus:

Methods of predicting criminal behaviour, whether clinical or statistical, are blunt instruments. Unlike the incipient tubercular, the potential recidivist does not carry easily spotted symptoms of his condition; the predictor has to rely on correlations between offenders' currently observed characteristics and any subsequent criminal behaviour on their part. The data will necessarily be crude: only grossly observable characteristics of the offender population can ordinarily be identified; and the measurement of outcome—subsequent criminal conduct—is notoriously unreliable, given the problems of undetected violations and selective enforcement.

If the conduct to be predicted occurs rarely in the sample, the crudity of these inputs takes its toll. With a predictive instrument of so little discernment and a target population so small, the forecaster will be able to spot a significant percentage of the actual violators *only if a large number of false positives is also included.* The process resembles trying to hit a small bull's-eye with a blunderbuss: to strike the centre of the target with any of the shot, the marksman will have to allow most of his discharge to hit outside it. A number of studies examining the accuracy of forecasts of recidivism thus report a high rate of false positives, ranging from one true positive for every eight false positives, to one true for every two false positives.[5]

There will be fewer false positives if less serious infractions are taken into account—for these are not so rare. Even a crude forecasting instrument will not overpredict much if the event to be predicted occurs frequently in the sample.[6] (It is like our marksman with the blunderbuss aiming at a very large target.) But to obtain this higher rate, one finds oneself fast descending the scale of seriousness toward lesser violations. As that happens, it becomes increasingly difficult to demonstrate a need for protecting society that is of sufficient urgency to warrant the extended deprivation of the offender's freedom.

Overprediction has disturbing implications. It suggests not merely that the predictions are fallible (what judgments are not?) but that they are prone to be grossly in error: most of those deemed to be risks—and confined on that account—may have been misclassified. Whatever the utility of holding those offenders who would in fact offend again, confining the false positives is dubious justice. Ostensibly, those spotted as potential recidivists are being deprived of their liberty to prevent them from infringing on the rights of others. But, to the extent the prediction is wrong, that infringement would not have occurred. Granted, we are speaking of persons who have already been convicted of an offence. But the objection persists where a convicted individual is, on the basis of a mistaken prediction, being held *longer* than he otherwise would have been, had the prediction not influenced his sentence.

A forecast, while overpredicting, will also spot persons who actually are dangerous (so-called true positives). Unless these are confined, innocent people will be hurt. But more false positives may be confined than victims spared—for, as we just noted, the false positives are apt to outnumber the true by a substantial margin. And mistaken intervention may be especially objectionable, because the individual who is the false positive is being injured by the state under claim of right. No recognition can be accorded him or the wrong he suffers—as his confinement necessarily prevents him from demonstrating that he would have done no harm had he remained at large. The true positive's victim is likewise injured—but at least the injury is not treated by society as *rightfully* inflicted.

Admittedly, there are other contexts where one's willingness to take risks diminishes as the gravity of the risk increases, irrespective of the number of false positives. One would withdraw the licence of an airplane pilot who became ill if there was even a slight chance that his health could affect the safety of his passengers. But predictive restraint poses special ethical problems. The fact that the person's liberty is at stake reduces the moral acceptability of mistakes of overprediction.

3.2(b) The False Positives Problem: Second Thoughts

When critics of positivism started questioning predictive sentencing in the early 1970s, they had two arguments: one that concerned overprediction, and the other, desert. Prediction of recidivism yielded an unacceptably high incidence of false positives. It also punished persons for wrongful choices not yet made. The two arguments, it was thought, fitted nicely together, and prediction restraint was obnoxious for both reasons. I took this stand myself (see Selection 3.2(a) above).

The attraction of the false-positives argument—the reason it seemed a useful supplement to the desert contention—is that it was less intellectually ambitious. To sustain the desert claim, one needed to justify a theory of punishment oriented to the past; to explain why it was wrong in principle to sentence on consequentialist grounds. The false-positive argument required no such philosophical underpinnings. One could, it seemed, simply hoist the prediction advocate by his own petard: even if the confinement of those who would recidivate were assumed justified, many of those predicted to be recidivists would *not* in fact return to crime. The unfairness arose from visiting predictive restraint on actually harmless persons.

Sometimes, prediction advocates responded by denying the existence of the false-positive problem. A prediction of dangerousness, it was said, is a statement of present condition, not a claim about future results (see Selection 3.5 below). To say A is dangerous is to say he is now able and possibly inclined to injure someone; and that claim is not falsified by the fact that he does not inflict the harm. The analogy sometimes cited is to unexploded bombs. After World War II, these were found at various sites in England and Germany, and had to be defused. There were few injuries—hence the rate of false positives was high. Yet no one could say that therefore the bombs were not dangerous.

The critics of prediction, however, had a ready reply. We can say bombs are dangerous because we can identify what makes them so—fuses, explosives, and so on. "Dangerous" individuals do not provide us with such

From A. von Hirsch *Past or Future Crimes* (New Brunswick, NJ: Rutgers University Press, 1986), pp. 176–8 with some textual changes.

convenient indica. The recidivist has not a perceptibly different makeup from the non-recidivist, and predicting dangerousness is almost exclusively a matter of following up offenders' subsequent conduct. Hence it *is* important how often the predicted conduct does actually occur. Moreover, bombs are not thought of as individuals with rights; the destruction of a bomb-shell that would not have exploded is not something that should trouble us. Offenders, by contrast, are persons with rights, and when confined they surely suffer. If that suffering is justified by reference to the injury they would have visited on others, it becomes a matter of legitimate concern whether the person would have committed the predicted misdeed. The bomb analogy fails.

Critics of predictive sentencing could be comfortable with the false-positive argument, moreover, because overprediction seemed so tenacious. Earlier prediction studies showed rates of up to eight false positives for every one true. Later prediction indices did somewhat better, but they still tended to show overprediction rates of 60 per cent or more: there were about two false positives for every true (see Selection 3.2(a)). The state of the predictive art seemed such that the false-positive objection could not be overcome. Critics had a simple, empirically-based reason for resisting individual prediction in sentencing.

Further reflection has brought out, however, that matters are not quite so simple. The two arguments, about false positives and desert, turn out to be in some conflict with one another. Pursuit of the desert line may lead to different conclusions than pursuit of the overprediction line, and vice versa.

The false-positive argument does not in principle question the appropriateness of predictive sentencing. The issue becomes only one of accuracy: were one able to reduce the number of false positives, selective incapacitation would become unobjectionable. The argument does not address the nature of prediction criteria—with sufficient accuracy, it would not matter whether those criteria relied on the current crimes, past crimes, or social factors; and whether or not sentences observed parity among offenders convicted for similar crimes.

Desert works differently. The acceptability of sentencing criteria depends on whether and to what extent these rely (chiefly at last) on the gravity of the criminal conduct, in determining the severity of the prescribed sanctions. Standards that rely on offence gravity would pass muster, even if poor predictors of recidivism; and those that rely chiefly on ulterior factors (say, the number of prior arrests or the offender's social history) would infringe desert criteria even if they happened to predict recidivism well.

Concentrating on the false-positive issue, with its emphasis on accuracy, therefore could have troublesome implications. To minimize the number of false positives, one needs a predictive device that is quite discriminating—that is, which accounts for a substantial percentage of variability in offender behaviour. To achieve that degree of sensitivity, one probably needs a highly selective prediction device: one that uses a combination of items about the offender's criminal and social past. Consequently, a preoccupation with false positives could lead one to prefer those prediction schemes that are most sensitive and selective—and hence potentially most in breach of the equal-treatment requirements of desert.

The most blatantly objectionable schemes, however, are those which both violate desert and have high false-positive rates. Individual prediction schemes that pick and choose particular offenders deemed dangerous from among those convicted of a given crime, and that do so with much overprediction, cannot be sustained by any concept of fairness.

Notes

1. Model Penal Code, §7.01(1)(a).
2. Model Sentencing Act, §§1, 5, 9 (see Selection 1.1 above).
3. Model Sentencing Act, Preface.
4. E. W. Burgess, "Factors Determining Success or Failure on Parole", in *The Workings of The Indeterminate Sentence Law of Illinois*, ed. by A. A. Bruce, A. G. Haino, and E. W. Burgess (Springfield, Ill.: State Board of Parole, 1928).
5. Ernst A. Wenk and James O. Robison, "Assaultive Experience and Assaultive Potential", National Council on Crime and Delinquency Research Center, Davis, Cal., 1971 (unpublished monograph); findings subsequently published in Ernst A. Wenk and Robert L. Emrich, "Assaultive Youth: An Exploratory Study of the Assaultive Experience and Assaultive Potential of California Youth Authority Wards", (1972) 9 *J. Research in Crime and Delinquency* 171; Harry L. Kozol, Richard J. Boucher, and Ralph F. Garofalo, "The Diagnosis and Treatment of Dangerousness", (1972) 18 *Crime and Delinquency* 371; J. Monahan, *Predicting Violent Behaviour* (Beverly Hills, Cal.: Sage, 1981).
6. The false-positive rate will decline as the "base rate" (that is, the rate in the sample of the events to be predicted) approaches 50 per cent. See Paul E. Meehl and Albert Rosen, "Antecedent Probability and the Efficiency of Psychometric Signs, Patterns and Cutting Scores", (1955) 52 *Psychol. Bull.* 194.

3.3

Incapacitation, Dangerousness and Forfeiture of Rights

NIGEL WALKER

The Presumption of Harmlessness

The harm someone has caused or attempted to cause is more than a predictor: it is part of the moral justification for subjecting that person to a precautionary measure. We are all at risk of being harmed by members of the free public who have not hitherto harmed anyone, or at least are not known to have done so. This is, in fact, the most frequent example of violence or sexual molestation which comes to official notice. Against this eventuality we can protect ourselves or our nearest and dearest only by taking our own unofficial precautions. It is not simply that society lacks the resources to interfere with possible attackers. Anti-protectionists argue that people who have not yet caused harm to others have a right not to be interfered with. This right is based on the presumption of harmlessness. One may recognise this right, but ask whether, like other rights, it can be renounced or forfeited. Someone who has harmed, or tried to harm, another person, can hardly claim a right to the presumption of harmlessness: he has forfeited that right, and given society the right to interfere in his life. (The presumption of harmlessness should not be confused with the presumption of innocence in criminal trials). The right to interfere need not be seen as a duty: courts should have discretion to decide, in the light of the nature of the apprehended harm and other considerations, whether to exercise that right, and how drastically. The justification is not a duty based on retribution but the offender's forfeiture of an immunity.

From N. Walker, "Ethical and Other Problems" in N. Walker (ed.), *Dangerous People* (London: Blackstone, 1996), at p. 7.

3.4

Incapacitation and "Vivid Danger"

A. E. BOTTOMS AND ROGER BROWNSWORD

We have taken a position in the dangerousness debate which has owed a great deal to Ronald Dworkin's (1977) seminal work on rights theory (see Bottoms and Brownsword, 1982). The ingredients of our position are these. We start by assuming that the State has the duty to treat its members with equal concern and respect; and the members have the correlative right against the State. Dworkin (1977, pp. 272–3) expresses the idea thus: "I presume that we all accept the following postulates of political morality. Government must treat those whom it governs with concern, that is, as human beings who are capable of suffering and frustration, and with respect, that is, as human beings who are capable of forming and acting on intelligent conceptions of how their lives should be lived. Government must not only treat people with concern and respect, but with equal concern and respect".

We would wish to argue that the right to equal concern and respect is axiomatic regardless of popular acceptance of the idea, but this apart we would adopt Dworkin's statement without qualification. The force of a right is that it shuts out appeals to expediency, or convenience, or public interest. A right can only be defeated by a competing right.

If A's exercise of his rights interferes with B's exercise of his rights, then we have a situation of competing rights. Suppose that A wishes to speak on some issue in a public place (we assume that A is exercising his right to freedom of expression) but that A's speech will precipitate large-scale public disorder which will result in B's subjection to physical aggression (we assume that B has the right not to be assaulted). Here we have a case of competing rights. It is, of course, no easy matter to decide which right should prevail. However, if the State limited A's right in the interests of safeguarding B's right then at least the *form* of the justification would be sound. A right can only be limited for the sake of a more pressing right.

From A. E. Bottoms, and R. Brownsword, "The Dangerousness Debate After the Floud Report" (1982) 22 *British Journal of Criminology* 229, with some textual changes.

Thus, our response to the various riddles thrown up by the dangerousness debate would have two stages: (i) to determine whether or not any rights are at stake; and (ii) to resolve any problems presented by competing rights. We can start by rehearsing the approach that we would take towards protective sentences.

The question of protective sentencing seems to us quite clearly to involve rights. An offender has a right to release at the end of normal term; equally we believe that citizens have, *inter alia*, the right not to be physically assaulted and the right to pursue an intelligent conception of the good life. So, we have a problem of competing rights. We suggest, following a rather under-developed remark by Dworkin (1977, p. 11), that a "vivid danger" test should be employed. The idea is that the offender's right to release should not be violated by imposing a protective sentence unless his release posed a vivid danger to other rights-holders. Therefore we set up a test with the following components: (i) *seriousness* (what type and degree of injury is in contemplation?); (ii) *temporality*, which breaks down into *frequency* (over a given period, how many injurious acts are expected?) and *immediacy* (how soon is the next injurious act?); and (iii) *certainly* (how sure are we that this person will act as predicted?) Within the vivid danger test the certainty component is absolutely crucial. For a protective sentence will certainly violate an offender's right to release, and will probably do so for a very long time; thus we need a pretty powerful reason for acting in this fashion. It simply will not do to say that there is an outside chance that some other person's rights will be infringed by the offender should he be released. So long as we are less certain about the offender violating somebody else's rights than we are about violating the offender's rights, then we have to tread extremely carefully in violating the latter's rights. Given the present state of the predictive art in relation to dangerousness sentences (a false positive rate of up to 66 per cent) we conclude that protective sentences would only *very exceptionally* be justified, the justification laying in the anticipated depth of the offender's violation of the rights of others (discounted by the degree of uncertainty) outweighing the depth of the known violation of the offender's rights.

References

Bottoms, A. E. and Brownsword, R. (1982), "Dangerousness and Rights", in J. Hinton (ed.), *Dangerousness: Problems of Assessment and Prediction* (London: Allen and Unwin).
Dworkin, R. (1977), *Taking Rights Seriously* (London: Duckworth).

3.5

Incapacitation Within Limits

NORVAL MORRIS

In the criminal law, if not in international relations, the pre-emptive strike has great attraction; to capture the criminal before the crime is surely an alluring idea. In a variety of ways, implicit and expressed, that idea has been pursued for centuries and is being more vigorously pursued today—and, of course, it is also at the foundation of the civil commitment of those mentally ill or retarded persons who are thought likely to be a danger to themselves or others.

My purpose here, as I have tried to define it, is not at all to attack the idea of the pre-emptive strike. I think one could easily attack it—it is far from invulnerable—but my effort is different, and is clearly more difficult. I will try to enunciate those principles under which such pre-emptive strikes would be jurisprudentially acceptable.

To discuss the definition and application of concepts of dangerousness in the criminal law, and in the law relating to mental health, may give the impression that I favour the widespread application of this concept. I certainly do not. My submission is different. It is that a jurisprudence that pretends to exclude such concepts is self-deceptive; they will frequently figure prominently in decision-making, whether or not they are spelled out in jurisprudence. One can pretend to ignore such predictions, but it will be a pretense. My view is that it is better to recognize the reality of such predictions and try to put them into their proper jurisprudential place, difficult though that may be.

But that is not the only reason for pursuing this topic of reliance on predictions of dangerousness. There is a larger justification. Suppose our present weak predictive capacity proves to be the best we can do for decades, which I think quite likely. Suppose for a high risk of a crime of violence

From Norval Morris, "On 'Dangerousness' in the Judicial Process", (1982) 39 *Record of the Association of the Bar of the City of New York* 102 with some textual changes. The original lecture was the Thirty-eighth Annual Cardozo Lecture of the Association of the Bar of the City of New York. Excerpted and reprinted by permission.

the best we can do at present is to predict one in three, in the sense that to be sure of preventing one crime we would have to lock up three people. My submission is, and it is a difficult one, that it is still ethically appropriate and socially desirable to take such predictions into account in many police, prosecutorial, judicial, correctional, and legislative decisions.

A statement of a prediction of dangerousness is a statement of a present condition, not the prediction of a particular result. The belief that it is the prediction of a result is an error that is constantly made and leads many astray. An analogy to a dangerous object rather than to a dangerous person may help clarify my point.

I remember the drab postwar days in London. The bombing had stopped but the scars of war were pervasive. And on occasion the risks of war returned in their earlier force. An unexploded bomb would be found and would have to be moved and rendered safe. Death and severe injuries were very rare; the base expectancy rate was very low; there were large numbers of "false positives" for every "true positive"—bombs that didn't go off, as distinguished from those that did. The area would be cleared; the bomb disposal crew would begin their delicate work and in all but a few instances manage it successfully. When the talk resumed that night in the neighbouring pub, would anyone say the bomb was not dangerous because it did not go off? Would anyone say that because it proved to be a "false positive" it was not dangerous? Of course not; that is not how words are used when the focus is on dangerous things as distinct from dangerous people. Yet the similarities of risk and analysis are great. Why the difference of usage? In part, I think, because we tend to think of dangerous people as those who intend harm—yet that view conceals the psychological reality. In sum, that the person predicted as dangerous does no future injury does not mean that the classification was erroneous.

False Positives and the Conviction of the Innocent

I want to defend three submissions, which are:

1. Punishment should not be imposed, nor the term of punishment extended, by virtue of a prediction of dangerousness, beyond that which would be justified as a deserved punishment independently of that prediction.
2. Provided the previous limitation is respected, predictions of dangerousness may properly influence sentencing decisions (and other decisions under the criminal law).

3. The base expectancy rate for the criminal predicted as dangerous must be shown by reliable evidence to be substantially higher than the base expectancy rate for another criminal, with a closely similar criminal record and convicted of a closely similar crime, but not so predicted as unusually dangerous, before any distinction based on his higher dangerousness may be relied on to intensify or extend his punishment.

These three submissions form an effort to state a jurisprudence of predictions of dangerousness for punishment purposes that would achieve both individual justice and better community protection. It would seem futile to deny the relevance and propriety of such predictions to a wide range of discretions exercised under the aegis of the criminal law, and in particular to decisions whether to imprison and for how long. Yet, if moral issues are to be taken seriously, the fact of approved use is not compelling and the morality of applying predictions based on group behaviour to predict the likely behaviour of the individual requires justification.

Thought has been led astray here, by equating the assumption of power (or of extra power) over the individual on a basis of a prediction of dangerousness to reluctance to risk convicting the innocent. The model of the criminal trial has confused analysis.

If it is true that it is better that nine guilty men be acquitted rather than one innocent man be convicted, why does not a similar though more compelling equation apply to the prediction of dangerousness—so that it is better that two men who would not in fact injure or threaten others (two false positives) should be released rather than one who would (one true positive) be detained? If one to nine is unacceptable in one case, how can two to one be acceptable in the other?

This line of reasoning, though it has persuaded many commentators and some judges, seems to me deeply flawed. The equation with the proof of guilt misses the point. Let us assume a properly convicted criminal, criminal X, with a one-in-three base expectancy rate of violence (as we have defined it), and another criminal, criminal Y, also properly convicted of the identical offence, but who has a very much lower base expectancy rate—same record, same offence. Unlike X, Y was not a school dropout; he has a job to which he may return and a supportive family who will take him back if he is not imprisoned, or after this release from prison. May criminal X be sent to prison while criminal Y is not? Or may criminal X be sent to prison for a longer term than criminal Y, despite the same record and the same gravity of offence, the longer sentence being justified by the utilitarian advantages of selective incapacitation? My answer to both questions is in the affirmative; he may. But since this appears to be the advocacy of locking up two "innocent" men to prevent crime by a third, I must offer a brief defence of my view.

The central idea that moves me in defining the foregoing submissions and the conclusion about criminal X is recognition of the imprecision of our moral callipers. In no exact sense can one say of punishment: "That was a just punishment". All I have ever been able to say about the justice of a particular sentence on a convicted criminal, and all I have ever thought people sensibly said was: "As we know our community and its values, that does not seem to be an unjust punishment". Retributive sentiments properly limit but do not define a just punishment.

The injustice of a punishment, assuming proper proof of guilt, is thus defined in part deontologically, in limited retributivist terms and not solely in utilitarian terms. The upper and lower limits of "deserved" punishment set the range in which utilitarian values, including values of mercy and human understanding, may properly fix the punishment to be imposed. There is always a range of a "not unjust" punishment, measured in relation to the gravity of an offence and the offender's criminal record. (See further, Selection 4.5 below.)

The philosophy of punishment I am offering is that of a limiting retributivist, and I suggest that punishments, and a just scale of punishment, should always allow for discretion to be exercised, under proper legislative guidance, by the judicial officer of the state.

The key to the argument I am advancing is my third submission—that the base expectancy rate for the criminal predicted as dangerous must be shown by reliable evidence to be substantially higher than the base expectancy rate for another criminal, with a closely similar criminal record and convicted of a closely similar crime, but not so predicted as unusually dangerous, before any distinction based on his higher dangerousness may be relied on to intensify or extend his punishment. This may seem a pallid and toothless proposition, but if accepted it would have a dramatically restrictive effect onto the acceptability of predictions of dangerousness in the criminal law. Rightly or wrongly, prior record and severity of the last offence are seen in all legal systems as defining the retributive range of punishment. Once criminal record and severity of the last offence are included, the definition of groups with higher base expectancy rates than those with similar crimes and similar criminal records becomes very much more difficult of proof.

Let me test this submission in relation to my criminals X and Y and show you one real defect in what I am offering.

Criminals X and Y had identical criminal records and had committed identical crimes, but Y was not a school dropout, Y had a job to which he could return if not sent to prison, and Y had a supportive family who would take him back if allowed to do so, while the unfortunate X was a school dropout, was unemployed, and lacked a supportive family. And let us suppose that past studies reveal that criminals with X's criminal record and with his environmental circumstances have a base expectancy rate of 1 in 10 of being involved in a crime of personal violence. While no such calculations have been made for criminals like Y, it is quite clear that they have a much lower base expectancy rate of future violent criminality. I suggest that X should be held longer than Y based on these predictions.

In fairness I must note that I have lured myself onto some very unpleasant terrain, for the reality in the USA at this time will be that my apparently aseptic principles will grossly favour the wealthy to the detriment of the poor, and will be used to justify even more imprisonment of blacks and other underclass minorities than at present obtains—as will the whole "selective incapacitation" process. Put curtly, without knowing more about our hypothetical criminals, we already confidently guess the pigmentation of X and Y. As a matter of statistical likelihood, Y is white and X is black.

I do not take lightly this line of criticism of the thesis I have offered here. I do not enjoy advancing principles which if accepted would have those effects. So let me offer one or two comments by way of explanation—not really apology—for my thesis. The sad fact is that in our society predictors of violence are not racially neutral. How could they be racially neutral, when at this moment one of every twenty black males in their twenties is either in prison or in jail? And that really underestimates the difference between blacks and whites in prisons and jails, since when black youths move into the middle class their crime rates are just the same as those of white youths. It is the black underclass, left behind, which has these enormously high rates of imprisonment and jailing and very much higher rates of violence. Predicting violence in the inner-city slum is grossly easier than predicting it in the dormitory suburb. And what else is characteristic of the inner-city ghetto? Much else that distinguishes our criminal X from our criminal Y—school absenteeism, unemployment, functional illiteracy, generations on welfare, no supportive families. Blackness and a higher base expectancy rate of violence overlap. And that is the problem of all these pre-emptive sentencing processes.

What, then, is the conclusion properly to be drawn from these sad realities? Some would say: "Don't base decisions in the criminal justice system at all on predictions of dangerousness; they are racially skewed, and we already lock up too many members of our minorities". I sympathize with the reason, but reject the conclusion. The criminal justice system cannot rectify racial inequalities and social injustices; it will do well if it does not exacerbate them. It is proper that predictions of violence should figure in many decisions in applying the criminal law, and if they are applied within principles that I am seeking to tease out, that is all that can be expected. My submissions may be in error, but if they are, then anyone seeking to apply predictions should offer alternative predictions. We cannot properly close our eyes to the different threats that criminal X and criminal Y pose to the community. But it is of first importance that we base our decisions about their respective dangerousness on validated knowledge and not on prejudice, particularly racial prejudice, and hence that we insist on the most careful validation of such stereotypes of dangerousness; my submissions are an effort to define what is required to achieve such validation. We must insist, if predictions are to be used, that they be reliable.

To conclude. As is so often the case with issues of justice, procedural and evidentiary issues become of central importance. Let me put the point curtly and again. Clinical predictions of dangerousness unsupported by actuarial studies should never be relied on. Clinical judgments firmly grounded on well-established base expectancy rates are a precondition, rarely fulfilled, to the just invocation of prediction of dangerousness as a ground for intensifying punishment.

I must admit that, if my submissions are accepted, I doubt the availability of sufficient knowledge to meet the necessary preconditions of just sentencing based on express predictions of violence. Further that gap in our knowledge should make us sceptical about our present widespread reliance on implicit and intuitive predictions of dangerousness in exercising discretion—in situations where we do not declare that usage as we do in the situations I have been discussing.

3.6

Selective Incapacitation

JAMES Q. WILSON

When criminals are deprived of their liberty, as by imprisonment (or banishment, or very tight control in the community), their ability to commit offences against citizens is ended. We say these persons have been "incapacitated", and we try to estimate the amount by which crime is reduced by this incapacitation.

Incapacitation cannot be the sole purpose of the criminal justice system; if it were, we would put everybody who has committed one or two offences in prison until they were too old to commit another. And if we thought prison too costly, we would simply cut off their hands or their heads. Justice, humanity, and proportionality, among other goals, must also be served by the courts.

But there is one great advantage to incapacitation as a crime control strategy—namely, it does not require us to make any assumptions about human nature. By contrast, deterrence works only if people take into account the costs and benefits of alternative courses of action and choose that which confers the largest net benefit (or the smallest net cost). Though people almost surely do take such matters into account, it is difficult to be certain by how much such considerations affect their behaviour and what change, if any, in crime rates will result from a given, feasible change in either the costs of crime or the benefits of not committing a crime. Rehabilitation works only if the values, preferences, or time-horizon of criminals can be altered by plan. There is not much evidence that we can make these alterations for large numbers of persons, though there is some evidence that it can be done for a few under certain circumstances.

Incapacitation, on the other hand, works by definition: its effects result from the physical restraint placed upon the offender and not from his sub-

From James Q. Wilson, "Dealing with the High-Rate Offender", (1983) 72 *The Public Interest* 52 with some textual changes. Reprinted by permission of the author and publisher. Copyright © 1983 by National Affairs, Inc.

jective state. More accurately, it works provided at least three conditions are met: some offenders must be repeaters, offenders taken off the streets must not be immediately and completely replaced by new recruits, and prison must not increase the post-release criminal activity of those who have been incarcerated sufficiently to offset the crimes prevented by their stay in prison.

The first condition is surely true. Every study of prison inmates shows that a large fraction (recently, about two-thirds) of them had prior criminal records before their current incarceration; every study of ex-convicts shows that a significant fraction (estimates vary from a quarter to a half) are rearrested for new offences within a relatively brief period. In short, the great majority of persons in prison are repeat offenders, and thus prison, whatever else it may do, protects society from the offences these persons would commit if they were free.

The second condition—that incarcerating one robber does not lead automatically to the recruitment of a new robber to replace him—seems plausible. Although some persons, such as Ernest van den Haag, have argued that new offenders will step forward to take the place vacated by the imprisoned offenders, they have presented no evidence that this is the case, except, perhaps, for certain crimes (such as narcotics trafficking or prostitution) which are organized along business lines.[1] For the kinds of predatory street crimes with which we are concerned—robbery, burglary, auto theft, larceny—there are no barriers to entry and no scarcity of criminal opportunities. No one need wait for a "vacancy" to appear before he can find an opportunity to become a criminal. The supply of robbers is not affected by the number of robbers practicing, because existing robbers have no way of excluding new robbers and because the opportunity for robbing (if you wish, the "demand" for robbery) is much larger than the existing number of robberies. In general, the earnings of street criminals are not affected by how many "competitors" they have.

The third condition that must be met if incapacitation is to work is that prisons must not be such successful "schools for crime" that the crimes prevented by incarceration are outnumbered by the increased crimes committed after release attributable to what was learned in prison. It is doubtless the case that for some offenders prison is a school; it is also doubtless that for other offenders prison is a deterrent. The former group will commit more, or more skillful, crimes after release; the latter will commit fewer crimes after release. The question, therefore, is whether the net effect of these two offsetting tendencies is positive or negative. In general, there is no evidence that the prison experience makes offenders as a whole more criminal, and there is some evidence that certain kinds of offenders (especially certain younger ones) may be deterred by a prison experience. Moreover, interviews with prisoners reveal no relationship between the number of crimes committed and whether the offenders had served a prior prison term. Though there are many qualifications that should be made to this bald summary, there is no evidence that the net effect of prison is to increase the crime rates of ex-convicts sufficiently to cancel out the gains to society resulting from incapacitation.

To determine the amount of crime that is prevented by incarcerating a given number of offenders for a given length of time, the key estimate we must make is the number of offences a criminal commits per year free on the street.[2] If a community experiences one thousand robberies a year, it obviously makes a great deal of difference whether these robberies are the work of ten robbers, each of whom commits one hundred robberies per year, or the work of one thousand robbers, each of whom commits only one robbery per year. In the first case, locking up only five robbers will cut the number of robberies in half; in the second case, locking up one hundred robbers will only reduce the number of robberies by 10 per cent.

In the late 1970s, researchers at the Rand Corporation had been interviewing prisoners (first in California, then in other states) to find out directly from known offenders how much crime they were committing while free.[3] No-one can be certain, of course, that the reports of the convicts constitute an accurate record of their crimes, undetected as well as detected, but the Rand researchers cross-checked the information against arrest records and looked for evidence of internal consistency in the self-reports. Moreover, the inmates volunteered information about crimes they had committed but for which they had not been arrested. Still, it is quite possible that the self-reports were somewhat inaccurate. However, it is reasonable to assume that inmates would be more likely to conceal crimes they did commit rather than admit to crimes they did not commit. Thus, any errors in these self-reports probably lead to an underestimate of the true rate of criminality of these persons.

The Rand Group learned that the "average" individual offence rate was virtually a meaningless term because the inmates they interviewed differed so sharply in how many crimes they committed. A large number of offenders committed a small number of offences while free and a small number of offenders committed a very large number of offences. In statistical language, the distribution of offences was highly skewed. For example, the median number of burglaries committed by the inmates in the three states was about 5 a year, but the 10 per cent of the inmates who were the highest-rate offenders committed an average of 232 burglaries a year. The median number of robberies was also about 5 a year, but the top 10 per cent of offenders committed an average of 87 a year. As Peter W. Greenwood, one of the members of the Rand group, put it, incarcerating one robber who was among the top 10 per cent in offence rates would prevent more robberies than incarcerating eighteen offenders who were at or below the median.[4]

All the evidence we have implies that, for crime-reduction purposes, the most rational way to use the incapacitative powers of our prisons would be to do so selectively. Instead of longer sentences for everyone, or for persons who have prior records, or for persons whose present crime is especially grave, longer sentences would be given primarily to those who, when free, commit the most crimes.

But how do we know who these high-rate, repeat criminals are? Knowing the nature of the present offence is not a good clue. The reason for this is quite simple—most street criminals do not specialize. Today's robber can be tomorrow's burglar and the next day's car thief.[5] When the police happen to arrest him, the crime for which he is arrested is determined by a kind of lottery—he happened to be caught red-handed, or as the result of a tip, committing a particular crime that may or may not be the same as either his previous crime or his next one. If judges give sentences based entirely on he gravity of the present offence, then a high-rate offender may get off lightly because on this occasion he happened to be caught snatching a purse. The low-rate offender may get a long sentence because he was unlucky enough to be caught robbing a liquor store with a gun.

Prosecutors have an understandable tendency to throw the book at persons caught committing a serious crime, especially if they have been caught before. To a certain extent, we want to encourage that tendency. After all, we not only want to reduce crime, we want to see criminals get their just deserts. Society would not, and should not, tolerate a system in which a prosecutor throws the book at purse snatchers and lets armed robbers off with a suspended sentence. But while society's legitimate desire for retribution must set the outer bounds of any sentencing policy, there is still room for flexibility within those bounds. We can, for example, act so that all robbers are punished with prison terms, but give, within certain relatively narrow ranges, longer sentences to those robbers who commit the most crimes.

If knowing the nature of the present offence and even knowing the prior record of the offender are not accurate guides to identifying high-rate offenders, what is? Obviously, we cannot ask the offenders. They may cooperate with researchers once in jail, but they have little incentive to cooperate with prosecutors before they go to jail, especially if the price of co-operation is to get a tougher sentence. But we can see what legally admissible, objective attributes of the offenders best predict who is and who is not a high-rate offender. In the Rand study, Greenwood and his colleagues discovered, by trial and error, that the following seven factors, taken together, were highly predictive of a convicted person being a high-rate offender: he (1) was convicted of a crime while a juvenile (that is, before age 16), (2) used illegal drugs as a juvenile, (3) used illegal drugs during the previous two years, (4) was employed less than 50 per cent of the time during the previous two years, (5) served time in a juvenile facility, (6) was incarcerated in prison more than 50 per cent of the previous two years, and (7) was previously convicted for the present offence.

Using this scale, Greenwood found that 82 per cent of those predicted to be low-rate offenders in fact were, and 82 per cent of those predicted to be medium- or high-rate offenders also were. To understand how big these differences are, the median California prison inmate who is predicted to be a low-rate offender will in fact commit slightly more than one burglary and slightly less than one robbery per year free. By contrast, the median California inmate who is predicted to be a high-rate offender will commit ninety-three burglaries and thirteen robberies per year free. In other states, this prediction scale may be more or less accurate.

Opinions differ as to the effect on the crime rate and prison population of making sentences for high-rate offenders longer than those for low-rate ones. Greenwood applied his scale to California and found that if all low-rate robbers received two-year prison terms (most now receive longer ones) and all high-rate robbers received seven-year terms (most now receive shorter ones), the number of robberies committed in the state would drop by an estimated 20 per cent with no increase in the prison population.

Obviously, a policy of reducing crime by selective incapacitation (that is, by adjusting prison terms to reflect predicted individual offence rates) raises a number of issues. Though these issues are important, one must bear in mind that they cannot be resolved by comparing selective incapacitation to some ideal system of criminal justice in which everyone receives exactly his just deserts. No such system exists or ever will. One must compare instead the proposed policy with what exists now, with all its imperfections, and ask whether the gains in crime reduction are worth the risks entailed when we try to make predictions about human behaviour.

The first issue is whether it is permissible to allow crime-control to be an objective of sentencing policy. Some persons, such as Andrew von Hirsch, claim that only retribution—what he calls "just deserts"—can be a legitimate basis for sentencing.[6] To some extent, he is undoubtedly correct. Even if we were absolutely certain that a convicted murderer would never murder again, we would still feel obliged to impose a relatively severe sentence in order to vindicate the principle that life is dear and may not be unlawfully taken without paying a price. Moreover, the sentences given low-rate offenders must reflect society's judgment as to the moral blame such behaviour deserves, and the sentences given high-rate offenders ought not exceed what society feels is the highest sentence appropriate to the crime for which the offenders were convicted. And low-rate offenders should get a sufficiently severe sentence to help persuade them, and others like them, not to become high-rate offenders. Still, after allowing for all of these considerations, there will inevitably remain a range of possible sentences within which the goal of incapacitation can be served. The range will exist in part because there is no objective way to convert a desire for retribution into a precise sentence for a given offence and in part because legislatures will almost invariably act so as to preserve some judicial discretion so that the circumstances of a case which cannot be anticipated in advance may affect the sentence. Among those circumstances is a concern for protecting society from the threat that a given offender represents.

The second issue is whether our prediction methods are good enough to allow them to influence sentence length. The answer to that question depends on what one will accept as "good enough". Absolute certainty will never be attainable. Moreover, criminal justice *now*, at almost every stage, operates by trying to predict future behaviour. When a prosecutor decides how much plea bargaining he will allow, he is trying to predict how a judge or jury will react to his evidence, and he is often trying to guess how dangerous an offender he has in his grasp. When a judge sets bail, he is always making a prediction about the likelihood of a person out on bail showing up for his trial and is frequently trying to predict whether the person, if out on bail, will commit another crime while free. When a defence attorney argues in favour of his client being released on his own recognizance, without bail, he is trying to persuade the judge to accept his prediction that the accused will not skip town. When the judge passes a sentence, he is trying, at least in part, to predict whether the convicted person represents a future threat to society. When a parole board considers a convict's application for early release, it tries to predict—often on the basis of a quantitative system, called a "base expectancy table"—whether the person will become a recidivist if released. Virtually every member of the criminal justice system is routinely engaged in predicting behaviour, often on the basis of very scant knowledge and quite dubious rules of thumb. The question, therefore, is this: are the kinds of predictions that scholars such as Greenwood make about future criminality better (more accurate) and thus fairer than the predictions prosecutors and judges now make?

A third issue is tougher. Is it fair for a low-rate offender who is caught committing a serious crime to serve a shorter sentence (because he is not much of a threat to society) than a high-rate offender who gets caught committing a relatively minor offence? Probably not. Sentences would have to have legal boundaries set so that the use of selective incapacitation could not lead to perverse sentences—armed robbers getting one year, purse-snatchers getting five.

Finally, there is bound to be a debate about the legal and even ethical propriety of using certain facts as the basis for making predictions. Everyone would agree that race should not be a factor; everyone would probably agree that prior record should be a factor. I certainly believe that it is proper to take into account an offender's juvenile as well as his adult record, but I am aware that some people disagree. But can one take into account alcohol or drug use? Suppose the person claims to be cured of his drinking or his drug problem; do we believe him? And if we do, do we wipe the slate clean of information about these matters? And should we penalize more heavily persons who are chronically unemployed, even if unemployment is a good predictor of recidivism? Some people will argue that this is tantamount to making unemployment a crime, though I think that overstates the matter. After all, advocates of pretrial release of arrested persons, lenient bail policies, and diverting offenders away from jail do not hesitate to claim that having a good employment record should be counted in the accused's favour. If employment counts in favour of some, then obviously unemployment may be counted against others. Since advocates of "bail reform" are also frequent opponents of incapacitation, selective or collective, it is incumbent on them to straighten out their own thinking on how we make use of employment records. Nonetheless, this important issue deserves thoughtful attention.

On one matter, critics of prison may take heart. If Greenwood and the others are correct, then an advantage of selective incapacitation is that it can be accomplished without great increases (or perhaps any increases) in the use of prisons. It is a way of allocating more rationally the existing stock of prison cells to produce, within the constraints of just deserts, greater crime-control benefits. Many offenders—indeed most offenders— would probably have their sentences shortened, and the space thereby freed would be allocated to the small number of high-rate offenders whom even the most determined opponents of prison would probably concede should be behind bars.

Notes

1. Ernest van den Haag, *Punishing Criminals* (New York: Basic Books, 1975), 52–60.
2. Scholars who study incapacitation call the numberr of crimes committed per offender per year free "lambda", or λ. To avoid technical terminology, I will refer to it as the "individual offence rate".
3. Mark A. Peterson and Harriet B. Braiker, *Doing Time: A Survey of California Prison Inmates* (Santa Monica, Calif.: Rand, 1980), vii, 32.
4. Peter W. Greenwood, *Selective Incapacitation* (Santa Monica, Calif.: Rand, 1982), 43–4.
5. Alfred Blumstein and Jacqueline Cohen, "Estimation of Individual Crime Rates", from Arrest Records", 70 *Journal of Criminal Law and Criminology* 581 (1979); Peterson and Braiker, *Doing Crime*, above n. 3, at 40; Marvin Wolfgang *et al.*, *Delinquency in a Birth Cohort* (Chicago: University of Chicago Press, 1972), 206.
6. Andrew von Hirsch, *Doing Justice: The Choice of Punishments*, a report of the Committee for the Study of Incarceration (New York: Hill and Wang, 1976). See also Selection 4.4 below.

3.7

Selective Incapacitation: Some Doubts

ANDREW VON HIRSCH

Prediction research in criminology has, by and large, focused on characteristics of offenders. Various facts about criminals are recorded: age, previous arrests and convictions, social history, and so forth. It is then statistically determined which of these factors are most strongly associated with subsequent offending.[1] The result is a "selective" prediction strategy: among those convicted of a given type of offence, some will be identified as bad risks and others not.

Traditional Prediction Methods

Traditional statistical prediction techniques pursued this selective approach. Generally, they found that certain facts about an offender—principally, previous criminal history, drug habits, and history of unemployment—were to a modest extent indicative of increased likelihood of recidivism.[2]

These techniques did not, however, distinguish between serious and trivial recidivism. Both the offender who subsequently committed a single minor offence and the individual who committed many serious new crimes were lumped together as recidivists. Moreover, the techniques offered no promise of reduced crime rates, as they did not attempt to estimate aggregate crime-prevention effects. Locking up the potential recidivist thus assured only that he or she would be restrained; since other criminals remained at large, it did not necessarily diminish the overall risk of victimization. By the 1970s, these limitations reduced penologists' interest in traditional prediction techniques.

This was published for the first time in the first edition of this book and has been edited somewhat for the present edition.

"Selective Incapacitation"

Surveys of imprisoned offenders, conducted in the United States in the early 1980s, found that a small number of such persons admitted responsibility for a disproportionate number of serious offences. If that minority of dangerous offenders could be identified and segregated, perhaps this could reduce crime rates after all. These surveys thus generated a renewed interest in prediction research.

The most notable product was a Rand corporation study published in 1982 by Peter W. Greenwood.[3] Greenwood named his prediction strategy "selective incapacitation". His idea was to target *high-rate, serious* offenders—those likely to commit frequent acts of robbery or other violent crimes in future. For that purpose he took a group of incarcerated robbers, asked them how frequently they had committed such crimes, and then identified the characteristics of those reporting the highest robbery rates. From this, he fashioned a seven-factor predictive index, which identified the high-rate offenders on the basis of their early criminal records and histories of drug use and unemployment.[4]

Greenwood also devised a method of projecting the crime reduction impact of this technique. On the basis of offender self-reports, he estimated the annual rate of offending of those robbers who were identified as high risks by his prediction index. He then calculated the number of robberies that, supposedly, would be prevented by incarcerating such individuals for given periods. By increasing prison terms for the high-risk robbers while reducing terms for the others, he concluded, one could reduce the robbery rate by as much as 15 to 20 per cent—without causing prison populations to rise.

Questions of Effectiveness

While the study initially attracted much interest, problems later became apparent. One difficulty is making the predictions hold up when official data of the kind a sentencing court has available are relied upon. The objective of selective incapacitation is to target the potential high-rate serious offenders, and distinguish them from recidivists who reoffend less frequently or gravely. To make this distinction, the Rand studies, including Greenwood's, relied upon offender self-reports. A sentencing court, however, is seldom in the position to rely upon the defendant facing sentence to supply the necessary information about his criminal past. The court would have to rely on officially recorded information about offenders' adult and juvenile records, and such records make the distinction poorly. When Greenwood's data were reanalyzed to see how well the potential high-risk serious offenders could be identified from information available in court records, the results were disappointing. The officially recorded facts—arrests, convictions, and meagre information about offenders' personal histories—did not permit the potential high-rate robbers to be distinguished from (say) the potential car thieves. The factors in the self-report study that had proved the most useful—such as early and extensive youthful violence and multiple drug use, were not reflected in court records.[5] To make the predictions work, the courts would have to obtain and rely on information in school and social-service files—with all the problems of practicability and due process that would involve.

Flaws were found, also, in the projections of preventive impact. Greenwood based his crime reduction estimates on the self-reported activities of *incarcerated* robbers, and then extrapolated those estimates to robbers generally. Incarcerated robbers, however, are scarcely a representative group; they may well rob more frequently than robbers generally in the community. (It is like trying to learn about the smoking habits of smokers generally by studying the self-reported smoking activity of admittees to a lung cancer ward.) When this extrapolation is eliminated, the projected crime reduction impact is reduced by about one-half.[6] Other defects in the projections exist. Greenwood assumed, for example, that his high-rate robbers would continue offending for a long time. When shorter and more realistic residual criminal careers are assumed instead, the estimated preventive effect shrinks.

These doubts are confirmed by the 1986 report of the National Academy of Sciences' panel on criminal careers.[7] The panel included several noted advocates of predictively-based sentencing, and the report endorses the idea of predictive strategies (within certain limits) *if* these could be shown to be effective. Nevertheless, the panel's conclusions on the crime-preventive effects of selective incapacitation are sceptical. After recalculating Greenwood's results and scaling his initial preventive estimates down considerably, the panel notes that even those revised estimates (1) do not hold up in two of the three jurisdictions studied; (2) would shrink further were the scale drawn from a broader and potentially more heterogeneous population than persons in confinement and were it to utilize officially recorded rather than self-reported information; and (3) could nearly disappear if the estimated length of the residual criminal career were scaled down. While the report urges further research, it does not claim that selective incapacitation methods now exist that yield more satisfactory results.

Prospects for Improvement

Can these difficulties be overcome? Greenwood's research was only the beginning, and future selective incapacitation studies might conceivably do better. The obstacles are considerable, however. If the aim is to distinguish potential high-rate, serious offenders from lesser potential criminals, this remains difficult to achieve using the scant official records courts have at their disposal. Records of early offending might become somewhat more accessible, with a change in the law concerning the confidentiality of juvenile records—but such records, notoriously, suffer from incompleteness and inaccuracy. Social histories, such as drug use and employment, will be even more difficult to ascertain accurately.

Estimation of the impact of selective incapacitation on crime rates involves difficult problems of sampling. Analyses of convicted or incarcerated offenders' criminal activities suffer from the difficulty mentioned already: it is not clear to what extent these persons' activities are representative of the activity of offenders in the community. Samples drawn from the general population are free from such bias, but may contain too small a number of active offenders.

Another obstacle concerns estimating the length of criminal careers. The serious offenders with whom selective incapacitation is concerned generally would be imprisoned in any event; the main policy issue is the length of their confinement. The strategy is to impose longer terms on the supposed high-risk offenders, but that assumes they will continue their criminal activities. Little prevention is achieved if the bad risks who are confined are those whose careers will end fairly soon. This means that selective incapacitation, to succeed, needs not merely to prick out high-risk offenders but *those who are likely to continue offending for an appreciable time*. But how much do we know about forecasting the residual career? The National Academy panel suggests that career termination may depend on new variables—not so much prior criminal history but later events, including steady employment and marriage. Those are scarcely matters concerning which a court can readily obtain information at time of sentencing.[8]

A valuable review of recent incapacitation research has been provided by Franklin Zimring and Gordon Hawkins[9] writing a decade after the National Academy Report. They note that the research problems mentioned above have yet to be resolved—and notes a variety of other problems for example, failure to deal adequately with the phenomenon of group offending (where confining one member of the group does not necessarily reduce the group's level of offending) and of substitution (where incarcerated offenders' criminal activities are taken up by other potential offenders). He notes also the tendency of incapacitative strategies to yield diminishing returns, if it is indeed true that only a limited number of offenders commit large numbers of crimes. He concludes that present projection methods "tend to invite overestimation of the amount of incapacitation to be expected from marginal increments of imprisonment".[10] Real improvements in ways of estimating incapacitative effects seem not yet to have occurred.

Proportionality Problems

Selective prediction strategies—whether the traditional sort or newer methods such as Greenwood's—suffer also from a serious ethical problem: their conflict with the requirements of proportionality. The conflict stems from the character of the factors relied upon to predict. Those predictive factors have little bearing on the degree of reprehensibleness of the offender's criminal choices.

Proportionality requires that penalties be based chiefly on the gravity of the crime for which the offender currently stands convicted. The offender's previous criminal record, if considered at all, should have only a secondary role and the offender's social status is largely immaterial to the penalty he or she deserves (see Selection 4.7).

With selective risk prediction, the emphasis necessarily shifts *away* from the seriousness of the current offence. Since the aim is to select the higher risk individuals from among those convicted of a specified type of crime, the character of the current crime cannot have much weight. Traditional prediction indices largely ignored the gravity of the current offence and concentrated on the offender's earlier criminal and social histories. The newer "selective incapacitation" techniques have a similar emphasis. Of Greenwood's seven predictive factors, three do not measure criminal activity of a significant nature at all, but the offender's personal drug consumption and lack of stable employment, instead. Of the four other factors, only two measure the offender's recent criminal record; and *none* measure the heinousness (e.g., the degree of violence) of the offender's current offence.

When one tries to take aggregate preventive impact into account, matters become worse. Selective incapacitation techniques, by their own proponents' reckoning, could promise significant crime reduction effects only by infringing proportionality requirements to a *very* great degree.

Greenwood's projection of a significant reduction in the robbery rate is made on the assumption that robbers who score badly on his prediction index would receive about *eight* years' imprisonment, whereas better-scoring robbers would receive only *one* year in jail.[11] This means a great difference in severity—one of over 800 per cent—in the punishment of offenders convicted of the same offence of robbery; and one that can scarcely begin to be accounted for by distinctions in the seriousness of the offender's criminal conduct. When this punishment differential is narrowed—when high-risk robbers receive only modestly longer terms than robbers deemed lower risks—the crime reduction payoff shrinks to slender proportions, even by Greenwood's estimation methods.[12]

Conclusions

Where does this leave us? A limited capacity to forecast risk has long existed: persons with criminal records, drug habits, and no jobs tend to recidivate at a higher rate than other offenders, as researchers have known for years. However, the limitations in that forecasting capacity must be recognized—for selective incapacitation as well as more traditional forecasting techniques. Identifying high-risk, serious offenders will be impeded by the quality of information available (or likely to become available) to sentencing courts. The potential impact of selective incapacitation on crime rates is far below proponents' initial estimates, and is likely to be modest. Considerations of proportionality limit the inequalities in sentence that may fairly be visited for the sake of restraining high-risk offenders; and limiting these permissible inequalities will, in turn, further restrict the technique's impact on crime. Selective incapacitation—far from being the near panacea some of its advocates have asserted it is—is both on empirical and ethical grounds a device of limited potential, at best.

Notes

1. For a description of prediction techniques, see D. M. Gottfredson, "Assessment and Prediction Methods in Crime and Delinquency", in President's National Commission for Law Enforcement and Criminal Justice, *Task Force Report: Juvenile Delinquency and Youth Crime* (Washington, D.C., 1967).
2. *Ibid.*
3. P. Greenwood, *Selective Incapacitation* (Santa Monica, Cal., 1982).
4. Greenwood's seven predictive factors are: (1) prior convictions of instant offence

type; (2) incarceration for more than half the preceding two years; (3) conviction before age of sixteen; (4) time served in a state juvenile facility; (5) drug use during preceding two years; (6) drug use as a juvenile; (7) employment for less than 50 per cent of the preceding two years. *Ibid*. He defines "high-risk" offenders as those for whom at least four of these factors are present.

5. M. Chaiken and J. Chaiken, "Offender Types and Public Policy", *Crime and Delinquency* 30 (1985): 195.

6. A. von Hirsch, *Past or Future Crimes* (New Brunswick, NJ., 1986), ch. 10. For the method of estimation, see A. von Hirsch and D. M. Gottfredson, "Selective Incapacitation: Some Queries on Research Design and Equity", (1983–4) *N.Y.U. Review of Law and Social Change* 12 11.

7. The panel's report is set forth in A. Blumstein, J. Cohen, J. Roth, and C. Visher, eds., *Criminal Careers and "Career Criminals"* (Washington, D.C., 1986), vol. 1, 1–209. For an examination of the report, see A. von Hirsch, "Selective Incapacitation Reexamined", (1988) 7 *Criminal Justice Ethics*, 19–35.

8. *Criminal Careers*, above n. 7, at 206.

9. F. E. Zimring and Gordon Hawkins, *Incapacitation* (New York, 1995).

10. *Ibid.*, 86.

11. Greenwood did not publish these proposed durations in his report, but they are estimated in the reanalysis of his data done for the National Academy of Sciences' panel. See *Criminal Careers*, above n. 7, at 131–2.

12. For his estimates, see Greenwood, *Selective Incapacitation*, above n. 3, at 78–9.

3.8

Selective Incapacitation: The Debate over Its Ethics

MICHAEL TONRY

Much of the debate over predictions of dangerousness in sentencing turns on the debaters' differing views of the importance of equality and proportionality in the distribution of punishment. These different views, in turn, derive from different theories of the justification and properties of criminal punishment.

Retributive and Utilitarian Theories

In the interest of efficiency, the issues commonly raised concerning prediction are considered here primarily from two polar hypothetical positions—that of the ultimate utilitarian (UU) and that of the thoroughgoing retributivist (TR), which are stereotyped exemplars of two kinds of philosophical views called, respectively, teleological (or "consequentialist") theories and deontological theories. In general, teleological theories are concerned with justification for actions as means to ends, deontological theories with justification of actions in themselves.

1. Utilitarian theories

Utilitarianism is the best-known teleological theory and is concerned ultimately with maximizing social utility and the aggregate public good. In the arcane reaches of utilitarianism, there is considerable debate about how one could best measure social utility, but for the purposes of this essay "the greatest good for the greatest number" should suffice. Applied to crime, UU would support the crime control strategy that costs least in

From Michael Tonry, "Prediction and Classification: Legal and Ethical Issues", in Don M. Gottfredson and Michael Tonry (eds.), *Prediction and Classification: Criminal Justice Decision Making* (Chicago: University of Chicago Press, 1987), with some textual changes. Copyright © 1987 by the University of Chicago. Reprinted and excerpted by permission.

economic and social terms when one takes fully into account the cost of crime and fear of crime; the cost of law enforcement and sanctioning; the cost to offenders, their families, and associates, and the state of the offender's being punished.

Utilitarians believe in incentives and rationality and therefore see the punishment of offenders as a device for reducing the incidence and cost of crime through deterrence, incapacitation, and rehabilitation. To UU, then, what is important in punishing individual offenders is not anything about them but rather the likely crime-preventive effects of their punishment. Strictly speaking, if no crime prevention effects would be realized from punishing an individual, no punishment would be justified. Conversely, if punishment of an individual will on balance increase social utility, then that punishment should be imposed even if, for example, a severe punishment is needed for a petty offence. Thus, for UU, equality and proportionality are relatively unimportant properties or objectives of punishment.

2. Retributivist theories

The thoroughgoing retributivist, TR, finds UU's views shocking and believes that people must be viewed as ends, not means. Punishments must be deserved; the relevant moral calculus concerns the offender and his culpability and not the consequences of his punishment. People deserve punishment because they knowingly and wrongly inflict injury to the person or interests of others. Exactly why this is so varies for different theorists, just as the methods for measuring social utility vary among utilitarian theorists.

A number of criticisms of prediction-based classifications have been offered. These are summarized in the following pages with, where appropriate, the different views of UU and TR set out alongside those of major contemporary writers.

Problems with Predictions

The mainstream case made for use of predictions of dangerousness goes something like this. Judges, parole boards, and correctional administrators have *always* taken an offender's apparent dangerousness into account in making critical decisions, although, of necessity, they have done so in an intuitionist way with wide divergence in the decisions reached; it is far better explicitly to rely on general predictive rules that are based on the best available evidence and that are systematically applied than to go on as before; so long as the resulting penalties do not exceed what the offender deserved, he has no ground for complaint, and the rest of us will be better off because crime will be incrementally reduced by virtue of the incapacitation of offenders predicted to be dangerous. If the accuracy of predictions can be significantly improved, we may be able to target resources on dangerous offenders, to extend greater leniency to non-dangerous offenders, to reduce prison populations, and thereby to achieve greater crime control at less financial cost. Thus the public's interests in crime control and economy will be served, sentencing (or bail release or parole release) disparities will be diminished, and offenders will suffer punishments that are not undeserved. It is not the best of all possible worlds, but it is better than what now exists.

Arguments for marginal improvements in justice and efficiency are hard to resist because we know that more ambitious efforts tend to fail. Nonetheless, powerful arguments have been offered against reliance on predictions.

1. Simple injustice

Some simply reject prediction's incapacitative premise. If, like TR, one believes that the offender's blameworthiness or culpability determines how much punishment he should suffer, an increase of that punishment for incapacitative reasons is, by definition, unjust. The promised decrease of punishment for the non-dangerous is not necessarily a good thing; the resulting differences between punishments of dangerous and non-dangerous offenders who have committed the same offence exacerbate existing inequalities in punishment.

A standard rejoinder is that, for obvious metaphysical reasons, it is impossible to say precisely what punishment is deserved for any particular offence and, consequently (barring aberrantly severe punishments), it is difficult ever to say that a punishment is undeserved. Norval Morris, for example, has argued that one can meaningfully speak of punishments as being "undeservedly lenient" or "undeservedly severe" but can say of punishments within the range thereby defined only that they are "not undeserved": "Hence, a deserved punishment must mean a not undeserved punishment which bears a proportional relationship in the hierarchy of punishments to the harm for which the criminal has been convicted" (1982, 150) (see also Selection 4.5 below).

Andrew von Hirsch has offered a surrejoinder to arguments like those of Morris. He concedes that no available moral calculus will allow one to identify the single punishment appropriate in any individual case. However, he argues that moral principles can give much more guidance than does Morris's "not undeserved" punishment. Von Hirsch distinguishes between "cardinal" and "ordinal" desert. With Morris he agrees that cardinal desert—that is, some absolute metaphysically appropriate punishment—is beyond the knowledge of mortal mind. Ordinal desert, however, deals with relations between punishments, and regarding this man's moral principles can offer guidance. Robbery, most people agree, is more serious than is petit larceny and should be more severely punished, and similar comparative statements can be made about most offences. If one concedes that, other things equal, more serious offences should precipitate more severe sanctions, then the logic of a comprehensive listing of offences scaled to reflect notions of their comparative seriousness carries with it an ordinal ranking of deserved punishments (see Selection 4.4 below).

Norval Morris responds to this by observing that the "ranges" for deserved punishments for particular offences must be quite broad and overlap substantially because the least severe version of higher-rated offences may be less deserving of punishment than the most severe version of lower-rated offences: "some rapes are less serious than some aggravated batteries that are not rapes" (Morris 1982, 151).

The force of Morris's response to some extent depends on the kind of criminal law sentencing system one has in mind. In systems in which criminal offences are defined broadly and in which judicial sentencing discretion is not structured by guidelines or a meaningful determinate sentencing law, surely Morris is correct. In a jurisdiction with tightly specified offence definitions, Morris's argument loses much of its force; various grades of rape could be distinguished, as could various grades of battery, and it would not be surprising if some battery subtypes were regarded as more serious than some rape subtypes.

Thus Morris's rebuttal can be avoided mechanically, if imperfectly. Inevitably, there must be marginal cases and grey areas, but in the main it should be possible to establish an offence ranking of sufficient detail to permit a coherent system of "ordinal" desert.

If one sees desert or retribution as defining principles governing the amount of punishment, then achievement of equality and proportionality in punishment are paramount goals. Predictive sentencing conflicts with achievement of equality and proportionality in outcomes and violates the limits set by concern for ordinal desert.

However, von Hirsch in my view wins the skirmish but loses the conflict unless he can persuade Morris or others to adopt his premise that desert *should* be both a justifying aim of punishment and the primary defining principle in determining amounts of punishment. Almost by definition, proponents of predictive sentencing subscribe to a significant degree to utilitarian premises of punishment and so, rejecting von Hirsch's premises, can reject his critique of predictive sentencing.

2. Past and future crimes

A second, more general, criticism of predictive sentencing is that it punishes people for crimes they have not yet committed and might not commit if released. On this point, TR and UU simply differ in principle. To TR, deserved punishment for the current crime can be calibrated reasonably precisely; extension of punishment beyond that amount is not deserved in respect of the current offence and can be seen as an additional increment of punishment for a crime not committed. Von Hirsch (1981) argues that some increase in punishment is permitted in respect of prior offences (actually, that offenders should be given the benefit of the doubt and given more lenient sentences than they deserve for the first, or first few, offences); to the extent that accumulated prior convictions predict future offending, some incapacitative effect will be coincident with increased penalties for successive convictions and is to that extent not objectionable. For von Hirsch, the values of equality and proportionality are not seriously undermined since all offenders convicted of the same offence and with the same criminal history will receive the same sentence (see Selection 4.7 below).

Norval Morris and Marc Miller would go further because their position of "limiting retributivism" does not require equality of suffering. It seems to them entirely proper "within the range of not unjust punishments, to take account of different levels of dangerousness of those to be punished; but the concept of the deserved, or rather the not undeserved, punishment properly limits the range within which utilitarian values may operate" (Morris and Miller 1985, 37). Thus, like the previous criticism that predictive sentencing is *prima facie* unjust, the argument against sentencing in respect of future crimes turns out to be another disagreement over the premises of punishment.

3. False positives and the "conviction of innocents" analogy

By this point in the argument, TR has rejected predictive sentencing. To Andrew von Hirsch, predictive sentencing is acceptable only insofar as it can be achieved in ways that are consonant with the limited scope that he would permit for increased sentence on account of prior convictions. For those who remain unconvinced or sceptical, another major problem remains—predictions of violence are not very accurate. The conventional wisdom for some years has been that for every three persons predicted to commit serious violent offences, only one will do so, and the other two will be "false positives". Perhaps this 33 per cent accuracy rate has improved, but even at 50 per cent accuracy, an argument can be made that this is too inaccurate to serve as the basis for denying liberty (see Selection 3.2 above).

To some extent, people's views of this criticism are subsumed within their views on "punishment for future crimes", but not completely. For Norval Morris and Marc Miller, even within the range of not undeserved punishments, predictive sentencing is appropriate only if the base expectancy rate of violence for the criminal predicted as dangerous is shown by reliable evidence to be *substantially higher* than the base expectancy rate of another criminal *with a closely similar criminal record* and *convicted of a closely similar crime* but not predicted as unusually dangerous (Morris and Miller 1985).

This is a very demanding test that few proposals for predictive sentencing could satisfy. Information concerning past criminality has repeatedly been shown to be the best predictor of future criminality. If, as the Morris-Miller formula prescribes, one controls for criminal history and the nature of the current crime, the offender's remaining characteristics are seldom likely to lead to predicted base expectancy rates "substantially higher" than those for other individuals with comparable criminal histories convicted of comparable crimes. Thus the Morris-Miller view concedes that the false positive problem is a serious problem and sidesteps it by setting a test for predictive sentencing that few, if any, systems could meet.

An argument sometimes offered by proponents of predictive sentencing is that the false positive problem is itself misconceived. This argument has two components. The first component is that "statistical predictions are made for groups and not for individuals" (Farrington and Tarling 1983, 20). The false positives, say Floud and Young (1981, 26), "are statistical errors and it is fallacious to think of them as misjudged individuals". All members of the group predicted to be violent (assuming reliable information) were correctly identified as having the characteristics that, in general, are possessed by those predicted to commit future violence. One could say that there was 100 per cent correct identification of members of a group that has a 33 per cent violence probability.

The second component of this argument is that "a statistical prediction of dangerousness, based on membership in a group for which a consistent and tested pattern of conduct has been shown, is the statement of a *condition* [membership in the group] and not the prediction of a result [future violence]" (Morris and Miller 1985, 18).

Clearly, neither component of this second argument would convince a desert theorist. I doubt that they would convince an agnostic or a sceptic either, for the distinctions offered beg the critical question. That this argument does not resolve the false positive problem can be shown by imagining that a criminal code expressly authorized an incremental prison term for dangerous offenders to be served after the "deserved" sentence imposed for the current offence (as English habitual offender laws once did). The question to be decided would be "is there an X per cent [possibly 33 per cent, possibly 50 per cent] probability that this individual will commit future acts of serious violence?" That the defendant had the attributes of membership in a group with a 33 per cent base rate would be admissible in evidence to show what is equivalent to membership—that the probability of that individual committing serious violence is 33 per cent. The legislative draftsmen in their wisdom could specify 33 per cent of 50 per cent or 90 per cent as the required probability, but the policy question concerning the punishment of individuals must surely be focused on the individual's probability of future violence, and that question is the same whether one considers group or individual probabilities.

A second argument put by proponents of predictive sentencing is that the seemingly low "false positive" rates are misleading. Some seeming false positives may be true positives who were overlooked either because their violent acts did not come to the attention of the authorities or researchers or because, for some reason, police, prosecutor, judge, or jury elected to overlook violent acts. Other false positives may in fact have committed no violent acts, not from innocence, but from the lack of appropriate opportunities or circumstances.

Here too I think the proponents of prediction offer a weak case. The effective argument is that the false positive problem is less serious than it appears to be because the predictions are more accurate than they appear to be. Given the attention that violence predictions have received, it seems reasonable to place on prediction's proponents the burden of proving predictive accuracy higher than the state-of-the-art appears to allow. If substantially more accurate predictions can be made, that could significantly alter the debates over predictive sentencing, and it seems only fair that the higher accuracy levels be demonstrated empirically rather than be surmised.

4. Inappropriate predictors

One major criticism of predictive sentencing (or paroling or bailing) is that many factors correlated with future violence are controversial. Although the Constitution apparently precludes use only of race, religion, ethnicity, political affiliation, and possibly sex as sentencing factors, many people object to other factors on policy grounds.

a) Factors beyond the offender's control. Many people believe it unjust to base punishment decisions on factors over which the offender has no control. For example, sex is seen by many to be an inappropriate factor, even though it is highly predictive of violence, because it has no moral relevance to punishment. Similarly, race, age, ethnicity, intelligence, and national origin are factors beyond the offender's control and are therefore not logically related to culpability. Some people would also place drug or alcohol addiction (as contrasted with non-addicted use) in the same category.

b) Status variables. A considerable number of social and economic status variables are correlated with recidivism and violence probabilities but are nonetheless widely regarded as inappropriate factors for consideration in punishment decisions. These include various measures of educational attainment, vocational skills and experience, residential stability, and income. Incorporation of such variables in decision-making criteria systematically adversely affects people of lower income and social status. On policy grounds, the sentencing commission in Minnesota expressly prohibited reliance on such factors in sentencing precisely because of their socially skewed impact.

Patently, retributivists in principle oppose consideration of such factors, and utilitarians in principle should not object, though in practice many do. Many people object to consideration of such factors, and, to the extent that they are purged from prediction formulas, their accuracy will be by that much reduced (and the false positive problem thereby exacerbated).

c) Non-conviction criminal history. Past involvement in crime is the best single predictor of future involvement in crime. Numerous research findings confirm this conclusion. Generally, however, researchers' analyses incorporate self-reports or information on arrests that did not result in convictions.

Arrests and alleged criminality not resulting in an arrest present one kind of problem. Researchers generally justify use of arrests in their analyses in three ways. First, arrests are much closer in time than are convictions to the commission of crimes, and in the aggregate they offer a fuller picture of crime. For analyses of aggregate data, the fullest picture of crime involvement is best, and it is not important to know which of those arrests proved unfounded. No harm will come to any individual because of research use of arrests (or self-reports) as indicators of crime. Second, relatively few arrests result in convictions, and reliance solely on convictions as crime indicators would impoverish the analyses. Third, there is no reason to doubt that most people who are arrested for crimes committed those crimes.

The problem results from the interaction of several of the preceding propositions. From a predictive perspective, the more indicators there are of past criminality, the more likely that a prediction of continued involvement in crime will be accurate. From the defendant's perspective, and from a civil liberties perspective, that is beside the point. If past crimes are to influence current sentencing, then they should be considered only when they have been admitted or proved beyond reasonable doubt. Reliance on arrests creates an unacceptable risk that the defendant will be additionally punished now for offences he did not commit (or could not have been proven to have committed) then.

From an incapacitative perspective, reliance solely on past convictions defeats the system. Many much-arrested individuals have been seldom convicted and, without arrest information, will escape the incapacitative net.

The split resembles that on many prediction issues. While UU would have little doubt about the appropriateness of use of arrests in making predictive judgments (though were he a proceduralist, he would want to establish procedures for assessing defendants' claims that their apparent arrest records were incorrect), TR would probably say that the benefit of the doubt should operate for the individual and against the state and, therefore, that taking liberty seriously requires that punishment be imposed or extended in respect only of criminal behaviour admitted or proved beyond a reasonable doubt.

To conclude, whether the ethical and policy criticism of predictive sentencing summarized here are regarded as devastating depends largely on the premises that shape one's views of punishment. Retributivists tend strongly to disapprove of predictive sentencing; utilitarians tend to accept it. However, almost every analyst of predictive sentencing is uncomfortable with some of its features.

References

Farrington, David, and Tarling, Roger (1983), *Criminal Prediction* Albany: State University of New York Press).

Floud, Jean, and Young, Warren (1981), *Dangerousness and Criminal Justice* (London: Heinemann).

Morris, Norval (1982), *Madness and the Criminal Law* (Chicago: University of Chicago Press).

Morris, Norval, and Miller, Marc (1985), "Predictions of Dangerousness", in *Crime and Justice: An Annual Review of Research*, vol. 6, edited by Michael Tonry and Norval Morris (Chicago: University of Chicago Press).

von Hirsch, Andrew (1981), "Desert and Previous Convictions in Sentencing", 65 *Minnesota Law Review* 591.

Suggestions for Further Reading

1. A Brief History of Prediction Methods in Penology

See Mannheim, H. and Wilkins, T., *Prediction Methods in Relation to Borstal Training* (1955); Dershowitz, M., "The Origins of Preventive Confinement in Anglo–American Law—Part 1: The English Experience", (1974) 43 *University of Cincinnati Law Review* 1.

2. Methodology of Prediction Techniques

Gottfredson, D. M., "Assessment and Prediction Methods in Crime and Delinquency", in President's Commission on Law Enforcement and Administration of Criminal Justice, *Task Force Report: Juvenile Delinquency and Youth Crime* (1967); Monahan, J., "The Prediction of Violent Criminal Behavior" in A. Blumstein, J. Cohen and D. Nagin (eds.), *Deterrence and Incapacitation* (1978); Floud, J., and Young, W. *Dangerousness and Criminal Justice* (1981), Appendix C; Monahan, J., *Predicting Violent Behavior: An Assessment of Clinical Techniques* (1981); Hinton, W. (ed.), *Dangerousness: Problems of Assessment and Prediction* (1983); Farrington, D. P. and Tarling, R. (eds.), *Prediction in Criminology* (1985); Gottfredson, S. D., "Prediction: An Overview of Selected Methodological Issues" in Gottfredson, D. M. and Tonry, M. (eds.), *Prediction and Classification: Criminal Justice and Decision Making* (1987); Tarling, R., *Analysing Offending* (1993), ch. 9; Zimring, F. E. and Hawkins, G., *Incapacitation* (1995), chs. 3 and 5.

3. General (i.e. Nonselective) Incapacitation Methods

Wilson, J. Q., *Thinking About Crime* (1975), chs. 8 and 10; Shinnar, R. and Shinnar, S., "The Effects of Criminal Justice on the Control of Crime", (1975) 9 *Law and Society Review* 581; Greenberg, D. F., "The Incapacitative Effect of Imprisonment: Some Estimates" (1975) 9 *Law and Society Review* 541; Cohen, J., "The Incapacitative Effect of Imprisonment: A Critical Review of the Literature", in A. Blumstein, J. Cohen and D. Nagin (eds.), *Deterrence and Incapacitation* (1978); Panel on Research on Deterrent and Incapacitative Effects, "Report" in *ibid.*; Brody, S. and Tarling, R., *Taking Offenders out of Circulation* (1980); Cohen, J., "Incapacitation as a Strategy for Crime Control: Possibilities and Pitfalls", in M. Tonry and N. Morris (eds.), *Crime and Justice: An Annual Review of Research*, (1983) vol. 5; von Hirsch, A., *Past or Future*

Crimes (1985), ch. 13; Tarling, R., *Analysing Offending*, above, ch. 9; Marvell, T. B., and Moody, C. E., "Prison Population Growth and Crime Reduction", (1994) 10 *Journal of Quantitative Criminology* 109; Spelman, W., *Criminal Incapacitation* (1994); Cohen, J. and Canela-Cacho, J. A., "Incarceration and Violent Crime: 1965–1988", in A. J. Reiss, Jr. and J. A. Roth (eds.), *Understanding and Preventing Violence* (1994), vol. 4.

4. Selective Incapacitation: Methods and Effects

Panel on Research on Deterrent and Incapacitative Effects, "Report" in A. Blumstein, J. Cohen, and D. Nagin, *Deterrence and Incapacitation*, supra: Greenwood, P. W., *Selective Incapacitation* (1982); Chaiken, M. and Chaiken, R., *Varieties of Criminal Behavior* (1982); von Hirsch, A. and Gottfredson, D. M., "Selective Incapacitation: Some Queries About Research Design and Equity", (1983–84) 11 *New York University Review of Law and Social Change* 12; Chaiken, J. and Chaiken, M., "Offender Types and Public Policy", (1984) 30 *Crime and Delinquency* 195; von Hirsch, A., *Past or Future Crimes,* above, chs. 9 and 10; Panel on Research on Criminal Careers, "Report", in A. Blumstein, J. Cohen, J. Roth and C. Visher (eds.), *Criminal Careers and "Career Criminals"* (1986); Visher, C., "The Rand Inmate Survey: A Reanalysis", in *ibid.*; Reiss, A. J., "Co-Offender Influences on Criminal Careers", in *ibid.*, von Hirsch, A., "Selective Incapacitation Re-examined: The National Academy of Sciences' Report on Criminal Careers and 'Career Criminals'" (1988) 7 *Criminal Justice Ethics* 19; Gottfredson, S. D. and Gottfredson, D. M., "Behavioral Prediction and the Problem of Incapacitation", (1994) 32 *Criminology* 441; Chaiken, J. Chaiken, M., and Rhodes, W., "Predicting Violent Behavior and Classifying Violent Offenders", in A. J. Reiss, Jr., and J. A. Roth (eds.), *Understanding and Preventing Violence*, vol. 4, above; Spelman, W., *Criminal Incapacitation*, above; Zimring, F. E. and Hawkins, G., *Incapacitation*, above.

5. Ethical and Policy Issues in Incapacitation

Dershowitz, A., "The Law of Dangerousness: Some Fictions About Predictions", (1970) 23 *Journal of Legal Education* 24; Morris, N., *The Future of Imprisonment* (1974), esp. 62–73; von Hirsch, A., *Doing Justice* (1976), esp. chs. 3 and 15; Radzinowicz, L. and Hood, R., "A Dangerous Direction for Sentencing Reform", (1978) *Criminal Law Review* 713; Sherman, M. and Hawkins, G., *Imprisonment in America* (1981), esp. chs. 4 and 5; Floud, J. and Young W., *Dangerousness and Criminal Justice* (1981); Radzinowicz, L. and Hood, R., "Dangerousness and Criminal Justice: A Few Reflections", (1981) *Criminal Law Review* 756; Walker, N., "Unscientific, Unwise, Unprofitable, or Unjust?" (1982) 22 *British Journal of Criminology* 276; Honderich, T., "On Justifying Protective Punishment", (1982) 22 *British Journal of Criminology* 268; Bottoms, A. E. and Brownsword, R., "The Dangerousness Debate After the Floud Report", (1982) 22 *British Journal of*

Criminology 229; Monahan, J., "The Case for Prediction in the Modified Desert Model for Criminal Sentencing", (1982) 5 *International Journal of Law and Psychology* 103; Bottoms, A. E. and Brownsword, R., "Dangerousness and Rights", in J. W. Hinton (ed.), *Dangerousness: Problems of Assessment and Prediction* (1983); Morris N. and Miller, M., "Predictions of Dangerousness", in M. Tonry and N. Morris (eds.), *Crime and Justice: An Annual Review of Research*, (1985) vol. 6; Moore, M. *et al., Dangerous Offenders* (1985); von Hirsch, A., *Past or Future Crimes,* above, chs. 11–13; Zimring, F. E. and Hawkins, G., "Dangerousness and Criminal Justice" (1986) 85 *Michigan Law Review* 481; Miller, M. and Morris N., "Predictions of Dangerousness: An Argument for Limited Use" (1988) 3 *Violence and Victims* 263; von Hirsch, A., "Selective Incapacitation Re-examined" above; Zimring, F. E., and Hawkins, G., *Incapacitation,* above chs. 4, 6, and 7.

4

Desert

Retributivist theories of punishment have a long history which includes the writings of Kant and Hegel, but their revival in modern times can be traced to various philosophical writings in the 1960s and early 1970s.[1] This increased philosophical interest percolated through into penal theory later in the 1970s—most notably, in the espousal of "just deserts" in the report of the Committee for the Study of Incarceration, *Doing Justice* (1976). Since then, desert theory has had a continuing (though sometimes disputed) influence on the sentencing policies of several countries, illustrated by the prominence it has achieved in the sentencing guidelines of Minnesota and Oregon, in the Swedish sentencing law of 1988 and in the English sentencing-reform statute of 1991.[2]

For present purposes, a desert theorist will be regarded as someone who claims that the seriousness of crimes should, on grounds of justice, be the chief determinant of the quantum of punishment. In terms of the three main issues in the justification of punishment—Why punish? Whom to punish? and How much to punish?—desert theorists will agree in principle about the second and third.

In response to the first question, Why punish? there appear to be at least two different approaches among modern desert theorists. One approach, advanced in Selection 4.1 by Michael Moore, is essentially that those who commit crimes deserve to be punished for the same reason that those who commit civil wrongs deserve to be made to pay damages: there is a fundamental intuitive connection between crime and punishment, of the same order as the promissory theory of contract or the corrective theory of tort liability. Punishment as a practice or institution needs no further justification than this. The second approach, adopted in the writings of von Hirsch (see Selection 4.4), regards desert as an integral part of everyday judgements of praise and blame, which is institutionalized in state punishment to express disapprobation of the conduct and its perpetrators.[3] This is the censuring function of punishment. But the other element of von Hirsch's justification is preventive: legal punishment provides a disincentive against engaging in certain conduct. Without the regular official punishment of crimes, "it seems likely that victimizing conduct would become so prevalent as to make life nasty and brutish, indeed".[4] For von Hirsch, therefore, the notion of deserved censure is necessary but not sufficient as a justification. General deterrence must also be invoked.[5] Critics of desert theory have argued that "a judgment that D has behaved wrongly does not involve or justify the further judgment that [he or she] should be punished".[6] Those who adopt von Hirsch's view would agree, since general prevention forms part of their justification. But those who follow Moore's view would disagree, as Selection 4.1 shows.

An interesting variant on these themes is provided by R.A. Duff in Selection 4.3. He agrees with von Hirsch that punishment's main justifying role is to convey censure of criminal conduct. However, he thinks this supports not only punishment's symbolic role of conveying disapproval of the offender's conduct, but also its "hard treatment" aspect of imposing deprivations on the offender. Punishment, he suggests, should be seen as a kind of secular penance, aiming not only at focusing the offender's attention on the wrongfulness of his conduct, but also at providing (through the suffering it inflicts) a vehicle through which the offender can reach a penitent understanding of his wrong. As such, the sanction is both backward-looking (to the wrongfulness of the conduct) and forward-looking (as repentance should involve efforts to desist in future). Seeing punishment as having this penitential function, he argues, need not involve an undue focus on the offender's spiritual condition, more suitable to a monastic institution than to a state in a free society. The scope of the criminal law can still be restricted to harmful conduct, and the concern about the actor's moral condition to culpability as expressed in such conduct. But does this suffice to distinguish Duff's secular penances from monastic ones? A penance involves not only confronting the actor with his wrongdoing, but also making him suffer as a way of allowing him to expiate his guilt. How can this latter function be justified, as a role appropriate to a secular state in a free society?[7]

Some writers, however, regard the idea of penal desert as having little or no merit. This perspective is set out in Selection 4.2, by Nigel Walker. He regards claims about deserved punishment as based on little more than shaky metaphors about "owing a debt to society", or "annulling the offence". As to arguments for deserved punishment based on notions of penal censure for wrongdoing, he argues that unless the censure can be shown to have social utility, its moral basis is obscure. Perhaps, he states, "our feelings about crime may well make us want to convey a [censuring] message to the criminal or others"; but that, he states, is only a psychological necessity, not a moral one. How convincing are Walker's arguments? To what extent do they assume the point in debate: inal policy may be justified only by its possible future crime-prev social benefits?

In answer to the second question, Whom to punish? desert theori agree that only those who have been proved to have committed an offence ought to be punished. This marks an important difference from deterrence theory, as noted in the introduction to Chapter 2 above. The reasons for limiting punishment to convicted offenders have been explored by H. L. A. Hart in his principle of "retribution in distribution",[8] and will not examined further here.

The third question, How much to punish? leads to the main distinguishing feature of desert theory. Desert theorists' answer to the question is the principle of proportionality: sentences should be proportionate in their severity to the seriousness of the criminal conduct. The proportionality principle's contours, and its difference from the deterrent and rehabilitative rationales, are set out in Selection 4.4 by Andrew von Hirsch. Within the general principle of proportionality, the major requirement is ordinal proportionality, which concerns how a crime should be punished compared to similar criminal acts, and compared to other crimes of a more or less serious nature. Thus, once the penal sanction has been established as a condemnatory institution to respond to criminal acts, its sentences ought to reflect the relative reprehensibleness of those acts. Crimes must be ranked according to their relative seriousness, as determined by the harm done or risked by the offence and by the degree of culpability of the offender. Ordinal proportionality is thus concerned with preserving a correspondence between relative seriousness of offence and relative severity of sentence.

Other writers have accepted only parts of desert theory's answer to the question, How much to punish? Thus Norval Morris, in Selection 4.5, argues that proportionality should merely set the outer limits of permissible punishment, allowing decisions within those limits to be taken on various other grounds which seem appropriate in particular cases. In Selection 4.4, however, von Hirsch points out that this would mean that persons committing equally reprehensible criminal conduct could receive quite unequal quanta of punishment. If punishment embodies blame as a central characteristic, he argues, it would not be unfair to visit such different severities (and thus unequal implicit blame) on offenders who commit comparably blameworthy transgressions. How might Morris reply to such an argument?

To establish a principled basis for desert theory is no more than the first step in fashioning a coherent theory of sentencing. Several of the elements

eed of further exploration, both in their own
theory itself. First, by what criteria can it be
cale is appropriately anchored—that is, how
of punitiveness be decided? The magnitude of a
rive from tradition and from the habit of associ-
ain gravity with penalties of a certain severity.
e reasons militating in favour of keeping overall
e levels. One reason is the idea of parsimony—that
ith moderation in inflicting deprivation on its citi-
, von Hirsch contends in Selection 4.4, derives from
the notion of ... nsure itself. The criminal sanction, he argues, should
serve primarily to support citizens' moral reasons for desisting from crime;
to perform this function of normative communication, he argues, the law's
threats should not be so harsh as to "drown out" that moral appeal.[10]

Second, by what criteria can it be assessed whether or not a sentencing
system achieves ordinal proportionality? How can we determine whether
robberies of a given kind should be regarded as more or less serious than
certain forms of burglary or of rape? Many would maintain that these are
largely uncontroversial matters: not only do most members of most societies rank most offences in a similar order of relative gravity, but also
those states which have recently introduced sentencing guidelines have not
found this to be a contentious part of the enterprise. Critics would assail
this cosy, consensus view from various angles. First, there is no agreement
on some matters such as the determinants of culpability (e.g., should
intoxication ever mitigate?) and the relevance of the presence or absence
of actual resulting harm (e.g., in attempted crimes). Second, the writings
of desert theorists have focused on "conventional" crimes, and it is unclear
whether and in what way so-called "white collar" crimes can be accommodated. Third, and more generally, the quantification of harms is both
a complex and a changing enterprise. Recent years have seen changes, for
example, in the assessment of such conduct as domestic violence, drinking and driving, and use of hard drugs. How can desert theory prescribe
criteria for offence seriousness in such changing social contexts? One
response to this challenge, based on a study by Andrew von Hirsch and
Nils Jareborg,[11] is sketched in Selection 4.6: it is to seek a framework for
rating crimes according to their effect on persons' "living standard". The
seriousness of a criminal offence depends on its degree of harmfulness (or
potential harmfulness) and on the degree of culpability of the perpetrator.
With harm, the problem has been to compare the injuriousness of criminal acts that invade different interests—to compare takings of property
with, say, invasions of privacy. Here, a broad notion of quality of life may

be helpful: invasions of different interests can be compared according to the degree to which they ordinarily affect a person's "living-standard" in the sense constituted by the standardized means and resources (both economic and non-economic) for living a good life. Such an analysis can also be applied, the Selection suggests, to rating the degree of onerousness of criminal penalties.

This living-standard approach is necessarily at a high level of generality. It may need to be supplemented by a more culturally specific examination of the values implicit in existing offence ratings, although even in pluralist societies there are probably some shared values which are relevant to crime seriousness. It may also need to be adapted to take account of the many crimes which do not have individual victims: there is a need to develop the theory so as to comprehend not only crimes against the state (such as espionage or perjury) but also offences which affect public welfare (such as pollution). Once it is accepted that ordinal proportionality is a requirement of fairness, the importance of pursuing this inquiry into how it is structured is beyond doubt.

Third, the effect of previous convictions on sentence remains an unsettled issue among desert theorists. Some argue that each offence should be treated in isolation, without prior record having any effect on sentence. On this view, any increases in sentence on account of prior record stem from aims of social protection (especially incapacitation) that are inconsistent with a desert rationale.[12] A counter-argument, developed by von Hirsch in Selection 4.7, is that a first offender ought to receive a reduced sentence because this recognizes humans as fallible and shows respect for their capacity to respond to censure. Such discount should diminish with the second and third convictions, and eventually be lost. Another disputed question is *how much* reduction in sentence is warranted for the absence of a criminal record. The approach suggested in Selection 4.7 would support only a modest adjustment for the previous criminal record, so that the primary (albeit not exclusive) emphasis would be on the current offence—thus retaining clear differentials between lesser offences (even when committed repeatedly) and serious crimes. Several further questions about the precise application of desert theory to prior record remain, about such matters as the similarity or dissimilarity of the previous offences, their relative seriousness, their frequency, and their recency or staleness.[13]

Fourth, it is argued that desert theorists have been preoccupied by serious crimes and custodial sentences, without devoting adequate attention to the bulk of less serious offences. It will be seen from Chapter 6 below that the deficiency is now being remedied by study of the application of desert theory to non-custodial measures (see particularly Selection 6.4 below). Rather less attention has been paid to the compatibility of policies of selective non-prosecution with the desert approach. Many sentencing systems now operate schemes for the formal cautioning of offenders or other forms of "diversion". In principle, they might be incorporated into desert theory by regarding them as proportionate responses to minor forms of law-breaking or to offences of certain kinds by persons of low culpability. So long as the criteria are clear and their use reflects ordinal proportionality, these schemes can be regarded as a manifestation of a lowering of the overall penalty level.

Fifth, desert theory may be criticized as an uncaring approach to the problems of crime and criminals, ignoring the causes of crime and showing little interest in constructive ways of tackling crime problems. As a general line of criticism this somewhat misses the target: desert theory is an approach to sentencing and not a set of prescriptions for the criminal justice system as a whole. There is no incompatibility between desert theory and the idea of new community correction programmes or innovative prison regimes, but the desert theorist would insist that sentences should not be prolonged so as to accommodate treatment programmes. A more specific question is whether desert theory has been little more than equivocal about sentences whose aim is to treat the particular needs of particular offenders, such as probation orders. As will be seen in Chapter 6 below, a desert model for non-custodial penalties such as that proposed by Wasik and von Hirsch (Selection 6.4) can accommodate the use of probation as an appropriate sanction for certain levels of offence. This would ensure that probation orders are used in a proportionate manner, while allowing the court to select probation on the overtly rehabilitative ground that there is "particular reason to believe that this type of offender is potentially responsive". A further criticism of a similar kind is that desert theorists have too little to say about the victims of crime, in terms of restitution and compensation. This question is taken up in Chapter 7 below.

Considerable interest has been shown in hybrid sentencing schemes, which combine desert theory with aspects of other approaches to punishment. Some hybrids that give primary emphasis to desert are sketched by von Hirsch in Selection 4.4. These would ordinarily require that the penalty be based on the gravity of the offence, but permit upward departures when extraordinary risks of crime are involved;[14] alternatively, they would allow departures from the deserved punishment to be made more routinely, but keep the amount of such departures modest.[15] Can such hybrids achieve a modicum of consistency with desert aims? And to what extent are they really needed as a practical matter?

An alternative way of constructing a hybrid sentencing scheme is sketched by Michael Tonry in Selection 4.8. Tonry would use the desert principles to set the *upper* limit on the punishment ordinarily permissible for a given offence. To set the actual penalty up to that limit, however, Tonry would rely on a principle of parsimony: the penalty should be the least severe appropriate for that kind of case. That raises the question, however, of how appropriateness should be determined. Should this be a matter of the degree of risk the offender poses?—in which case the scheme is close to that sketched by Norval Morris in Selection 3.5 above. Or is Tonry proposing a less preventively-orientated approach, in which what matters is not risk but such things as the defendant's efforts to remedy the damage done, his efforts to return to a law-abiding existence, or the impact of the penalty on the defendant's family. These are matters going beyond the gravity of the offence, but nevertheless seem to be justice-related in a broad sense.[16] How could such considerations be defined more fully?

A final issue, addressed in Selection 4.9 by Barbara Hudson, concerns "just deserts in an unjust society". The distinctive feature of proportion-alist sentencing schemes is that they purport, not merely to prevent unde-sired conduct, but to punish fairly. How can they do so in a society that does not treat its socially-deprived members equitably? An early response to this objection by desert theorists was that a proportionalist sentencing scheme, at least, does not treat deprived offenders any worse than others who commit comparable offences, whereas predictively-based sentencing approaches would impose extra constraint on deprived offenders because they represent greater risks.[17]

This, however, scarcely seems a sufficient answer: the issue is whether deprived offenders should in a fair system receive less punishment, if any. Hudson does propose penalty reductions for the deprived. Her argument is not that deprivation makes the person unable to choose, but rather that culpability is reduced because deprivation makes compliance so much more difficult.[18] Could this culpability-based argument be spelled out more fully? What practical problems would arise from trying to imple-ment it? If no discount of the kind Hudson proposes is granted, would that make the system totally unfair? Or would it make it a kind of hybrid scheme—where desert generally remains the guiding criterion, but deprived offenders (for whatever practical reasons may be cited) are, by being denied the discount, thus receiving somewhat more than they deserve?

The strengths of desert theory may be recognized in its basis in every-day conceptions of crime and punishment, in its close links with modern liberal political theory, in its insistence that state power be subject to limitations, in its model of individuals as autonomous, choosing beings, and in its protagonists' insistence that sentencing systems should have coherent aims and predictable sentences. Desert theory would seem ordinarily to rule out considerations of race, culture, family circumstances, and employment in determining the severity of sentence: it sets out to be non-discriminatory and, insofar as it results in clear sentencing guidance, it should exclude such factors from the calculation of sentence. But matters such as social deprivation might be relevant to culpability and might therefore tell in mitigation of sentence.

A.A.

Notes

1. e.g., K. G. Armstrong, "The Retributivist Hits Back", (1961) 70 *Mind* 471; H. G. McCloskey, "A Non-Utilitarian Approach to Punishment", (1965) 8 *Inquiry* 249; J. Kleinig, *Punishment and Desert* (1973).

2. See, A. von Hirsch, *Censure and Sanctions* (1993), ch. 10; see also, the discussion of the Minnesota and Oregon guidelines in selection 5.2, and the Swedish statute in Selection 5.3 below. For an analysis of the aims of the 1991 English statute, see A. Ashworth, *Sentencing and Criminal Justice*, 2nd edn. (1995), ch. 3.

3. For fuller discussion, see von Hirsch, above n. 2, ch. 2.

4. A. von Hirsch, *Past or Future Crimes* (1985), 55.

5. von Hirsch, above n. 2, 12–14; also, Selection 4.4.

6. N. Lacey, *State Punishment* (1988), 21.

7. For more on this question, see von Hirsch, above n. 2, 72–7.

8. H. L. A. Hart, *Punishment and Responsibility* (1968), ch. 1.

9. For fuller discussion of parsimony as it relates to desert-based sanctions, see von Hirsch, above n. 2, 109–11; Ashworth, above n. 2, 80–1.

10. See also von Hirsch, above n. 2, 38–46. In his discussion of anchoring a penalty scale, this author introduces two kinds of conceptions. One is that of "cardinal proportionality"—which sets broad outer limits on the potential severity of the scale (*ibid.*, 36–8); the other is the argument (referred to in the text) concerning not "drowning out" the censure's moral appeal (*ibid.*, 38–46). This latter argument furnishes grounds for scaling punishments downward *within* the broad limits set by cardinal proportionality.

11. A. von Hirsch and N. Jareborg, "Gauging Criminal Harms: A Living-Standards Analysis", (1991) 11 *Oxford Journal of Legal Studies* 1.

12. See G. Fletcher, *Rethinking Criminal Law* (1978), 460–6.

13. For discussion of these issues, see A. von Hirsch, "Desert and Previous Convictions in Sentencing", (1981) 65 *Minnesota Law Review* 591; M. Wasik,

"Guidance, Guidelines, and Criminal Record", in M. Wasik and K. Pease (eds.), *Sentencing Reform: Guidance or Guidelines?* (1987); J. V. Roberts, "The Role of Criminal Record in the Sentencing Process", (1997) 22 *Crime and Justice: A Review of Research* 303.

14. For discussion of such hybrid schemes, see von Hirsch, above n. 2, 48–53; P. Robinson, "Hybrid Principles for the Distribution of Criminal Sanctions" (1987) 82 *Northwestern Law Review* 19; and A. E. Bottoms and R. Brownsword, "Dangerousness and Rights", in J. W. Hinton (ed.), *Dangerousness: Problems of Assessment and Prediction* (1983).

15. See, von Hirsch, above n. 2, 53–6.

16. See the discussion of such "quasi-desert" factors in A. von Hirsch, "Sentencing Guidelines and Penal Aims in Minnesota", (1994) 13(1) *Criminal Justice Ethics* 39, 46–8.

17. A. von Hirsch, *Doing Justice* (1976), ch. 17.

18. See also, discussion of this issue in von Hirsch, above n. 2, 106–8; and from a different perspective Norrie (in Selection 8.1 below).

4.1

The Moral Worth of Retribution

MICHAEL S. MOORE

Retributivism is a very straightforward theory of punishment: we are justified in punishing because and only because offenders deserve it. Moral culpability (desert) is in such a view both a sufficient as well as a necessary condition of liability to punitive sanctions. Such justification gives society more than merely a right to punish culpable offenders. It does this, making it not unfair to punish them, but retributivism justifies more than this. For a retributivist, the moral culpability of an offender also gives society the *duty* to punish. Retributivism, in other words, is truly a theory of justice such that, if it is true, we have an obligation to set up institutions so that retribution is achieved.

Retributivism, so construed, joins corrective justice theories of torts, natural right theories of property, and promissory theories of contract as deontological alternatives to utilitarian justifications; in each case, the institutions of punishment, tort compensation, property, and contract are justified by the rightness of fairness of the institution in question, not by the good consequences such institution may generate. Further, for each of these theories, moral desert plays the crucial justificatory role. Tort sanctions are justified whenever the plaintiff does not deserve to suffer the harm uncompensated and the defendant by his or her conduct has created an unjust situation that merits corrective action; property rights are justified whenever one party, by his or her labour, first possession, or intrinsic ownership of his or her own body, has come by such actions or status morally to deserve such entitlements; and contractual liability is justified by the fairness of imposing it on one who deserves it (because of his or her voluntary undertaking, but subsequent and unexcused breach).

Once the deontological nature of retributivism is fully appreciated, it is often concluded that such a view cannot be justified. You either believe punishment to be inherently right, or you do not, and that is all there is to be said about it. As Hugo Bedau (1978) once put it:

> "Either he [the retributivist] appeals to something else—some good end—that is accomplished by the practice of punishment, in which case he is open to the criticism that he has a nonretributivist, consequentialist justification for the practice of punishment. Or his justification does not appeal to something else, in which case it is open to the criticism that it is circular and futile".

Such a restricted view of the justifications open to a retributivist leads theorists in one of two directions: Either they hang on to retributivism, urging that it is to be justified "logically" (i.e., non-morally) as inherent in the ideas of punishment (Quinton, 1954) or of law (Fingarette, 1977); or they give up retributivism as an inherently unjustifiable view (Benn and Peters, 1959). In either case, retributivism is unfairly treated, since the first alternative trivializes it and the second eliminates it.

Bedau's dilemma is surely overstated. Retributivism is no worse off in the modes of its possible justification than any other deontological theory. In the first place, one might become (like Bedau himself, apparently) a kind of "reluctant retributivist". A reluctant retributivist is someone who is somewhat repelled by retributivism but who nonetheless believes: (1) that there should be punishment; (2) that the only theories of punishment possible are utilitarian, rehabilitative, retributive, or some mixture of these; and (3) that there are decisive objections to utilitarian and rehabilitative theories of punishment, as well as to any mixed theory that uses either of these views in any combination. Such a person becomes, however reluctantly, a retributivist by default.

In the second place, positive arguments can be given for retributivism that do not appeal to some good consequences of punishing. It simply is not true that "appeals to authority apart, we can justify rules and institutions only by showing that they yield advantages" or that "to justify is to provide reasons in terms of something else accepted as valuable" (Benn and Peters, 1959, 175–6). Coherence theories of justification in ethics allow two non-consequentialist possibilities here:

1. We might justify a principle such as retributivism by showing how it follows from some yet more general principle of justice that we think to be true.
2. Alternatively, we can justify a moral principle by showing that it best accounts for those of our more particular judgments that we also believe to be true.

In a perfectly coherent moral system, the retributive principle would be justified in both these ways, by being part of the best theory of our moral sentiments, considered as a whole.

The first of these deontological argument strategies is made familiar to us by arguments such as that of Herbert Morris (1976), who urges that retributivism follows from some general ideas about reciprocal advantage in social relations. Without assessing the merits of these proposals one way or another, I wish to pursue the other strategy. I examine the more particular judgments that seem to be best accounted for in terms of a principle of punishment for just deserts.

These more particular judgements are quite familiar. I suspect that almost everyone at least has a tendency—one that he may correct as soon as he detects it himself, but at least a tendency—to judge culpable wrong-doers as deserving of punishment.

Most people react to [atrocious crimes] with an intuitive judgment that punishment (at least of some kind and to some degree) is warranted. Many will quickly add, however, that what accounts for their intuitive judgment is the need for deterrence, or the need to incapacitate such a dangerous person, or the need to reform the person. My own view is that these addenda are just "bad reasons for what we believe on instinct anyway", to paraphrase Bradley's general view of justification in ethics.

To see whether this is so, construct a thought experiment of the kind Kant originated. Imagine that [atrocious] crimes are being done, but that there is no utilitarian or rehabilitative reason to punish. The murderer has truly found Christ, for example, so that he or she does not need to be reformed; he or she is not dangerous for the same reason; and the crime can go undetected so that general deterrence does not demand punishment (alternatively, we can pretend to punish and pay the person the money the punishment would have cost us to keep his or her mouth shut, which will also serve the ends of general deterrence). In such a situation, should the criminal still be punished? My hypothesis is that most of us still feel some inclination, no matter how tentative, to punish.

The puzzle I put about particular retributive judgments is this: Why are these particular judgments so suspect—"primitive", "barbarous", "a throwback"—when other judgments in terms of moral desert are accorded places of honour in widely accepted moral arguments? Very generally, there seem to me to be several explanations (and supposed justifications) for this discriminatory treatment of retributive judgments about deserved punishment.

1. First and foremost there is the popularly accepted belief that punishment for its own sake does no good. "By punishing the offender you

cannot undo the crime", might be the slogan for this point of view. I mention this view only to put it aside, for it is but a reiteration of the consequentialist idea that only further good consequences achieved by punishment could possibly justify the practice. Unnoticed by those who hold this position is that they abandon such consequentialism when it comes to other areas of morals. It is a sufficient justification not to scapegoat innocent individuals, that they do not deserve to be punished; the injustice of punishing those who did not deserve it seems to stand perfectly well by itself as a justification of our practices, without need for further good consequences we might achieve. Why do we not similarly say that the injustice of the guilty going unpunished can equally stand by itself as a justification for punishment, without need of a showing of further good consequences? It simply is not the case that justification always requires the showing of further good consequences.

Those who oppose retributivism often protest at this point that punishment is a clear harm to the one punished, and the intentional causing of this harm requires some good thereby achieved to justify it; whereas *not* punishing the innocent is not a harm and thus does not stand in need of justification by good consequences. Yet this response simply begs the question against retributivism. Retributivism purports to be a theory of justice, and as such claims that punishing the guilty achieves something good— namely, justice—and that therefore reference to any other good consequences is simply beside the point. One cannot defeat the central retributivist claim—that justice is achieved by punishing the guilty—simply by assuming that it is false.

The question-begging character of this response can be seen by imaging a like response in areas of tort, property, or contract law. Forcing another to pay tort or contract damages, or to forgo use and possession of some thing, is a clear harm that corrective justice theories of tort, promissory theories of contract, or natural right theories of property are willing to impose on defendants. Suppose no one gains anything of economic significance by certain classes of such impositions—as, for example, in cases where the plaintiff has died without heirs after his cause of action accrued. "It does no good to force the defendant to pay", interposed as an objection to corrective justice theories of tort, promissory theories of contract, or natural right theories of property simply denies what these theories assert: that something good *is* achieved by imposing liability in such cases—namely, that justice is done.

This "harm requires justification" objection thus leaves untouched the question of whether the rendering of justice cannot in all such cases be the good that justifies the harm all such theories impose on defendants. I accordingly put aside this initial objection to retributivism, relying as it does either on an unjustifiable discrimination between retributivism and other deontological theories, or upon a blunderbuss assault on deontological theories as such.

2. A second and very popular suspicion about retributive judgments is that they presuppose an indefensible objectivism about morals. Sometimes this objection is put metaphysically: There is no such thing as desert or culpability (Mackie, 1982). More often the point is put as a more cautious epistemological modesty: "Even if there is such a thing as desert, we can never know who is deserving". For religious people, this last variation usually contrasts us to God, who alone can know what people truly deserve. We might call this the "don't play God" objection.

A striking feature of the "don't play God" objection is how inconsistently it is applied. Let us revert to our use of desert as a limiting condition on punishment: We certainly seem confident both that it is true and that we can know that it is true, that we should not punish the morally innocent because they do not deserve it. Neither metaphysical scepticism nor epistemological modesty gets in our way when we use lack of moral desert as a reason not to punish. Why should it be different when we use the presence of desert as a reason to punish? If we can know when someone does *not* deserve punishment, mustn't we know when someone *does* deserve punishment? Consider the illogic in the following passages from Karl Menninger (1968):

> "It does not advance a solution to use the word *justice*. It is a subjective emotional word . . . The concept is so vague, so distorted in its applications, so hypocritical, and usually so irrelevant that it offers no help in the solution of the crime problem which it exists to combat but results in its exact opposite—injustice, injustice to everybody" (10–11).

Apparently Dr. Karl knows injustice when he sees it, even if justice is a useless concept.

Analogously, consider our reliance on moral desert when we allocate initial property entitlements. We think that the person who works hard to produce a novel deserves the right to determine when and under what conditions the novel will be copied for others to read. The novelist's labour gives him or her the moral right. How can we know this—how can it be true—if desert can be judged only by those with godlike omniscience, or worse, does not even exist? Such scepticism about just deserts would throw out a great deal that we will not throw out. To me, this shows that no one really believes that moral desert does not exist or that we could not know it if it did. Something else makes us suspect our retributive judgments than supposed moral scepticism or epistemological modesty.

References

Bedau, H. (1978), "Retribution and the Theory of Punishment", 75 *Journal of Philosophy* 601.

Benn, S. I., and R.S. Peters (19659), *Social Principles and the Democratic State* (London: Allen and Unwin).

Fingarette, H. (1977), "Punishment and Suffering", 50 *Proceedings of American Philosophical Association* 499.

Mackie, J (1982), "Morality and the Retributive Emotions", 1 *Criminal Justice Ethics* 3.

Menninger, K (1968), *The Crime of Punishment* (New York: Viking Press).

Moore, M. S. (1982), "Moral Reality", *Wisconsin Law Review* 1061.

Morris, H. (1976), *On Guilt and Innocence* (Berkeley and Los Angeles: University of California Press).

Quinton, A. M. (1954), "On Punishment", 14 *Analysis*.

4.2

Desert: Some Doubts

NIGEL WALKER

The Retributive Justification

It is not hard to see why "just deserts" has proved attractive. Most Benthamite techniques seem to be of the hit-or-miss sort, offering no certainty of success in particular cases. What retributivism appears to offer is an aim that is achievable with virtual certainty in every case.

At first sight anyway. But Portia and Hegel raise an awkward question. Is retribution achieved if more or less than the exact amount of flesh is forfeited? As Hegal put it, "Injustice is done at once if there is one lash too many, or one dollar or one cent, one week in prison or one day too many or too few".[1] Can we ever be sure that the suffering, hardship, or inconvenience actually imposed on the offender is commensurate with his or her culpability? It is hard enough to measure either, let alone construct a scale which lays the measures side by side.

Nowadays the task is made all the harder by the recognition of a third dimension, although it is usually ignored by philosophers of punishment. It was the utilitarian Bentham who pointed out that offenders' "sensibility" to penalties (we would call it "sensitivity") varies with their age, gender, and other circumstances.[2] Today even retributive sentencing is expected to take account, and does. Commensurability is a problem with three, not two, dimensions.

Led by Hegel, or more precisely Rupert Cross's interpretation of Hegel,[3] modern retributivists have substituted "proportionality" for commensurability. What the proportionalist envisages is two ladder-like scales whose rungs roughly correspond. On the penalty ladder each rung is meant to differ in severity from its neighbours. There is of course no way of being sure that the intervals between rungs are in all cases the same. A two-year

From N. Walker, "Modern Retributivism", in H. Gross and R. Harrison (eds.), *Jurisprudence: Cambridge Essays* (Oxford: Oxford University Press, 1992), with some textual changes.

custodial sentence exceeds an 18-month sentence by the same amount as the latter exceeds a one-year sentence; but the two-year sentence may be served in a pleasanter prison than shorter ones. A short sentence may not lose a man his job when a slightly longer one would. In this and other ways the measurement of the intervals on the scale depends on the offender's circumstances. "Overlap" too is a problem, especially acute when a sentencer is hesitating between a custodial and a non-custodial sentence. The former is not always the more severe. Some offenders prefer a short time "inside" to paying a heavy fine, and demonstrate this by defaulting. The rungs on the ladder are not merely loose: "sensibility" means that some are interchangeable. There can be no penalty-ladder which holds good for a whole society: only one which holds good for an individual. Yet what proportionalists offer is the former.

The other scale is usually even cruder, although it could be improved if proportionalists took the trouble. Its rungs consist of offences distinguished by legal definitions: murder, rape, robbery, and so forth. This is crude because legal definitions do not distinguish degrees of harm: after all there are murders and murders. Better would be a ladder in which the rungs were precisely defined harms. And since retributivists are concerned with culpability they ought to be not harms done but harms intended or knowingly risked. Yet if culpability is what matters the rungs need to be elastic, so as to take into account mitigating and aggravating considerations such as provocation, extreme temptation, good intentions, and unnecessary cruelty. No wonder proportionalists are vague in their descriptions of this ladder.

Now the proportionalist juxtaposes his two scales. If he hopes that they will tell him the appropriate penalty for a mercy killing by an aged wife, or a robbery by a mentally dull teenager, he will be disappointed. They may tell him that one should be punished more severely than another, but not by how much; and in some cases they will not even tell him which should be punished more severely. They will certainly help to induce sentencers to reason less idiosyncratically when choosing penalties, and so to be more consistent. But that is all.

A retributive theory needs to explain why the guilty party "ought" to be punished, in the moral sense of "ought". Retributivists have offered quite a few answers.

Some are intuitionist: the duty to inflict desert is simply perceived by our moral sense (see Selection 4.1 above). The perception that tells us we ought not to kill people also tells us that we ought to kill those who do, or at least inflict some serious harm on them. Perceptions of this kind, however, seem to be less unanimous than sense-perceptions. There is more agreement about the sweetness of sugar than about the sweetness of revenge or of legitimate punishment, let alone their morality.

Most retributivists concede the need for an explanation. Their explanations tend to be either superstitious or metaphorical. the superstitious kind need not detain us for long. In some cultures, more common in the past than in the present, a grave crime such as homicide or incest is seen as creating a sort of contamination that can be sanitized only by some transaction which gets rid of the offender (whether by death, by banishment, or by some nasty magic). Some forms of some religions see the offender's suffering as needed to carry out the will of a deity (which makes it legitimate to speculate about the deity's reasoning). Some Christian theologians justify punishment on the ground that it may promote spiritual improvement.[4] This is not necessarily Benthamist utilitarianism: it is the offender's immortal soul they have in mind, not his temporal future. Yet spiritual improvement is highly improbable unless he accepts or can be brought to accept the justice of his suffering. If he cannot, his punishment must be either unjustifiable or justifiable by some other reasoning. This is the point at which theologians, like philosophers, tend to resort to metaphors.

Metaphors are treacherous friends, turning tail when one needs help most. (They are, after all, just a special kind of analogy, and so by definition not precisely what is meant.) Consider, for instance, the popular explanation that offenders "owe a debt", usually "to society" rather than the victim. (Even retributivists who want victims to be compensated may also believe that the offenders owe something to society.) The debt is not literal. If I try to borrow and am refused, I owe no debt; but if I attempt a crime unsuccessfully, I am said to owe something to society. Again, what a debtor owes is something that will benefit the creditor; but it is not easy to see what benefit an afflictive penalty will confer on society.

Another metaphor talks of "annulling" or "cancelling" the offence; that is, it seems, restoring a status quo ante in which the crime had not been committed. Certainly in the case of theft or criminal damage it is usually possible for restitution to undo virtually all the harm, if one ignores fear and outrage; but nobody can be unmurdered, unraped, or unmugged. Nor, again, would this broken-backed analogy justify the punishment of inchoate crimes. As Bosanquet realized,[5] the most that punishment can be claimed to do on these lines is to *symbolize* cancellation, not achieve it.

Should metaphors be accepted as genuine currency in a transaction of this kind? Metaphorizing retributivists could plead that they are trying to describe something so special that its nature can be grasped only by intuition, but that a metaphor—or two, or three—can guide the interlocutor's intuition to the point at which he should be able to say, "Now I see". This would be more convincing, however, if they had done their best to guide us with literal statements before resorting to metaphors.

At least two inter-war philosophers did so. W. D. Ross suggested that when the state punishes it is keeping promises made in its criminal code.[6] The aim of the code is to protect citizens' rights; but the obligation to punish lies in the nature of a promise. J. D. Mabbott's suggestion was very similar.[7] If a disciplinary code prescribes penalties for infringements, this is a sufficient and compelling reason for imposing them on infringers. These explanations were non-superstitious and non-metaphorical. They allowed that the institution called "punishment" may have been included in the criminal code (or in other disciplinary codes) for utilitarian reasons, yet accounted for the retributivist's feeling that there is an obligation to penalize.

Modern retributivists could have done worse than develop Mabbott's point. Post-war ethnomethodologists have demonstrated the extent to which people are rule-making and rule-following animals.[8] All sorts of social transactions, even speech, are rule-governed, and breaches of the rules arouse feelings which range from outrage to embarrassment. Formal codes of conduct such as the criminal law and disciplinary codes include rules which specify penalties for breaches of the substantive rules. If a substantive rule has been breached, a failure to apply the appropriate penalizing rule adds one more breach. This may well be the logical core of the feeling that penalizing is obligatory, and it is often reinforced by dislike of the offender because of what he has done. There are awkwardnesses to be overcome. In particular, many (but not all) penalizing rules are nowadays permissive rather than prescriptive: they do not specify what *must* be done to the transgressors, only what *may* be done. Even so, the sentencer (or other disciplinary authority) may regard himself as bound by other rules to choose one of the permitted penalties (for example by the guidelines of the Magistrates' Association or by the dicta of appellate courts).

Yet post-war retributivists who have seen the need for non-superstitious, non-metaphorical explanation of desert have overlooked the need to preserve the element of obligation. Robert Nozick, for example, resorts to symbolism.[9] He takes great care to make clear that it is not merely the consequentialist sort that holds out hope of improving crime-rates:

> "The hope is that delivering the message will change the person so that he will realize he did wrong, then start doing things because they are right . . . Yet, if it does not do this, still, punishment does give the correct values some significant effect on his life . . . The nonteleological [sc. non-utilitarian] retributive view . . . sees punishment as effecting a connection between the wrongdoer and the correct values that he has flouted".

In other words, if the message has a good effect on the wrongdoer's behaviour so much the better, but that is not essential.

This gets rid of the metaphorical bathwater, but loses the vital baby: a reason why we should feel an obligation to inflict desert. Why *ought* a "connection" to be effected between the wrongdoer and the correct values which he has flouted, if it does not matter whether this improves his behaviour?

Von Hirsch thinks he can save his message of "censure" from this criticism. The state is under an obligation to respond in some way to criminal law-breaking. This obligation need not be a retributive one: von Hirsch seems to regard it as utilitarian. But "it should do so in a manner that testifies to the recognition that the conduct is wrong. To respond in a morally neutral fashion, to treat the conduct merely as a source of costs to the perpetrator, is objectionable because it fails to provide this recognition". This sounds like a utilitarian argument for "censure"; but he goes on: "Even if we failed to discover evidence confirming that the criminal sanction reinforces people's desire to be law-abiding . . . the sanction should still express blame as an embodiment of moral judgments about criminal conduct" (see Selection 4.4 below). This has narrowed the gap, but still fails to show us how to cross it. If the censorious message need have no utility, why is it morally necessary? It is not hard to find a *psychological* necessity. Our feelings about a crime may well make us want to convey such a message to the criminal or others, but that is not a moral necessity.

Notes

1. See Hegel, *Philosophy of right* (1854), tr. T. M. Knox (Oxford, 1942).
2. See J. Bentham, *Introduction to the Principles of Morals and of Legislation* (London, 1789).
3. See R. Cross, *The English Sentencing System* (London, 1971).
4. See e.g. E. Moberley, *Suffering, Innocent and Guilty* (London, 1978).
5. See B. Bosanquet, *Some Suggestions in Ethics* (London, 1918).
6. In an appendix to W. D. Ross, *The Right and the Good* (Oxford, 1930), which received little attention.
7. J. D. Mabbott, "Punishment", (1939) 48 *Mind*, 190 ff.
8. e.g. H. Garfinkel, in *Studies in Ethnomethodology* (Englewood Cliffs, NJ, 1967), and, more systematically, R. Harré and P. Secord, in *The Explanation of Social Behaviour* (Oxford, 1972).
9. See R. Nozick, *Philosophical Explanations* (Oxford, 1981).

4.3

Desert and Penance

R. A DUFF

In this essay I wish to sketch an account of punishment as a mode of rational, transparent[1] communication and persuasion: an account which does justice to the anti-consequentialist, retributivist thought that punishment must not use those who are punished merely as means to some social benefit, but must be justified as being deserved for their past wrongdoing, but which also recognizes the persuasive force of the non-retributivist thought that punishment must also be justified as a means of preventing future crime. For punishment, on the account I will offer, looks both back towards the crime which is punished, as a justified response to that crime, and forward towards the offender's repentance and self-reform. It does indeed aim, in a sense, to "prevent" crime: but to prevent crime by persuading offenders to recognize and repent their past wrongdoing.[2] (One merit of a communicative account of punishment, of the sort that I will sketch, is thus that it undercuts the traditional distinction between purely retributivist, or backward-looking, and purely consequentialist, or forward-looking, accounts: it shows how punishment which is justified as a merited response for a past offence can also, by virtue of its very character as punishment, have a future-oriented goal; and how we can give punishment a future-oriented goal without portraying it solely as an instrumental technique for achieving that goal.)

We could perhaps imagine a system of criminal law without a penal system, or at least without a system of punishments at all like those with which we are familiar. What is harder (if not impossible) to imagine is a system of criminal law which made no provision for any kind of formal or authorized response to crime: a system which declared certain kinds of conduct to be public wrongs, but which neither provided for formal responses to such conduct, nor authorized informal responses by others. The reason for this is simple: a state or society which, through its

This essay is published here for the first time.

criminal law, condemns certain kinds of conduct as wrong in advance cannot be sincere in that condemnation if (at least or especially in the case of
more serious wrongs) it ignores or is silent in the face of commissions of
such wrongs: to ignore manifest breaches of what we have declared to be
important norms is in effect to deny what we claim to have declared.

But what form might this response take? The obvious answer (one that
both von Hirsch and I have emphasized) is that the immediate or primary
response should be *censure*.[3] For if someone has committed a public
wrong (especially a serious wrong; but moderate censure is also called for
in respect of lesser wrongs), an appropriate response to him as a responsible agent is to censure his conduct. If the state (and the law) should treat
its citizens as responsible agents, it should therefore respond to their criminal wrongdoings with censure; and this, I suggest, is central to the meaning of a criminal conviction. A conviction does not merely record a finding
that this person committed the crime charged: it condemns him for that
crime; it is a communicative act, communicating censure to the convicted
defendant.

Now we could say that a conviction itself, as a communicative act of
censure, has as its goal a certain kind of "transparent persuasion", aimed
at the convicted person; and that in that qualified sense it has a preventive aim. For, first, internal to censure is the aim or aspiration of modifying future conduct: to censure someone for a past wrong is not only to
condemn that wrong, but also to urge or imply that he should not act thus
in the future; and someone who accepts the censure as justified must
thereby commit himself to trying to avoid such conduct in future. Of
course, this is not to say that censure is justified only if and when it is in
fact likely to achieve such a future effect: we can properly censure those
who will have no chance to repeat their wrong; or those who, having
already repented for themselves, do not need our censure to persuade them
to change their ways; or those who will, we are sure, remain unpersuaded.
But the fact still remains that internal to censure is the message not just
that the person censured should not have acted as they did, but that they
should not act thus in future.

Second, that modification of future conduct is to be wrought by *transparent* persuasion—at least if censure is to address and treat the other as
a responsible agent. That is to say, the aim must be not merely to bring
about, by whatever means or techniques may be effective, a suitable
change in the other's attitudes and conduct: but to persuade him to modify his future conduct by bringing him, rationally, to recognize (or to
renew or reinforce his recognition of) the wrongfulness of what he did,
and thus the need to avoid repeating such conduct; and to do this by offer-

ing him or reminding him of the reasons which justify the censorious judgement that his conduct was wrongful.

Can we also talk in this context, as we could in the context of the declared law, of an aim of transparent *general* persuasion? It would seem that we can: for in censuring this particular defendant we can also surely communicate an appropriate message to others—that this kind of conduct is criminally wrong and to be avoided. Now it is true that, once we see the verdict of a trial as a communicative act, we can see it as being addressed to an audience wider than the individual defendant (compare Feinberg on the various expressive functions of punishment):[4] it assures the victim, and other concerned participants or observers, that the law's demands are taken seriously, thus helping to vindicate the victim; it shows the public at large that—at least to this extent—the law means what it says. However for the kinds of roughly Kantian reason which are often mobilized against an account of punishment as general deterrence, I think that we should see such effects on or messages to the larger public as at most a kind of secondary or side-effect, rather than as our principal justifying aim: for otherwise we will be "using" the offender as a means to a larger social end. What justifies censuring him is the wrong that he has done; and the communicative purpose internal to the act of censure is that *he* should come to recognize that he did wrong and must avoid such conduct in future.

I would add two further points about censure. First, while there is clearly room, and need, for empirical investigation into the actual impact of criminal censure on offenders and on the wider public (what message is actually heard, and to what further effect); and whilst there is also room, and need, for empirical investigation into the effects of different kinds or styles of censuring; the justification of censure I have offered does not depend on such empirical facts. Second, and relatedly, this account is neither purely retributivist, nor purely forward-looking or consequentialist. Its independence of empirical testing might seem to justify the charge that what I present as a forward-looking goal for punishment turns out to be nothing other than retribution more or less thinly disguised. But my argument is that censure, whilst retributive in that it is focused on and justified by the past wrongdoing which is censured, is also and essentially forward-looking, in that it aims to persuade the wrongdoer to amend his ways. It is, we could say, not so much consequentialist (which implies a purely contingent or external relation between "means" and "end"), as purposive.

Now one could portray censure itself, as formally administered by a court, as a species of punishment: for it is imposed on an (alleged) offender, for his (alleged) offence, by a formal authority; and it is intended to be unpleasant. But criminal punishment typically consists, of course, in something more than this—in the infliction of something unpleasant, that is, in "hard treatment".

A central task for a communicative theory of punishment is to explain why punishment should take the form of hard treatment (or to follow an abolitionist path and argue that hard treatment punishments *cannot* be justified). Penal hard treatment *can* communicate censure: but since censure can also be communicated by the offender's conviction itself, or by purely symbolic measures which are burdensome or unwelcome *solely* by virtue of the censure which they communicate, we must ask what could justify the state in using hard treatment as the method of communication.

Von Hirsch thinks that we cannot answer this question purely by appeal to the communicative, censorial purpose of punishment.[5] Beyond punishment's primary role as moral communication, he argues, we should see penal hard treatment as adding a (modest) prudential supplement to the law's moral voice. It serves as a deterrent, in that it aims to reduce crime by creating a prudential disincentive that might dissuade from crime at least some of those who are insufficiently motivated by the law's moral appeal. However, it should not replace or drown (as a system of *purely* deterrent hard treatment punishments replaces or drowns) the moral tones of censure: it offers an *additional*, prudential reason for obedience, as being suitable to moral agents who are capable of being moved by moral censure but also susceptible to temptation—a reason which is not (or should not be) intended to be persuasive by itself (as the reasons offered by purely deterrent punishments are intended to be), but which can add additional persuasive force to the law's primarily moral appeal (see Selection 4.4 below).

I wish, however, to suggest an alternative understanding of penal hard treatment, which shows how it too can serve the communicative aims of punishment. Hard treatment punishment, in my view, should be understood as a secular species of *penance*. A penance serves several, closely interrelated, purposes. It aims to focus (indeed, to force) the wrongdoer's attention onto his wrongdoing: he is not allowed to turn his attention away from the wrong that he has done (a turning away which is, as we all know, tempting for human beings), but is forced to confront it. It aims to communicate to him not merely the judgement that he did wrong, but a symbolic portrayal of the character and implications of that wrong: thus, for instance, a term of imprisonment (which on this account should be reserved for the most serious offences) communicates the way in which the offender's crime broke the essential bonds of community with his fellow-citizens, separating him from them; a vandal who is required to undertake Community Service repairing of others' vandalism is confronted with the effects of his crime. It aims to persuade him to accept this judgement on, and this understanding of, his crime (but *not* to force him to accept it, for it must still address him as a moral agent who remains free to reject the message which is communicated to him): to come to recognize and repent the wrong he has done. And, if he does come to such a repentance, his punishment also then becomes a vehicle of self-reform (for to recognize and repent his past wrongdoing must also be to set himself to improve his future conduct): it enables him to strengthen that penitent understanding of what he has done, to express it to others, and thus to reconcile himself with them. On this view, punishment (including its element of hard treatment) is a communicative process which aims to induce repentance, (self-)reform and reconciliation. It addresses the offender as a moral agent, and as a member of the community, who has done wrong, and who should recognize and repent that wrong: it looks back, as censure of its nature looks back, to the past offence on which it is focused; but it also looks forward, to the penitential result that it aims to achieve.

As thus barely sketched, this account will seem radically implausible to many people; and I do not have the space to try to render it much more plausible here. However, I would note three points which might help to make it a little less implausible.

First, it is not meant to provide an account of what the punishments administered in our existing penal systems either actually achieve or are (for the most part) plausibly designed to achieve; nor, therefore, does it aim to offer a justification of the penal status quo. Rather, it is intended to provide an account of what punishment *ought* to be—of what it would need to be if it is to treat offenders with the respect that is due to them as moral agents (and with the concern that is due to them as members of the community); and thus also to provide an ideal against which we can judge our existing penal institutions and practices.

Second, it does not warrant oppressive punishments which aim to grind the offender down until he repents; or indeterminate sentences which last until he repents. For punishment, as a communication of deserved censure, must be proportionate to the offence. Furthermore, it must always address the offender as a moral agent, who must come to his own judgement and his own understanding: it compels his attention, but must not coerce his understanding; and, like any process of rational persuasion, it is essentially fallible, in that the offender must remain free to be unpersuaded and unrepentant.

Third, talk of penance readily conjures up the image of a monastic order, in which the abbot imposes penances on members of the order in order to improve the condition of their souls; and in which he properly takes a close interest in every aspect of their spiritual well-being. This then might suggest that an account of criminal punishment as a secular species of penance allots to the state a role like the abbot's: that it would authorize the state to take a close, and oppressively intrusive, interest in the moral condition of its citizens, and to use punishment to remedy every kind of moral failing. But this is surely not the kind of role that, if we have any regard for liberal values, we should allow a secular state. The account I am offering, however, need not allot the state such an extensive or intrusive role, and can respect at least some of the liberal concerns which the picture of the abbot will arouse. For it is quite consistent with my account that we should set strict limits on the scope of the criminal law, using it to prohibit only those kinds of conduct which seriously threaten interests or values that are of central importance to the community and its members. It is also quite consistent with this account that the law's interest in the offender's moral condition should be strictly limited to those aspects of his character which are fully displayed in (indeed are actualized by) his criminal conduct: that the courts and penal authorities should not be allowed to engage in an all-encompassing inquiry into his moral state, but should attend only to his criminal dispositions as manifested in his criminal conduct.

Much more would need to be said to explicate this kind of account— let alone to render it more plausible. That "more" would need to include a detailed discussion of the kinds of punishment which could play the communicative and penitential role that, on this account, punishment should play; a discussion and defence of the communitarian conception of the state and of society on which this account depends (for it portrays punishment as a mode of communication between fellow members of a moral community); and a discussion of the various political and social preconditions on which the very possibility of such a practice of punishment must depend.

Notes

1. Persuasion is "transparent" when it appeals to the very reasons which justify the attempt to persuade. Thus while a deterrent system of punishment aims at rational persuasion, it does not aim at "transparent" persuasion: for the prudential

reasons that it offers for obeying the law are not the moral reasons which justify the claim that citizens should obey the law, or the attempt to persuade them to do so. See J. Bickenbach, "Critical Notice of Duff, *Trials and Punishments*" (1988) 18 *Canadian Journal of Philosophy* 765.

2. See R. A. Duff, *Trials and Punishments* (1986), ch. 9; R. A. Duff, "Penal Communications", (1996) 20 *Crime and Justice: A Review of Research* 1.
3. See Selection 4.4 below; see also A. von Hirsch, *Censure and Sanctions* (1993), ch. 2.
4. Joel Feinberg, "The Expressive Function of Punishment" in J. Feinberg, *Doing and Deserving* (1970), ch. 5.
5. Von Hirsch, above n. 3, pp. 12–15, 38–46; see also, U. Narayan, "Adequate Responses and Preventive Benefits", (1993) 13 *Oxford Journal of Legal Studies* 13.

4.4

Proportionate Sentences: a Desert Perspective

ANDREW VON HIRSCH

Criminologists' interest in desert dates from the mid-1970s, with the publication of a number of works arguing that this notion should be seen as the central requirement of justice in sentencing. Once broached, the idea of desert quickly became influential. A number of American states' sentencing-guidelines systems (most notably, those of Minnesota and Oregon) have explicitly relied on it; some European sentencing-reform efforts (particularly those of Finland, Sweden and more recently, England) have done likewise, although these latter schemes make use of statutory statements of guiding principle, rather than specific, numerical guidelines.[1]

The groundwork for this revival of interest in desert was laid already in the post-Second World War literature of analytical moral philosophy. These writings supplied a principled critique of purely instrumental ways thinking about social and penal issues, suggesting how such reckonings were capable of sacrificing individual rights to serve majority interests. The philosophical literature also began exploring the conception of desert, suggesting how it constitutes an integral part of everyday moral judgements.[2]

The movement toward a proportionality-based sentencing theory began, perhaps, in 1971 with the publication of the Quaker-sponsored American Friends Service Committee report, *Struggle for Justice* (1971). The report recommended moderate, proportionate punishments, and opposed deciding sentence severity on predictive or rehabilitative grounds. The Friends Committee report did not rely explicitly on the idea of desert as the basis for its proposals; that was left to subsequent writings, including the Australian philosopher John Kleinig's *Punishment and Desert* (1973), my own *Doing Justice* (1976), and the British philosopher R.A. Duff's *Trials and Punishments* (1986). A number of influential British and Scandinavian penologists have also contributed to this literature, includ-

This essay is published here for the first time.

ing A.E. Bottoms, Andrew Ashworth, Martin Wasik, and Nils Jareborg.[3] The present essay is designed to summarize recent writing in this area, including subsequent work of Duff's and mine (Duff (1996); von Hirsch (1993)).

Desert theories for sentencing have had the attraction that they purport to be about *just* outcomes: the emphasis is on what the offender should fairly receive for his crime, rather than on how his punishment might affect his future behaviour or that of others. It also seems capable of providing more guidance: the sentencer, instead of having to address elusive empirical questions of the crime-preventative effect of the sentence, can address matters more within his or her ken, concerning the seriousness of the criminal offence—how harmful the conduct typically is, how culpable the offender was in committing it (see Selection 4.6 below).

Censure and Penal Desert

There have been a variety of retributive or desert-based accounts of punishment, ranging from intuitionist theories (see Selection 4.1 above), to talionic notions of requiting evil for evil, to conceptions that see punishment as taking away the "unjust advantage" over others which the offender obtains by choosing to offend (see Finnis (1980), pp. 263–4).[4] The desert-based conception examined in this essay, however, relies on a different account: one emphasizing the communicative features of punishment.

The criminal sanction censures: punishing consists of doing something unpleasant to someone, because he purportedly has committed a wrong, under circumstances and in a manner that conveys disapprobation of the person for his wrong. Treating the offender as a wrongdoer, Richard Wasserstrom (1980) has pointed out, is central to the idea of punishment. The difference between a tax and a fine, for example, does not rest in the material deprivation imposed—which is money in both cases. It consists, rather, in the fact that with the fine, money is taken in a manner that conveys disapproval or censure; whereas with a tax, no disapproval is implied.

A sanction that treats the conduct as wrong—that is, not a "neutral" sanction—has two important moral functions that are not reducible to crime prevention. One is to recognize the importance of the rights that have been infringed. The censure in punishment conveys to victims and potential victims the acknowledgment that they are wronged by criminal conduct, that rights to which they properly are entitled have been infringed. The other (and perhaps, still more important) role of censure is that of addressing the offender as a moral agent, by appealing to his or her sense of right and wrong. This is not just a crime-prevention strategy, however, for otherwise there would be no point in censuring actors who are repentant already (since they need no blame to make them regret their actions and to try to desist in future) or who seemingly are incorrigible (since they will not change despite the censure). Any human actor, this communicative perspective suggests, should be treated as a moral agent, having the capacity (unless clearly incompetent) of evaluating others' assessment of their conduct. A response to criminal wrongdoing that conveys blame gives the individual the opportunity to respond in ways that are typically those of an agent capable of moral deliberation: to recognize the wrongfulness of the action; feel remorse; to make efforts to desist in future—or to try to give reasons why the conduct was not actually wrong. What a purely "neutral" sanction not embodying blame would deny, even if no less effective in preventing crime, is precisely this recognition of the person's status as a moral agent. A neutral sanction would treat offenders and potential offenders much as beasts in a circus—as beings which must be restrained, intimidated, or conditioned into submission because they are incapable of understanding that predatory conduct is wrong (von Hirsch (1993), ch. 2; Narayan (1993))

Relying on this idea of censure helps remove some of the seeming mysteriousness of penal desert judgements: censure or blaming involves everyday moral judgments used in a wide variety of social contexts, of which punishment is just one. This account also helps address another objection traditionally raised against retributive penal theories, namely, their seeming harshness—their apparent insistence on an eye for an eye. Once the paying back of evil for evil is not seen as the underlying idea, penal desert does not demand visitation of suffering equal to the harm done. What is called for instead is punishments that are *proportionate* to the seriousness of the criminal conduct. Proportionate punishments—even if not involving harm-for-harm equivalence—would suffice to convey blame for various crimes according to their degree of reprehensibleness. Indeed, several advocates of the desert perspective (including myself) have advocated substantial reductions of penalty levels.[5]

Can the institution of punishment be explained purely in terms of censure? Punishment does convey blame, but does so in a special way— through visitation of deprivation ("hard treatment") on the offender. That deprivation is, of course, the vehicle through which the blame is expressed. But why use this vehicle, rather than simply expressing blame in symbolic fashion? Some adherents of the communicative view of desert, most notably R.A. Duff, hold that the hard-treatment component of the penal sanction can itself be explained in desert terms: Duff treats the deprivations involved in punishment as providing a kind of secular penance (see Selection 4.3 above).[6] I have my doubts, however. The reason for having the institution of punishment (that is, for expressing disapproval through hard treatment, instead of merely censuring) seems to have to do with keeping predatory behaviour within tolerable limits. Had the criminal sanction no usefulness in preventing crime, there should be no need to visit material deprivation on those who offend. True, we might still wish to devise another way of issuing authoritative judgements of blaming, for such predatory behaviour as occurs. But those judgements, in the interest of keeping state-inflicted suffering to a minimum, would no longer be linked to purposive infliction of suffering (von Hirsch 1993, 14).

If the criminal sanction thus serves to prevent crime as well as censure, how is this consistent with treating offenders and potential offenders as moral agents? The hard-treatment in punishment, on my view, serves a prudential reason for obedience to those insufficiently motivated by the penal censure's moral appeal. But this should *supplement* rather than replace the normative reasons for desisting from crime conveyed by penal censure—that is, it provides an *additional* reason for compliance to those who are capable of recognizing the law's moral demands, but who are also tempted to disobey them. The law thus addresses *ourselves*, not a distinct "criminal" class of those considered incapable of grasping moral appeals. And it addresses us neither as perfectly moral agents (we are not like angels), nor as beasts which only can be coerced through threats; but rather, as moral but fallible agents who need some prudential supplement to help us resist criminal temptation (von Hirsch (1993) pp. 12–14; see also Narayan (1993)). However, this account (as will be discussed further below) calls for moderation in the overall severity in punishment levels. The harsher the penalty system is, the less plausible it becomes to see it as embodying chiefly a moral appeal rather than a system of bare threats.

The Rationale for Proportionality

In a minimal sense, proportionality always had a role in sentencing policy: penalties that were grossly excessive in relation to the gravity of the offence were perceived as unfair. Statutory maximum sentences reflected that understanding, and it also had a constitutional dimension: some jurisdictions adopted a constitutional bar against grossly excessive punishments.[7] This, however, gave the notion of proportionality only the outer, constraining role of barring draconian sanctions for lesser offences. Short of these (rather high) maximum limits, proportionality had small weight in theories about how sanctions should be determined, with consequentialist concerns (about rehabilitation, incapacitation, and deterrence) counting chiefly instead.

What is distinctive about contemporary desert theory is it moves notions of proportionality from this merely peripheral to a central role in deciding sanctions. The primary basis for deciding quanta of punishments, under this theory, is the principle of proportionality or "commensurate deserts", requiring the severity of the penalty to be proportionate to the gravity of the defendant's criminal conduct. The criterion for deciding the quantum of punishment is thus retrospective rather than consequentialist: the seriousness of the offence for which the defendant stands convicted.

What is the basis for this principle? The censure account, just discussed, provides the explanation. If punishment embodies blame, then how much one punishes will convey how much the conduct is condemned. If crime X is punished more severely than crime Y, this connotes the greater disapprobation of crime X. Punishments, consequently, should be allocated consistently with their blaming implications. When penalties are arrayed in severity according to the gravity of offences, the disapprobation thereby conveyed will reflect the degree of reprehensibleness of the conduct. When punishments are arrayed otherwise, this is not merely inefficient (who knows?—it might sometimes "work"), but unfair; offenders are being visited with more or less censure than the comparative blameworthiness of their conduct would warrant (von Hirsch 1993, ch. 2).

Equity is sacrificed when the proportionality principle is disregarded, even when this is done for the sake of crime prevention. Suppose that offenders A and B commit and are convicted of criminal conduct of approximately the same degree of seriousness. Suppose B is deemed more likely to re-offend, and therefore is given a longer sentence. Notwithstanding the possible preventative utility of that sentence, the objection remains that B, through his more severe punishment, is being treated as more to blame than A, though their conduct has the same degree of blameworthiness.

A possible objection (see Dolinko (1992)) to this argument might run as follows: if the component of "hard treatment" in the criminal sanction serves a crime-preventative as well as a purely censuring function (as argued earlier in this essay), then why cannot one allocate the relative severities of punishment in part on preventative grounds rather than purely on the basis of offence seriousness? The reply is that punishment's deprivations and its reprobative connotations are inextricably intermixed: it is the threatened penal deprivation that expresses the degree of censure.

If the deprivations visited on a given type of crime are increased, even for preventative reasons, this (necessarily) increases the severity of the punishment. But changing the severity, relative to other penalties, alters the implicit censure—which would not be justified if the seriousness of the conduct is itself unchanged (von Hirsch 1993, pp. 16–17).

Desert as "Determining" or "Limiting"?

If the principle of proportionality is so important, is it a "determining" or merely a "limiting" principle? While our sense of justice tells us that criminals should be punished as they deserve, there do not seem to be definite quanta of severity associated with our desert-judgements. Armed robbers have committed a serious offence, deserving of substantial punishment, but it is not apparent whether that should consist of two years' confinement, three years, or some shorter or longer period.

One response to this problem has been Norval Morris's: to say that desert is merely a limiting principle (see Selection 4.5 below). It tells us, he asserts, not how much robbers deserve, but only some broad limits beyond which their punishments would be *un*deserved. Within such limits, the sentence can be decided on other (for example, predictive) grounds. This view, however, would mean that persons who commit similar crimes could receive quite different amounts of punishment. If punishment embodies blame as a central characteristic, it becomes morally problematic to visit such different degrees of severity, and hence of implicit blame, on comparably blameworthy transgressions.

A conceivable opposite response, but scarcely a plausible one, would be the heroic intuitionist stance: that if we only ponder hard enough we will perceive deserved quanta of punishments: that robbers ordinarily deserve so-and-so many months or years of confinement, and so forth. Our intuitions, however, fail to provide such answers.

The way out of this apparent dilemma is to recognize the crucial difference between the comparative ranking of punishments on one hand, and the overall magnitude and anchoring of the penalty scale on the other. With respect to comparative rankings, *ordinal* proportionality provides considerable guidance: persons convicted of similar crimes should receive punishments of comparable severity (save in special aggravating or mitigating circumstances altering the harm or culpability of the conduct in the particular circumstances); and persons convicted of crimes of differing gravity should suffer punishments correspondingly graded in onerousness. These ordinal-proportionality requirements are no mere limits, and they are infringed when equally reprehensible conduct is punished markedly unequally in the manner that Morris suggests (von Hirsch 1986, ch.4).

Desert provides less constraint, however, on the penalty scale's overall dimensions and anchoring points. This is because the censure expressed through penal deprivations is, to a considerable degree, a convention. When a penalty scale reflects the comparative gravity of crimes, making *pro rata* decreases or increases in the prescribed sanctions constitutes a change in that convention.

This distinction helps resolve the dilemma just mentioned. The leeway which desert allows in fixing the scale's overall degree of onerousness explains why we cannot perceive a single right or fitting penalty for a crime. Whether X months, Y months, or somewhere in between is the appropriate penalty for robbery depends on how the scale has been anchored and what punishments are prescribed for other crimes. Once those anchoring points are decided, however, the more restrictive requirements of ordinal proportionality apply. This explains why it would be inappropriate to give short prison terms to some robbers and long ones to other robbers, on the basis (say) of predictive factors not reflecting the degree of seriousness of the criminal conduct.

Does this purported solution still leave the anchoring of the scale too wide open? Could it not permit a very severe penalty scale, as long it is not *so* harsh as to impose drastic penalties on manifestly trivial crimes? My suggested answer to this question has been that high overall severity levels are inconsistent with the moral functions of penal censure. Through punishments' censuring features, the criminal sanction offers a normative reason for desisting to human beings seen as moral agents: that doing certain acts is wrong and hence should be refrained from. Punishments' material deprivations can then be viewed (as noted earlier) as providing a supplemental disincentive—as providing humans (given human fallibility and the temptations of offending) an additional prudential reason for complying with the law. The higher penalty levels rise, however, the less the normative reasons for desisting supplied by penal censure will count, and the more the system becomes in effect a bare system of threats (in Hegel's apt words, a stick that might be raised to a dog). To the extent this argument is accepted, it points toward keeping penalties at moderate levels (von Hirsch 1993, ch. 5).[8]

Inclusion of Crime-Control Aims?

Desert theory sets priorities among sentencing aims: it assumes that it is more important to have proportionately ordered sanctions than to seek other objectives—say, incapacitating those deemed higher risks. This understandably evokes discomfort: why cannot one seek proportionality *and* pursue other desired ends, whether they be treatment, incapacitation or something else?

To some extent, a desert model permits consideration of other aims: namely, to the degree this is consistent with the proportionate ordering of penalties. Thus when there is a choice between two non-custodial sanctions of approximately equivalent severity (say, a unit-fine of so many days' earnings and intensive probation for a specified duration), proportionality constraints are not offended when one of these is chosen over the other on (say) treatment grounds. Desert theorists thus have come forward with schemes for scaling intermediate, non-custodial penalties; these sanctions would be ranked in severity according to the gravity of the crime, but penalties of roughly equivalent onerousness could be substituted for one another when treatment or feasiblity concerns so indicate (see more fully, Selection 6.4 below). Nevertheless, a pure desert model remains a constraining one: ulterior aims may be relied upon only where these do not substantially alter the comparative severity of penalties. Giving substantial extra prison time to persons deemed high risks would thus breach the model's requirements. Why not, then, relax the model's constraints to allow greater scope to such other aspirations?

A possibility —sometimes referred to as a "modified" desert model— would be to relax the constraints to a limited degree. Proportionality would ordinarily determine comparative punishment levels, but deviations would be permitted in case of the gravest risks of crime (see Robinson (1987); von Hirsch (1993) pp. 48–53). Here, the idea is that avoiding extraordinary harms is so important a goal as to warrant some sacrifice of fairness. This position differs from ordinary penal consequentialism, however, in that departures from desert requirements could be invoked only exceptionally, to deal with threats of an extraordinary nature (von Hirsch 1993, pp. 48–53).[9] Alternatively, deviations could more regularly be permitted, but these would be restricted ones: say, a deviation of no more than 10 or 15 per cent from the deserved sentence. While departures from proportionality involve a sacrifice of equity, the extent of that sacrifice depends on the degree of the deviation from desert constraints. Limited deviations, it might be argued, would permit the pursuit of ulterior objectives without "too much" unfairness (von Hirsch 1993, pp. 54–56).

These mixed approaches still make desert the primary determinant for the ordering of penalties, but give some extra scope for ulterior purposes. Even such schemes remain constraining, however: especially dangerous offenders might be given substantial extra prison time, but not the ordinary potential recidivist; some extra leeway might be granted to suit a non-custodial penalty to the offender's apparent treatment needs, but not a great deal.

Could still more scope be given to non-desert considerations? In a hybrid rationale, either desert will predominate or something else will. If—in the ordinary case—the seriousness of the crime is the penalty's primary determinant, the system remains desert-dominated. If other (say, crime-preventive) aims are given the greater emphasis, however, that creates a system dominated by those aims. That will re-introduce the familiar problems of consequentialist sentencing schemes—for example, those relating to equity among offenders, and those of insufficient systematic knowledge of preventive effects (see Chapters 1 to 3 above).

In assessing these alternatives, it needs to be borne in mind that even a "purely" desert-based sentencing scale is likely to have collateral crime-prevention benefits—in such deterrence as its penalties achieve, and in the possible incapacitative effects of the prison sentences it prescribes for serious crimes. Departing from proportionality for the sake of crime prevention, then, will call not just for a showing that preventative effects might be achieved (for a desert-based system may achieve these too); instead, it would call for a showing that the departures are likely to yield *enhanced* preventative effects—which is no easy matter to establish. And here, one is likely to confront a fairness/effectiveness trade-off: because crime rates tend to be rather insensitive to small variations in punishment, modest departures from proportionality are likely to have relatively little impact; large departures might possibly work better, but these precisely are the ones that are most troublesome on moral grounds (see Selection 3.7 above).

Other Issues: Severity and Social Deprivation

Must desert lead to harsh penalties? As the theory emerged and became influential at a time when penalty levels rose in many jurisdictions, some critics have argued that the theory must in part be responsible for such increases (Hudson 1987). However, desert theory itself does not require a severe sentencing policy—indeed, as noted earlier, it permits (indeed, arguably points toward) considerable penalty reductions. Moreover, the sentence-reform schemes which rely explicitly on notions of desert tend not to be severe ones: the Minnesota and Oregon sentencing guidelines, for example, call for relatively modest penalties by American standards; European desert-oriented sentencing standards, such as those of Finland

and Sweden, are likewise associated with penal moderation (von Hirsch 1993, ch. 10). Measures which most clearly call for tougher sanctions tend to utilize criteria inconsistent with proportionality: mandatory sentences, for example, select particular offence categories for harsh treatment, without regard to the gravity of the offence involved, or the penalties imposed for other offences (see Chapter 9 below).

Another issue is that concerning just punishment and social deprivation (see Murphy 1973). Many offenders live in grim social environments that restrict their opportunities for living tolerable and law-abiding lives. Should such persons be punished differently? The penal law is a poor instrument for rectifying social ills: it is social policy, rather than criminal policy, that is the appropriate instrument for addressing problems of social deprivation. But the question remains disturbing, nevertheless. If social policy fails to alleviate poverty and deprivation, how should the deprived offender be sentenced?

It has been pointed out that desert theory at least does not *add* to the punishment imposed on deprived persons—whereas penal consequentialism would do so, to the extent that social deprivation is a sign (say) of greater dangerousness (von Hirsch 1976, ch. 17). But the question remains whether such persons deserve *reduced* punishments. Arguably, reductions could be warranted on grounds of reduced culpability—in view of the greater obstacles such persons face in leading law-abiding lives (see Selection 4.9 below).[10] Granting such mitigation would, however, create a host of practical and political difficulties—so that the perplexity remains.

Notes

1. For an analysis of the Oregon and Minnesota Guidelines, see von Hirsch (1994) and von Hirsch, Knapp and Tonry (1987), ch. 5; for the Swedish sentencing scheme, see Jareborg 1994; for the English system after the Criminal Justice Act 1991, see Ashworth (1995). For guidelines and statutory sentencing principles generally, see Chapter 5 below.
2. For a critique of utilitarianism, see Williams (1973); for writings on the idea of desert, see Armstrong (1961); H. Morris (1968).
3. See Suggestions for Further Reading, this chapter, for references.
4. For a critique of the "unjust advantage" theory, see von Hirsch (1986) pp. 57–9; Duff (1986), ch. 8.
5. See, e.g., Singer (1979); Ashworth (1995), ch. 9; Duff (1986); Jareborg (1995); von Hirsch (1993).
6. On Duff's view, the hard treatment in punishment should serve to bring the

criminal to understand, and repent of his wrongdoing—and also to provide a vehicle which will enable him to work through and express his penitent understanding.

7. The U.S. Supreme Court has formerly held that grossly excessive punishments violated the Constitutional ban on cruel and unusual punishments (see *Weems v. U.S.* [(1910) 217 U.S. 349]), but the Court later overruled that doctrine (see *Rummel v. Estelle* (1980) 445 U.S. 263).The German Consitutional Court has adopted doctrines barring gross disproportionality of sentence in relation to the seriousness of the crime.

8. There exists a conceptually separate further reason for keeping penalty levels low—namely, the idea of "parsimony"—of keeping state-inflicted suffering to a minimum; see von Hirsch (1993), p. 111.

9. For another defence of such a position, see Bottoms and Brownsword (Selection 3.4 above). Unlike those authors, however, I do not see the issue as one involving conflict of rights—for reasons set forth in von Hirsch (1993), p. 51.

10. For the pros and cons of granting such mitigation, see von Hirsch (1993), pp. 106–8.

References

American Friends Service Committee (1971) *Struggle for Justice* (New York: Hill & Wang).

Armstrong, K. G. (1961) "The Retributivist Hits Back" 70 *Mind* 471.

Ashworth, A., *Sentencing and Criminal Jsutice* (2nd edn., 1995).

Dolinko, D. (1992) "Three Mistakes of Retributivism", 39 *UCLA Law Review* 39.

Duff, R. A. (1986) *Trials and Punishments* (Cambridge: Cambridge University Press).
—— (1996) "Penal Communications", in M. Tonry (ed.), *Crime and Justice; & Review of Research*, Vol. 20, p. 1.

Dworkin, R. (1977) *Taking Rights Seriously* (Cambridge, Mass.: Harvard University Press).

Finnis, J. (1980) *Natural Law and Natural Rights* (Oxford: Oxford University Press).

Hudson, B. (1987) *Justice Through Punishment* (London: St. Martin's Press).

Jareborg, N. (1995) "The Swedish Sentencing Reform", in C. M. V. Clarkson and R. Morgan (eds.), *The Politics of Sentencing Reform* (Oxford: Oxford University Press).

Kleinig, J. (1973) *Punishment and Desert* (The Hague: Martinus Nijhoff).

Morris, H. (1968) "Persons and Punishment" 52 *The Monist* 475.

Murphy, J. G. (1973), "Marxism & Retribution", 2 *Philosophy and Public Affairs* 217.

Narayan, U. (1993) "Adequate Responses and Preventive Benefits" 13 *Oxford Journal of Legal Studies* 13.

Robinson, P. (1987) "Hybrid Principles for the Distribution of Criminal Sanctions" 82 *Northwestern Law Review* 19.

Singer, R. (1979) *Just Deserts* (Cambridge, Mass.: Ballinger Publishing Co.).

von Hirsch, A. (1994) "Proportionality and Parsimony in American Sentencing

Guidelines", in C. M. V. Clarkson and R. Morgan (eds.), *The Politics of Sentencing Reform* (Oxford: Oxford University Press).

—— (1993) *Censure and Sanctions* (Oxford: Oxford University Press).

—— (1986) *Past or Future Crimes* (Manchester: Manchester University Press).

—— (1976) *Doing Justice* (New York: Hill and Wang).

von Hirsch, A., Knapp, K., and Tonry, M. (1987) *The Sentencing Commission and Its Guidelines* (Boston, Mass.: Northeastern University Press).

Wasserstrom, R. (1980) "Punishment", in R. Wasserstrom, *Philosophy and Social Issues: Five Studies* (Notre Dame, Ind.: University of Notre Dame Press).

Williams, B. (1973) "A Critique of Utilitarianism" in J. S. C. Smart and B. Williams, *Utilitarianism: For and Against* (Cambridge Univeristy Press).

4.5

Desert as a Limiting Principle

NORVAL MORRIS

There is an important element in the recommendations of just desert theorists which cannot be as cursorily dismissed as can the argument for mandatory minimum sentences. Their recommendations lead to an issue of principle central to the relationship between equality and desert. They all favour, as do I, a system of sentences which is primarily retributive, which does not pretend to a personal curative effect on the criminal, and in which the proper sentence to be imposed is strongly influenced by what the criminal has done. Thus, concepts of just desert are of overwhelming importance. Indeed, these theorists build their entire sentencing system on a *defining* relationship between the deserved and the imposed punishment. My view is different: It is that desert is not a *defining* principle, but is rather a *limiting* principle; that the concept of a just desert properly limits the maximum and the minimum of the sentence that may be imposed, but does not give us any more fine-tuning to the appropriate sentence than that.

Is this only a quibble, or does it push to issues of principle concerning just sentencing? I think the latter, of course, and hope to prove that conclusion to you today. Let me offer some examples where it seems to be accepted, and is in my view proper and just, not to treat like cases alike. The exemplary sentence is such a case. As Professor Nigel Walker put it, judges "will sometimes impose sentences which are markedly more severe than the norm for the express purpose of increasing their deterrent effect".[1] He gives as an example the imposition of a sentence of four years imprisonment on each of nine young white men who were involved in attacks on blacks in the Nottinghill District of London in 1958. This sentence was at least double the sentence normally imposed for their offences, and was stated by the sentencing judge to be in excess of his normal sentence for such offences, but it was within the legislatively prescribed

From Norval Morris, *Punishment, Desert, and Rehabilitation* (Washington, D.C.: U.S. Government Printing Office, 1976), with some textual changes.

maximum for those offences. It was imposed expressly as an exemplary punishment, to capture public attention and to deter such behaviour by a dramatic punishment. It needs no refined analysis to demonstrate that these nine offenders were selected for *unequal* treatment before the law. Please do not misunderstand me, I am not opposing such sentences, quite the contrary. Rather, I am arguing that if the increased penalty is within the legislatively prescribed range, then any supposed principle of equality does not prevent such a sentence from being in the appropriate case a just punishment. There are many such examples, they occur in all countries and are generally accepted. Let me give you just one more example. Annually, in Chicago, there is what is called a "crackdown on drunken driving". It occurs in the latter weeks of November and the early weeks of December. It is designed expressly to reduce the carnage from drunken driving in Chicago over the Christmas period. Often, those selected for punishment during this crackdown commit their offences in the summer or autumn months, when the thought of the allegedly jolly penury of Christmas is far from their minds; but such are the delays in the courts that an opportunity to serve their country as recipients of exemplary punishment is vouchsafed them—in this instance, a jail term for what would at other times be punished by lesser sanctions. Exemplary punishment is surely discordant to the principle that like cases should be treated alike, if that principle is regarded as either a limiting or defining principle of just punishment.

Let us consider another hard case for that principle. Let us suppose what is, no doubt, wildly unlikely, that six medical practitioners in Denver are discovered to have a preference for patients who pay them in cash and who do not require receipts. Let us suppose that on full investigation we discover that all six doctors have understated their income last year by, say, $20,000 each. For some time we have been doubtful of the precision of tax returns by medical practitioners in this city and, as advisers to the Internal Revenue Service, we discuss what should be done about the six doctors. Well, to start with, it is quite clear that all six must pay tax on the income they have failed to declare, interest at appropriately high rates on that tax, and substantial financial penalties for their criminality. All this can, of course, be arranged without the need for their prosecution before a federal district court. Most of the six and their tax advisers will be happy indeed to arrange such settlements with IRS agents or, if necessary in relation to disputed issues of fact, through the tax court. Do we need to prosecute all six in the federal district court and do we need to send all six to prison? I submit not. Our purposes are utilitarian, deterrent. We wish, as Voltaire said of the English practice of killing an occasional admiral to encourage the others to bravery, publicly to punish by sending to prison an occasional medical practitioner "to encourage the others" to integrity in their tax returns. We do not need to send all six to prison. The extra increment of deterrence would be bought at too high a cost. It would be wasteful of our own resources, wasteful of the court's time and, what is perhaps also in point, it would inflict unnecessary suffering on those doctors whose punishment did not substantially increase the deterrent impact we would gain by the imprisonment of, say, two of their number. The principle of parsimony overcomes the principle of equality.

How should we select those to be imprisoned? Perhaps we should struggle for some distinguishing characteristic of deserved severity or some opportunity of extra deterrent utility in the punishment of some among the six; but what is important to recognize is that we are involved in a conscious breach of a principle that like cases should be equally punished. It may be that we would select those doctors whose lives had achieved the larger contribution to social welfare and who, as a consequence, were the better known of the six; their punishment would thus achieve the larger deterrent impact. *That* can hardly be a reason of equality for selecting them for the larger punishment.

This principle of parsimony in the imposition of punishment is, I think, of great importance, and is too often neglected. Let me offer some figures to demonstrate the frugality with which the Internal Revenue Service in practice applies its massive punitive powers. In 1975, throughout this vast country, only 1,391 defendants were indicted for federal income tax violations, of whom 1,158 were convicted and sentenced, and of whom only 367 were sent to prison or jail. This is an astonishingly selective and cautious use of the sanction of imprisonment for deterrent purposes. Is it unjust? It cannot be treating like cases alike if any reasonable concepts of the quality of guilt and deserved suffering are to be applied. In my view, on the data that have been published about the imposition of the prison term in federal district courts, the system is both unequal and just, and it is precisely that apparent paradox I am seeking to defend.

Our entire present criminal justice system is infested with discretion in the exercise of the punishment power, and much of this discretion must continue to be exercised, guided but not determined by principles of equality in punishment. At present, the shortage of police, prosecutorial, defence, judicial, and punishment resources compels the discretionary selection of cases to be prosecuted; but the constraint that the principle of parsimony in punishment properly imposes on the principle of equality in just punishment would remain were such resources unlimited. Equality would still remain only a guiding principle; even with adequate resources in the criminal justice system, equality would neither define nor limit just punishment. By contrast, the principle of a deserved punishment is and should remain a limiting principle of just punishment. Let me try to unpack that blunt affirmation.

Let me propose that the death penalty be the mandatory sentence for anyone convicted of abortion. I am not talking only about an abortion in which the mother dies but the run-of-the-mill legally unjustified abortion in which the life of the well-grown, third-trimester fetus is terminated. Well, why do you not leap to accept such a proposition? Why does no one, so far as I know, advocate *that* punishment? Not even the most per-fervid advocates of the right-to-life position seem to take themselves that seriously in relation to abortion being murder. On deterrent utilitarian grounds there would be a great deal to be said for such a penalty if you are a true believer in the right to life. It would certainly push the price of the backyard abortion up to a very high figure; it would greatly reduce the number of fetuses whose existence was terminated; it would greatly increase the number of tickets that were purchased on international air-lines and I would, for my own part, immediately reinvest in TWA. Well, why not? The answer must surely be that no one would see such a pun-ishment as an appropriately *deserved* punishment, even those who are both in favour of protecting the fetus and in favour of capital punishment for convicted murderers. The limiting principle is the principle of desert. As elsewhere, it is hard to quantify this principle, but it clearly operates in this case to hold that such a punishment would be undeserved.

Desert thus operates categorically to limit the maximum of punishment. Sometimes it operates to limit the minimum, when it is argued that a too lenient punishment would unduly depreciate the seriousness of the offence that the accused has committed. An example of this was the sentencing of former U.S. Vice-President Spiro Agnew which, in my view, was entirely correct for utilitarian and governmental practical reasons, but which cer-tainly strained at the lower level of the deserved punishment.

By contrast, I am suggesting that the principle of equality, that like cases should be treated alike, is not a limiting principle at all, but is only a guid-ing principle which will enjoin equality of punishment unless there are other substantial utilitarian reasons to the contrary; such as those that favour exemplary punishment or the parsimonious punishment of some of my six doctors, or in situations where there are inadequate resources for or high costs attached to the application of equal punishments. The equal-ity principle neither restricts nor limits; it merely guides. The principle of desert is not much of a guide, but it does restrict and limit.

When we say a punishment is deserved we rarely mean that it is precisely appropriate in the sense that a deterrent punishment could in principle be. Rather we mean it is not undeserved; that it is neither too lenient nor too severe; that it neither sentimentally understates the wickedness or harmfulness of the crime nor inflicts excessive pain or deprivation on the criminal in relation to the wickedness or harmfulness of his crime. It is not part of a utilitarian calculus, in the properly restricted sense of utilitarianism. The concept of desert defines relationships between crimes and punishments on a continuum between the unduly lenient and the excessively punitive within which the just sentence may on other grounds be determined.

Note

1.   Nigel Walker, *Sentencing in a Rational Society* (London: Penguin Press, 1969), 69.

4.6

Seriousness, Severity, and the Living Standard

ANDREW VON HIRSCH

The principle of proportionality requires the *severity* of penalties to be determined by reference to the *seriousness* of crimes. That means we need a way of gauging the two predicates of crime-seriousness and punishment-severity. Suppose someone proposes that crime X be visited by punishment Y. To tell whether this is a proportionate sanction, one needs to be able to judge how grave X is compared to other crimes, and how onerous Y is compared to other sanctions.

Judging Crimes' Seriousness

Ordinary people, various opinion surveys have suggested, seem capable of reaching a degree of agreement on the comparative seriousness of crimes.[1] And rule-making bodies that have tried to rank crimes in gravity have not run into insuperable practical difficulties. Several American state sentencing commissions (those of Minnesota, Washington State and Oregon), for example, were able rank the seriousness of offences for use in their numerical guidelines (see, e.g., von Hirsch, Knapp and Tonry (1987), ch. 5). While the grading task proved time-consuming, it did not generate much dissension within the commissions.

Less satisfactory, however, has been the state of the theory. What criteria should be used for gauging crimes' gravity? The gravity of a crime depends upon the degree of harmfulness of the conduct, and the extent of the actor's culpability. Culpability can be gauged with the aid of clues from the substantive criminal law. The substantive law already distinguishes intentional conduct from reckless and from criminally negligent

This essay is published here for the first time. For a fuller account of the analysis, see A. von Hirsch and N. Jareborg, "Gauging Criminal Harm: A Living-Standard Analysis", (1991) 11 *Oxford Journal of Legal Studies* 1; see also, A. von Hirsch, *Censure and Sanctions* (Oxford: Oxford University Press, 1993), ch. 4.

behaviour. It should not be too difficult in principle to develop, for sentencing doctrine, more refined distinctions concerning the degree of purposefulness, indifference to consequences, or carelessness in criminal conduct. The doctrines of excuse in the substantive criminal law could also be drawn upon to develop theories of partial excuse—for example, of partial duress, and diminished capacity.

The harm dimension of seriousness is more puzzling, however, as the substantive law fails to provide assistance: it does not formally distinguish degrees of harm. How, then, can one compare the harmfulness of acts that invade different interests: say, compare crime X that invades property interests with crime Y that chiefly affects privacy?

To answer that question, victimizing harms might be ranked in gravity according to how much they typically would reduce a person's *standard of living* (see more fully, von Hirsch and Jareborg (1991)). That term is used here in the broad sense suggested by Amartya Sen (1987), which reflects both economic and non-economic interests.

The living standard is one of a family of related notions, including well-being, that refer to the quality of persons' lives. Well-being, however, can be highly personalized: my well-being depends on my particular focal aims, and to the person who wants to devote his life to contemplation and prayer, material comfort and ordinary social amenities may matter little. However, the living standard, in Sen's sense, does not focus on actual life-quality or goal achievement, but on the *means or capabilities* for achieving a certain quality of life. Some of these means are material (shelter and financial resources) but others are not (good health, privacy, and the like). It is also standardized, referring to the means and capabilities that would *ordinarily* promote a good life. Someone has a good standard of living if he has the health, resources and other means that people ordinarily can use to live well.

Using the living-standard as a way of gauging harms has a number of advantages. First, it seems to fit the way we usually judge harms. Why is mayhem more harmful than burglary? It is because the overall quality of the person's life has been more adversely affected. Second, the living-standard idea permits drawing from a rich array of experience—including experience outside of the criminal law. We can ask how the harm in an arson compares with that in an accidental fire. Finally, a living-standard analysis would allow for cultural variation. Different social living-arrangements can affect the consequences of a criminal act, and normative differences among cultures can affect the impact of those consequences on the quality of persons' lives. The harmfulness of burglary, for example, depends on the degree to which the home is ordinarily the focal point for people's private existences, and on the degree to which privacy is valued. A living-standard analysis thus could, in another culture, lead to a different rating for burglary—if the home has a different social role and if a different valuation is given to privacy.

Our suggested analysis begins with parcelling out the various kinds of interests that offences typically involve. After the interests involved in a given type of offence are identified, their importance is judged by assessing their significance for the living standard.[2]

Most victimizing offences involve one or more of the following interest-dimensions: (1) physical integrity, (2) material support and amenity, (3) freedom from humiliation, and (4) privacy. A simple residential burglary, for example, chiefly involves material amenity and privacy. The material loss would consist of what is stolen, plus the inconvenience and expense of repairs. The privacy-loss consists of the intrusion of a stranger into the person's living-space. To rate the harmfulness of the conduct, the living-standard criterion should be applied to each dimension, successively. In the case of the burglary, the analysis would thus begin with its material-amenity dimension. Here, the impact on the living standard would be rather small: not much is taken in the typical burglary, so that the person's material well-being would normally not be much affected. Next, the privacy dimension would be considered. Here, the rating might well be somewhat higher, given the importance of privacy to a good existence, and the extent to which an intrusion into the home affects privacy. The attraction of this mode of analysis is that each dimension involved—physical integrity, material support, privacy, or whatever—can ultimately be assessed in terms of a common criterion: that of impact on the living standard. This means that, in the burglary, one can compare the living-standard impact of the material loss (rather minor) with that of the privacy-intrusion (arguably, somewhat greater). One could also compare a burglary with another victimizing offence involving different interests: say, an assault, where physical integrity and freedom from humiliation are primarily involved.

To aid in this analysis, the living-standard itself can be graded. One might use three living-standard levels: (1) subsistence, (2) minimal well-being, and (3) "adequate" well-being. The first, subsistence, refers to survival but with maintenance of no more than elementary human capacities to function—in other words, barely getting by. The remaining levels refer to various degrees of life quality above that of mere subsistence. The function of the gradations is to provide a rough measure of the extent to which a typical criminal act intrudes upon the living standard. To take an obvious example, aggravated assault threatens subsistence, and thus is substantially more harmful than a theft that still leaves the person with an "adequate" level of comfort and dignity.

This analysis is to be used chiefly in gauging the standard harm involved in various categories or subcategories of offence. The point is to assess the injuriousness of typical instances of (say) residential burglary, or residential burglary of a certain kind (one might, say, distinguish simple burglary from ransacking); not to gauge the injury done to an individual, Mary Smith, when her apartment was broken into and her favourite vase was stolen. The living-standard relates, as we noted, to the *standardized* means or capabilities for a good life—not to the life-quality of particular persons. Deviations from such standardized assessments should be made only in certain kinds of special circumstances, where the differences from the ordinary case are fairly apparent. (While assessments of harm are thus to be standardized to a degree, culpability judgements need not be. A desert-based sentencing system may—indeed, should—afford room for pleas of reduced personal culpability on a variety of grounds such as, for example, that of provocation (see Narayan and von Hirsch (1996)).

This harms analysis is no formula providing ready answers, because the impact of a crime on the living standard is itself very much a matter of factual and normative judgement. But it still may be helpful as a guide to thinking about rating harms.

Gauging Punishments' Severity

Grading sanctions presupposes an ability to judge their comparative severity. While prison sanctions can be compared by their duration, the onerousness of non-custodial sanctions depends on their intensity as well. Three days of community service may be tougher than three days' probation but not as tough as three days of home detention.

A number of studies have attempted to measure sanction severity through opinion surveys. A selected group of respondents is shown a list of penalties of various sorts, and asked to rate their severity on a numerical rating scale. The surveys tend to show a degree of consensus.[3] These ratings, however, do not attempt to elucidate what is meant by severity; to elicit respondents' reasons for their rankings; or to assess the plausibility of those reasons. It is necessary to consider what *should* be the basis of comparing penalties—i.e., to develop a theory of severity.

A possible account of severity would be that it depends upon how disagreeable the sanction typically is experienced as being. On this view, surveys would be the best way to assess penalties: they should simply ask people how unpleasant they think various penalties would be. Unpleasantness or discomfort, arguably, is ultimately subjective: a matter of how deprivations typically are experienced. If penalty Y is generally perceived to be more unpleasant than penalty Z, this simply makes it so.

This approach, however strikes me as being misconceived. What makes punishments more or less onerous is not any identifiable sensation; rather, it is the degree to which those sanctions interfere with people's interests. The unpleasantness of intensive probation supervision, for example, depends—not on its "feeling bad" in some immediate sense—but on its interfering with such important interests as being in charge of one's own life or moving about as one chooses.

It would thus seem preferable to apply an interests analysis comparable to the one just suggested for gauging crime-seriousness. The more important the interests intruded upon by a penalty are, on this theory, the severer the penalty should be considered to be. Penalties could be ranked according to the degree to which they typically affect the punished person's freedom of movement, earning ability, and so forth. The importance of those interests could then be gauged according to how they typically impinge on persons' "living standard"—in the sense of that term sketched earlier in this essay. Such an interests-analysis seems to fit the way we often discuss punishment's severity. When asked to explain why long-term imprisonment is a severe sanction, for example, one is tempted to answer in terms of how its deprivations typically impinge on the quality of someone's life.[4]

Adopting an interest-analysis approach means that the assessment of severity is not made dependent on the preferences of particular individuals. The living-standard, as noted earlier, refers to the means and capabilities that *ordinarily* assist persons in achieving a good life. If a given interest is important in this sense to a good existence, it would warrant a high rating—notwithstanding that some persons choose to go without it. Imprisonment qualifies as a severe penalty—because the interests in freedom of movement and privacy it takes away are normally so vital to a decent existence—despite the fact that a few defendants might happen to be claustrophiliacs. This helps answer an objection that Nigel Walker has raised to desert theory: namely, that one never can grade penalties' onerousness, because people's subjective perceptions of painfulness vary so much (see Selection 4.2 above).

Notes

1. For citations, see Ashworth (1995), pp. 90–2.
2. For a fuller description of this method of analysis, see von Hirsch and Jareborg (1991). The analysis is designed to apply to crimes that typically involve identifiable victims, as burglary and robbery do. For the possibility of carrying this technique over to crimes that risk injury to unidentified persons, or which affect "collective" interests, see *ibid.*, pp. 32–5.
3. For citations to these studies, see Wasik and von Hirsch (1988), at p. 563, n. 20.
4. To apply the living-standard idea to penalties, there would have to be modifications in the analysis. When rating harms, the main interests are (as noted above) those of physical integrity, material amenity, and so forth. For punishments, some other interests also need to be taken into account: for example, the interest in freedom of movement that is affected by incarceration, home detention, and intensive probation supervision.

References

Ashworth, A. (1995) *Sentencing and Criminal Justice*, 2nd edn. (London: Butterworths).

Narayan, U., and von Hirsch, A. (1996) "Three Conceptions of Provocation" 15(1) *Criminal Justice Ethics* 15.

Sen, A. (1987) *The Standard of Living* (Cambridge: Cambridge University Press).

von Hirsch, A. (1993) *Censure and Sanctions* (Oxford: Oxford University Press).

von Hirsch, A., and Jareborg, N. (1991) "Gauging Criminal Harm: A Living- Standard Analysis" 11 *Oxford Journal of Legal Studies* 1.

von Hirsch, A., Knapp, K. and Tonry, M. (1987) *The Sentencing Commission and Its Guidelines* (Boston, Mass.: Northeastern University Press).

Wasik, M. and von Hirsch, A. (1988) "Punishments in the Community and the Principles of Desert" [1988] *Criminal Law Review* 555.

4.7

Desert and Previous Convictions

ANDREW VON HIRSCH

In traditional discretionary sentencing systems, most judges adjusted the sentence to take account of the offender's previous convictions. However, the weight to be given to the criminal record was uncertain. Should the criminal record be the primary determinant of the sentence? Or should the sentence chiefly reflect the seriousness of the current crime, with only a modest adjustment made for the person's previous convictions? Under a discretionary system, different judges answered such questions differently. As jurisdictions move toward more explicit guidance for sentencing decisions, however, it becomes essential to decide how much weight the record should have, and why.

The question has no simple answers. One sometimes hears it asserted, for example, that the criminal record should not be considered at all, because the offender has been "punished already" for his previous crime. However, this argument is circular. If some feature of having been previously convicted affects the basis for his present punishment, then adjusting his sentence is not penalizing him twice for his past crime. If, for example, the offender has received a discount in the penalty for his first offence, removing that discount if he subsequently reoffends is not necessarily punishing him twice over.

The significance of the prior record will vary, depending on which rationale for sentencing is used. A rationale emphasizing prediction and incapacitation would give the record primary weight. Prediction studies tend to show that the statistical likelihood of someone's re-offending is influenced primarily by his previous criminal history, rather than by the seriousness of his current criminal act. What predicts recidivism best (or rather, least badly) is the person's previous record of arrests (especially,

This essay is published here for the first time, but the main arguments are taken from A. von Hirsch, *Past or Future Crimes* (New Brunswick, N.J.: Rutgers University Press, 1985); and A. von Hirsch, "Criminal Record Rides Again", (1991) 10(2) *Criminal Justice Ethics* 2, 55–7.

early arrests), plus certain facts about his social history, such as use of drugs and lack of regular employment (see Selection 3.7 above).

I wish in this essay, however, to assume a desert rationale—according to which punishments should be proportionate to the seriousness of the criminal conduct. On that perspective, what should the role of the criminal record be? There has been disagreement on this subject among desert theorists. One school of thought, represented by George Fletcher (1978) and Richard Singer (1979) holds that the prior record should not be considered at all. Another, which includes Andrew Ashworth (1995) and Martin Wasik (1987) favours a theory of "progressive loss of mitigation". The offender who is convicted for the first time gets a discount, but then that discount gradually diminishes—so that by a certain number of repetitions (say, the third) it is lost entirely. Thereafter, record should not matter; the sixth shoplifting should be treated no differently than the fourth. The discount, on this theory, would also be limited in magnitude—so that the seriousness of the current crime, rather than the criminal record, primarily determines the onerousness of the penalty.

My view is similar to Ashworth's and Wasik's. The offender should get somewhat less when first convicted, but the discount should progressively be reduced thereafter. The question is why so. The explanation needs to be one that comports with notions of desert—in particularly, with a communicative (i.e., censure-based) conception of desert discussed earlier (see Selections 4.3 and 4.4 above).

Explanations Directed to the Present Act

Could the fact of a prior conviction or convictions alter the seriousness of the current crime? To do so, the prior offence would have to affect the harm or the culpability involved in the current conduct.

The harmfulness of the conduct does not seem affected. Obviously, the conduct's direct consequences or risks are unaltered. Possibly, it might be argued that there is a special kind of harm involved—namely defiance: the repeater is flouting the law when he reoffends after having been punished already. But as George Fletcher rightly points out, "in a liberal society, defiance should not constitute a wrong that justifiably enhances what a recidivist deserves" (Fletcher 1982, p. 57). Treating defiance in itself as an extra harm presupposes authoritarian assumptions about the state and the criminal law.

What about the culpability of the current offence? I did once claim that culpability was affected (von Hirsch 1976, ch. 10). Before one has been convicted, I argued, one is simply part of the general audience of people to whom the legal prohibition is addressed. One may not have paid the prohibition much attention or understood its scope and applicability to oneself. Once one has been formally censured for the conduct through a criminal conviction, however, it is rather like having one's nose rubbed in what one has done: the punishment for the first offence serves as a dramatic way of confronting the actor with the wrongfulness of the conduct. Thereafter, claims to possible ignorance or inattention to the prohibition become less plausible.

Later, I became aware that this argument was problematic. Granted, in some instances, a first offender may not have been fully aware of the prohibition or understood its scope or applicability. In Anglo-American criminal law, ignorance of law has generally been no excuse. Sentencing theory might work differently, and give ignorance (or partial ignorance) some mitigating effect—on grounds that culpability is reduced. The difficulty is, however, that the person who is convicted for the first time may have been perfectly aware of the prohibition or of the wrongfulness of the act, but simply done it anyway. Ignorance, or failure fully to understand or take notice, does not support a *generally* applicable discount for first offenders.

"Tolerance" and the Prior Record

Further reflection has convinced me to approach the issue differently. The discount for the first offender does not rest on claims of lack of full knowledge or appreciation of the prohibition; it is, rather, a concession we make to the fallibility of human nature. The reduced response for the first offence serves to accord some respect for the fact that the person's inhibitions functioned before, and to show some sympathy for the all-too-human weakness that can lead to a first lapse. The idea is thus one of a limited tolerance for human frailty.

Notice that we have this tolerance only because we have certain expectations, or should have them, about human beings and their nature. If we were angels, we would not have or need it. If I remember my Milton, Lucifer was a first offender when he fell, but he did not get or claim a discount—because for an angel, once is too much. Were one sufficiently puritanical about humans, one would also deny the discount: frailty, on this view, is something to be abominated and confronted with vigour. But because humans are not angels, and should not be judged as though they were, a certain tolerance seems appropriate.

But such a tolerance theory raises its own questions which need to be addressed (see Stuart (1986), Durham (1987)). How, precisely, does the fact of human frailty link with notions of censure and desert? And if one wishes to be so tolerant, why not keep it up? Since it is also a fact of human nature that some people keep on offending, why not continue to grant discounts even to frequent repeaters?

The "Why" of Tolerance

Our everyday moral judgements include the notion of a *lapse*. A transgression (even a rather serious one) is judged less stringently when it occurs against a background of prior compliance. The idea is that even an ordinarily properly-behaved person can have his or her moral inhibitions fail in a moment of weakness or wilfulness. Such a loss of self-discipline is the kind of human frailty for which some understanding should be shown.

In sentencing, the lapse of which we are speaking is not just any moral failure, but an infringement of the standards of the criminal law. And the prior compliance in question is that of not having committed and been convicted for a criminal offence. It is not the offender's whole moral life that should be the subject of inquiry, but only his criminal record.[1] The logic of the first-offender discount, however, remains that of dealing with a lapse somewhat more tolerantly.

A reason for so treating a lapse is respect for the process by which people can respond to others' censure. A first offender, after being confronted with blame or censure, is capable of reflecting on the propriety of what he has done and of making the effort to show greater restraint. What the discount does is recognize the importance of this kind of phenomenon, and give the offender a "second chance".

Why, however, should we lose patience—that is, stop giving the discount after the offender has been reconvicted a few times? The repeated offence can less and less plausibly be characterized as a lapse—an aberrational failure of moral inhibition. Repetition after confrontation with penal censure also suggests a failure on the part of the offender to make the extra effort at self-restraint—the effort which should be the response to being faced with censure.

In this connection, we might bear in mind the normative functions of penal censure. One thing censure does is simply express judgements of disapproval. Beyond this expressive function, however, censure has a communicative role—it is a form of discourse that is addressed to a person as a moral agent. It serves to confront the agent with the censuring person's or agency's sense of the wrongfulness of the act (see Selections 4.3 and 4.4). What is thereby hoped is that the actor not merely desist in future (which mere restraint could accomplish) but desist because he shares that recognition. This is not a question of notice or knowledge, for the actor may have known all along that the act was wrong. It is, rather, that the condemnation constitutes reason for the actor's taking known moral rules more seriously in his own case. This communicative account illuminates, I think, the questions at issue here. Thus:

1. Why should we scale down the condemnatory and punitive response initially? It is because it is assumed that humans are both fallible and capable of doing something worthy of respect—namely, attending to others' censure. The fallibility calls for a limited tolerance of failure, expressed through some diminution of the initial penal response. The respected process, on account of which the discount is also granted, is that by which a person can attend the disapproval visited upon him and alter his conduct accordingly. In viewing the person as a moral agent, we initially assume him capable of such a response and thus give him his "second chance".

2. Why give up the discount after a certain number of repetitions? It is because that respected process has not occurred. The person has chosen to disregard the disapproval visited on him through his punishment, and thus seems not to have made the requisite additional effort at self-restraint. However, due consideration to human fallibility calls for gradual loss of the discount. Its complete loss after a second offence would be suggestive more of a different and more authoritarian theory: that the person has been warned and that his repetition thereafter is an act of defiance.

Have I just reinvented rehabilitation? The "second chance" sounds like a rehabilitative argument, but it is not. I do not claim that the discount for first offending will in fact induce future compliance by the actor better than a full dose of punishment would. The first-offender discount reflects, instead, an ethical judgement: it is a way of showing respect for any person's capacity, as a moral agent, for attending to the censure in punishment.

What has been so troublesome about traditional penal rehabilitationism is that punishment is not made to depend on the blameworthiness of the offender's actual criminal choices, but on his supposed future amenability to treatment. On this rehabilitationist view, the availability of any discount would depend on how responsive the offender is expected to be to his sentence. If he is deemed the "amenable" type—who would learn better self-control from a scaled-down first dose of punishment (and whatever treatment programme seems indicated)—he would be punished less. If he is deemed the "unamenable" type, the discount would be denied. On my suggested account, however, no such picking and choosing on the basis of anticipated future conduct would be permitted. The discount is available to *every* first offender until he has accumulated the requisite number of prior convictions to lose it; it does not depend on the offender's expected amenability. The reason why is, again, suggested by the communicative view of desert: every offender, as a human being, is to be deemed a moral agent capable of understanding the censure expressed through punishment. The person forfeits the tolerance, and loses the associated penal discount, only through his actual subsequent criminal choices.

While this account is not a reinvention of the rehabilitative sentence, it embodies (I think) something we instinctively feel is legitimate behind the idea of rehabilitation. This is not the conventional positivist idea that sentences should be based on offenders' diagnosed treatability. It is, rather, that people's capacity to take condemnation of their acts seriously is something that has a moral dimension and should be acknowledged in the criminal law.

The foregoing account shares with desert theory in general the assumption that criminal conduct constitutes wrongdoing, and that punishment expresses justified censure for that wrongdoing. Perhaps, its claims are even stronger, in that it asserts that the offender has a duty to attend to the censure and make extra efforts at self-restraint. That raises, squarely, questions of the morality of the criminal law itself. The core conduct which the criminal law addresses—namely, victimizing behaviour of various sorts—does seem *prima facie* morally reprehensible. But the criminal law has wider scope than that, and the ethical basis of some of its prohibitions seems seriously questionable.[2] Moreover, the status of the criminal law in a society having serious inequalities in its distribution of goods, opportunities, and power needs also to be reflected upon (see Selection 4.9 below).

There are, moreover, three particular issues that call for more thought. One is whether the account sketched here properly applies to any criminal conduct, however grave. Might not the most heinous conduct—for example, the more brutal homicides—fall outside the scope of human fallibility discussed here? (see Ashworth (1995), pp. 159–60).

Another question is whether there might be special instances where one would be reluctant to treat continued offending as I have—as a failure to take the previous condemnation seriously. Arguably, there might—where the continued offending is linked with other special indicia of reduced culpability. A case of such reduced culpability might be that of the repeat offender of limited intelligence (albeit not intellectually deprived enough to qualify as completely excusable). His continued offending might be attributable to an inability to grasp fully the censure that the previous conviction conveys. More debatable are cases of repeat offending that are grounded in a special degree of social deprivation—for example, the homeless petty repeat offender (see Selection 4.9 below).

A third question is what should be done with those who build up *extraordinary* criminal records. On the theory of "progressive loss of mitigation" defended here, the discount is simply lost after (say) the third offence, so that the sixth would be treated no differently. What, however, of the offender who had 20 or 30 prior convictions? Might it be argued that such "incorrigibility" shows a special dimension of contempt for law or for others' rights that merits extra punishment? I am inclined to be quite sceptical of such a claim, and in any event it would call for arguments different from those set forth here. Nevertheless, the issue may be worth debating.

Notes

1. For discussion of why only the offender's criminal record should be considered, and not the broader merits or demerits of his life, see von Hirsch (1981), pp. 607–13.
2. That seems so, for example, with respect to the remaining criminal prohibitions relating to consensual sexual behaviour among adults.

References

Ashworth, A. (1995) *Sentencing and Criminal Justice* (London: Butterworths).

Durham, A. (1987) "Justice in Sentencing: The Role of Prior Record of Criminal Involvement", 78 *Journal of Criminal Law & Criminology* 614.

Fletcher, G. (1978) *Rethinking Criminal Law* (Boston: Little, Brown).

——— (1982) "The Recidivist Premium" 1(2) *Criminal Justice Ethics* 54.

Singer, Richard (1979) *Just Deserts* (Cambridge, Mass.: Ballinger).

Stuart, J.D. (1986) "Retributive Justice and Prior Offenses" 18 *Philosophical Forum* 40.

von Hirsch, A. (1976) *Doing Justice* (New York: Hill & Wang).

——— (1981) "Desert and Previous Convictions in Sentencing" 65 *Minnesota Law Review* 591.

Wasik, M. (1987) "Guidance, Guidelines and Criminal Record", in M. Wasik and K. Pease (eds.), *Sentencing Reform: Guidance or Guidelines?* (Manchester: Manchester University Press).

4.8

Parsimony and Desert in Sentencing

MICHAEL TONRY

The Importance of Non-Desert Factors

A desert-based sentencing guidelines system such as Minnesota's allows little play for non-criminal-record factors to influence penalties. Consider a minority offender who grew up in a single-parent, welfare-supported household, who has several siblings in prison, and who was formerly drug-dependent but who has been living in a common law marriage for five years, has two children whom he supports, and has worked steadily for three years at a service station—first as an attendant, then an assistant mechanic, and now a mechanic. Under Minnesota's desert-oriented guidelines, none of these personal characteristics are supposed to influence the sentencing decision, and certainly not to justify imposition of a non-custodial sentence on a presumed prison-bound offender. For people who believe in individualized sentences, on either utilitarian or retributive grounds, Minnesota's refusal to consider my hypothetical offender's promising features will seem regrettable. For people concerned by the gross over-representation in courts, gaols, and prisons of deeply disadvantaged people, Minnesota's refusal to consider evidence that my hypothetical offender is overcoming the odds will seem deeply regrettable.

A numerical guidelines system, such as Minnesota's, attaches no significance to the collateral effects of a prison sentence on the offender, or on the offender's family or children, what Nigel Walker (1991, 106–8) calls incidental (on the offender) and obiter (on the offender's dependants and associates) effects of punishment. Incarceration of an employed father and husband may mean loss of the family's home and car, perhaps the break-up of a marriage, perhaps the creation of welfare dependency by the wife and children. To ignore that incidental and obiter effects of punishments

From M. Tonry, "Proportionality, Parsimony, and Interchangeability of Punishments" in [R.]A. Duff, S. Marshall, R. E. Dobash, R. P. Dobash (eds.), *Penal Theory and Penal Practice* (Manchester: Manchester University Press, 1992), with some textual changes.

vary widely among seemingly like-situated offenders is to ignore things that most people find important.

Problems of objectification of crimes, offenders, and punishments are especially stark in a numerical guidelines system. In systems that feature written policy guidelines, they lurk beneath the surface. The Minnesota illustration is generally relevant to analysis of proportionality in punishment, however, because it makes real world implications of strong proportionality conditions starkly apparent. If proportionality is an, or the, overriding principle in the distribution of punishment in practice, then the imperfections of objectification that I describe are presumably regrettable but acceptable costs to be paid for a principled punishment system. If they appear unacceptable, the problem may be that the principle of proportionality offers less helpful guidance than its proponents urge.

Parsimony

Proponents of strong proportionality conditions necessarily prefer equality over minimization of suffering. For two decades, Andrew von Hirsch and Norval Morris have been disagreeing over the role of parsimony in punishment. Von Hirsch (1985) has argued for strong desert limits on punishment and high priority to pursuit of equality and proportionality in punishment. Morris (1974) has argued that desert is a limiting, not a defining, principle of punishment and that policy should prescribe imposition of the least severe "not undeserved" sanction that meets legitimate policy ends. Within these outer bounds of "not undeserved" punishments Morris has consistently argued for observance of a principle of parsimony.

To some extent Morris and von Hirsch have argued past each other. Morris argues that a desert approach is unnecessarily harsh and von Hirsch responds by noting that he personally favours relatively modest punishments and, in any case, desert schemes are not inherently more severe than other schemes. In turn, von Hirsch argues that Morris's "not undeserved" proportionality constraints are vague, the breadth of allowable ranges of sentencing discretion is never specified, and Morris responds by noting that absolute measures of deserved punishment are unknowable and that his aim is to minimize imposition of penal suffering within bounds that any given community finds tolerable.

The problem is that they start from different major premises—von Hirsch's is the "principle of proportionality", Morris's the "principle of parsimony". The difference between them can be seen by imagining a comprehensive sentencing guidelines punishment scheme. Imagine that policy-makers have conscientiously classified all offenders into ten categories and, using von Hirsch's ordinal/cardinal magnitude and anchoring points approach (see Selection 4.4 above), have decided that all offences at level VII deserve 23 to 25-month prison terms. Imagine further that reliable public opinion surveys have shown that 90 per cent of the general public would find a restrictive non-custodial punishment "not unduly lenient" and a 36-month prison term "not unduly severe" for level VII offences.

Von Hirsch would, I presume, argue that for non-exceptional cases concern for proportionality requires that persons convicted of level VII crimes receive at least a 23-month prison term, even though public opinion would support much less severe punishments. To achieve greater proportionality, von Hirsch would punish some offenders much more severely than is socially or politically required.

Morris, by contrast, would presumably argue that imposing 23-month terms on all level VII cases would be unjust because it would constitute imposition of punishment that is not required by public attitudes or preventive considerations. Morris would argue that, barring exceptional circumstances, no level VII offender should receive more than 25-months' incarceration but that many should receive less than 23 months. To achieve less aggregate suffering, Morris would punish some offenders much less severely than concern for proportionality would suggest.

The preceding hypothetical is overstated. Von Hirsch would, at least for exceptional cases, approve departures from the 23- to 25-month range or perhaps approve a wider range (for example, 18 to 28 months). Morris would almost certainly want to establish a normal upper bound lower than 36 months and would want to devise some system for assuring that level VII offenders receive roughly equivalent punishments.

Sorting out principles

Disagreements about just punishments, like disagreements about the death penalty or abortion, are often in the end disagreements about powerful intuitions or deeply embedded values. It may be that differences in view between those who give primacy to proportionality and those who give primacy to parsimony cannot be bridged.

The burden of persuasion should rest, however, it seems to me on those who reject Isaiah Berlin's observations that "not all good things are compatible, still less all the ideals of mankind" (1969, 167) and that "the necessity of choosing between absolute claims is then an inescapable characteristic of the human condition" (1969, 169).

Punishment raises at least two important conflicts between ideals—between the principles of proportionality and parsimony, between the quests for criminal justice and social justice.

Punishment is not unique in this respect. *Justice, Equal Opportunity, and the Family* (1983) by James Fishkin shows similar irreconcilable conflicts in ideals that are posed by family policy. Even in ideal theory, he argues, values inherent in support for equal opportunity conflict with values inherent in support for family autonomy. Notions of equal opportunity, he argues, must include a "principle of merit" that "there should be a fair competition among individuals for unequal positions in society" (p. 19), and a "principle of equal life chances specifying roughly equal expectations for everyone regardless of the conditions into which they are born" (p. 20). Without equal life chances, both common experience and modern sociology instruct, scarce social goods will not be distributed according to merit. As Fishkin observes, "if I can predict the outcomes achieved by an individual merely by knowing his or her race, sex, ethnic origin, or family background, then equality of life chances has not been realised" (p. 34).

If we were single-mindedly devoted to equal opportunity, then we should view equalization of life chances as an overriding goal of social policy. However, Fishkin argues, efforts to equalize life chances run head on into another powerful principle, that the value of autonomy in a private sphere of liberty encompasses a principle of family autonomy, of nonintrusion by the state into the family's sphere of private liberty.

In other words, equal opportunity and family autonomy conflict fundamentally. Full respect for equal opportunity would involve intrusion into the family that would widely be seen as objectionably intrusive. Full respect for family autonomy would widely be seen as cruel disregard for children's basic needs.

And so it may be with punishment. Principles of proportionality and parsimony may simply conflict, with resolutions between them necessarily partial and provisional.

Reconciling Proportionality and Parsimony

A middle ground exists on which a punishment scheme can be built that honours both proportionality and parsimony—development of sentencing guidelines that establish presumptive sentencing ranges in which the upper bounds are set in accordance with the proportionality principle and the lower bounds are sufficiently flexible to honour the parsimony principle. This would discourage disparately severe punishments, including aggravation of sentences on predictive or rehabilitative grounds beyond what would otherwise be deemed appropriate. If von Hirsch is correct as a social psychologist of punishment when he insists that desert schemes are not necessarily more severe than other schemes, use of proportionality constraints to set upper bounds (within higher statutory maxima) should result in upper-bound penalties that are no harsher than would occur in a scheme with narrow ranges. Below those upper bounds, however, judges could set sentences not premised on "standard cases" or "standard punishments".

The challenge is not to decide between proportionality and parsimony, but to balance them in ways that preserve important elements of each. This is not the place to discuss mechanics at length. A reconciliation can be sketched.[1]

Use proportionality to establish presumptive maximum sentences

Much of von Hirsch's proportionality analysis can be used in setting maximum bounds of sentencing authority for ordinary cases. By using standardized measures of offence severity, proportionate maximum sentences can be specified, the gap between those upper bounds and statutory maxima to be reserved for extraordinary cases subject to the provision of reasons and the possibility of appellate sentence review. The Advisory Council on the Penal System (1978) proposed such a scheme, albeit not in the vocabulary of guidelines. The worst injustices in sentencing and the worst disparities are those suffered by people who receive aberrantly long or severe penalties. Presumptive guidelines for maximum sentences scaled to proportionality could both lessen the likelihood of aberrantly severe penalties and achieve proportionality among those offenders receiving the most severe presumptive sentences.

Parsimony presumption

Within the authorized bounds, judges should be directed to impose the least severe sentence consistent with the governing purposes *at* sentencing (e.g., Morris and Tonry 1990, 90–2). Within, for example, any category of offences encompassed in an offence severity level in the above-mentioned sentencing guidelines grid, judges should be directed to consider monetary penalties or their equivalents (e.g., community service) when retribution or deterrence is the governing purpose, stringent community controls when incapacitation is at issue, and community controls with treatment conditions when sex or drug or alcohol treatment is called for, reserving incarcerative sentences only for cases when deterrence, public attitudes, or incapacitation seem to indicate. If the parsimony presumption favoured the least restrictive alternative, judges would have to devise particularized reasons for doing otherwise—including imposition of sentences for incapacitative or deterrent reasons (see more fully, Selection 6.5 below).

Rough equivalence

Efforts to devise ways to make punishments interchangeable have foundered on proportionality's shoals. If prison is used as the norm, and all other penalties must be converted to carceral coin, interchangeability soon collapses. Almost inexorably, one day in prison equals two or more days of house arrest equals two or more days of community service. Something about the process seems to force literal thinking. If sentences must be proportionate in incarceration time, the scope for use of non-custodial penalties necessarily is limited.

Thinking about equivalences becomes easier if proportionality constraints are loosened. If any prison sentence up to 24 months can be imposed in a given case, then the range for substitution is broadened immensely.

Thinking about equivalences also becomes easier if prison is replaced by money, say a day's net pay, as the basic unit from and to which sanctions are converted.

Thinking about equivalences becomes easier if we think about different purposes to be served *at* sentencing in a given case. If the goals are retribution and deterrence, then prison and financial penalties ought to be fully interchangeable as might also, for the indigent, a combination of residential controls, community service, restitution, and supervision.

If, for normative reasons, sentencing guidelines and guidance are to be scaled proportionately to the severity of crime, objectively measured, and expressed in standardized units of incarceration, objectively characterized, the scope for non-custodial penalties will necessarily be slight. It is not easy to devise non-custodial penalties that are objectively equivalent to 23 months' incarceration.

If non-custodial penalties are to be widely adopted and used, proportionality constraints must be loosened to take account of the almost infinite variety of offender circumstances, offence contexts, and punishment dimensions. If ways can be devised to institutionalize principles of both proportionality and parsimony in punishment, we are likely to do less injustice than if we establish systems that seek an illusion of equality of suffering for offenders in whose lives equality in most other things has been conspicuously absent.

Note

1. Among the issues that might be discussed: the strengths and weaknesses of the punishment units approach; whether sentencing grids should have two, three, four, or more "bands" representing different presumptions concerning the appropriate type of sentence; at what offence severity level the normal offence is so serious that only incarceration sentences should be authorized; the widths of bands of authorized sentences for categories of cases; whether equivalences should be conceptualized in terms of suffering, intrusiveness, or some other measure (for discussion of some of these issues, see Selection 6.5 below).

References

Advisory Council on the Penal System (1978), *Sentences of Imprisonment: A Review of Maximum Penalties* (London: HM Stationery Office).

Berlin, Isaiah (1969), *Four Essays on Liberty* (Oxford: Oxford University Press).

Fishkin, James S. (1983), *Justice, Equal Opportunity, and the Family* (New Haven, Conn.: Yale University Press).

Morris, Norval (1974), *The Future of Imprisonment* (Chicago: University of Chicago Press).

—— and Tonry, Michael (1990), *Between Prison and Probation: Intermediate Punishments in a Rational Sentencing System* (New York: Oxford University Press).

Von Hirsch, Andrew (1985), *Past or Future Crimes* (New Brunswick, NJ: Rutgers University Press).

Walker, Nigel (1991), *Why Punish?* (Oxford: Oxford University Press).

4.9

Mitigation for Socially Deprived Offenders

BARBARA A. HUDSON

An aspect of the "just deserts in an unjust society" debate with which desert theorists have engaged is that of whether or not criminal justice should involve itself in wider questions of social injustice. One of their most persuasive arguments has been that fair punishment of offences committed is likely to be less disadvantageous to the poor and to minority groups than sentencing rationales directed towards future offending. It is true that most schemes whose prime aim is to prevent re-offending would include factors such as poor employment record and perhaps ethnicity as indicating likely future offending, and thus it has been easy to see desert rationales as more likely to reduce discrimination in sentencing (although this argument rests on identification of the crimes of the poor as the crimes which need to be deterred, as opposed to employee crime, corporate crime etc.).

This argument for proportionality reflects the spectre of crime control punishment schemes which haunt the vision of deserts theorists, since it is only concerned with protection of the disadvantaged against *additional* punishment that may be imposed because of poor prognoses under crime control systems, or judicial prejudice in the absence of restrictions on discretion. Critics of desert from other vantage points, however, have in mind the possibility of *reduced* punishment for the poor and otherwise disadvantaged, and it is the presumption of punishment for every crime, and the difficulties of imposing penalties lower than the "going rate" with which they take issue. Michael Tonry, for instance, sketches an example of [the formerly drug-dependent minority offender from a deprived background who] "has been living in a common-law marriage for five years, has two children he supports, and has worked steadily for three years at a service station" [see Selection 4.8 above—eds.] Tonry argues that should

From B. A. Hudson, "Beyond Proportionate Punishment: Difficult Cases and the 1991 Criminal Justice Act", (1995) 22 *Crime, Law and Social Change* 59–78, with some textual changes.

such a person commit an offence, he should be given credit for his efforts to "overcome the odds".

The danger of this approach, however, is that it divides the poor into the deserving and the undeserving. What if the individual had not found work? What if he—or even more significantly, she—had not supported the children? Defendants would be vulnerable to disparate punishment depending on their abilities to construct a "sympathetic self", and we have enough information from research on the tendency of probation officers and others who present the court with its picture of the offender to know that factors such as unemployment, domestic arrangements, demeanour are constructed differently for black defendants, women defendants, or residents of certain estates. Deserts theory had considerable force in opposing itself to the way in which personal-social characteristics have influenced sentencing in the past, yet Tonry is surely right that some way should be found to accommodate these factors, for they are essentially relevant to questions of culpability.

As punishment is inescapably a moral phenomenon in that it is pain inflicted for *wrong* done, and as desert theory is linked to morality in its basic premise that punishment should be distributed according to the extent to which it is *deserved*, then an approach to sentencing which rules out consideration of individual circumstances and motivations cannot be satisfactory. The way to bring these considerations into sentencing theory in a more principled, systematic manner involves reconsidering the ideas of equalities or inequalities in liability to punishment, and of freedom of choice to commit or refrain from crime.

If difference of race, gender, class and so forth are ruled irrelevant, the criterion that is ruled relevant is moral agency: we are all presumed equally possessed of free will. The very strong notion of free will that is embedded in law is crucial to proportionality.

In other words, assessment of the *degree* of choice exercised by an offender in the decision to commit or refrain from crime is deemed irrelevant, so that in theory as well as in legislation, desert is collapsed into proportionality to offence.

These very robust notions of free will and choice seem far from the mark when one considers the people who fill our courts. Women shoplifting groceries or not declaring to the social service authorities their earnings from early morning cleaning jobs; young burglars who have never had the chance of a job; young mothers who turn a blind eye to the provenance of the money these young men give them to provide for their children; even the joyriders for whom performing in a car may be the only free source of excitement and esteem—the offences may be dangerous, over-prevalent and may destroy the quality of life for their victims, but it is difficult to imagine the perpetrators as making positive, unconstrained choices to be criminal. If given the choice between a "real job" and crime, the majority would undoubtedly take the job.

What is needed first of all, then, is a means of applying parsimonious penalties to those whose personal-social circumstances indicate limited freedom of choice and therefore reduced culpability. Tonry's "overcoming the odds" example is problematic because it looks to selective downward departures for people who can present themselves as specially deserving cases. Such selective leniency may make for more severe outcomes for those who do not present themselves so favourably, a dilemma familiar to lawyers and probation officers representing female defendants, who know that telling the court of the defendant's virtues as a mother, encouraging her to dress in a conventionally feminine manner, may make things worse for other women whose children are in state care, who do not fit feminine stereotypes. Similar considerations apply to employed and unemployed males, where a good job record, or a promising career, may exempt someone from the punishment that an unemployed offender would have to endure. Rather than a return to this prejudicial discretion, the sort of disparities which made desert seem so appealing, what is desired is to build into criminal justice decision-making systematic recognition that the majority of offenders are from disadvantaged groups. To parallel debates about incapacitative sentencing, categorical leniency is preferable to individual leniency.

One way of achieving this would be to have a desert system where those crimes which are statistically correlated with poverty and unemployment are ranked as of lesser seriousness. This would bring about considerable penal deflation, since high-incidence crimes such as burglary, shoplifting, car theft are highly correlated with unemployment (which may or may not be a satisfactory measure of poverty). Crimes against the person show considerably less correlation with unemployment; the most serious violent crimes show the least correlation of all, so this would not conflict with a harm notion of seriousness.

Whatever the levels of penalties, however, my argument is that there will always be differences in culpability between offenders because of differences in freedom of choice of action, and that these differences should be taken into consideration in sentencing practices. Even if the "going rate", the normal penalty for crimes correlated with poverty were to be (much) lower than currently, there should still be provision for reduced sentencing in cases of reduced culpability, or no punishment at all if the defendant seems so constrained by poverty, or other disadvantage or situation that the "reasonable person" would have been unable to refrain from crime in similar circumstances.

The concept of "fair opportunity to resist" which law recognizes in the defences of physical duress or mental incapacity, should be widened to include an economic incapacity. "Economic duress" could be a *prima facie* defence in cases where the perpetrator has no income at all, or has no access to or control over their supposed income. In England and Wales now, young people of 16 and 17 are not eligible for welfare benefits if they are not on a government training scheme: the young homeless and those with chaotic lifestyles have no incomes at all. Whether one poses the argument in terms of economic duress, or in term of balance of social rights and social obligations, it is difficult to see how such people should be considered liable to punishment. The actions they must engage in order to survive—begging, squatting—are, however, at the present time being criminalized in ever more inventive ways, and penalties are increasing. Women whose menfolk do not give them any money, people leaving penal or residential institutions who receive benefits in arrears but who have to find food and shelter immediately, would seem to be other categories eligible for a defence of economic duress.

Enquiries about the financial means of defendants are undertaken by probation officers in their pre-sentence reports, but, firstly, not all defendants are the subject of such reports, and secondly, these considerations are usually linked to recommendations of appropriate sentence (generally, whether a fine is feasible or not) rather than to questions of culpability. This means that lack of money can lead to sentencing involving greater restriction of liberty (probation, community service, even imprisonment rather than a fine) if financial enquires are used to assess sentence feasibility, a difficulty that would be removed if they are undertaken to determine culpability.

Suggestions for Further Reading

1. The Theory of Proportionality and Desert

Armstrong, K. G., "The Retributivist Hits Back", (1961) 70 *Mind* 471; McCloskey, H., "A Non-Utilitarian Approach to Punishment", (1965) 8 *Inquiry* 249; Hart, H. L. A., *Punishment and Responsibility* (1968); Feinberg, J., *Doing and Deserving* (1970), ch. 5; Finnis, J., "The Restoration of Retribution", (1972) 32 *Analysis* 131; Murphy, J. G., "Marxism and Retribution", (1973) 2 *Philosophy and Public Affairs* 217; Kleinig, J., *Punishment and Desert* (1973); von Hirsch, A., *Doing Justice: The Choice of Punishments* (1976); Bedau, H., "Retribution and the Theory of Punishment", (1978) 75 *Journal of Philosophy* 601; Murphy, J. G., *Retribution, Justice, and Therapy* (1979); Morris, H., "A Paternalistic Theory of Punishment", (1981) 18 *American Philosophical Quarterly* 263; Mackie, J., "Morality and the Retributive Emotions", (1982) 1 *Criminal Justice Ethics* 3, reprinted in his *Persons and Values* (1985), ch. 15; Davis, M., "How to Make the Punishment Fit the Crime", (1983) 93 *Ethics* 726; Hampton, J., "The Moral Education Theory of Punishment", (1984) 13 *Philosophy and Public Affairs* 230; Murphy, J. G., "Retributivism, Moral Education, and the Liberal State", (1985) 4 *Criminal Justice Ethics* 3; von Hirsch, *Past or Future Crimes* (1985), chs. 3–5; Sadurski, W., *Giving Desert Its Due* (1985); Duff, R. A., *Trials and Punishments* (1986); Sher, G., *Desert* (1987); Duff, R. A., "Punishment and Penance: A Reply to Harrison", (1988) 62 *Aristotelian Society-Supplemental Volume* 153; Primoratz, I., "Punishment as Language", (1989) 64 *Philosophy* 187; Sadurski, W., "Theory of Punishment, Social Justice and Liberal Neutrality", (1989) 7 *Law and Philosophy* 351; Scheid, D. M., "Davis and the Unfair Advantage Theory of Punishment: A Critique", (1990) 18 *Philosophical Topics* 143; Russel, P., "Hume on Responsibility and Punishment", (1990) 20 *Canadian Journal of Philosophy* 539; von Hirsch, "Proportionality in the Philosophy of Punishment", (1990) 1 *Criminal Law Forum* 259; Dolinko, D., "Some Thoughts about Retributivism", (1991) 101 *Ethics* 537; Kleinig, J., "Punishment and Moral Seriousness", (1991) 25 *Israel Law Review* 401; Husak, D. N., "Why Punish the Deserving?", (1992) 26 *Nous* 447; Walker, M. T., "Punishment: a Tale of Two Islands", (1993) 6 *Ratio* 69; von Hirsch, A., *Censure and Sanctions* (1993), chs. 2, 3 and 5; Dagger, R., "Playing Fair with Punishment", (1993) 103 *Ethics* 473; Moore, M. S., "Justifying Retribution", (1993) 27 *Israel Law Review* 15; Davis, M., "Criminal Desert and Unfair Advantage: What's the Connection?", (1994) 12 *Law and Philosophy* 133; Dolinko, D., "Measuring Unfair Advantage: a Response to Michael Davis", (1994) 13 *Law and Philosophy* 493; Scheid, D. E., "Davis, Unfair Advantage Theory and Criminal Desert", (1995) 14 *Law and Philosophy* 303; Duff, R. A., "Penal Communications: Recent Work in the Philosophy of Punishment", (1996) 20 *Crime and Justice: a Review of Research* 1; Scheid, D. E., "Constructing a Theory of

Punishment, Desert, and the Distribution of Punishments", (1997) 10 *Canadian Journal of Law and Jurisprudence* 271; Dimock, S., "Retributivism and Trust", (1997) 16 *Law and Philosophy* 37.

2. Applying Desert to Sentencing Policy

American Friends Service Committee, *Struggle for Justice: A Report on Crime and Punishment in America* (1971); von Hirsch, A., *Doing Justice* (1976); Gardner, M., "The Renaissance of Retribution: An Examination of Doing Justice", (1976) *Wisconsin Law Review* 781; Clarke, D., "Marxism, Justice, and the Justice Model", (1978) 2 *Contemporary Crises* 27; National Swedish Council for Crime Prevention, *A New Penal System: Ideas and Proposals* (1978); Twentieth Century Fund, Task Force on Sentencing Policy toward Young Offenders, *Confronting Youth Crime* (1978); Singer, R., *Just Deserts: Sentencing Based on Equality and Desert* (1979); von Hirsch, *Past or Future Crimes,* above, chs. 6–8, 11–12, 14; Galligan, D., "The Return to Retribution in Penal Theory", in C. Tapper (ed.), *Crime, Proof, and Punishment: Essays in Memory of Sir Rupert Cross* (1981); Jareborg, N., "The Coherence of the Penal System", in his *Essays in Criminal Law* (1988); Ashworth, A., "Criminal Justice and Deserved Sentences", (1989) *Criminal Law Review* 340; von Hirsch, "The Politics of Just Deserts", (1990) 32 *Canadian Journal of Criminology* 397; Braithwaite, J., and Pettit, P., *Not Just Deserts* (1990); von Hirsch and Ashworth, "Not Not Just Deserts: A Response to Braithwaite and Pettit", (1992) 12 *Oxford Journal of Legal Studies* 83; von Hirsch, "Proportionality in Punishment: Some Philosophical Issues", in M. Tonry and N. Morris (eds.), *Crime and Justice: An Annual Review of Research,* vol. 16 (1992); von Hirsch, *Censure and Sanctions,* above, chs. 3–4; Frase, R. S., "Sentencing Principles in Theory and Practice", in M. Tonry and N. Morris (eds.), *Crime and Justice: a Review of Research,* vol. 22 (1997).

3. Hybrid Theories

Monahan, J., "The Case for Prediction in a Modified Desert Model of Sentencing", 5 *International Journal of Law and Psychiatry* 103 (1982); Morris, N., and Miller, M., "Predictions of Dangerousness", in M. Tonry and N. Morris (eds.), *Crime and Justice. An Annual Review of Research,* vol. 6 (1986); Tonry, M., "Prediction and Classification: Legal and Ethical Issues", in M. Tonry and D. M. Gottfredson (eds.), *Crime and Justice: An Annual Review of Research,* vol. 7 (1987); Robinson, P. H., "Hybrid Principles for the Distribution of Criminal Sanctions", (1987) 82 *Northwestern University Law Review*; Primoratz, I., "The Middle Way in the Philosophy of Punishment", in R. Gavison (ed.), *Issues in Contemporary Legal Philosophy* (1987); von Hirsch, "Proportionality in Punishment: Some Philosophical Issues", above; von Hirsch, *Censure and Sanctions,* above, ch. 6; Tonry, M., "Proportionality, Parsimony and Interchangeability of Punishments", in R. A. Duff *et al., Penal Theory and Practice* (1994).

4. Desert and Prior Criminal Record

Von Hirsch, *Doing Justice* (1976), ch. 10; Fletcher, G., *Rethinking Criminal Law* (1978), 460–6; Singer, *Just Deserts,* above, ch. 5; von Hirsch, "Desert and Prior Convictions in Sentencing", (1981) 65 *Minnesota Law Review* 591; von Hirsch, *Past or Future Crimes,* above, ch. 7; Stuart, J. D., "Retributive Justice and Prior Offenses", (1986) 18 *Philosophical Forum* 40; Wasik, M., "Guidance, Guidelines and Criminal Record", in K. Pease and M. Wasik, *Sentencing Reform* (1987); von Hirsch, "Criminal Record Rides Again", (1991) 10 (2) *Criminal Justice Ethics* 2; Roberts, J. V., "The Role of Criminal Record in the Federal Sentencing Guidelines", (1994) 13 *Criminal Justice Ethics* 21.

5

Structuring Sentencing Discretion

Now that four of the leading aims of sentencing have been examined, it is time to turn to the translation of aims and policies into practical sentencing systems. How can sentencing be organized effectively so that it achieves one of the above aims, or a carefully constructed hierarchy of aims?

The question seems to have been little discussed until the last two decades. There was considerable debate about consistency in sentencing one hundred years ago in England, with calls in 1892 for an appellate court to review sentences. In fact, a Court of Criminal Appeal was created in 1907, but six years earlier Lord Chief Justice Alverstone had responded to public debate by overseeing the preparation of a "Memorandum on Normal Punishments", a kind of informal sentencing tariff which the High Court judges agreed to.[1] This debate did not, however, result in any clarification of the general aims or principles to be applied, and for most of the twentieth century sentencing in England and the USA has been characterized by wide judicial discretion. The notion of a sentencing "system" was either not used or, if it was used, it would be applied to an agglomeration of sentencing powers provided by legislatures for courts. The normal approach in most jurisdictions was for the legislature to establish maximum penalties for offences, to create a range of sentencing options including imprisonment, and then to leave the courts to exercise discretion within the wide ranges provided. In a few jurisdictions, most notably England and Wales, the availability of appellate review led to the development of some sentencing principles through case law. In many American jurisdictions, by way of contrast, there was virtually no authoritative guidance beneath the legislative maxima. The result was what Judge Frankel, in Selection 5.1, denounced as "lawlessness in sentencing": decisions on sentence directly concern the basic liberty of citizens—for example, whether those convicted of crimes should go to prison and, if so, for how long—and yet the protections of the rule of law seemed to be absent. No standards for sentencing existed, there was no requirement of giving reasons, and therefore no protection was provided from inconsistent or ill-founded decisions.

One justification advanced in support of the wide discretion enjoyed by sentencers was that it enabled the judge to select a rehabilitative sentence based on a diagnosis of the offender's "needs". This justification began to wear thin as the claims of rehabilitative sentencing were increasingly questioned in the early 1970s (see Chapter 1 above). Interest in sentencing reform was kindled, and the arguments advanced by Judge Frankel and others began to win acceptance. What approach should be taken to the structuring of sentencing discretion? In the last 20 years, many countries have introduced or proposed reforms. It is now possible to identify a number of key factors in the process of structuring. Decisions must be taken on the *content* of guidance, on the *source* of guidance, on the *authority* by which it should be laid down, and the *style* in which it should be formulated; and attention must also be paid to the *mechanics* of putting the guidance into practice. However, before introducing each of these topics, the constitutional dimensions of the subject need to be aired.

In a system which has some attachment, however loose, to the doctrine of separation of powers, which organ of the state should have authority in matters of sentencing? It is widely accepted that the legislature has supreme authority over sentencing policy, at least to the extent that it may lay down maximum penalties for offences and may decide what forms of sentence are to be available to the courts.[2] It also seems that legislatures may provide for mandatory sentences or mandatory minimum sentences for any offence: mandatory sentences for murder are common to many jurisdictions, without a suggestion that they involve an unconstitutional exercise of power by the legislature, and mandatory minimum sentences have also been held constitutional.[3] However, when legislatures have begun to impinge on what was hitherto a wide sentencing discretion of the judiciary, this has sometimes led to claims that the judiciary has some quasi-constitutional right to discretion in matters of sentencing. These claims, heard in many jurisdictions at different times,[4] have sometimes been bolstered by suggesting that sentencing discretion is required by the constitutional principle of the independence of the judiciary. But all such claims are dubious. If mandatory and mandatory minimum sentences are accepted as constitutional, the only claim of the judiciary can be to whatever discretion the legislature leaves. The principle of judicial independence is surely designed to protect the impartiality of judges and their freedom from pressure, influence, and bias;[5] it cannot be used to deny the propriety of legislatively authorized restrictions on sentencing, and therefore of legislative supremacy in sentencing matters. The correct position is surely that stated in the 1990 English White Paper:

"No Government should try to influence the decisions of the courts in individual cases. The independence of the judiciary is rightly regarded as a cornerstone of our liberties. But sentencing principles and sentencing practice are matters of legitimate concern to Government".[6]

Turning to the structuring of guidance for sentencers, an initial question concerns the *content* of the guidance. One of the consequences of the widespread discretion which has characterized sentencing for much of the twentieth century is that a whole variety of principles and policies have influenced sentencing, largely according to the inclinations of the particular sentencer. One of the aims of structuring discretion should be to ensure that it is exercised in a principled manner, as argued in Selection 5.2 below, and one essential step must be to decide upon a rationale for sentencing. A choice should be made between deterrence, rehabilitation, incapacitation, reparation (see Chapter 7 below) or desert as the leading aim of the system. Once the leading aim is chosen, then a decision should be taken about whether any other aim or aims should be allowed to influence sentences, to what degree, and in what types of case. Unless decisions of principle are taken on priorities and spheres of application of two or more sentencing aims, the resultant uncertainty would be a recipe for disparity: Selections 5.2 and 5.3 show how these points have been accepted and acted upon in England and in Sweden, respectively.

There are other decisions of principle to be taken, too. One concerns the promotion of principles such as equality before the law, particularly if there has been evidence of discriminatory sentencing in the past: a declaration that courts may not have regard to such factors as race, colour, gender, employment status, and religion might be a first step toward this goal. Another issue concerns the use of imprisonment: if there is to be a policy of restraint in the use of imprisonment, this may be implemented, for example, by means of specific legislative declarations (for the English experience, see Selections 5.2 and 5.4 below) or by introducing a prison capacity constraint into the fixing of the sentencing guidance itself (as in Minnesota).

What should be the *source* of any guidance on sentencing? In other words, if guidance is to be given, who should undertake the inquiries necessary to decide upon and formulate the guidance most appropriate to a particular system? The typical English approach, in times of legislative abstention, has been for the senior judiciary in the Court of Appeal to develop guidance through their judgments. However, the perspective of the senior judiciary is narrow and is unlikely to demonstrate sensitivity to wider criminal justice policies: in the Criminal Justice Act 1991 the British legislature introduced new policies itself, leaving the judiciary to develop those policies through appellate judgments, but the new Government's desire to see greater guidance from the Court of Appeal seems likely to lead to the creation of a new advisory machinery (see Selection 5.2). In several other jurisdictions, governments entrusted the task to a specially appointed drafting committee as a prelude to legislation (as in Sweden); or to a commission acting with legislatively delegated rule-making authority (as in Minnesota, for example). The membership of such bodies can be broadly based, drawing upon the experience of some judges and also including others with wider correctional and criminal justice experience.

Once proposals for the structuring of sentencing have been drawn up, there is the question of the *authority* by which they should be promulgated. Should all the standards be contained in legislation, or should use be made of some other form of law or regulation? Some jurisdictions, such as California, have placed all the detailed guidance in primary legislation; this might appear to ensure maximum control by a democratically elected institution, but it brings the danger that a carefully contrived scheme of guidance can be distorted by individual and piecemeal amendments, often proposed for political gain. Another approach, adopted in Minnesota and Oregon, is for the legislature to set out some basic principles in primary legislation, and to establish a rule-making commission to formulate detailed guidance in the form of regulations, which will then take effect unless the legislature resolves otherwise. Much depends here on the competence and sense of commitment of the commission, and its ability to devise a coherent system of guidance which sentencers can be persuaded to adopt. The traditions and legal culture of the jurisdiction will clearly be a significant factor. A third approach would be for the primary legislation to set out the basic principles, and leave the judiciary to develop the detailed guidance through appellate judgements. This approach, adopted in the 1988 Swedish sentencing law (see Selection 5.3) and in the 1991 English legislation (see Selection 5.2), depends for its success on the judiciary's willingness to take the principles seriously and to develop them sympathetically.

The next question is what *style* of guidance should be chosen. Mandatory minimum sentences for certain crimes have become increasingly attractive to politicians in recent years: the UK Parliament has now followed the example of others, such as the USA and Singapore, by introducing another mandatory sentence and a form of prescribed (i.e. minimum) sentence. There is ample evidence that mandatory minimum sentences have little effect on the crime rate and that sentencers strive to avoid the injustice of having to treat different cases as if they were the same: these and other criticisms are developed in Selection 5.2, and are placed in their political context in Chapter 9 below.

Determinate or "fixed point" sentencing has been the technique used in certain American jurisdictions which place their sentencing guidance in primary legislation, such as California. Once the judge has categorized the crime, there are usually two stages of decision-making. The first is whether to impose a prison sentence or a non-custodial penalty, and that decision is (at least, in California) largely discretionary. But if the judge chooses prison, the next stage is narrowly restricted: only three sentences will be available—the standard, the aggravated, and the mitigated. The judge may not go outside that threefold choice, which leaves little scope for taking account of unusual combinations of circumstances.

Perhaps the best-known style of guidance in recent times in the USA, however, has been numerical guidelines. In Minnesota these take the form of a grid of normal sentence ranges, with scores for the seriousness of the crime and the prior record of the offender. Departure from this range is possible, upon reasons given and subject to appellate review, and a body of jurisprudence on permissible reasons for departure has grown up. In the American federal system the guidelines are more complex and more restrictive of judicial discretion: some details and some criticisms will be found in Selection 5.2.

Another approach, adopted in some European countries, is that of setting out in legislation detailed principles, including guidance on how to resolve conflicts of principles, and leaving the courts to translate those into actual sentencing levels: this is the approach of Swedish law, described in Selection 5.3(a) by Andrew von Hirsch and supplemented by a translation of the law in Selection 5.3(b). It will be evident from Selection 5.2 that the approach taken in the English legislation of 1991 was somewhat similar, although the principles were less carefully spelt out.

These various styles of guidance differ in the extent to which they reduce judicial discretion, but it would be wrong to assume that the pursuit of principled sentencing means that the most constraining approach is necessarily the best. The point is that there will inevitably be questions of detailed application which can be answered differently by different sentencers, so that even if all sentencers were conscientiously pursuing the same aim or set of aims, inconsistencies could result. For example, if the overall aim of the system were incapacitation, it would still be important to have guidance on the types of offence and offender for whom predictive restraint might be justified, on whether limits should be placed on sentences in certain types of cases, and on whether class- or race-related factors such as employment history might be taken into account. If the overall aim is desert, it would be important to have parameters for determining the relative seriousness of different crimes, and for deciding how much weight to give to an offender's prior record. Beyond that, the choices are familiar. "The more detailed the rules and the less room for discretionary choices, the more cumbersome the system becomes, and the more it tends to deal inappropriately and unjustly with unforeseen contingencies. The less the detail and the more interstitial the discretion, the greater the risk of inconsistent treatment of similar cases."[7] Much will depend, in practice, on what is deemed appropriate in the context of the legal and political culture of the jurisdiction.

Devising guidance is not, however, sufficient to achieve the structuring of decisions on sentence. Whatever the content, source, authority, and style of sentencing guidance, it will only be worthwhile if it operates in practice in the way intended. It is abundantly clear that compulsion may not bring this about: the experience of courts circumventing mandatory minimum sentences is sufficient to substantiate this.[8] Where the degree of compulsion is reduced and courts are given the opportunity to depart from guideline sentences upon giving reasons, there may be substantial compliance; but the experience of "adaptive behaviour" by both judges and prosecutors in Minnesota demonstrates that the element of flexibility may be exploited to some extent.[9] Appellate review of sentences may be expected to contribute to the practical enforcement of sentencing guidance, but the extent of its contribution will depend on three points. First, the appeal court will need to take a strong line against unwarranted deviations from guidance by lower courts. Second, its decisions should not merely decide the particular case, but serve as precedents for later cases. And third, it must be willing to address issues of principle in its judgments. In terms of achieving consistency, the ideal position is that sentencers be persuaded of the desirability of the policies and principles underlying the sentencing system, and also that they be fully trained in the approach which it adopts. These training functions can be performed by an academy or institute for judges—such as England's Judicial Studies Board. However, judicial training cannot contribute to principled sentencing unless there are clear principles in existence. Another approach to securing consistency is the introduction of technical aids for sentencers, such as computerized systems with databases which help the judge to discover the relevant laws, policies, and current practice relating to a particular type of case. Information systems of this kind may be particularly useful in collating and presenting relevant guidance from different sources, for example, legislation, judicial decisions, and common practice.[10]

Having surveyed a range of possible methods for structuring sentencing, so as to bring practice into conformity with the rationales and principles of a given sentencing system, it remains to emphasize that sentencing forms only a part of the criminal justice process. Any structuring would therefore need to be related to the stages of the criminal process occurring before and occurring after the sentencing decision. This is not the place to develop these arguments in detail,[11] but a few examples can be given. Clearly those cases that come before the courts for sentence are those selected for prosecution by the police and Crown Prosecution Service, who have powers to "divert" cases from the courts and who do so in considerable numbers. Likewise, the offence-labels attached to the conduct for which courts pass sentence stem from those earlier prosecution decisions, and from any bargains struck by prosecution and defence in relation to guilty pleas and the reduction of charges. Moving to the post-sentence phase, the impact of sentences may be affected by the decision of the English Parole Board on early release, in those cases over which the Board has powers. It follows from these examples that any approach to sentencing guidance which neglected the stages of decision-making before and after sentence would be limited in its effect. At the least, there should be an attempt to ensure congruity with prosecution guidance and parole guidance.

A.A.

Notes

1. See L. Radzinowicz and R. Hood, *The Emergence of Penal Policy* (1990), 755–8, and D.A.Thomas, *Constraints on Judgment* (1978).
2. For further discussion of the constitutional aspects, see C.Munro, "Judicial Independence and Judicial Functions", in C. Munro and M. Wasik (eds.), *Sentencing, Judicial Discretion and Training* (1992), and A. Ashworth, "Sentencing Reform Structures", in N. Morris and M. Tonry (eds.), *Crime and Justice*, vol. 16, 181.
3. *Palling* v. *Corfield* (1970) 123 C.L.R. 52, a decision of the High Court of Australia.
4. e.g. the statement of Lord Halsbury, as Lord Chancellor, in 1890, quoted by Radzinowicz and Hood, above n. 1, 754. A century later a similarly vigorous assertion may be found in a memorandum of the judges of Victoria (Australia) on sentencing: see Victorian Sentencing Committee, *Sentencing* (1988), vol. 3, Appendix 1.
5. See the declaration of the United Nations, *Basic Principles on the Independence of the Judiciary*, adopted at the Seventh United Nations Crime Congress, 1985, paras 1 and 2: "—The independence of the judiciary shall be guaranteed by the State

and enshrined in the constitution or law of the country.—The judiciary shall decide matters before them with impartiality on the basis of facts, in accordance with the law, without any improper influences or pressures".

6. Home Office, *Crime, Justice and Protecting the Public* (1990), para. 2.1. For the USA, see the dictum of Justice Blackmun in *Mistretta* v. *U.S.* (1989) 109 S.Ct. 647, at 654, that "the scope of judicial discretion with respect to a sentence is subject to congressional control"; also *Rummel* v. *Estelle* (1980) 445 U.S. 263.

7. A. von Hirsch, "Commensurability and Crime Prevention: Evaluating Formal Sentencing Structures and their Rationales", (1983) 74 *Journal of Criminal Law and Criminology* 209, at 245.

8. See M. Tonry, *Sentencing Matters* (1996), ch.5, and Selection 5.2.

9. For evidence from Minnesota, see D. Parent, *Structuring Criminal Sentencing* (1989), p.184; see more generally Tonry, *Sentencing Matters*, ch. 6.

10. For a recent development in Scotland, see N. Hutton, A. A. Paterson, C. Tata, and J. N. Wilson, *A Sentencing Information System for the Scottish High Court of Justiciary* (1996); earlier systems are reviewed by A. Ashworth, "Sentencing Reform Structures" (above n.2) at pp. 227–30.

11. For detailed discussion of pre-trial processes, see A. Ashworth, *The Criminal Process*, 2nd edn. (1998); for post-sentences processes, see G. Richardson, *Law, Process and Custody: Prisoners and Patients* (1993).

5.1

Lawlessness in Sentencing

MARVIN FRANKEL

The common form of criminal penalty provision confers upon the sentencing judge an enormous range of choice. The scope of what we call "discretion" permits imprisonment for anything from a day to one, five, 10, 20, or more years. All would presumably join in denouncing a statute that said "the judge may impose any sentence he pleases". Given the mortality of men, the power to set a man free or to confine him for up to 30 years is not sharply distinguishable.

The statutes granting such powers characteristically say nothing about the factors to be weighed in moving to either end of the spectrum or to some place between. It might be supposed by some stranger arrived in our midst that the criteria for measuring a particular sentence would be discoverable outside the narrow limits of the statutes and would be known to the judicial experts rendering the judgements. But the supposition would lack substantial foundation. Even the most basic sentencing principles are not prescribed or stated with persuasive authority. There is, to be sure, a familiar litany in the literature of sentencing "purposes": retribution, deterrence ("special" and "general"), "denunciation", incapacitation, rehabilitation. Nothing tells us, however, when or whether any of these several goals are to be sought, or how to resolve such evident conflicts as that likely to arise in the effort to punish and rehabilitate all at once. It has for some time been part of our proclaimed virtue that vengeance or retribution is a disfavoured motive for punishment. But there is reason to doubt that either judges or the public are effectively abreast of this advanced position. And there is no law—certainly none that anybody pretends to have enforced—telling the judge he must refrain, expressly or otherwise, from trespassing against higher claims to wreak vengeance.

Moving upward from what should be the philosophical axioms of a rational scheme of sentencing law, we have no structure of rules, or even

From Marvin E. Frankel, "Lawlessness in Sentencing", (1972) 41 *Cincinnati Law Review* 1. Excerpted and reprinted by permission.

guidelines, affecting other elements arguably pertinent to the nature or severity of the sentence. Should it be a mitigating factor that the defendant is being sentenced upon a plea of guilty rather than a verdict against him? Should it count in his favour that he spared the public "trouble" and expense by waiving a jury? Should the sentence be more severe because the judge is convinced that the defendant perjured himself on the witness stand? Should churchgoing be considered to reflect favourably? Consistent with the first amendment, should it be considered at all? What factors should be assessed—and where, if anywhere, are comparisons to be sought—in gauging the relative seriousness of the specific offence and offender as against the spectrum of offences by others in the same legal category? The list of such questions could be lengthened. Each is capable of being answered, and is answered by sentencing judges, in contradictory or conflicting, or at least differing, ways. There is no controlling requirement that any particular view be followed on any such subject by the sentencing judge.

With the delegation of power so unchannelled, it is surely no overstatement to say that "the new penology has resulted in vesting in judges and parole and probation agencies the greatest degree of uncontrolled power over the liberty of human beings that one can find in the legal system". The process would be totally unruly even if judges were superbly and uniformly trained for the solemn work of sentencing.

The *kadi*, unfettered by rules, makes his decrees swiftly and simply. But we learned long ago that the giving of reasons helps the decision-maker himself in the effort to be fair and rational, and makes it possible for others to judge whether he has succeeded. And so we require our federal district judges and many others to explain themselves when they rule whether a postal truck driver was at fault in crumpling a fender and, if so, how much must be paid to right the wrong.

There is no such requirement in the announcement of a prison sentence. Sometimes judges give reasons anyway, or reveal in colloquy the springs of their action. The explanations or revelations sometimes disclose reasoning so perverse or mistaken that the sentence, normally unreviewable, must be invalidated on appeal. Most trial judges (to my impressionistic and conversational knowledge, at least) say little or nothing, certainly far less than a connected "explanation" or rationale of the sentence. Many, sharing a common aversion to being reversed, are perhaps motivated by the view (not unknown on trial benches) that there is safety in silence. It is likely that the judge, not expected to explain, has never organized a full and coherent explanation even for himself. Some judges use the occasion of sentencing to flaunt or justify themselves by moral pronunciamentos and excoriations of the defendant. This has no relation to the serious and substantial idea that the community's "denunciation" is a—possibly the—chief aim of sentencing. It is, in any event, not kin to the reasoned decisions for which judges are commissioned.

The state I have described as lawlessness calls for some immediate, if not immutable, remedies by law-making. At least some principles of sentencing should by now be attainable. Both by substantive controls and through procedural revisions the unchecked powers of the untutored judge should be subject to a measure of regulation. The vague, indefinite, and uncritical use of indeterminate sentences calls for restriction through meaningful definitions and discriminating judgements. Matters like the "apportionment of punishment" and its "severity" are peculiarly questions of legislative policy. Believing it has been time long since to start abhorring the vacuum that exists in this area, I propose here to suggest only some beginnings, leaving for wiser heads and fuller time the continuous task of completion and betterment.

Despite all the philosophizing on this most fundamental of subjects in scholarly works and random judicial opinions, we have virtually no meaningful or specific legislative declarations of the principles justifying criminal sanctions.

Beyond dealing with the bedrock subject of sentencing purposes a new code of sentencing should begin to weigh and decide numerous issues of mitigation or aggravation on which judges are now free to go their disparate ways. It is not acceptable to leave for the normally unspoken and diverse judgements of sentencing courts such questions as: whether a plea of guilty should be considered in mitigation; whether (what is not the converse) standing trial should be considered aggravating; whether waiving a jury or seemingly lying on the stand should be taken into account; whether disruptive behaviour and tactics at trial should be considered aggravating; or whether "co-operation" with the prosecutor (furnishing evidence for other investigations, testifying against codefendants, etc.) should be considered mitigating. In addition to such matters of in-court behaviour, there are, of course, more fundamental questions touching the criminal acts and the general character and history of the defendant. Students of the subject recall, and generally scorn these days, the efforts of scholars in times past to catalogue such factors—the relative gravity of the specific offence, the cruelty or stealth or deliberateness of the behaviour, defendant's age, prior record, character traits, etc.—and evolve a kind a calculus for computing sentences. The short answer to such proposals for detailed sentencing codes has been the familiar, and weighty, aversion to illusory certainty bought at the cost of inflexible laws that torture disparate people and events into identical molds. But, like other short answers, this one is too short. There has not yet been a sufficient investment of energy and imagination in the attempt to codify precise, detailed factors governing sentences. Until the attempt has been made, with at least a measure of the resources and attention befitting a moon-voyaging society, the vague, futile, helpless wailing about disparity remains hypocrisy. Believing this, and risking the misunderstanding likely to greet a proposition conceded to be rudimentary and tentative, I mean to outline (a) the reasons for a detailed sentencing code and (b) the general nature of the contents and uses of such a code.

(a) The argument for codifying sentencing criteria is, very simply, that they now exist and operate, whether we like this or not, in an arbitrary, random, inconsistent, and unspoken fashion. Factors I have repeatedly mentioned—guilty pleas, prior record, defendant's age and family circumstances—are considered every day by sentencing judges, but in accordance with uncontrolled and divergent individual views of what is, after all, the "law" each time it applies. Every factor of this kind calls for a judgement of policy, suited exactly for legislative action and surely not suited for random variation from case to case. It is not a question, then, of seeking out and attempting to apply artificial criteria. It is a question of making explicit and uniform what is now tacit, capricious, and often decisive.

Making such determinations, a detailed sentencing code would eliminate some of the obscurity and the futility now attending the subject. Counsel would have some basis for knowing what to do and how to argue. The sentencers—the single judge or a group, as well as probation officers—would face a task similarly defined and capable of similarly focused appraisal. The defining of concrete issues would lead in turn to the possibility of meaningful appellate review.

(b) To posit at least a theoretical ideal, subject to revision of all kinds in the pursuit, I suggest the goal of codification might be conceived as a fairly detailed calculus of sentencing factors, including such use of arithmetical weightings as experimental study might reveal to be feasible. Again, I disclaim anything beyond the crude diagramming of a preliminary hypothesis. The hypothesis begins with the thought that every sentence under the code, as heretofore urged, would be classified in accordance with its basic purpose or purposes—as deterrent, rehabilitative, etc. For each such category, the code might contain some initial or tentative sentencing guides—for example, that a purely deterrent sentence should presumptively fall (subject to aggravating factors) in the lowest quartile of the sentencing range for the particular crime, or that a rehabilitative sentence might be categorized initially in terms of the defined need and proposed form of treatment.

Thereafter, within each broad sentencing category or group of categories, particular factors of mitigation or aggravation would be enumerated in the proposed code. Where possible, as I have suggested, numerical weights or ranges would be assigned—as, for example, for the relative gravity of the offence, the defendant's past criminal record, the favourable or unfavourable character of the defendant's work history and abilities. However unromantic numbers sound, or however misleading they may be in foolish hands, their proper uses may guide and regulate judgement. The physician who speaks of a grade 3 heart murmur may not be reporting a measurement as precise as the number of feet in a yard. But he says a meaningful thing that gives information and guidance to others professionally trained. Similarly, at least over time, a score of 5 on a scale of 1 to 5 for "gravity of particular offence" would help to tell what the sentencing judge thought and to test whether his thoughts made sense for the particular case.

For lack of time and competence, I have not attempted to think through how far a scheme of quantification might be carried. Depending upon the resolution of this basic problem, the aim of the sentencing code would be a sentencing form or chart giving possibly an overall "score" or, more likely, a profile of factors and their weights. The end product thus recorded by the sentencing tribunal could be preceded by proposed forms on charts submitted by counsel, probation officers, and others seeking to affect or determine the sentence. All, as I have urged, would have concrete things to aim at and talk about. All would have bases for comparison in assessing differences of ultimate judgement.

If this sounds crass and mechanical, I press it nonetheless as a goal preferable to the void in which we now operate. Outside the sombre field of sentencing, it has not been our way to make a fetish of vagueness. Whether numbers and scores are useless is a judgement that ought to follow, not precede, earnest study.

The aspects of sentencing that strike me as most flawed and most urgently in need of law revision have led to the few, somewhat scattered suggestions for legislative reform outlined above. There are needs, however, for action of a more thorough and continuous nature. Ignorance being one of the greatest problems, there is a need to marshal resources and talent for research and experimentation. Because the subject of sentencing is not steadily exhilarating or profitable to political officials, there is a need to fill the gaps in attention between sporadic moments of concern in times of crisis. Another aspect of the same essential point is the lack of political power suffered not only by convicted persons but by their keepers as well. Finally, the need for revision of the law is not a one-time thing: the gross inadequacies of the existing situation require continuing study and reform.

Thoughts along these lines lead to the very possibly impractical but earnest final recommendation of this paper. I propose that there be established a national commission charged with permanent responsibility for (1) the study of sentencing, corrections, and parole; (2) the formulation of laws and rules to which the results of such study may lead; and (3) the actual enactment of rules subject to congressional veto. When I suggest details of the commission's proposed composition and functions, it will be to invite thought rather than to claim anything like certainty or finality. With these caveats I sketch the proposal and its rationale.

Starting with the latter, I have mentioned the need for continuous and prestigious attention to problems of sentencing. The commission, properly launched and populated, could serve in a sense as a lobby within the government of those sentenced and for those charged with their custody and treatment. Other interests, politically significant, have such representation. Agriculture, labour, business, investors, and others have their spokesmen in various departments and agencies. Lately, reflecting a variety of things we seem to care about as a nation, the consumer is elbowing his way into the power structure. Prisoners and jailers, like the poor and others who seemed so distant a while ago, are headed for participation unless we mean to deflect sharply the lines of our recent development. But whether or not that is so, the stakes of everyone in a system of rational sentencing are too great for contentment with the dishevelled status quo. The improvements needed will not be achieved through fitful bursts of activity. The task requires the continuous attention of a respected agency.

Membership of the commission would be a matter for discussion. Obvious possibilities suggest themselves—lawyers, judges, criminologists, penologists, more generally-based sociologists, psychologists, and, not least but least traditional, former or present prison inmates. This is not to stump for government of prisoners by consent. It is to say we have gone too long without paying much attention to the actual impact upon the recipients of our well-intentioned but ineffectual "treatment" programmes.

The commission would not pretend to supersede existing scholarly efforts in universities and elsewhere. Like other agencies of government, the commission would draw upon such enterprises, generate additional ones, and engage in its own study programmes. Early in its career, the commission would chart a programme of inquiry and action and would set priorities. From this would follow decisions on the commissioning of outside studies and the organization of the agency's own projects.

I envision a highly prestigious commission or none at all. The calibre of those to be sought as commissioners would be a crucial concern. Their roles would be as philosopher-statesmen, charged with both basic scholarship and the formulation of rules, but leaving administrative and operating responsibilities to others. It is conceived, however, that the commission would have significant impact upon the shape and functioning of the affected administrative institutions. It may well be, for example, that the commission would want to consider whether there is any sound reason why the attorney general, the chief prosecutor, should have the Bureau of Prisons and Board of Parole under this jurisdiction. The phrasing here, if it implies a view as to the answer, is accurately revealing, but the commission might discover two sides to the question. The list of provocative possibilities could be extended, but the result might not be to enhance the palatability of my basic suggestion.

Sentencing is today a wasteland in the law. It calls, above all, for regulation by law. There is an excess of discretion given to officials whose entitlement to such power is established by neither professional credentials nor performance. Some measures already in existence—such as sentencing councils and appellate review—seem desirable because they operate to channel the exercise of discretion. On the other hand, the evil of unbounded discretion is enhanced by the uncritical belief that a beneficent "individualization" is achieved through indeterminate sentencing. Indeterminancy in its most enthusiastic forms takes on its literal dictionary quality of vagueness; it means the conferring of power to extend or terminate confinement where the grounds of the power have been misconceived and the occasions for its exercise are not ascertainable. Some aspects of sentencing and the treatment of convicted persons call for prompt legislative attention—in the choice of basic substantive principles, the prescription of basic procedures, and provisions for appellate review. The entire subject, however, is one for study and a steady process of law revision led by an imminent and permanent federal commission.

5.2

Four Techniques for Reducing Sentence Disparity

ANDREW ASHWORTH

The distinctive English contribution to the structuring of sentencing has been the development of judicial guidance and guidelines. In this essay, the approach of the English Court of Appeal is examined, and it is then contrasted with three other techniques for structuring sentencing discretion—statutory sentencing principles, numerical guideline systems, and mandatory sentences. In conclusion, the 1992 recommendations of the Council of Europe are outlined.

Judicial Self-Regulation

For many years the English courts were able to regulate their own sentencing practices, within the boundaries set by the legislature. Since the latter part of the nineteenth century, Parliament had done little more than lay down maximum penalties, leaving a broad judicial discretion with few restrictions on what courts might and might not do. Such an expanse of judicial discretion leaves the way open for disparate approaches to sentencing, and public and political concern about disparity was widespread towards the end of the nineteenth century.[1] This was one reason for the creation in 1907 of the Court of Criminal Appeal, now the Court of Appeal. In its judgments on appeals against sentence the Court, occasionally in the early years and much more frequently in recent years, has given its authority to various general principles of sentencing. For example, the Court has held that judges should pass concurrent, not consecutive, sentences where two or more crimes could be said to arise from the same transaction; and it has held that it is wrong for a court to impose a financial penalty (e.g. a fine or compensation order) on a wealthy offender where a poor offender would receive a more severe measure. It has also been claimed that the Court's decisions establish the "normal range" of

This essay is published here for the first time.

sentences for most crimes,[2] although until 1988 the Court heard only defence appeals against undue severity, and the balance of its decisions has not been greatly altered since then.

This kind of self-regulatory system has also existed in Scotland, Ireland, Canada, New Zealand and Australian jurisdictions, and there are many other common law countries in which the appeal court's decisions constitute binding precedents for other judges. Through appellate review, a collection of sentencing principles develops over time, enabling the judiciary to claim that discretion in sentencing is desirable and that it can correct disparity and promote principle through self-regulation.

A system of guidance that is dependent on appellate review does have certain drawbacks. One is that it is unlikely to lead to a rounded consideration of sentencing principles as a whole: a case law approach does not conduce to overall harmonization of principle. A second drawback is that the system tends to be reactive: the appellate court will make statements of principle in response to the issues raised by the cases under consideration. However, the English Court of Appeal has now broken away from this fetter. The policy-making role of the Court of Appeal was developed in the 1980s under Lord Lane, C.J. From time to time he would select a particular appeal case in which to deliver a guideline judgment, setting out the parameters of sentencing for a whole range of variations of the crime in question. To take the example of the guideline judgment on sentencing for rape, two main starting points for sentencing are indicated—eight years' imprisonment where one of four aggravating features is present, and five years in other cases—and then the judgment sets out eight aggravating factors and three mitigating factors which courts should take into account when deciding how much higher or lower than the starting-point the sentence should be. The decision also identifies three factors which are not to be treated as mitigating.[3] The strengths of this kind of judgment are that it provides judges with a framework within which they can locate the individual case, without depriving them of the discretion to deal differently with a case which has unusual features. The guidance is also narrative, having the familiar form of an appellate court's judgment rather than presenting a stark table of numbers. One internal weakness is that the judgment may give little indication as to the weight and effect of aggravating and mitigating factors, and this is the very problem most likely to be encountered in practice.[4] As a policy instrument, the guideline judgment has further disadvantages. The tendency has been for these judgments to be delivered sporadically and without any sense of an overall strategy. They may therefore succeed in improving the consistency of sentencing within an offence category, such as rape, without considering the proper relationship of sentence levels for that offence to sentence levels for other crimes such as robbery, burglary and manslaughter. And, at least in English law, they cover only a small area of sentencing, leaving many common offences untouched.

Despite these disadvantages, the guideline judgment is a significant innovation and an important tool for the development of consistent sentencing. Guideline judgments appear to be followed by most courts, and are not subjected to the suspicion and hostility that sentencers sometimes show towards legislative attempts to structure sentencing. In strict legal terms, most of the contents of guideline judgments are *obiter dicta*—pronouncements which run beyond the case under consideration, and which are therefore non-binding—but English judges tend to treat them as binding because they normally have the authority of the Lord Chief Justice. An interesting implication of guideline judgments is that they dispose of one much-trumpeted judicial objection to sentencing guidance: that each case is unique, and has its own individual combination of factors, and therefore guidance will invariably be crude and unhelpful. This is often the last line of defence for those who favour unfettered judicial discretion in sentencing. It assumes that it is merely the different combinations of facts in cases that lead to different sentencing outcomes, and ignores the possibility of differing judicial evaluations of the facts, differing judicial views of the relative seriousness of offences, different notions of the aims of sentencing, etc. Guideline judgments embody a recognition that these other differences do enter into sentencing, and their purpose is to deal with the main issues so as to foster consistency. Guideline judgments have been welcomed by most English judges, as providing a common framework while preserving flexibility for individual cases, and this demonstrates that sensible guidance is possible.

Much of the success of the technique of guideline judgments stems from the fact that they are constructed *by* judges *for* judges. But the technique was not widely used in the 1980s, particularly for the most numerous types of offence, and by the end of that decade the Government began to consider the introduction of a statutory framework for sentencing—encouraging the continued development of guideline judgments by the Court of Appeal, but within an overall sentencing structure established in legislation. This development is discussed next.

Statutory Sentencing Principles

Since 1976, article 6 of the Finnish Penal Code has contained a provision which declares that "punishment shall be measured so that it is in just proportion to the damage and danger caused by the offence and to the guilt of the offender manifested in the offence". Many other jurisdictions have a legislative declaration of sentencing aims, but those aims are sometimes conflicting (as in the German Penal Code). The Finnish Code not only articulates a primary rationale but also contains a list of aggravating and mitigating factors which relate to that aim. Beyond that, the application of the guidance in individual cases is left to the courts.

A more sophisticated version of the same approach is to be found in the Swedish Penal Code, as revised in 1988. The new chapters of the Code identify proportionality (desert) as the primary rationale for sentencing, and require the judge to assess the "penal value" (i.e. seriousness) of the offence. Some aggravating and mitigating factors are specified, as are other factors which the court may take into account. There is also guidance on the choice among forms of sentence. The Swedish law is discussed in detail by Andrew von Hirsch and Nils Jareborg in Selections 5.3(a) and 5.3(b) below.

The Finnish and Swedish approaches are notable in that they leave the judge to apply and individuate the general norms declared in the legislation. In one sense the judges have considerable discretion, because they are subject to few legislative restrictions. In another sense the discretion is structured, because they are expected to evaluate the factors in individual cases by reference to the principles of sentencing declared in the legislation—they are not free to impose exemplary deterrent sentences, for example, because that would be inconsistent with those principles. The structuring of discretion is therefore achieved through an approach which ties their patterns of reasoning to particular aims and principles, rather than through numerical guidance of the kind used in some American systems.

In 1991 England and Wales also enacted statutory sentencing principles, albeit in a less clear way than the Finnish and Swedish legislation. The origins of the Criminal Justice Act 1991 were in the Government's White Paper of 1990, which stated that desert should be the primary aim of sentencing, and that rehabilitation and deterrence should not be used as general aims of sentencing.[5] However, the 1991 Act was not drafted so as to enunciate its principles clearly. References to "the seriousness of the offence" as the principal criterion in sentencing were as far as the Act went. Thus, the provision on calculating the length of prison sentences, in section 2(2), reads:

"The custodial sentence shall be (a) for such term (not exceeding the permitted maximum) as in the opinion of the court is commensurate with the seriousness of the offence."

The provisions on community sentences and fines use the same formula. One might argue that this is a sufficiently clear *allusion* to the principles of proportionality and desert, particularly when read in conjunction with the White Paper of 1990, even if it does not spell out the principles with the same clarity as the Finnish and Swedish laws. However, the formula did not survive a hostile reception from the Court of Appeal. When Lord Taylor, C.J. came to construe section 2(2)(a), he did decide that it prevents courts from imposing exemplary sentences in individual cases, but he went on to state that "commensurate with the seriousness of the offence" should be interpreted so as to mean "commensurate with the punishment and deterrence which the seriousness of the offence requires".[6] This set the tone for a reading-down of many parts of the 1991 Act, in which the judges made sure that it affected their daily sentencing as little as possible.[7]

Reference to the White Paper of 1990 shows that the Government had hoped that the courts would play an equal part in developing guidance within the broad statutory framework. For example, this was the intention behind section 1(2) of the 1991 Act, which reads:

> "the court shall not pass a custodial sentence on the offender unless it is of the opinion (a) that the offence . . . was so serious that only such a sentence can be justified for the offence".

It was hoped that the Court of Appeal would develop more specific guidance, in line with the spirit of the subsection. In practice, the Court soon took refuge in the vapid approach of stating that an offence passes the seriousness threshold if this is what "right-thinking members of the public" would think. This test offers no guidance to lower courts,[8] and thus undermines another of the Act's intentions.

The new Labour Government of 1997 has signified its intention to keep faith with the judicial development of guidelines, within the broad statutory framework, but has proposed the creation of a Sentencing Advisory Panel to advise the Court of Appeal of the need for guidelines on sentencing for various types of crime. It is not yet clear how the new machinery will work, but the Crime and Disorder Bill contains provisions along these lines which seem designed to prompt the Court of Appeal to greater activity as a guidance-giving body.

Numerical Guideline Systems

In the USA, the predominant approach to guidance on sentencing has been to adopt numerical guidelines. Several variations on this approach may be found in different American jurisdictions: they vary in the form in which they are promulgated, in the presence or absence of overall aims or policies, and in the degree of latitude left to courts in individual cases. The best-known system is that of Minnesota, which has been adapted for use in other states. This will be contrasted with the distinctly less successful federal guidelines, emanating from the U.S. Sentencing Commission.

The sentencing commission in Minnesota began work in the late 1970s.[9] One of its earliest determinations was to decide upon a primary rationale for sentencing: desert. It then went on to make some crucial policy decisions. Sentences for property offenders were to be made less severe, and those for violent offenders correspondingly more severe. Prior criminal record was to be less influential than the seriousness of the offence. And overall sentence levels were to be calculated so as to ensure that the numbers sentenced to imprisonment remained within the capacity of the prisons.[10] The Commission then divided all serious offences into ten categories of relative gravity, and developed a seven-point scale for calculating the seriousness of an offender's criminal history. The result was Minnesota's "Sentencing Guidelines Grid", in operation since 1981, which enables a judge to find the presumptive sentence for each case by placing the offence within the appropriate category, calculating the offender's criminal history score, and then locating the cell where the two intersect. The judge is obliged to impose a sentence within the range of presumptive sentences unless there are substantial and compelling circumstances in the individual case for departing from that range. In such circumstances, departure is permitted upon giving reasons, and the guidelines include a list of factors which may and factors which may not be used as reasons for departure.

The Minnesota system has been reasonably successful in attaining its objectives. Sentencing consistency was improved, property offenders have been sent to prison less frequently, and the state's Supreme Court has developed a jurisprudence of permissible and impermissible departures. On the other hand, the division of all serious offences into only ten categories is rather crude, and the elements of discretion remaining in the Minnesota system have enabled judges and prosecutors to circumvent some of the guidelines.[11] In recent years some of the policies underlying the original guidelines have been altered for political reasons, but that does not weaken the effectiveness of the guidelines approach as a model, and it has been adapted successfully in other states, most notably Oregon.[12]

The approach of the U.S. Sentencing Commission was different, as have been the consequences of the guidelines they drafted. The Commission was established by the federal Sentencing Reform Act of 1984 and was directed to draft, within certain legislative constraints, guidelines for the sentencing of federal offences. The guidelines became law in 1987, but from the outset their structural defects were manifest in practice. Four areas of difficulty might be mentioned briefly.

First, the Commission declined to declare a primary rationale for sentencing, and instead opted for a scheme with an indiscriminate mixture of rationales. This is not a mere matter of academic elegance: it is a matter of fundamental practical importance when it comes to deciding what factors should aggravate or mitigate and how judges should exercise the discretion left to them by the system. Without a guiding aim, consistency is a forlorn hope.

Second, the Commission declined to adopt a principle of restraint in the use of imprisonment, despite a reference to resource constraints in the Sentencing Reform Act. This position has been worsened by the mandatory and mandatory minimum sentences enacted by Congress, particularly for drug offenders and career criminals. Federal imprisonment rates are high, and the mandatory sentences (to which many judges are opposed) have had a further distorting effect on the guidelines.

Third, the federal guidelines are high on complexity and low on clarity. The Commission's "Sentencing Table" has some 43 "offence-levels" on one axis and six "criminal history categories" on the other. For each type of offence a "base level" is indicated by the guidelines; then there are various "enhancements", for which the judge must raise the offence level if they are present; and there are also some factors such as "acceptance of responsibility" (an ambiguous and practically troublesome reference to a plea of guilty) which reduce the offence level where they are present. A practical example may be used to show how the guidelines operate.[13] Robbery carries a base level of 18 on the scale. The amount stolen increases this, so that if $100,000 were taken, this would add three points to the offence level. There are further enhancements if a weapon was involved: if a gun was brandished but not used, for example, this would add three further points. Then if the judge thought that the offender's plea of guilty showed acceptance of responsibility, the offence level would be reduced by two. Next the judge would turn to the offender's prior record: the calculation takes account not only of the number of previous convictions but also of their seriousness.[14] There are also augmentations for "career criminals". The result of this should lead the judge to a cell in the "Sentencing Table" indicating the appropriate range of sentences. Courts may depart from the range wherever it seems "reasonable" to do so. The guidelines specify some factors which may not and others which may justify departures, and there are also certain "policy statements" whose authority has at times caused judicial confusion.

A fourth difficulty is that the apparent rigidity of the guidelines in practice (with a compliance rate of some four-fifths of cases) has resulted, as the Federal Courts Study Committee found in 1990,[15] in a transfer of considerable power to federal prosecutors. Although this is a natural consequence of rigidly-drafted guidelines, the situation has been more complex because of the uncertainty about sentencing discounts for guilty pleas. Nevertheless, early research found a significant degree of guideline evasion through plea bargaining.[16]

The federal guideline system has been subject to an extraordinarily voluminous amount of judicial and academic criticism, much of it predictable in view of the defects inherent in the original conception.[17] Few would regard the system as a suitable model for future reforms.

Mandatory and Mandatory Minimum Sentences

One of the difficulties in American federal sentencing has been the increasing number of mandatory and mandatory minimum sentences for which Congress has legislated, adding to the restrictiveness of the guidelines themselves. Mandatory sentences have proved attractive to legislatures in several jurisdictions in the 1990s, and are to be found in recent British legislation in the shape of the Crime (Sentences) Act 1997. Section 2 of that Act requires a court to impose a sentence of life imprisonment on any person found guilty of a second serious sexual or violent offence (as listed), unless the court finds "exceptional circumstances" for not doing so. Sections 3 and 4 of the Act provide for "prescribed sentences" of seven years for the third class A drug dealing offence and three years for the third offence of residential burglary: these provisions are less restrictive than section 2, since the courts need not impose the prescribed sentence if it would be "unjust in all the circumstances" to do so. The new sections were originally based on the "three strikes and you're out" laws in some American jurisdictions. Sections 2 and 3 have already been implemented: cases in which section 3 is relevant will be rare, since most such offences attract sentences in excess of seven years anyhow, but the mandatory life sentence in section 2 will have a major impact on sentencing for serious offences. On the basis of evidence of their use in American jurisdictions, what are the difficulties with such sentences?

From the detailed study by Michael Tonry,[18] four principal objections can be identified. First, "there is little basis for believing that mandatory penalties have any significant effects on rates of serious crimes". This is a firm inference from the various American initiatives,[19] and one obvious reason is that low detection rates would tend to off-set any expected increase in deterrent effect. In respect of drugs, there is a powerful view that other approaches which target a reduction of demand are likely to be far more effective in reducing crime rates than higher sentences. In respect of the "serious offences" targeted by section 2 of the 1997 Act, there is little evidence that it will have a significant incapacitative effect.[20] Second, mandatory sentences and mandatory minimum sentences have considerable potential for injustice: "such laws sometimes result in the imposition of penalties in individual cases that everyone involved believes to be unjustly severe." While the "prescribed" minimum sentences for drug dealing and burglary in the 1997 Act have a sufficiently wide escape clause, the mandatory life sentence introduced by section 2 can only be avoided where there are "exceptional circumstances", and this phrase is intended to be construed narrowly. Third, this potential for injustice often leads prosecutors and judges to find ways of circumventing the mandatory provisions. The American studies cited by Tonry show all kinds of "adaptive behaviour" by judges and others, in order to avoid outcomes which are agreed to be unjust. It seems likely that similar behaviour will take hold in England and Wales if "exceptional circumstances" is interpreted narrowly by the courts. And fourth, a related but distinct effect is that there are fewer guilty pleas where the penalty is mandatory. Thus Tonry reports that "the U.S. Sentencing Commission found that trial rates were two-and-a-half times higher for offences bearing mandatory minima than for other offences", and there were similar effects in state jurisdictions. This both increases anxiety for victims and other witnesses, and acts as a further drain on resources in a criminal justice system under strain. Some might be prepared to accept this if a substantial deterrent or incapacitative effect were likely to follow from the mandatory sentences: but, as we saw earlier, the prospects for this seem poor.

Despite these weaknesses of mandatory sentences, they continue to hold considerable attraction for politicians and legislators: they are one of the manifestations of the resurgent politics of "law and order", discussed in Chapter 9 below. Many American states have enacted mandatory or mandatory minimum sentences for drugs or gun offences. Many others have introduced "three strikes" laws, which impose a long mandatory sentence on those who repeat certain types of offence. The practical implications of the English versions, introduced by the Crime (Sentences) Act 1997, remain to be observed in the coming years.

Conclusions

Disparity of sentencing occurs when similar cases are dealt with differently, and where different cases are treated without reference to those differences. Disparity is a manifest form of injustice, which may bring a sentencing system into public disrepute. However, the choice of techniques to reduce disparity and to promote consistency is not a simple matter. Much will depend on the political climate and on the legal tradition of the country or state. Any sentencing reform should be formulated and promulgated in the most appropriate way for each jurisdiction, and it must have the support of the judiciary if it is to achieve its objectives.

Judicial self-regulation offers an excellent basis for the development of principles that are closely sensitive to the practical problems of sentencers and, because the guidance is in narrative form and emanates from other judges, it is likely to have the support of sentencers. As a technique of guidance, judicial self-regulation is likely to work best in those jurisdictions where the appellate courts are experienced at delivering principled judgments. However, judicial self-regulation is not a suitable means for deciding upon the overall aims of sentencing or on policies to be pursued with respect to imprisonment, victims, and so on.

On such matters of overall policy there is a need for a more dynamic machinery which permits changes in sentencing policy to be brought about. For this, a preferable approach is the enactment of statutory principles, formulated after appropriately wide consultation and presented as a framework for judicial sentencing. The approach of formulating general statutory principles and leaving the courts to apply them, as in Finland and Sweden, is likely to work best where the judiciary feels an obligation to follow the spirit of legislation, and not in a jurisdiction (such as England and Wales) where the judiciary feels little awkwardness about resisting and frustrating the spirit of legislation. Greater compulsion may be exerted through a numerical guideline system, either on the Minnesota model or, more rigidly, on the model of the U.S. Sentencing Commission. There seems little to recommend the U.S. Commission's guidelines, but the Minnesota model can be adapted and refined so as to provide principled guidance without undue compulsion.

In 1992 the Council of Ministers of the Council of Europe approved a recommendation on "Consistency of Sentencing" which sets out a number of principles for the structuring of sentencing in member states.[21] The first point is that legislation ought to articulate the basic principles of sentencing and, where more than one such principle is enunciated, it should state the order of priority among those principles. Whilst the Finnish, Swedish and English legislation complies with this recommendation—for example, the Swedish law allows deterrent sentencing for the offence of drink-driving while maintaining proportionality as the leading criterion elsewhere—other examples (such as Canada) show that legislatures sometimes proclaim several inconsistent principles without prescribing much in the way of an order of priority or separate spheres of application.[22] The Council of Europe's recommendations go on to declare various principles of sentencing: the principle of proportionality between the seriousness of the offence and the sentence, the principle of humanity, and the principle of non-discrimination. Perhaps the most innovative recommendations, relevant to this chapter, are B3 and B4, as follows:

> "3. (a) Wherever it is appropriate to the constitution and traditions of the legal system, some further techniques for enhancing consistency of sentencing should be considered.
>
> (b) Two such techniques which have been used in practice are "sentencing orientations" and "starting points".
>
> (c) *Sentencing orientations* indicate ranges of sentence for different variations of an offence, according to the presence or absence of various aggravating or mitigating factors, but leave courts with the discretion to depart from the orientations.
>
> (d) *Starting points* indicate a basic sentence for different variations of an offence, from which the court may move upwards or downwards so as to reflect aggravating and mitigating factors.
>
> 4. (a) In particular for frequently committed or less serious offences or offences which are otherwise suitable, consideration may be given to the introduction of some form of orientations or starting points for sentencing as an important step towards consistency in sentencing.
>
> (b) Wherever it is appropriate to the constitution or the traditions of the legal system, one or more of the following means, among others, of implementing such orientations or starting points may be adopted:
>
>   (i) legislation;
>   (ii) guideline judgments by superior courts;
>   (iii) an independent commission;
>   (iv) Ministry circular;
>   (v) guidelines for the prosecution.

The Council of Europe's recommendations proceed to deal with a range of issues, including previous convictions, custodial sentencing, aggravation and mitigation. But the above proposals on approaches to structuring sentencing, which studiously avoid giving any prominence to the term "guidelines" because of its American association with numbers, deserve serious consideration.

Notes

1. Sir Leon Radzinowicz and Roger Hood, *The Emergence of Penal Policy* (Oxford University Press, 1990), ch. 23.
2. Notably by D.A.Thomas, *Principles of Sentencing*, 2nd edn. (1979), whose pioneering work in rationalizing and reconstructing the Court of Appeal's decisions has had a considerable influence on the development of its jurisprudence.
3. See *Billam* (1986) 86 *Criminal Appeal Reports* 347, and the general discussion by A. Ashworth, *Sentencing and Criminal Justice*, 2nd edn. (1995), pp. 26–32.
4. Cf. R. Ranyard, B. Hebenton and K. Pease, "An Analysis of a Guideline Case as applied to the Offence of Rape", (1994) 33 *Howard Journal of Criminal Justice* 203.
5. Home Office, *Crime, Justice and Protecting the Public* (H.M.S.O., 1990), ch. 2.
6. *Cunningham* (1993) 14 Cr.App.R.(S) 444.
7. One exception to these strictures concerns the Court of Appeal's handling of s. 2(2)(b), which permits longer than proportionate sentences for sexual and violent offenders where this is thought necessary for public protection. The Court has made a conscientious effort to interpret the section according to its objectives, although there are some respects in which its approach might be improved: for discussion, see A. von Hirsch and A. Ashworth, "Protective Sentencing under Section 2(2)(b); the Criteria for Dangerousness" [1996] Crim.L.R. 175.
8. For discussion, see A. Ashworth and A. von Hirsch, "Recognising Elephants: the Problem of the Custody Threshold" [1997] Crim.L.R. 187.
9. For the history and the experience of the early years, see Dale G. Parent, *Structuring Criminal Sentences* (1989).
10. For detailed analysis and discussion, see Andrew von Hirsch, "Structure and Rationale: Minnesota's Critical Choices", in A von Hirsch, K. Knapp and M. Tonry, *The Sentencing Commission and its Guidelines* (1987), ch. 5.
11. See K. Knapp, "Implementation of the Minnesota Guidelines: Can the Innovative Spirit be Preserved?", in von Hirsch, Knapp and Tonry (above n. 10), ch. 8.
12. For discussion of recent developments, see the essays by Andrew von Hirsch and by Richard S. Frase, in C. Clarkson and R. Morgan (eds.), *The Politics of Sentencing Reform* (1995), and M. Tonry, *Sentencing Matters* (1996), ch. 5.
13. For another practical example, with greater detail, see the essay by A. Doob in Clarkson and Morgan (above n. 12), at pp. 218–26.
14. For discussion of issues relating to previous convictions, see Selection 4.7 below.
15. Federal Courts Study Committee, *Report* (Washington, D.C., 1990).
16. S. Schulhofer and I. Nagel, "Negotiated Pleas under the Federal Sentencing Guidelines: the first 15 months", (1990) 27 *American Criminal Law Review* 231.
17. Among these, see e.g. the criticisms of Michael Tonry, drawn together in his *Sentencing Matters* (1996); Daniel J. Freed, "Federal Sentencing in the Wake of Guidelines: Unacceptable Limits on the Discretion of Sentencers", (1992) 101 *Yale L.J.* 1681; and the essay by Doob in Clarkson and Morgan (above n. 12).
18. M. Tonry, *Sentencing Matters* (1996), ch. 5, from which all quotations in this paragraph are taken.

19. For greater detail, see M. Tonry, *Sentencing Reform Impacts* (National Institute of Justice, 1987).

20. For a careful study, see R. Hood and S. Shute, "Protecting the Public: Automatic Life Sentences, Parole and High Risk Offenders" [1996] Crim.L.R. 788.

21. Council of Europe, Recommendation No. R (92) 17, *Consistency of Sentencing* (Strasbourg, 1993).

22. e.g. the Sentencing Act 1991 in Victoria, Australia, discussed in A. Freiberg's essay in Clarkson and Morgan (eds.), *The Politics of Sentencing Reform* (1995), at p. 62.

5.3

The Swedish Sentencing Law

5.3(a) The Principles Underlying the New Law

ANDREW VON HIRSCH

[This first extract describes the principles underlying the Swedish reforms, and was written at the time when they were proposed. The actual law as enacted in 1988, which differs little from the proposals, is set out and explained in Selection 5.3(b)—eds.]

The Rise of Swedish "Neoclassicism"

In the decades after the Second World War, Sweden became internationally noted for its interest in penal rehabilitation. Actually, it did not go so far as foreigners imagined: the idea of a graded tariff of penalties retained considerable influence. Indeterminate sentences were used only for special offender categories, such as youthful offenders, and habitual criminals. The Swedish Penal Code did not have much to say on choice of sentence for offenders outside these narrow categories. It mentioned rehabilitation and general prevention in broad terms, but provided scant advice on how those aims should be implemented by the courts.

During the 1970s and 1980s, Sweden witnessed growing disenchantment with its law and conceptions of sentencing. The Penal Code, it was felt, gave insufficient guidance for choosing the sanction. It began to be recognized that only limited capacity exists to fashion sentences for rehabilitative effect. Questions were raised about the fairness of basing sanctions on supposed responsiveness to treatment or on likelihood of future offending. There was a strong revival of interest in the idea of proportionality—of

From Andrew von Hirsch, "Guiding Principles for Sentencing: The Proposed Swedish Law", (1987) *Criminal Law Review* 746, with some textual changes. Excerpted and reprinted by permission.

punishments that fairly comport with the seriousness of the defendant's criminal conduct.

The new thinking received considerable stimulus with the publication in 1977 of *A New Penal System: Ideas and Proposals*.[1] This report, written for the Swedish National Council on Crime Prevention by a working group of judges and penologists, attracted widespread debate and comment. The report emphasized ideas of structuring sentencing discretion and proportionate sanctions. Similar ideas—sometimes referred to as "neoclassical"—were echoed in an influential essay collection that appeared three years later. Such ideas continued to surface in the Swedish literature, affected in part by Finnish writings and by English-language writings on "just deserts".

Writing the Proposed Law

The Swedish neoclassicists' first success was in their campaign against the indeterminate sentence. We have, they asserted, neither the capacity to identify persons who are long-term risks nor the ability to treat such persons, that these measures assumed. Above all, they argued, indeterminacy was unfair, in its potential disregard of the seriousness of the offender's conduct in deciding whether and how long to confine. Indeterminate confinement for youths was abolished in 1979, and "internment" for adults eliminated in 1981.

The next step was to address the Penal Code's general provisions on sentencing. In 1979, the Swedish minister of justice appointed a study commission, the Committee on Imprisonment (*Fängelsestraffkommittén*) to examine the matter. The Committee issued its report, *Sanctions for Crimes*, six years later, in the spring of 1986. The report, among other things, recommended a lowering of the statutory maxima and minima for many crimes, an expansion of the system of unit fines, and changes in the rules on parole release. Its most notable proposal, however, concerned the principles governing the choice of sentence. The Committee put forward two wholly new draft chapters of the Penal Code, dealing with the subject. The chapters emphasize notions of proportionality in sentencing.

As is customary with study commissions in Sweden, the Committee circulated its proposals to a wide group of scholars, judges, prosecutors, lawyers, correctional administrators, union officials, and other interested parties. The provisions on choice of sentence received generally favourable comment—and early in 1987 the Ministry of Justice, after reviewing the responses, tentatively decided to support those proposals. Ministry

242 Structuring Sentencing Discretion

support means that the proposed new chapters—after some technical amendments to reflect comments received—will became a government bill, with reasonably good chances for passage. [In fact they were enacted in 1988 and came into force in 1989: the key provisions are set out in Selection 5.3(b), which follows—eds.]

How Much Guidance?

The previous provisions of the Swedish Penal Code, as I mentioned, provided little guidance to sentencing judges. The so-called penalty scales (that is, the ranges between the statutory maxima and minima) were fairly wide, especially for the more serious crimes—albeit not as wide as they have been in the USA. The Penal Code provided that sentences should (1) promote general obedience to law and (2) foster the defendant's rehabilitation. It is far from clear, however, how the courts are to accomplish these potentially conflicting aims—especially given the paucity of effective treatments and the tenuous connection between general law-abidingness and the sentence in any particular case. The Code failed to suggest what features of the offender or his offence should ordinarily be given emphasis. And it left important issues unaddressed—especially, the issue of proportionality between the gravity of crimes and the severity of punishments. Guidance was thought necessary, therefore, to supply a coherent policy for sentencing: to help choose which penal aim should predominate, and thereby to help decide what features of the offender or his offence should be given most weight.

How much guidance should there be, and who should supply it? The Imprisonment Committee considered various solutions. At one extreme was the traditional English approach—of leaving the task of guidance to the appellate courts, without substantial assistance provided by statute or regulation. At the other was Minnesota's approach of a numerical sentencing grid that prescribes specific terms or narrow ranges as the normally recommended sentences. The Committee adopted an intermediate solution: the legislation should provide general principles but no numbers. The courts are then to apply those principles in deciding the quantum of sentence.

The Swedish Imprisonment Committee's proposals on choice of sentence consist, therefore of *principles*. The primary factors to be considered in deciding the sentence are set forth, not the actual sentencing outcomes. The proposed statute thus provides that the seriousness of the crime should be given principal emphasis, directs how seriousness ("penal value") should be judged, and gives general directives on the use of imprisonment and lesser sanctions. The numbers—the actual quanta of sentences—are to be evolved later by the courts. This is designed to permit the statute to focus on what is most important: the *policy*. The Imprisonment Committee's proposals offer a general policy: since the seriousness of the crime should count most, lesser offenders with long criminal records ordinarily should not receive the severe sanction of imprisonment. Such a general statute need not specifically address the extraordinary cases: what should happen if the offender's criminal record is extremely long—for instance, the case of the person convicted of a routine theft for the twentieth time. The courts would deal with such extraordinary cases, bearing the statute's general principles in mind. The drafters did not need to distort the general principles to supply a politically "acceptable" solution for the special cases.

Rationale

The proposed statute—as the Imprisonment Committee's report makes clear—rests on the idea of proportionality: that the offender's punishment should be fairly proportionate in its severity with the seriousness of the criminal conduct for which he stands convicted.

Why should punishments comport with the gravity of crimes? As I have addressed the question elsewhere (see Selection 4.4 above), let me just summarize. The idea of proportionate punishments presupposes no deep "metaphysical" notions of requital for evil or of guilt and atonement. There is, instead, a simpler explanation. Punishment is a *condemnatory* institution. The difference between a criminal and a civil sanction lies, generally, in the fact that the former levies censure on the actor. Penalties should, in fairness, be allocated consistently with their blaming implications.

Swedish neoclassicists tended also to feel that proportionality in punishment might serve general preventive aims. American and some English general preventionists have focused on deterrence, that is, the intimidating effect of punishment—a notion which may offer little support for principles of commensurability and desert. Scandinavian neoclassicists have taken a different tack: their discussion of general prevention focused on punishment's "moral" and "educational" effects in reinforcing people's inhibitions against criminal behaviour. People's sense of moral self-restraint, the authors of *A New Penal System* argued, might well be enhanced if they are treated as responsible for their conduct, and are sanctioned in a proportionate manner that reflects an ordinary persons sense of justice.

Penal Value

How, then, should proportionate sentences be determined? The proposal's central concept is that of a crime's penal value, and the draft begins with a general definition: "The penal value *(straffvärde)* of a crime is determined by its seriousness". To determine a crime's seriousness, the statute goes on to state, special regard should be given to (1) the harmfulness of the conduct and (2) the personal culpability of the actor. This definition—of seriousness in terms of the conduct's harm and culpability—is standard in the recent literature on desert.

Harm

That harm is an important element in a crime's seriousness should be obvious. Murder is more serious than assault because the harm characteristic of such conduct is greater: death instead of injury or attempted injury. Harm has always been important in determining the statutory penalty scales—which is why the legal maximum and minimum for murder are so much higher than those for assault. What the proposed law would do is to direct the judge to give more careful consideration to the conduct's harmfulness *within* the applicable scale: that is, to try to distinguish among types of assaults in terms of the degree of actual or potential injuriousness. Giving harm this central role should stimulate the development of more sophisticated doctrines on how to assess harm. (An attempt to develop a fuller theory for grading harm is to be found in Selection 4.6 above.)

Culpability

It is a peculiarity of the Swedish language that the word "culpability" does not exist. Hence the drafters had to resort to the more old-fashioned term "guilt". While the word "guilt" may for some readers evoke theological connotations, those are *not* intended. When the draft speaks of "the offender's guilt manifested in the conduct", it is *not* referring to an elusive evil state in the criminal's soul which the conduct reflects. The draft is referring, instead, to what in English would be denoted by the more neutral word culpability: the degree of intent, recklessness, or negligence involved, the presence of partial excuses, and so forth.

Criteria for Choice of Sanctions

The proposal sets forth, for the first time in Swedish law, criteria for the use of imprisonment. These criteria indicate when imprisonment ordinarily is to be imposed, in preference to the lesser sanctions of probation or conditional sentence. The criteria—when read together with the draft's other provisions—prescribe imprisonment in two main kinds of cases. The first is where the crime of conviction is serious: in the words of the draft, where it has "considerable penal value". The courts will have to assess which crimes thus qualify as serious, but crimes of violence such as armed robbery would be included, as would major economic offences. Those convicted of such crimes could expect to be imprisoned, unless they were able to establish mitigating circumstances indicating reduced culpability for the crime. The fact that the defendant was a first offender would *not* justify withholding imprisonment. The rationale is plain enough. If punishment is to reflect the gravity of the conduct, then the system's most severe type of sanction, imprisonment, becomes appropriate for the worst conduct.

The second type of case where imprisonment would be invoked concerns the criminal record. The Committee's proposals generally attempt to restrict the role of the prior record: serious offenders would be confined even if not previously convicted, and lesser offenders would be given non-custodial sanctions even if recidivists. However, the prior record would continue to play a role with respect to offences in the middle range of seriousness, such as, perhaps, burglary. Offenders convicted of such crimes would ordinarily be imprisoned only after having accumulated a significant criminal record.

The draft contains parallel provisions on the use of non-custodial penalties. The fine would continue to be the sanction most extensively utilized. It would be the sanction of choice for crimes of low penal value. It would also be so for crimes of intermediate penal value except where the defendant's prior criminal record was extensive. The more substantial fines would be unit fines, scaled according to the offender's income (see also Selections 6.2 and 6.4 below).

Between the fine, below, and actual imprisonment, above, would be the two other alternatives—conditional sentence and probation. To ensure that these sanctions are more onerous than a fine alone, they could be supplemented by monetary penalties.

Supplementary Principles

A few other provisions of the proposed statute are worth noting:

1. The draft contains a list of aggravating and mitigating circumstances, as noted already. These are generally desert-related—concerning increased or decreased harm or culpability of the conduct.
2. The draft calls also for reduced sanctions when special circumstances make the penalty uncharacteristically onerous. Ill health or advanced age are included. So, more controversially, are situations where specially adverse employment consequences are involved. The rationale still is one of proportionality—these questions bear (albeit indirectly) on the severity of the sanction. The employment provision may present problems of implementation, however, since punishment can so readily have employment consequences.
3. The draft authorizes deterrent penalties (in excess of what the conduct's penal value would indicate) for certain crimes, such as drinking and driving. This authorization, however, is restricted to conduct which the Swedish Parliament has found (a) to have unusually harmful consequences and (b) to be more than usually amenable to deterrence. The imposition of such sanctions is treated as a departure from the normal standards, for which a special burden of justification must be met.[2]

These supplemental principles would permit the court to address, in sophisticated fashion, a variety of issues that have long been of concern to courts in other countries. Only now, the applicable principles would be spelled out, and would reflect a consistent set of purposes. Mitigation of sentence, for example, would no longer have to be treated ad hoc. Instead, the courts would have statutory guidance in developing coherent doctrines of extenuation.[3]

Notes

1. Brottsförebyggande Rådet, *Nytt Straffsystem: Ideer och Förslag* (1977). For english summary, National Swedish Council for Crime Prevention: *A New Penal System: Ideas and Proposals* (1978).
2. For discussion of such hybrid systems, see Selection 4.4 above.
3. For discussion of the implementation of the statute since enactment, and for

further detail on the law itself, see Nils Jareborg, "The Swedish Sentencing System", in C. M. V. Clarkson and R. Morgan, *The Politics of Sentencing Reform* (Oxford: Clarendon, 1995).

5.3(b) The Details of the New Law

ANDREW VON HIRSCH AND NILS JAREBORG

The proposed Swedish law, with certain changes, was enacted in June 1988, to take effect in the following year. The statute consists of two main parts. Chapter 29 addresses "punishments". In Swedish legal tradition, only two sanctions are termed "punishments": fines and imprisonment. Where an offender qualifies for a fine, only the provisions of this chapter apply. If the case is somewhat more serious and a fine alone is not appropriate, then the reader must turn also to the next chapter, chapter 30. This chapter addresses the choice between (1) actual imprisonment and (2) substitutes for imprisonment—viz., conditional sentence or probation.

The statute thus creates three graded levels of sanction. The lower level is the fine—which includes unit fines levied as a proportion of income (see also Selection 6.2 below). The next level is conditional sentence or probation—which may be supplemented by monetary penalties. The highest level is incarceration in a penal institution.

The distinctions are significant, because the statute becomes confusing when they are overlooked. There are, for example *two* provisions governing prior criminal record. Chapter 29, § 4, addresses how prior record affects the choice between fines and imprisonment and how it affects the amount of fines or imprisonment. Chapter 30, § 4, governs how prior record affects the choice between probation or conditional sentence and actual imprisonment.

Swedish legal tradition permits (indeed, requires) the courts to consult legislative history in interpreting a statute. The statute, therefore, needs to be read in the light of the report of the Committee on Imprisonment, and of the Ministry of Justice's report accompanying submission of the bill. Those texts clarify certain language that may appear ambiguous on the statute's face:

From Andrew von Hirsch and Nils Jareborg, "Sweden's Sentencing Statute Enacted", (1989) *Criminal Law Review* 275, with some textual changes. Excerpted and reprinted by permission.

1. *Reasons for Imprisonment* (Chap. 30, § 4). This section addresses the choice between imprisonment and its substitute sanctions, probation and conditional sanction. It has applicability, therefore, only to the higher-ranking offences—for which fines would not be the sanction of choice. For these crimes, according to the section's second paragraph, imprisonment may be invoked in three kinds of situations. The first is where the crime has a high penal value—that is, is quite serious—irrespective of whether the offender has a record. The second is where the penal value (seriousness) is of the upper-middle range (that is, high enough to preclude a fine alone) and the person has a significant criminal record. The third (referred to by the "nature of the criminality" clause) is a restricted authorization for deterrent penalties for certain crimes—an important instance being drinking and driving.

2. *Predicted Risk* (chap. 30, § 7). The statute generally rules out predictive sentencing: proportionality is sacrificed when those defendants who seem good risks are given substantially less punishment than equally culpable offenders who seem bad risks. The objection diminishes, however, when prediction is used to change the character of the penalty but not its severity by much. This provision thus allows the sentencing judge, when choosing between a conditional sentence and probation, to opt for conditional sentence—if the offender appears unlikely to offend again. Probation with its supervision of the offender, may be unnecessary for low-risk offenders—and is not much more severe than a conditional sentence. However, this provision is *not* intended to permit the court to substitute conditional sentence for imprisonment on predictive grounds, as those sanctions differ so greatly in their severity.

Changes in the Final Version of the Law

The law, as proposed by the Ministry of Justice and enacted by the Swedish Parliament, contains certain changes from the recommendations of the Committee on Imprisonment (described in Selection 5.3(a) above). However, those changes are of limited scope.

1. *Definition of "Penal Value"* (chap. 29, § 1). The seriousness of a crime depends on the harmfulness (or risk of harm) of the conduct and the culpability of the actor. The Swedish language lacks the term "culpability", so the Committee on Imprisonment used the old-fashion term "guilt". That term's connotations evoked objections, so the law has substituted, "What the accused realized or should have realized . . . and the intentions and motives of the accused". However, no substantive change is intended,

and the idea remains what is denoted in English by "culpability".

2. *Prior Record* (chap. 29, § 4). The Committee on Imprisonment proposed narrow restrictions on considering the criminal record. For upper-middle level crimes, as noted, a criminal record would be grounds for invoking actual imprisonment, instead of conditional sentence or probation. It would also affect the severity of fines. However, the record could not be used to affect the duration of imprisonment. The Ministry's proposals, and the statute as enacted, have relaxed this latter restriction, so that the record could affect the duration of imprisonment to a limited degree.

3. *Rehabilitation* (chap. 30, § 9). The Committee on Imprisonment's draft authorized reduction of sentence in situations where "through the offender's own efforts, a considerable improvement has occurred in his personal and social situation that bears on his criminality". The intention, apparently, was to qualify the statute's general emphasis on proportionality, in order to permit treatment-based sentences in the most plausible and sympathetic-seeking kind of case, viz., where the change was wrought by efforts of the offender himself or herself. The enacted version eliminates the reference to the offender's own efforts. The legislative history, however, makes clear that any departures from the statute's proportionality requirements on rehabilitative grounds should be quite sparingly invoked.

The Statute

The text of the statute is as follows:

"Chapter 1   *On Crimes and Sanctions* . . .

§ 3   In this code, sanctions for crime are the punishments of fine and imprisonment, as well as conditional sentence, probation, and commitment to special care . . .

§ 5   Imprisonment is to be regarded as a more severe punishment than a fine.
   The relation between imprisonment and conditional sentence and probation is regulated in chapter 30, § 1.

§ 6   No one may be sentenced to a sanction for a crime he committed before he has reached fifteen years of age . . .

Chapter 29   *On the Measurement of Punishment and Remission of Sanctions*

§ 1   The punishment shall be imposed within the statutory limits according to the penal value of the crime or crimes, and the interest of uniformity in sentencing shall be taken into consideration.
   The penal value is determined with special regard to the harm, offence, or risk

which the conduct involved, what the accused realized or should have realized about it, and the intentions and motives of the accused.

§ 2   Apart from circumstances specific to particular types of crime, the following circumstances, especially, shall be deemed to enhance the penal value:

1. whether the accused intended that the criminal conduct should have considerably worse consequences than it in fact had,
2. whether the accused has shown a special degree of indifference to the conduct's adverse consequences,
3. whether the accused made use of the victim's vulnerable position, or his other special difficulties in protecting himself,
4. whether the accused grossly abused his rank or position or grossly abused a special trust.
5. whether the accused induced another person to participate in the deed through force, deceit, or abuse of the latter's youthfulness, lack of understanding, or dependent position, or
6. whether the criminal conduct was part of a criminal activity that was especially carefully planned, or that was executed on an especially large scale and in which the accused played an important role.

§ 3   Apart from what is elsewhere specifically prescribed, the following circumstances, especially, shall be deemed to diminish the penal value:

1. whether the crime was elicited by another's grossly offensive behaviour,
2. whether the accused, because of mental abnormality or strong emotional inducement or other cause, had a reduced capacity to control his behaviour,
3. whether the accused's conduct was connected with his manifest lack of development, experience, or capacity for judgement, or
4. whether strong human compassion led to the crime.

The court may sentence below the statutory minimum when the penal value obviously calls for it.

§ 4   Apart from the penal value, the court shall, in measuring the punishment, to a reasonable extent take the accused's previous criminality into account, but only if this has not been appropriately done in the choice of sanction (see chap. 30, § 4) or revocation of parole (see chap. 34, § 4). In such cases, the extent of the previous criminality and the time that has passed between the crimes shall be especially considered, as well as whether the previous and the new criminality is similar, or whether the criminality in both cases is especially serious.

§ 5   In determining the punishment, the court shall to a reasonable extent, apart from the penal value, consider

1. whether the accused as a consequence of the crime has suffered serious bodily harm,
2. whether the accused according to his ability has tried to prevent, or repair, or mitigate the harmful consequences of the crime.

3. whether the accused voluntarily gave himself up,
4. whether the accused is, to his detriment, expelled from the country in consequence of the crime,
5. whether the accused as a consequence of the crime has experienced or is likely to experience discharge from employment or other disability or extraordinary difficulty in the performance of his work or trade,
6. whether a punishment imposed according to the crime's penal value would affect the accused unreasonably severely, due to advanced age or bad health,
7. whether, considering the nature of the crime, an unusually long time has elapsed since the commission of the crime, or
8. whether there are other circumstances that call for a lesser punishment than the penal value indicates.

If, in such cases, special reasons so indicate, the punishment may be reduced below the statutory minimum.

§ 6   The punishment is to be remitted entirely when, with regard to circumstances of the kind mentioned in § 5, imposition of a sanction is manifestly unreasonable.

§ 7   If someone has committed a crime before the age of 21, his youth shall be considered separately in the determination of the punishment, and the statutory minimum may be disregarded.

Life imprisonment is never to be imposed in such cases.

Chapter 30   *On the Choice of Sanctions*

§ 1   In choosing sanctions, imprisonment is considered as more severe than conditional sentence and probation.

Provisions on the use of commitment to special care are set forth in another chapter.

§ 2   Unless otherwise provided, no one is to receive more than one sanction for the same crime.

§ 3   Unless otherwise provided, someone convicted of more than one crime is to be given one sanction.

If there are special reasons, however, the court may combine a fine for some criminal conduct with another sanction for other conduct, or combine imprisonment for some conduct with conditional sentence or probation for other conduct.

§ 4   In choosing the sanction, the court shall especially pay need to circumstances that suggest a less severe sanction than imprisonment. In so doing, the court shall consider circumstances referred to in chapter 29, § 5.

As a reason for imprisonment the court may consider, besides the penal value and the nature of the criminality, the accused's previous criminality.

§ 5   For a crime committed by someone before the age of 18, imprisonment may be imposed only if there are extraordinary reasons.

For a crime committed by someone between the age of 18 and the age of 21, imprisonment may be imposed only if there are, with respect to the penal value of the crime or other grounds, special reasons.

§ 6   For a crime committed by someone under the influence of mental disease, mental deficiency, or other mental abnormality of such a substantial nature as to be comparable to mental disease, the court may only impose commitment to special care, a fine, or probation.

If no such commitment or sanction should be imposed, the accused shall be free from sanction.

§ 7   In choosing sanction, the court shall consider, as a reason for conditional sentence, whether there is no special reason to fear that the accused will relapse in criminal conduct.

§ 8   Conditional sentence shall be combined with day fines, unless a fine would be unduly harsh, considering the other consequences of the crime, or there are other special reasons that militate against imposition of a fine.

§ 9   In choosing sanction, the court shall consider, as a reason for probation, whether there is reason to suppose that such sanction can contribute to the accused's not committing crimes in the future.

As special reasons for probation the court may consider.

1.   whether a considerable improvement has occurred in the accused's personal or social situation that bears upon his criminality,
2.   whether the accused is being treated for abuse or other condition that bears upon his criminality, or
3.   whether abuse of addictive substances, or other special condition that calls for care or other treatment, to a considerable degree explains the criminal conduct and the accused has declared himself willing to undergo adequate treatment, in accordance with an individual plan that can be arranged in connection with the execution of the sentence.

§ 10   In judging whether probation should be combined with day fines, the court shall consider whether this is called for with regard to the penal value or nature of the criminal conduct or the accused's previous criminality.

§ 11   Probation may be combined with imprisonment only if it is unavoidably called for, with regard to the penal value of the criminal conduct or the accused's previous criminality . . .

Chapter 34   *Certain Provisions concerning Concurrence of Crimes and Change of Sanction*

§ 4   . . . In judging whether parole should be revoked and in deciding on duration of reconfinement on revocation, it shall be considered whether the previous criminality and the new criminality are similar, whether the criminality in both cases is serious, and whether the new criminality is more or less serious than the previous criminality. In addition, the time that has passed between the crimes shall be considered.

Suggestions for Further Reading

1. Structuring Sentencing Decisions

Frankel, M., *Criminal Sentences: Law without Order* (1972); A. von Hirsch, *Doing Justice* (1976), ch. 12; Twentieth Century Fund, Task Force on Criminal Sentencing, *Fair and Certain Punishment* (1976); Gottfredson, D. M., Wilkins, L T., and Hoffman, P. B., *Guidelines for Parole and Sentencing* (1978); Forst, R. L. (ed.), *Sentencing Reform: Experiments in Reducing Disparity* (1982); Blumstein, A., *et al.*, *Research on Sentencing: The Search for Reform* (1983); Ashworth, A., "Techniques of Guidance on Sentencing", (1984) *Criminal Law Review* 519; Martin, S. E., "Interests and Politics in Sentencing Reform: The Development of Sentencing Guidelines in Minnesota and Pennsylvania", (1984) 29 *Villanova Law Review* 21; Shane-Dubow, S., Brown, A. P., and Olsen, E., *Sentencing Reform in the United States: History, Content, and Effects* (1985); von Hirsch, A., "Principles for Choosing Sanctions: Sweden's Proposed Sentencing Statute", (1987) 13 *New England Journal of Civil and Criminal Confinement* 171; Pease, K. G., and Wasik, M. (eds.), *Sentencing Reform: Guidance or Guidelines?* (1987); Tonry, M., *Sentencing Reform Impacts* (1987); von Hirsch, A., Knapp, K., and Tonry, M., *The Sentencing Commission and Its Guidelines* (1987); Robinson, P., "A Sentencing System for the 21st Century?" (1987) 66 *Texas Law Review* 1; Parent, D., *Structuring Criminal Sentences: The Evolution of Minnesota's Sentencing Guidelines* (1988); Council of Europe, *Disparities in Sentencing: Causes and Solutions* (1989); Lovegrove, A., *Judicial Decision-Making, Sentencing Policy, and Numerical Guidance* (1989); von Hirsch, "Federal Sentencing Guidelines: Do They Provide Principled Guidance?", (1989) 27 *American Criminal Law Review* 367; Nagel, I., "Structuring Sentencing Discretion: The New Federal Sentencing Guidelines", (1990) 80 *Journal of Criminal Law and Criminology* 883; Bogan, K., "Constructing Felony Sentencing Guidelines in an Already Crowded State", (1990) 36 *Crime and Delinquency* 467; von Hirsch, "The Politics of Just Deserts", (1990) 32 *Canadian Journal of Criminology* 397; Wasik, M., and von Hirsch, A., "Statutory Sentencing Principles: The 1990 White Paper", (1990) 54 *Modern Law Review* 508; Tonry, "The Politics and Processes of Sentencing Commissions", (1991) 37 *Crime and Delinquency* 307; Wasik, M., and Taylor, R. D., *Blackstone's Guide to the Criminal Justice Acts 1991–93* (1993); Alschuler, A., "The Failure of Sentencing Guidelines: A Plea for Less Aggregation", (1991) 58 *University of Chicago Latv Review* 901; Frase, R. S., "Sentencing Reform in Minnesota: Ten Years After", (1991) 75 *Minnesota Law Review* 727; Lappi-Seppala, T., "Penal Policy and Sentencing Theory in Finland", (1992) 5 *Canadian Journal of Law and Jurisprudence* 95; Freed, D. J., "Sentencing in the Wake of the Guidelines: Unacceptable Limits on the Discretion of Sentencers", (1992) 102 *Yale Law Journal* 1681.

Munro, C., and Wasik, M. (eds.) *Sentencing, Judicial Discretion and Training* (1992); Wasik, M., "Sentencing: a Fresh Look at Aims and Objectives", in Stockdale, E., and Casale, S. (eds.), *Criminal Justice under Stress* (1992); Duff, R. A., Marshall, S. E., Dobash R. E., and Dobash, R. P. (eds.), *Penal Theory and Practice* (1994); Ashworth, A., *Sentencing and Criminal Justice*, 2nd edn. (1995); Clarkson, C., and Morgan, R. (eds.), *The Politics of Sentencing Reform* (1995); Tonry, M., *Sentencing Matters* (1996); Tonry, M. (ed.), *Sentencing Reform in Overcrowded Times* (1997); Robinson, P. H., and contributors, (1997) 91 *Northwestern University Law Review* 1231, special issue on the Federal Sentencing Guidelines.

2. Official Reports

United States Sentencing Commission, *Sentencing Guidelines and Policy Statements* (1987); Canadian Sentencing Commission, *Sentencing Reform: A Canadian Approach* (1987); Report of the Standing Committee on Justice and Solicitor General on Its Review of Sentencing, Conditional Release, and Related Aspects of Corrections, *Taking Responsibility* (Canada, 1988); Victoria Sentencing Committee, *Report* (1988); Law Reform Commission of Australia, *Sentencing* (1988); Home Office, *Crime, Justice, and Protecting the Public* (England and Wales, 1990); Government of Canada, *Directions for Reform* (1990); Council of Europe, *Consistency of Sentencing* (Recommendation No. R(92) 17, Strasbourg, 1993); Home Office, *Protecting the Public: the Government's Strategy on Crime in England and Wales* (1996).

6

Community Punishments

Sentencing options, in English-speaking Western countries, traditionally were few. This was particularly true in the USA, where the offender was either sent to prison or jail, or else was placed on probation—usually as part of a large caseload, with perfunctory supervision. Such extremes are ill-suited for crimes of the middle range of gravity, where incarceration seems unduly harsh and probation scarcely punitive enough.

Dissatisfaction with this state of affairs (and with rising rates of imprisonment and their associated costs) has fuelled interest in intermediate sanctions—that is, non-custodial penalties having an intermediate degree of punitive bite. Monetary penalties (particularly, unit or "day" fines measured by income), community service, intensive probation supervision, required attendance at day-reporting centres, and home detention, are all being or have been tried, especially in the period since the mid-1980s. The present chapter examines such sanctions.

Initially, it was believed that the new options needed merely to be made available to the courts. The judge who invoked imprisonment because he or she was dissatisfied with the alternative of probation or a small fine would gladly resort to sanctions of intermediate onerousness if authorized to do so. This strategy proved illusory—for reasons examined by James Austin and Barry Krisberg in Selection 6.1. It is not only the absence of other options that creates the tendency to prefer imprisonment, they point out, but also political and ideological pressures within the criminal justice system. Reducing the use of imprisonment will necessitate a variety of legal and administrative measures that restrict the permitted use of the prison sanction and require intermediate non-custodial sanctions to be employed instead. Such measures may encounter considerable resistance.

Non-custodial sanctions have often been spoken of as "alternatives" to incarceration. This perspective is misleading—as it implies that the only value of such sanctions' is as possible replacements of imprisonment. Intermediate sanctions should, instead, be thought of as sanctions in their own right, suited to offences in the middle range of gravity. As such, they would replace imprisonment where that is (inappropriately) being used to penalize such offences; and they would also replace traditional non-custodial measures (such as, in the USA, routine probation supervision) to the extent that the latter provides an insufficient sanction. An offender convicted of (say) car theft should receive not a prison term but, instead, a substantial intermediate penalty.

Devising a middle range of sanctions requires fashioning non-custodial penalties suitable to this purpose. Here, a particularly important measure is the fine. Financial penalties, in view of their quantitative nature, can readily be scaled to offence gravity. The problem, of course, has been that a given fine amount has differing punitive impacts on people having different incomes. To deal with this problem, a number of European countries—Germany and Sweden, for example—have been using the *unit fine* (or, in American parlance, "day fine"). This involves determining fines not in currency amounts, but rather in units related to the person's daily earnings. Two persons convicted of a lower-intermediate offence might be fined, say, 15 fine units—corresponding to 15 days' earnings less deductions for necessary living expenses. If their earnings are unequal, they will pay different amounts—but the intended effect is to equalize the punitive impact.

How a unit-fine system is constructed, and what its functions are, is sketched in Selection 6.2, by Judith Greene. Such a scheme should involve two major components. One (which most European unit fine systems possess) is a formula according to which a fine unit is translated (depending on the person's earnings) into actual currency amounts. The other component (which some European systems lack) is a set of guidelines (or other form of explicit policy guidance) that assists the court in determining how many fine units to impose—in view of the gravity of the offence, the criminal record, and any other relevant factors. Ms Greene explains how such guidance might be structured. A few American jurisdictions have now established such a scheme; England had a system of unit fines for a brief period in the early 1990s, but then abandoned it for reasons seeming to have more to do with politics than the merits (see discussion in that Selection).

The next selection, Selection 6.3, by Todd Clear and Patricia Hardyman, addresses another kind of non-custodial penalty—intensive supervision probation (ISP). The essay points out some of the hazards encountered when developing intermediate sanctions, and thus supplements Austin and Krisberg's warnings in Selection 6.1. To overcome judicial and public resistance, the sponsors of ISP in various American states have tried to make this measure as attractive and uncontroversial as possible. This search for "acceptability" has taken several forms:

(1) Eligibility criteria are restrictively drawn, to ensure the recruitment of tractable participants who would prompt little public anxiety. Those criteria require ISP participants to have modest crimes of conviction and brief criminal records or none at all.

(2) To dispel potential judicial objections, broad discretion is retained for judges to decide whether actually to sentence eligible defendants to ISP.

(3) To provide reassurance that ISP participants are not "getting off too easily", the routines of supervision are fairly stringent—including substantial punitive conditions (e.g. numerous hours of community service) and extensive risk controls (e.g. regular urine tests for drug use).

(4) For similar reasons, offenders who default on these requirements can be promptly removed from the programme and imprisoned.

The trouble with these four features, Clear and Hardyman point out, is that they tend to defeat the aims of the programme. Thus:

(1) the narrow eligibility criteria mean that offenders convicted of middle-level offences—that is, those who should participate—are largely excluded. The criteria mainly permit recruitment of lesser offenders.

(2) Leaving judges wide discretion aggravates this problem: only the "easy" (i.e. least serious) cases will tend to receive ISP.

(3) Tough supervision routines, when applied to the lesser offenders recruited in the programme, merely escalate the overall severity of the response.

(4) Easy resort to imprisonment for breach of programme conditions is particularly problematic. Programmes such as ISP monitor offenders' activities much more closely than did traditional probation. Closer monitoring means that technical violations are more frequently uncovered. If incarceration is frequently invoked as the sanction, the upshot may be that more defendants end in prison than would have, had the programme not existed at all.

How does one avoid the pitfalls which Clear and Hardyman describe? What is needed is clearer objectives that target intermediate sanctions to middle-level offenders, not lesser ones—and guidelines or other guidance methods that help ensure that this targeting is implemented. This, however, makes the political and institutional obstacles more formidable. It is easy to promote the new programmes for the most tractable offenders, whose crimes cause only minimal public anger or anxiety. It is harder to

secure implementation of non-custodial sanctions aimed at the more substantial crimes in the middle range: for example, at defendants whose
crimes are not violent but are still significant wrongs, such as burglary. It
is also harder to insist that such participants should not be imprisoned for
routine breaches of programme rules but only for quite substantial new
infractions. The warning of Austin and Krisberg in Selection 6.1 still
holds: securing a meaningful system of intermediate punishments may well
evoke considerable resistance.

Suppose, however, that such resistance could be overcome; that it were
feasible, in a given jurisdiction, to establish guidelines or other criteria for
the use of non-custodial sanctions. Then, the critical question becomes:
what should the *content* of these standards be? To what extent should the
seriousness of the crime determine which penalties should be used, and to
what extent should other factors count also? How much "interchangeability" among punishments should be permitted? Such questions are
addressed in the final two selections of this chapter.

The first of these two selections, Selection 6.4 by Martin Wasik and
Andrew von Hirsch, addresses the scaling of non-custodial sanctions
under a desert model. The article deals in systematic fashion with a number of key issues that need to be considered in developing a principled system—and thus may be of use even to those who do not subscribe to a
desert-oriented rationale. Some of the issues are as follows.

1.   *The role of rationale.*   A desert rationale, the article points out, permits extensive use of non-custodial penalties—namely, for all offences but
those of a fairly high degree of seriousness. It would call for non-custodial sanctions to be graded in severity according to the gravity of the criminal conduct—as the illustrative grids in the selection show. Intermediate
sanctions would specifically be targeted to crimes of middling or upper-
middling gravity. Changing the rationale, as the article points out at the
end, could alter the architecture of the scheme considerably.

2.   *Interchanges—desert constraints.*   The authors' scheme does permit interchange among penalties—but only where those penalties are of
roughly equivalent onerousness. This follows the desert-based requirement
(see Selection 4.4 above) that criminal conduct of equal seriousness should
be punished roughly equally. To the extent that this constraint is relaxed,
interchanges among sanctions of different punitive bite would become permissible.

3.   *Interchanges—other policy limits.*   Should desert requirements constitute the *only* constraint on substitution among penalties? Then (as the
"full substitution" model in Figure 2 of Selection 6.4 shows) there could
be very extensive interchangeability, even under a desert rationale. Indeed,

a whole smorgasbord of penalties, with extensive mixing, could be employed—so long as the net severity visited on the defendant achieves approximately the prescribed level. The authors point out various problems with such extensive substitutability—for example, that it makes comparisons among penalties difficult. They propose, instead, limited substitutability—wherein one type of penalty is the normally recommended penalty for a given band in the grid, and other sanctions (of comparable onerousness) are permitted only for special reasons. Mixing and matching—that is, imposing several diverse sanctions in a particular case—would also generally be ruled out.

4. *Breach sanctions.* As pointed out already, the greater intensity of intermediate penalties will cause technical violations by offenders to be uncovered more frequently. Unless limits are placed on the severity of the sanctions for such violations—and particularly, on the use of imprisonment as the breach sanction—the net result could be an *escalation* of severity. The authors discuss breach sanctions under a desert rationale, and propose that technical breaches ordinarily should call for only a modest increase in the severity of the response. On their view, imprisonment should be used as the breach sanction only in exceptional cases.

The Wasik-von Hirsch scheme is a complex one, and it does raise a number of issues. The central question, of course, has been addressed already in Chapter 4 above—the acceptability of the desert rationale. While the authors do make suggestions about how their model might be altered to accommodate more utilitarian conceptions, it is clearly conceived of in desert terms. The model also assumes an ability to make severity comparisons among different possible sanctions. While the living-standard approach (discussed in Selection 4.6 above) might help make such assessments, this may not sustain more than approximate comparisons. To be made practicable, the authors' approach may thus need to provide more accommodation for the uncertainties of rating and comparing crimes and penalties involved. Another issue is whether there might need to be some softening of the scheme's severity-equivalence requirements to allow treatment-oriented supervision to be substituted for the normally-prescribed unit fine or other applicable penalty—since it might often be the case that the normal penalty and the supervision are somewhat different in onerousness. Here, however, there is a conceptual framework available, and it is discussed in Selection 4.4 above: namely, to allow *limited* deviations from desert constraints. With such limited deviations, such substitutions might be easier. A final question is the workability of the authors' proposals on breach. They suggest that breach penalties should ordinarily involve only a single severity-step upward on the grid—

meaning that these will still be quite lenient if the original penalty was low on the scale. Would more rigorous sanctions be necessary as a practical matter? If so, how does one avoid the hazard of breach penalties becoming a source of increased use of imprisonment? Could the answer be to permit imprisonment as a back-up sanction of last resort, but to strictly limit its duration—say, to no more than a few days or weeks? But to what extent would such limitations be acceptable as a practical political matter? Devising fair and practicable breach penalties is a problem not only for this scheme, but for other efforts to promote non-custodial penalties.

The next selection, Selection 6.5, by Michael Tonry addresses the use of non-custodial sanctions under a different rationale, Norval Morris's "limiting retributivism" (see Selection 4.5 above). The principles Tonry puts forward derive from a 1990 work by Morris and himself.[1] There, these authors propose permitting extensive interchangeability among penalties. An offender convicted of a crime in the upper-intermediate range of seriousness, for example, might receive either a short prison term or else a non-custodial sanction such as a stint of home detention or intermittent confinement on evenings or weekends. Unlike in the Wasik-von Hirsch scheme, these punishments need not be of even roughly equivalent onerousness, as long as the differences in severity are not so great as to breach the desert limits of Morris's theory—i.e., so long as none of those penalties are disproportionately harsh or lenient relative to the gravity of the conduct involved.

How defensible Morris and Tonry's stance on interchangeability is depends, of course, on the underlying assumption—that desert supplies only outer limits on permissible punishments. The assumption—versus a more thoroughgoing desert rationale—has been debated already in Selections 4.4 and 4.5 above. The workability of their scheme depends also on their ability to delineate what the applicable desert limits are. There are at least two possibilities.

(1) The desert limits (while more permissive than under a full desert model) might still be significantly confining; that is, these limits would substantially shape (albeit not fully determine) the gradation of penalties. The guidelines might, for example, classify intermediate penalties into several bands according to their degree of punitiveness: say, into various gradations of "mild", "lower-intermediate", "upper-intermediate", and "onerous". Substitutions might be permitted *within* a given band (even if the penalties differ somewhat in punitive bite) but would be restricted among different bands. Thus a short stint in jail and a period of home detention might be interchangeable as both are fairly tough, albeit not

equally severe; but a prison term could *not* be interchanged with moderate financial penalties because the disparity in punitiveness would be too great. Such a view would set some meaningful limits on what interchanges are permissible and what are not.

(2) Alternatively, the desert limits could be much more permissive—and bar only *manifest* disproportion. Limits of this kind would serve mainly as a supplement to the statutory maxima and minima. Under such a view, almost any interchange would be permissible—as it largely is today in many jurisdictions.

Which view of desert limits, (1) or (2), is being espoused here? In his formulation of his punishment theory, Morris gives little guidance on what the width of the desert limits should be or how those widths should be determined.[2] However, at the end of Selection 6.5, Tonry makes some practical recommendations (derived from a 1997 publication of his[3]) which seem to opt for the first option—for a scheme in which desert constraints would significantly constrain the choice of sanctions. He thus recommends four—or preferably, six—severity bands (or in his terminology, "zones of discretion") for the guidelines, based on the seriousness of the offences involved. Substitutions among unequally-severe penalties may be made within a given band, but not outside it. Substantial desert-based limits would thus be placed on what interchanges would be permissible and what would not.

This is an important clarifying step; and it will enhance the workability of the scheme. Offence-seriousness will now provide a substantial degree of guidance in deciding the permissible range of intermediate punishments. But it also lessens the difference between this kind of approach and a desert-based one such as Wasik and von Hirsch's. Both approaches now would make offence seriousness an important criterion, and both would bar large disparities in severity for comparably serious criminal conduct. Their remaining difference concerns smaller severity-disparities: these would continue to be permissible under Tonry's approach, but barred by a full fledged desert scheme such as Wasik and von Hirsch's. Such lesser disparities might, however, be permissible under the "modified" desert model discussed also in Selection 4.4 above; in such a modified model, limited deviations from the proportionate sentence would be permissible.

This last possibility raises the question whether Tonry's four-to-six severity band scheme can best be rationalized by Morris's "limiting retributivism" or by such a "modified" desert model instead. Morris's view gives plenty of scope for inequalities in punishment, but the question is whether it gives too much scope—since it seems to give so little guidance on the width of the desert limits. A modified desert model, on the other hand, permits some inequalities in penalties—whilst still providing grounds for argument why large disparities in the punishment of comparably serious crimes would not be appropriate. What response might an adherent of Morris's view make to such a suggestion?[4]

Within the bands set by offence seriousness, Tonry suggests, interchanges among penalties would be determined not by a criterion of equivalent severity, but of equivalence *of function* instead: one penalty may be substituted for another when they both serve the same penological aim. The judge would also be called upon to specify the aim he seeks to achieve in setting the sentence in the particular case: to declare the purpose *at* sentencing. To decide whether two sentences are functionally equivalent, however, one needs to ascertain what those functions should be. How should one determine this? The guidelines might, Tonry suggests, contain certain presumptions indicating the purpose at sentence for different kinds of cases. But on what basis should the drafters of the standards decide what purposes at sentencing to authorize or encourage? An incapacitative aim might seem to be appropriate when the defendant represents a higher than normal risk, and a rehabilitative one when the offender seems in need of treatment and an effective treatment is at hand. But Tonry cites a number of illustrations in which the purposes at sentence are said to be "retributive and deterrent". How does one tell when deterrence should be a primary aim? And what of "retribution" as the primary function for a particular sentence? The latter notion seems particularly puzzling, since Tonry simultaneously asserts that retribution (i.e., desert) provides only limits and little or no guidance in setting the particular sentence within these limits.

It should be possible to develop other models for deciding the use of community penalties, besides the two set out in Selections 6.4 and 6.5. The aims of any such alternative model should be clearly specified, however. In the area of non-custodial penalties, principled sentencing means having principles which inform the system of guidance that is adopted.

A.v.H.

Notes

1. Norval Morris and Michael Tonry, *Between Prison and Probation: Intermediate Punishments in a Rational Sentencing System* (1990).

2. For a critique concerning the failure of Morris's theory to specify the nature of the desert limits, see Andrew von Hirsch, *Censure and Sanctions* (1993), 53–4, 65–6.

3. Michael Tonry, *Intermediate Sanctions in Sentencing Guidelines* (U.S. National Institute of Justice, 1997).

4. See, e.g., the discussion of the applicability of the two models in the Minnesota guidelines in Richard Frase, "Sentencing Principles in Theory and Practice", (1997) 22 *Crime and Justice: A Review of Research* 363. But for a different view from Frase's, see Andrew von Hirsch, "Sentencing Guidelines and Penal Aims in Minnesota", (1994) 13(1) *Criminal Justice Ethics* 39.

6.1

"Alternatives" to Incarceration: Substitutes or Supplements?

JAMES AUSTIN AND BARRY KRISBERG

The research literature on alternatives to incarceration suggests that their promise remains largely unmet. In each instance, the non-incarcerative options were transformed, serving criminal justice system values and goals other than reducing imprisonment. Sentencing alternatives, such as restitution and community service, are employed to enhance the increasingly criticized sanctions of probation and fines. There is little evidence that sentencing alternatives have substantially displaced incarceration. Similarly, post-incarceration release programmes often escalate the level of control over clients and have served primarily to control populations within prison systems. Increasing the availability of community facilities has not reduced populations in secure confinement . . .

An analysis of why these non-incarceration schemes have failed must confront the question of goals. In each attempted reform, significant criminal justice actors added other objectives to, displaced, or replaced the original goals. An even more troubling problem facing reform efforts is the inherent ambiguity in what constitutes successful alternatives to incarceration. Reviews of enabling legalisation as well as programme descriptions illustrate how multiple and often conflicting objectives characterized these reforms.[1] Harland notes that advocates of restitution often fail to anticipate conflicts with traditional criminal justice goals and procedures.[2] Sentencing occurs within a system dominated by the values of law enforcement, community protection, and punishment. Other values enter the sentencing process during stages of plea negotiation and presentence investigation. Most criminal justice personnel do not endorse the value of reducing incarceration. Quite the contrary, imprisonment itself is valued, and milder forms of punishment such as probation or diversion rest on the threat that incarceration may be applied if the offender fails to conform.

From James Austin and Barry Krisberg, "The Unmet Promise of Alternatives to Incarceration", (1982) 28 *Crime and Delinquency* 374. Copyright © 1982 by National Council on Crime and Delinquency. Reprinted by permission of Sage Publications, Inc.

Alternatives are employed to the extent that they fit the structure of power and values within specific criminal justice systems and the variety of goals pursued by actors within the system.

Generally, the values of police, judges, and prosecutors are predominant. In correction, the strongest influence is exercised by administrators of prison and jail systems, who control large budgets and often share law enforcement values. Probation and parole agencies exert less influence than do police, court, and correctional organizations; often they are subordinate parts of judicial or prison bureaucracies. Thus, alternatives as a means to reduce imprisonment are advocated by the less powerful divisions of the criminal justice system—or by private reform organizations with minimal political and economic influence, which must rely on the media and the presentation of "new knowledge" to promote decarceration policies and legislation. Within this milieu, alternatives are attractive to law enforcement, court, and prison officials as tools to supplement non-incarcerative sanctions (e.g., probation, fines, and parole). Public opinion opposing the use of socially defined "lenient" alternatives for serious offenders intensifies the system's reluctance to expand the use of alternatives except in crisis situations (e.g., following riots or federal court orders).

In the typical hierarchy of agency values and power within the criminal justice system, it is predictable that sentencing alternatives will be employed for minor offenders whose dispositions rarely produce strong conflict between agencies, or reflect a compromise between competing values. Alternatives tend to become integrated into plea bargaining rituals as part of the local scale of punishments assigned to various constellations of offences and offenders. The supplementing of probation and jail sentences by "alternatives" reflects a process of compromise between the values of punishment and rehabilitation. Since the rehabilitative ideology has little support from within the criminal justice system or among members of the public, the compromise position embodied by alternatives is likely to consist of the application of more restrictive conditions to minor offenders. Should the rehabilitative ideal gather greater strength in the future, alternatives might be applied to "tougher" cases. Exceptions to this pattern may occur when strong financial incentives such as federal grants or agency budget crises induce shifts in philosophy and practice. The dilemma of criminal justice reform involves restructuring policy at many complex decision points and persuading key decision-makers to choose more enlightened sanctioning strategies that sustain desired values.

Changing values and translating these new orientations into practice are difficult enterprises. Traditionally, proponents of non-incarcerative sanctions have made rational and moral arguments to various publics, including criminal justice personnel. Non-incarcerative sanctions are presented as a means of expanding the social control tools of the criminal justice system. Many observers now openly question the strategy of providing a broader range of social control mechanisms, instead proposing to shrink or regulate discretion exercised within the criminal justice system. Harland, for example, argues that community service should be given statutory authorization that specifies the kinds of offences and offenders appropriate.[3] Furthermore, he argues for legislation equating hours of community service with specific terms of incarceration. Legislation must make it clear that a key aim of community service is to reduce imprisonment. This view is echoed by Galaway, a 10-year veteran of restitution research, who argues that restitution will reduce incarceration only when it is recognized as the fair penalty for certain classes of offences.[4]

Yet, the promise of such alternatives will not be enhanced merely by legislative enactments. The history of mandatory, presumptive, and determinate sentencing schemes is replete with examples of how new forms of discretionary behaviour emerge to frustrate the law-maker's intent. This can be well understood from observing the role of prosecutors and law enforcement in creating sentencing policies. New efforts to implement non-incarcerative sanctions must examine and respond to the interests and ideology of the powerful segments of the criminal justice system.

This is not simply a matter of waiting for prevailing values to change. Values influence and are influenced by alteration in the ideology, power, and economic forces within the criminal justice system and society at large. Structural changes may precipitate the reordering of values to enable change in social conditions. For example, the pressures of bulging prisons and scarce public funds may force government officials to re-examine the value of imprisonment versus other forms of social control. Judicial orders mandating reduced prison and jail populations may provide incentives for the system to employ non-incarcerative sanctions for certain classes of offenders. Likewise, legislation forbidding prison administrators from incarcerating more than a specified number could help in expanding alternatives to incarceration by constricting the ability of criminal justice actors to employ imprisonment as punishment.[5] The significance of capping correctional capacity is in its redistribution of resources from the construction and maintenance of correction facilities to non-incarcerative sanctions. It may, moreover, be necessary to create independent public agencies charged with planning, implementing, and monitoring diverse sentencing alternatives that reduce the use of imprisonment.[6]

Explicit legislative delineation of alternatives, substantially greater resources, and more powerful organizational bases might go far in realizing the promise of alternatives to incarceration. To achieve any success in the political arena, the proponents of alternatives must have much better evidence to support their claims that (1) alternatives do not significantly increase risks to public safety, and (2) non-incarcerative sanctions are acceptable to the public, criminal justice practitioners, and victims. Furthermore, we must learn more about how the dynamic criminal justice nets support or impede rational reform efforts.

A radical shift in correctional policy toward the presumptive use of non-prison sanctions, together with fixing (or reducing) custodial capacity, deserves serious debate. One can anticipate intense resistance from actors with opposing ideologies, who stand to forfeit considerable power from such rearrangements. The prospects that change will emanate from within the criminal justice system seem dismal. We might more productively concentrate on forging a new political consensus in which the values of punishment and public safety are rationally balanced with fiscal limits and competing claims for public revenue. Although most elected officials are sympathetic to traditional criminal justice values, their concerns about the costs of punishment provide an opening for discussion.

Notes

1. James Austin, "Instead of Justice: Diversion" (Ph.D. diss., University of California at Davis, 1980); A. T. Harland, "Court-ordered Community Service in Criminal Law", *Buffalo Law Review* (Summer 1980), 426–86.
2. Alan T. Harland, "Goal Conflicts and Criminal Justice Innovation: A Case Study", *Justice System Journal* (Spring 1980), 291–8.
3. Harland, "Court-Ordered Community Service in Criminal Law", above n. 1.
4. Burt Galaway , "Restitution as an Integrative Punishment", in Randy Barnett and John Hagel (eds.), *Assessing the Criminal: Restitution, Retribution, and the Legal Process* (Cambridge, Mass.: Ballinger, 1977), 331–47.
5. National Council on Crime and Delinquency, *A New Correctional Policy for California: Developing Alternatives to Prison* (San Francisco: Research Centre West, 1980).
6. *Ibid.*

6.2

The Unit Fine: Monetary Sanctions Apportioned to Income

JUDITH GREENE

A number of European countries—Germany and Sweden, for example—make extensive use of monetary penalties. In Germany, the fine is used for most offenders convicted of property crimes, and for a substantial proportion of those convicted of assault.

A major reason why fines can be used so extensively in those jurisdictions is the device of the unit fine (or, as it is termed in the USA, the "day fine"). The most obvious drawback of the ordinary fine of a specified monetary amount is that its punitive bite varies with the resources of the offender. A $1,000 (or £1,000) fine is a devastating penalty to a poor defendant, but trivial to the millionaire. The unit fine addresses this problem by assessing the fine in income units: the offender is assessed the equivalent of so many days' work (or so many days' worth of disposable income), instead of so many dollars or pounds. The actual monetary amount per fine unit is then calculated on the basis of the offender's income.

Assessing unit fines involves two steps: (1) deciding how many fine units (that is, how many days' worth of income) should be assessed against a defendant; and (2) deciding the actual monetary amount involved per unit, given that defendant's earning power. European unit fine systems have guidelines for the second step: a fine unit consists of the estimated daily income, minus certain specified deductions (e.g., for child support). However, few of these countries have guidelines for step one: it is largely up to the judge to decide, within broad statutory limits, how many day fine units are to be imposed on a particular defendant.[1]

A pilot project[2] undertaken during the 1980s by the Vera Institute of Justice for the New York City Borough of Staten Island attempted to make good this latter deficiency. It did so by supplying benchmarks concerning the number of fine units appropriate for various types of offences. Misdemeanours, under these benchmarks, are classified in seriousness into

This essay is published here for the first time.

six "bands". The recommended number of fine units is graded according to the "band" involved—that is, according to the gravity-level of the offence. A modest downward adjustment in the number of day fine units is then authorized for defendants who lack a significant criminal record; and further adjustments are also permitted for aggravating and mitigating circumstances relating to the offence. The result is a scheme with a coherent (mainly desert-oriented) rationale, and with meaningful guidance provided regarding the number of fine units to assess. The scheme is not a full sentencing guideline scheme, however, in that it does not apply to felonies, and also in that the judge retains discretion on whether to invoke unit fines at all. Under a full-fledged sentencing guideline scheme, the guidelines would prescribe when the unit fine is the recommended penalty, as well as how many fine units are owed (see, e.g., Selection 6.4 below).

A system of unit fines results, of course, in offenders convicted of the same crime paying different amounts: the rich defendant pays more per unit than the defendant with only modest means. Is that a disparity? The theory of the unit fine is that it is not, but rather a way of *avoiding* disparity: the proportion of income taken from the two defendants is the same, making the punitive bite comparable. Yet the measure of punitiveness used—namely, units of income—is an objective and readily measurable one. Purely subjective differences in sensitivity to punishment would not be considered: the miserly defendant would be fined as many units for a given offence as the prodigal one, though payment might subjectively "hurt" more.

The unit fine is best suited for defendants with regular, measurable (and legal) income flow. Staten Island, where this experimental project was tried, generally has lower-middle- and working-class neighbourhoods, where most defendants are employed. The judge in Staten Island also retains discretion to choose a penalty other than a day fine, if the particular defendant is indigent. With a full system of guidelines, however, the solution is not so simple: where day fines are normally prescribed but the defendant is indigent, a sanction of comparable onerousness may need to be imposed (see Selection 6.4 below). The day fine system also requires an efficient system of collection. In Sweden, fines are collected by the agency that enforces tax liabilities and other debts owed to the state—and that agency has wide powers of attachment, garnishment, etc. Other jurisdictions, which lack such an agency, would have to develop alternative collection mechanisms.

The Staten Island pilot project did not become institutionalized as a regular programme, because the state legislature refused to raise the (rather low) statutory fine maxima to a monetary amount that would suffice for unit fines to be applied to more affluent defendants. However, analogous schemes have been put into operation in some other American jurisdictions.[3]

The Staten Island scheme makes use of numerical benchmarks to guide the number of fine units ordinarily to be imposed. An alternative, however, would be to utilize statutory guiding principles, providing these offer a reasonable degree of guidance. This is Sweden's approach. That country's 1989 sentencing reform law calls for proportionate sentences (see Selection 5.3 above), with unit fines to be used as the normally-applicable sentence for a wide band of intermediate-level offences. Based generally on the guidance provided by this statute, the courts have adopted the practice of imposing varying numbers of fine units depending on the seriousness of the offence involved.

Between 1991 and 1993, England and Wales had a unit fine system. This scheme was authorized by the Criminal Justice Act 1991, which also made proportionality the primary criterion for choice of sentence.[4] Unfortunately, the details of the programme were less carefully worked out than in Sweden. The Act, while endorsing proportionality in general terms, provided less guidance than its Swedish counterpart on how the appropriate sanction was to be ascertained. Procedures for implementing the unit-fine scheme also were not well designed—and included a provision that refusal by the defendant to inform the court of his earnings would result in the highest level of earnings being assumed for purposes of calculating the amount to be paid per fine unit. As a result, some ordinary persons who had committed rather minor offences were reported as having to pay large amounts, in consequence of their refusal to declare their earnings. Such deficiencies, the opposition of some influential popular newspapers, and the shift of English criminal justice politics in 1993 toward a "law and order" stance,[5] led to the repeal of the unit fine provisions in that year.[6] English judges may still take the defendant's earnings into consideration in setting the amount of a fine,[7] but it is unfortunate that the unit fine system was dropped instead of being remedied to remove its technical deficiencies.

In 1991, Superior Court Judges in Phoenix, Arizona began using a unit fine system. The "FARE Probation Program" in Phoenix uses a 14-level unit penalty scale (which ranks more than 250 criminal code offences by severity) to calculate the amount of a comprehensive monetary penalty "package" for use as an intermediate sanction for non-violent felony offenders.[8] The unit fine method is used to determine the *total* amount of a monetary sanction designed to encompass a range of financial orders authorized or mandated under Arizona laws: fines, probation service fees, restitution and victim compensation fund contributions, court costs, and various other assessments and fees commonly imposed on sentenced offenders. Judges are encouraged to use the FARE Probation order as an alternative to standard probation in felony cases where an offender does not appear to need either community supervision or specialized probation services (e.g. substance abuse treatment; literacy training) and where imposition and collection of an appropriately-scaled monetary penalty can serve as the sole sanction. FARE Probationers are released from any reporting obligations so long as they mail their agreed-upon instalment payments to the probation department until the required amount is paid in full.

An evaluation of the FARE Probation Program conducted by the RAND Corporation has produced evidence that the sanction is being used by judges as intended.[9] During the evaluation period only half of the court's judges were authorized to use the sanction. A matched comparison group of offenders was drawn from the sentencing dockets of non-participating judges. Both FARE Probationers and the control group were tracked for a period of one year after receiving their sentences. The data produced by this experiment demonstrates that the targeted sanction is reaching the intended population—offenders bound for standard probation supervision—and has not "widened the net" by drawing in those who receive lesser sanctions (summary probation or discharge).

While the average total monetary assessment was roughly the same for FARE probationers as for the comparison group ($1,015 compared with $1,186), their compliance with financial payment orders was much improved. Almost *all* FARE probationers made at least some payment (96 per cent, compared with 77 per cent for the comparison group) and the average amount paid within one year was markedly *higher* for FARE probations ($694) than for controls ($447). FARE Probationers were quicker to discharge their financial obligation—53 per cent had paid in full within one year of sentencing, compared with only 20 per cent of the controls. Recidivism rates were low for both groups (only 11 per cent of FARE probationers were rearrested within a year of sentencing; 17 per cent were rearrested among the control group), providing court officials with reassurance that use of unit-fine penalties has not diminished the effectiveness of the sentencing functions in this busy urban court jurisdiction.

Notes

1. In Sweden, however, the use of unit fines is guided by that country's system of statutory sentencing principles. See discussion of the Swedish approach later in this Selection.

2. The programme is described in Judith A. Green, "Structuring Criminal Fines: Making an 'Intermediate' Penalty More Useful and Equitable", (1988) 13 *Justice System Journal* 37, which was excerpted as Selection 6.3 in the 1st edition of this book. The description of unit fines in the present Selection has been drawn from the Introduction to Chapter 6 of the 1st edition.

3. See, e.g., the description of the Phoenix scheme later in this Selection.

4. See Selection 5.4 above, and for a fuller description, Andrew Ashworth, *Sentencing and Criminal Justice*, 2nd edn. (1992), ch. 10.

5. For "law and order" generally, see Chapter 9 below. For a thoughtful account of the change in character of criminal-justice politics in England in 1993, see Lord Windlesham, *Responses to Crime: Legislating with the Tide* (1996), ch. 1.

6. *Ibid.*

7. Criminal Justice Act 1991, s. 18.

8. Judith A. Greene, *The Maricopa County FARE Probation Experiment* (New York: Vera Institute of Justice, 1996) (unpublished).

9. Susan Turner and Joan Petersilia, *Day Fines in Four U.S. Jurisdictions* (Santa Monica Cal: RAND, 1996) (unpublished).

Intensive Supervision Probation: How and for Whom?

TODD R. CLEAR AND PATRICIA L. HARDYMAN

There have been two quite distinguishable intensive supervision move-ments in the last quarter century. The first, which occurred in the 1960s, has been characterized as the "search for the magic number" (Carter and Wilkins, 1984) because it was primarily a series of experimental projects designed to determine the optimal number of clients to be supervised in a single caseload. The second movement, which began in the mid-1980s and continues today full force, might be called a "response to crowded pris-ons" because most of these new programmes have resulted from alarm about crowding in U.S. prisons and jails. The difference in the nature of these two movements is significant because it helps to make understand-able the considerable contrast between the traditional meaning of inten-sive supervision programmes (ISPs) common to the 1960s and today's versions of the same general idea.

The impetus for the new ISP movement does not come from careful study of the literature on community corrections. It is instead a product of the serious problem of prison crowding in the 1980s. Without jail and prison crowding, it is hard to imagine that the current support for ISP would have materialized of its own accord. In most jurisdictions in the United States, courts are imposing levels of control or punishment for which the system simply lacks resources, and ISP is presented as an alter-native that occupies the crevice between available resources and demands for them. In short, overwhelming institutional crowding created an irre-sistible demand for alternatives to incarceration. But because of its extremely limited public credibility, probation was poorly equipped to meet the need. The solution to this dilemma was approached in part as a public relations problem: Corrections would bring about a version of

From Todd R. Clear and Patricia L. Hardyman, "The New Intensive Supervision Movement", (1990) 36 *Crime and Delinquency* 42. Copyright © 1990 by Sage Publications, Inc. Reprinted by permission.

"new, improved probation" that would be so richly endowed and tightly run that it could do what regular probation could not.

With a few exceptions, most of the new ISPs are quite brazen in their claims about the clients served. Partly as justification for the intensive methods employed, the client target group is referred to as the "serious", "dangerous", "recidivist", or "high-risk" offender. The image is created of a predatory group of offenders who must receive close supervision so as to keep the community from peril. These labels are often applied as broad generalizations about the persons who will be eligible for ISPs. It is important to clarify the use of these labels.

The term "high-risk" offender refers to a person whose characteristics, including the length and diversity of criminal record, indicate that he or she has a high probability of some future, serious law violation (Gottfredson and Gottfredson, 1986). This is normally established through the use of a statistical assessment instrument, but it can also be the result of a clinical assessment of certain types of offenders (Monahan, 1981). A "dangerous" offender is a subclass of high-risk offenders for whom there is some reason to believe that any future criminality will involve violence. Thus, ISPs that claim to work with "high-risk" or "dangerous" offenders are really saying that they tap the high end of a spectrum of offenders arrayed according to probability of a new, serious offence.

A person is defined as a "serious" offender due to the nature of the current offence. Usually, the label "serious" is restricted to designate only the most heinous, predatory personal crimes. Thus, when an ISP is focused on a serious offender, it selects criminals from among those whose current offences are the most repugnant.

In the specification of target group criteria, most ISPs establish certain bases for exclusion. One common reason for exclusion is a violent (i.e., "serious") current offence—and some programmes go so far as to exclude a person with any prior history of violence. Another common requirement for exclusion is a long criminal record or an otherwise unusual risk to the community. New Jersey's ISP, for example, is available only to "low risk inmates who are sincerely motivated to change" (New Jersey Administrative Office of the Courts, 1985).

When the new ISP establishes exclusionary criteria based on current offence and prior record, it restricts itself to a target group that is not likely to tap either high-risk or serious offenders, not to mention dangerous ones. ISP administrators may be pleased that they can avoid responsibility for these offenders, but the irony is that regular probation usually cannot. In many cases, offenders who are ineligible for ISP due to their record or risk are nonetheless eligible for regular probation. Remarkably, some of those who would be ineligible for ISP because of their purported risk level or crime seriousness instead are placed on regular probation. In Georgia, for instance, over 30 per cent of the ISP (there called "IPS" clients) score as "minimum risk" on their assessment instrument, while less than 20 per cent are "maximum" risk (Erwin, 1986). This profile is not very different from that of regular probationers across the state.

In other words, there are almost certainly numerous persons on regular probation who represent a considerably higher public safety problem than the ISP client. Yet markedly greater time and attention—in the order of three to 10 times the commitment of resources—is invested in the ISP client. Stated in another way, this example of an ISP programme has been able to develop a concentrated level of supervision heretofore unheard of, with a degree of community control that exceeds any previously experienced in this country. This supervision is applied to a target group of client volunteers, one-third or one-half of whom represent a minimal level of community risk—this, while the ordinary probationer (who looks much the same in terms of risk) receives the usual degree of (often scant) attention.

Advocates of ISPs respond that while this may be true, the real justification of these programmes lies in the prison space they save and, hence, in tax dollars. These offenders are being diverted from prison, and that is the main intent of the ISP. Such claims of programme priority are certainly legitimate, but they leave unanswered a troubling question. If these ISP clients are truly bound for incarceration and yet look not remarkably different from regular probation cases in terms of risk and crime seriousness, then why are they bound for incarceration? And how much of the current crisis of prison crowding is a product of irrational allocation of incarcerative resources rather than a scarcity of those resources? More to the point, if ISP clients look like regular probation cases except for being prison-bound, then why do they need such intensive supervision?

The problem of target group criteria has already been described. Especially when a programme is new and vulnerable to criticism, there is considerable pressure to apply exclusions to the target group such that those with lengthy criminal records and/or serious current offences are ineligible. When this is done, the vast majority of incarceration-bound offenders are excluded.

The methods of the new ISP movement are unapologetically strict. The typical programme calls for at least twice-weekly contact, home visits at night, community service, and restitution; many programmes use curfews, urine monitoring, and electronic surveillance. Surveys of ISP requirements have shown them to be quite varied but truly intensive by any reasonable criteria (Byrne, 1986).

One impressive aspect of the new ISP movement is the degree of intensity it appears to have achieved. The use of stringent methods combined with strict enforcement raises three issues: appropriateness of conditions, interaction effect, and costs.

In many of the ISPs, conditions are applied across-the-board without much attention to the individual circumstances of the case. For instance, a punitive condition such as community service may be required, even though similarly situated offenders on regular probation would not face a similar requirement. Conversely, risk-control conditions such as urinalysis are applied even when there is no evidence that the use of drugs has ever been a problem in an offender's life.

The inordinate use of punitive conditions means that the scale of punitive sanctions is further muddied under the ISP. If every ISP offender performs 140 hours of community service regardless of the offence, then the service loses much of its punitive value as a sanction because everyone gets it. One of the reasons it is so hard to justify ISPs for serious offenders is that the scale of punishments is already thrown off by the heavy unnecessary reliance upon prison as a core sanction. Overly punitive ISP conditions exacerbate this problem as it applies to community supervision.

A different, but equally serious, problem is created by the unrestrained use of risk-control conditions. Once information exists that a rules violation is occurring, a response is necessary, even if it is unwise. In Georgia, for example, routine use is made of urine screening, even for offenders for whom there is little reason to be concerned about drug use. A large proportion of urines come back dirty, many of them indicating marijuana use only. When this happens, it puts agents of the law in a bind. The use of marijuana is still against the law in Georgia, and the urine is clear evidence of continuing law violation. Yet for many offenders, the adjustment to supervision has been otherwise acceptable (or even laudable) and to return the person to prison would be ridiculous, given the goals of the programme. So the probation officer is forced to play a type of game—warning the offender and noting the violation but trying to avoid action unless something else happens in the case.

The problem here is both conceptual and practical. The imposition of a condition is a "threat"—that the offender should either abide by the requirement or suffer the consequences. When the threat is hollow because there can be no intent to follow it with action, or when it appears arbitrary because it is out of scale with other threats, the law is mocked. The resources simply do not exist to carry out all the threats made in the ISPs—and body in the new ISPs would claim they should all be fully enforced. The primary role of the threats is to show how "tough" the new alternative really is and to thereby generate public support for it. Whether it is appropriate to use conditions in this way, with their enforcement left to discretion and potential abuse, is a troubling question.

There are only two types of savings that can occur as a result of an ISP alternative: Actual dollars are saved because a facility is closed down or substantially reduced in its use, or costs are avoided because the need to build a new prison is reduced due to diversion. Most of the claims of savings will take the latter form, and so they are more symbolic than actual tax savings.

However, even cost avoidance can be reduced by close enforcement strategies.

Assume that an ISP is supervising 1,000 offenders who, as a group, would have served an average of 9 prison months each—a total possible savings of 9,000 cell months. Assume as well that offenders who fail under an ISP serve a premium of an average of 24 months per offender, and assume further that 25 per cent fail.[1] That reduces the net savings to merely 3,000 cell months. If the true diversion rate for those original 1,000 offenders is only 70 percent, then the net saving is only 300 cell months. If 33 per cent of the non-diversion are low-risk cases who otherwise would have failed at a rate of 15 per cent without the close supervision and would have received a lesser premium for a penalty for failure of, for example, 12 months, then there is actually a net *loss* of 120 cell months. Whether these assumptions are completely accurate is open to debate, but as speculations they are certainly not outlandish. In any event, they show how an ISP that is very successful at diversion can, through interaction effect and overenforcement, result in a net loss in prison space at financial cost to the public.

Note

1. This is the percentage of failures the new ISP's commonly produce.

References

Byrne, James (1986), "The Control Controversy: A Preliminary Examination of Intensive Probation Supervision in the United States", 50 *Federal Probation* 2–16.
Carter, Robert, and Leslie T. Wilkins (1984), "Caseloads: Some Conceptual Models",

in *Probation, Parole, and Community Corrections*, 2nd edn., edited by Robert Carter and Leslie T. Wilkins (New York: Wiley).

Erwin, Billie S. (1986), *Final Report of the Georgia Intensive Probation Supervision Project* (Atlanta: Department of Corrections).

Gottfredson, Stephen E., and Don M. Gottfredson (1986), "Accuracy of Prediction Models", in *Criminal Careers and Career Criminals, Vol. II*, edited by Alfred Blumstein, Jacqueline Cohen, Jeffrey Roth, and Christy A. Visher (Washington, D.C.: National Academy Press).

Monahan, John (1981), *Predicting Violent Behavior: An Assessment of Clinical Techniques* (Beverly Hills, Calif.: Sage).

New Jersey Administrative Office of the Courts (1985), *Intensive Supervision Program* (Trenton, N.J.: Author).

6.4

Non-Custodial Penalties and the Principle of Proportionality

MARTIN WASIK AND ANDREW VON HIRSCH

This article attempts to apply a penal rationale to the development of, and choices among, non-custodial penalties. It concentrates on one such rationale—desert—and discusses how that conception might illuminate the use of non-custodial penalties. To remain concise, we will assume the reader's understanding of the basic tenets of desert theory in sentencing (sketched in Selections 4.4, 4.6 and 4.7 above). At the end, we will see how much our conclusions might change if desert constraints are relaxed in favour of more utilitarian positions.

In this article, we will be using grids to explicate our position. It should be emphasized that this is for heuristic purposes only, as a grid best illustrates the relationship between the various elements of the system. Our arguments in no way presuppose the actual establishment in law of such grids or their use by sentencers, since other techniques—such as Swedish-style statutory sentencing principles (see Selection 5.3 above), might be a preferable way of guiding judges' choices.

Desert and Non-Custodial Sentences

Two features of desert theory are worth emphasizing at the outset. The first is that the theory permits most offences to be dealt with by non-custodial penalties. A custodial sentence is severe, and the theory requires severe sanctions only for serious crimes (see Selection 4.4 above). For other crimes, a less severe, non-custodial penalty may ordinarily be the sanction of choice.

From Martin Wasik and Andrew von Hirsch, "Non-Custodial Penalties and the Principles of Desert" [1988] *Criminal Law Review* 555 with some textual changes. A version of that article, written for American audiences, appeared as Andrew von Hirsch, Martin Wasik, and Judith Greene, "Punishments in the Community and the Principles of Desert", (1989) 20 *Rutgers Law Journal* 595; that article appeared in excerpted form as Selection 6.6 in the 1st edition of this book.

Secondly, a desert rationale addresses only the severity of penalties, not their particular form. This permits considerable flexibility to use non-custodial sanctions of various types, as we shall see. It also potentially permits substitution among penalties. If A is a sanction that is appropriate for crimes of a given degree of seriousness, and B is a sanction of another type that is approximately of equal severity, then B can be substituted for A without infringing desert constraints. One may then even choose between the two severity-equivalent sanctions, A and B, on utilitarian grounds—since doing so would not alter the onerousness of the punishment. How much substitution, if any, there should be is one of the main topics which we shall address.

The "No Substitution" Model

How might non-custodial sanctions be arrayed on a penalty scale? The simplest model can be illustrated by a grid which sets out graded sanctions in the manner represented in Figure 1A. In accord with usual desert principles, the two axes relate to offence seriousness and the prior record, and the relatively flat lines demarcating divisions between different bands reflect the predominance of offence seriousness in deciding the sanction. The sentence, on a desert rationale, should be determined chiefly by the present criminal act, but qualified to a limited extent by judgements addressed to the defendant's previous criminal behaviour (see Selection 4.7 above). Penalties could be divided into mild, intermediate, and severe. For the purposes of illustration and for the moment intuitively, we might place discharge and warning in the mild band, fines in the intermediate band, and custody in the severe band. To achieve ordinal proportionality, there would have to be ranking within these bands, in respect of the severity of the particular sanction involved.

This very simple model permits no substitution between different non-custodial sentences or between non-custodial and custodial sentences. It would envisage a diminution in the number of non-custodial sentences available to the courts, and only one penalty would be found within each band. Even this simple model, however, would permit a substantial reduction in the use of custodial sentences—since the intermediate-level crimes which now often receive custody would receive fines instead.

The model could be elaborated through subdividing some of the bands, without departing from the basic design. Custodial sentences could be divided into two bands, one more severe requiring residential custody, and one less severe calling for intermittent custody for prescribed numbers of

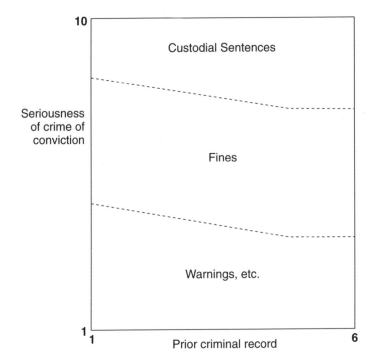

Figure 1A—Simple "No Substitution" model

hours of the day or weekends. Fines could be elaborated further, with substantial monetary penalties for upper-intermediate crimes, and more modest ones for lower-intermediate crimes. These monetary penalties could be expressed as unit fines, to achieve greater equity of impact (see Selection 6.2 above). The lowest band could likewise be subdivided, with small, flat fines in its upper portion and warnings in its lower portion. The model, thus elaborated, is shown in Figure 1B.

By increasing the number of bands in this way, the scheme could further restrict the use of full custody, and would provide more gradual transitions in prescribed severity. However, the model would still rule out substitutions between penalties, and this probably renders it unworkable. The prescribed sanctions may, for example, not be feasible for certain types of offenders, for administrative reasons. Consider the substantial unit fines prescribed for the upper-intermediate band. While this sanction is suitable for most offenders to whom it would apply, it cannot be used for those who have no means for payment. A substitute sanction of equivalent severity would be needed in such cases.[1]

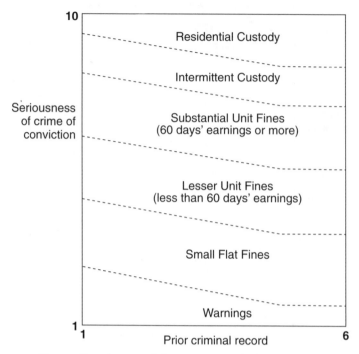

10

Residential Custody

Intermittent Custody

Seriousness
of crime of
conviction

Substantial Unit Fines
(60 days' earnings or more)

Lesser Unit Fines
(less than 60 days' earnings)

Small Flat Fines

Warnings

1
1

Prior criminal record

6

Figure 1B—A more elaborate "No Substitution" model

The "Full Substitution" Model

Let us, then, consider the opposite extreme: a grid with full substitutability. This model is envisaged in Figure 2. The grid uses penalty bands computed on the basis of "sanction units", rather than specific types of sentences. Thus the mild penalty band could be indicated by sanction units between 1 and 20, the lower-intermediate by sanction units between 21 and 40, the upper-intermediate between 41 and 80, the moderately severe between 81 and 120, and the severe between 121 and 200. All available custodial and non-custodial sentences would, in a separate translation scale, be assigned sanction units, reflecting their comparative severities. This model would operate quite differently from that previously described, since it would allow extensive substitution amongst penalties. It would be possible, by reference to the translation scale, to equate penalties, and to impose the appropriate sanction-unit sentence through a variety of sentencing options. Also, the model would allow the combining of different penalties together, so as to achieve the prescribed sanction-unit

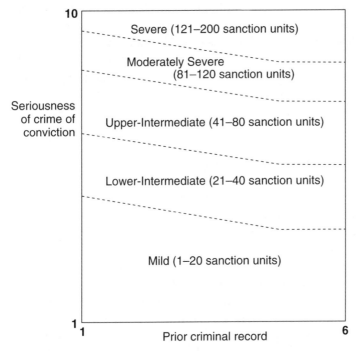

Figure 2—"Full Substitution" model

total. Combination of penalties would not be possible under the earlier models.

The full-substitution model would have a number of drawbacks. First, it presupposes a degree of sophistication in our ability to compare and calibrate severities of different species of sanctions that does not now exist and is not likely to exist. In our non-substitution models shown in Figures 1A and 1B, it is not difficult to make the judgement that the sanctions are arrayed in ascending order of severity. It would be vastly harder, however, to make penalty-unit comparisons among a large and heterogenous variety of possible sanctions.

Second, the need for full substitutability is far from obvious. Unless one has an heroic belief in individualisation, cafeteria-style sentences may accomplish little that a more restricted substitutability could not achieve. We have seen that substitutability is sometimes needed because the normally-prescribed penalty cannot feasibly be applied to a particular defendant—as in the case of substantial fines for indigent defendants. But such cases can be accommodated by prescribing a standard substitute—say, community service, instead. A limited substitutability might also be useful for preventive ends—say, in order to supervise offenders, convicted of middle-level crimes, who seem particularly amenable to such treatment. However, our present capacity to affect offenders' criminal behaviour through supervision is fairly limited—and supervision targeted to a few discrete subcategories of offenders would probably be all that could accomplish results.

The "Partial Substitution" Model

What remains—and strikes us as more sensible—is *limited* substitutability. A standard type of punishment would be prescribed for each band in the grid, and would be the normally-recommended type of disposition. However, there would be substitution rules which allow that sanction to be replaced, in specified types of cases, with another of equivalent severity.

A limited-substitution model might have the form of Figure 3. A presumed sentence-type would be indicated for each penalty band. However, a limited substitution would be permitted. The substitute penalty would have to be of equivalent severity, and it could be invoked only for certain stated reasons. Those reasons could be crime-preventive (where, for example, the sentencer has special reason for believing that the alternative sanction would be more effective in terms of reducing recidivism), or administrative (where, for example, the defendant would be unable to perform the presumptive sentence). Desert requirements would be satisfied nevertheless, because the substituted penalty is of approximately the same onerousness as the normally-prescribed grid sanction.

The normally-recommended sanctions in Figure 3 might be the same as those in Figure 1B. However, the substitution rules might permit the following possibilities:

(1) The severe band would involve full custody, for periods of (say) six months or more. No substitution of non-custodial penalties would be permitted, as these would be less severe.

(2) The moderately-severe band would normally involve intermittent custody—served perhaps, at specified hours at day-attendance centres. However, periods of full custody, of substantially less than six months, would be the permitted substitute in prescribed situations—for example, for offenders whose previous records indicate that they would not appear at attendance centres. The duration of such full custody, however, would be calibrated so as to be comparable in onerousness to the normally-applicable sentence.

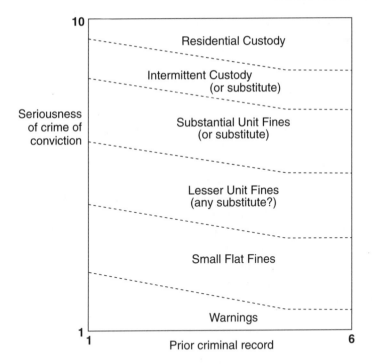

Figure 3—"Partial Substitution" model

(3) In the upper-intermediate band, the normally-prescribed penalty might be a substantial unit fine. (By "substantial" we mean unit fines representing a substantial number of days' earnings—perhaps 60 days' earnings or more.) However, other sanctions of comparable severity might be substituted to a limited extent. These might include intensive supervision for amenable individuals, and community service for those lacking the income on which such fines are based.

(4) The lower-intermediate band would normally have more modest unit fines—say, those involving less than 60 days' earnings. Substitution would seldom be needed, here. Fewer offenders would lack the means to pay, and community service may now be too severe to be the substitute sanction. Supervision, to be comparable in severity to the fine, would have to be light—too light, perhaps, to have much prospect for effectiveness.

(5) The lowest bands would consist of warnings, and small, flat fines. Little need for substitution would exist here.

The reader should note that the particular penalties mentioned here are only for the sake of illustration. One could construct a limited-substitution model using other sanctions as the normally-recommended ones or their substitutes.

Gauging Sentence Severity

The limited-substitution model requires the substitute sanction to be of comparable severity with the normally-prescribed one. How should the requisite comparisons in severity be done? One possibility would be to resort to opinion surveys: to describe the various sanctions to a sample of the public, and ask how they would rate the sanctions in degree of onerousness. A preferable approach, in our view, would be to rate severities in terms of the importance of the interests of a person typically interfered with through the operation of the penalty. The more important the interest infringed, and the greater the extent of the infringement, the severer the penalty. This would call for a "living standard" analysis of various sanctions (in the manner summarized in Selection 4.6 above).

Back-up Sanctions

Non-custodial penalties require back-up sanctions for wilful defaulters—as in the case of the individual who refuses to pay his day fine, although capable of paying. How should those back-up sanctions be devised?

Traditionally, back-up sanctions have relied on imprisonment. The form of the non-custodial penalty often called for such a response: the offender received a conditional sentence whereby, if he failed to perform the prescribed penalty in the community, the condition was violated and the prison sentence held in reserve could be invoked. Such a response is troublesome both for pragmatic reasons and in principle.

The pragmatic difficulty is that, to the extent that non-custodial sentences are meant to diminish reliance on imprisonment, systematic resort to confinement as a back-up sanction would be self-defeating. A considerable number of lesser and intermediate-level offenders would be confined as defaulters, for periods that could substantially exceed the terms they might have received, had imprisonment been the initial response to their crimes. Such a severe sanction, moreover, is likely to be invoked unevenly: some defaulters will go to prison when others, whose default is no more flagrant, are allowed to remain in the community.

The theoretical difficulty is that reliance on imprisonment as a potential back-up sanction can infringe desert principles. Suppose an offender commits an offence in the lower-intermediate band of the grid, receives the prescribed non-custodial sanction, and then defaults without good excuse. Since he has not fully undergone his penalty, he still "owes" its not-yet-completed portion, in some comparable form. Imprisonment will not serve this purpose, however, as it is much more severe than his original penalty, and could not have been imposed, under the grid, for his crime. One might argue that his act of default (although not necessarily a statutory offence) itself is a reprehensible act, for which he "owes" more. But how much more? Unless one is prepared to argue that default *per se* is *very* reprehensible, it would not suffice as grounds for invoking the severe sanction of imprisonment. We need, then, to devise non-incarcerative measures as back-up sanctions. How, under a desert model, should their severity be determined?

We might begin by trying to identify a penalty that is equivalent in severity to, but more readily enforceable than, the initially-imposed punishment. Where the offender has completed a portion of his non-custodial penalty before defaulting, the substitute would correspond to the severity of the unserved portion. Next, one might treat the act of default (if wilful) to be itself a reprehensible act, deserving of some increase in the punishment. How serious that act is considered to be would depend on one's general criteria for gauging seriousness. However, default *per se* does not strike us as greatly reprehensible, and would not warrant more than a modest increase in the severity of the sanction. The increase might involve, perhaps, a step-up to the next band in the grid immediately above the band in which the initial penalty was located.

Were our suggested "partial substitution" model (see Figure 3) employed, and such a one-band-upward standard used for defaults, it might have the following consequences. A person convicted of a lower-intermediate level offence, for which a modest unit fine is the normally-recommended penalty, would upon wilful default be subjected to the penalty prescribed for the upper-intermediate band—a substantial unit fine. To ensure the penalty was paid, measures of distraint (i.e. attachment or garnishment) could be employed. Defaulters convicted of crimes in the upper-intermediate band, for which substantial unit-fines would be the normal sanction, would similarly face the penalty in the next band up. This would consist of intermittent confinement in an "attendance centre" (or else, for the sufficiently recalcitrant, a short, equivalently-severe period of actual confinement).

Impact on Use of Imprisonment

How much could our proposed scheme of non-custodial sanctions reduce reliance upon imprisonment? We suspect the reduction might be considerable. Full custody would be invoked routinely only for the serious offences in the top band of the grid. Its only additional permitted use would be rather selective—as a substitute sanction (but for short periods) for the next-most-serious band, and as a back-up sanction for defaulters in the band below that). Lesser offenders—who now often face incarceration if considered poor risks—would not be confined, and incarceration would not be invoked to back up lesser non-custodial penalties as it may be today.

One could only have confidence that the reduction in custodial penalties would occur, however, by conducting prison-impact analyses of the kind pioneered in Minnesota.[2] Unless one stimulates the application of the proposed standards to a representative caseload of offences—one likely to be encountered by the courts which are to use the standards—predictions about the standards' impact on the use of imprisonment will necessarily be speculative.

Effects of Shifting toward a More Utilitarian Rationale

In the foregoing sketch of non-custodial penalties, we have assumed full adherence to desert principles. Crime prevention aims, in our model, may be considered only insofar as their use does not infringe proportionality requirements.

Not everyone will agree with these assumptions, however. Some will prefer a rationale giving less emphasis to desert constraints and more to utilitarian concerns. What would the effects of such a shift be on the penalty structure? The answer will depend, of course, on which utilitarian concerns are focused upon. A deterrence rationale may produce a different array of non-custodial penalties than a rationale emphasizing restraint of potential recidivists. Let us consider the latter for present purposes—as more is known about prediction than about deterrence or treatment. As predictive concerns are given more weight, how would the penalty structure change?

First, the seriousness of the current crime would have less influence, and the prior criminal record more, as it tends to be the better predictor of future criminality (see Selection 3.7 above). On a grid, this would be reflected by altered slopes of the bands of the grid. Those bands—particularly the band containing custodial sentences—would tilt more toward the vertical, so as to emphasize the prior record. In addition, the horizontal axis of the grid may come to include additional factors, other than the criminal record, that are found to be useful predictors.

The back-up sanctions may also change. When wilful default is indicative of increased probability of offending, a stiffer sanction would be invoked where that would be useful to restrain the offender. Relaxing desert requirements would thus allow the system to be more permissive with back-up sanctions.

Two features of our suggested scheme should be retained, however. First, a limited-substitution system would remain preferable to one that allows unlimited substitution. Even if one accepts a rationale that gives more emphasis to incapacitation and less to desert, there is no obvious reason why cafeteria-style sentencing would be needed.

Secondly, when one penalty is substituted for another, it should still be considered whether it is of equal severity. Even on a more predictively-oriented rationale, there is an important difference between (1) replacing a sanction with another equally-severe one, and (2) replacing one sanction with another that is *more* severe. Where one is increasing severity on the basis of a prediction, we need firmer supporting evidence as to the reliability of the prediction.[3]

Conclusions

We have tried to show that it is indeed feasible to design a sentencing framework based on desert principles which makes extensive use of non-custodial penalties. Such penalties, then, can be scaled and interrelated in a more coherent and consistent manner than is the case at present. They would no longer be associated primarily with rehabilitative aims nor be regarded merely as substitutes for incarceration. They would instead be seen as penalties in their own right, ranged on a scale below immediate custody, and involving varying degrees of punitiveness.

Extensive reliance upon non-custodial sanctions is to be distinguished from mere proliferation of such sanctions. We have argued for a system involving a relatively small standard group of penalties, with limited substitution. Such a system would be conceptually coherent and would avoid many of the problems which beset the present system.

There are some areas in which further research needs to be done—particularly, in measuring the comparative severities of different non-

290 Community Punishments

custodial penalties. Work along these lines would facilitate judgements concerning the substitutability of penalties.

Ours is only a brief sketch, and more thinking needs to be done—both about the structure of penalties and the practical problems of their administration. Desert theory *can* provide a useful framework in scaling non-custodial penalties, but only with more thought than has been given to the subject in the past.

Notes

1. The substitutes being of no more than equivalent severity with the normally-applicable penalty is essential here—not only on desert principles, but to avoid class bias.
2. These techniques are described in Andrew von Hirsch, Kay A. Knapp and Michael Tonry, *The Sentencing Commission and its Guidelines* (1987), ch. 6.
3. Thus Norval Morris recommends that predictively-based increases in sentencing severity need to be supported by stronger statistical evidence (see Selection 3.5 above).

6.5

Interchangeability, Desert Limits and Equivalence of Function

MICHAEL TONRY

Many offenders are jailed or imprisoned because credible community punishments do not exist and judges believe their crimes *too serious* to be sanctioned solely by an ordinary probation sentence. Many offenders are given routine probation because community sentences do not exist and judges believe their crimes *not serious enough* to be sanctioned by a jail or prison sentence. In both cases, credible, community-based punishments are lacking. By "intermediate punishments" I mean punishments lying between imprisonment and "ordinary" probation. These include fines, community service orders, intermittent confinement, "split" sentences combining a short term of confinement with a non-custodial disposition, and intensive supervision probation buttressed where appropriate by electronic and other monitoring techniques.

If fairness, rationality, and improved crime control are to be achieved in our systems of justice, the near vacuum between ordinary probation and incarceration must be filled by a graduated series of intermediate punishments imposed in a principled way. Until judges have adequate guidance directing them, to use intermediate punishments in appropriate cases and to select among them, and between them and jail or prison terms, these sanctions will continue to be underused and little respected.

Some Principles

A principled system should allow for interchangeability between imprisonment and intermediate punishments, and for interchangeability among intermediate punishments. Interchanges should be governed not by notions of equivalences in severity, as desert theorists urge, but of interchangeability of function. The appropriate role of desert would not be

This selection is published here for the first time.

defining, but limiting: to establish bounds within which interchanges take place. Norval Morris and I have sketched the relevant principles in a 1990 volume,[1] but let me enumerate them briefly here.

1. The role of desert

This should reflect Morris's philosophy of "limiting retributivism" (sketched in Selection 4.5 above). Desert, on this view, establishes the limits on the permissible range of punishments, given the seriousness of the offence; it does not define the appropriate quantum of penalty within that range. When we say a punishment is deserved we rarely mean that it is precisely appropriate to the seriousness of the offence. Rather we mean that it is not *undeserved*; that it is neither too lenient or too severe. The concept of desert defines relationships between crimes and punishments on a continuum between the unduly lenient and the excessively punitive— within which the just sentence may on other grounds be determined. In a system of intermediate punishments, desert principles would thus define the upper and lower limits on the severity of the permissible sanction; and it would also help define the punishment relationship between offences of substantially differing gravity. Within these constraints, however, there should be considerable room to consider utilitarian concerns of social protection and of economizing with scarce punishment resources, and humanitarian concerns of minimizing the suffering imposed on criminals.

2. Interchangeability

A system which treats desert as providing only the limits on permissible punishment will give considerably more scope for interchangeability among intermediate punishments, and between such punishments and custodial sentences, than will a desert-based system (such as that suggested in Selection 6.4 above). Below a level of severity punishable by a substantial prison term, extensive interchanges would thus be allowed. Subject to the applicable desert limits, different intermediate penalties could be substituted for one another, and short periods of confinement and (the more substantial) non-custodial penalties could also be exchanged.

3. Equivalence of function

In making these interchanges, equivalence of *severity* would not be required—that is the strict desert criterion (suggested in Selection 4.4 above) which Morris and I would reject. Instead, the focus would be on interchangeability of *function*. One penalty may be substituted for another if they both serve the same or alternately appropriate penological purposes in the circumstances. For a drug-using repetitive thief, for example, a sentence having some incapacitative effect might be desirable. The sanctions having this function, and hence functionally equivalent, might be a period of confinement, or house arrest with electronic monitoring and frequent unannounced drug-testing. One of these penalties may be substituted for the other, even if their penal bite is different. For a white-collar offender, deterrent and retributive functions may be more worth emphasizing; here, a short period of confinement and a large fine might equally achieve those functions.

If the function of the sentence in the particular type of case is to have this role, it is no longer enough to talk of the purposes *of* sentencing— that is, the systematic aims which a sentencing system should aim to achieve. Purposes *at* sentence become important: what kind of aim or function this particular kind of sentence, addressed to this particular kind of offender, should seek. For the drug-using offender in the preceding illustration, incapacitation is the purpose at sentence; for the white-collar offender, retribution and deterrence may be. In setting the purpose at sentence, the sentencing judge ought to have an important role—as he or she is best familiar with the case before him, and the aims that might practicably be achieved in that kind of situation.

Some Suggestions for Scaling Intermediate Sanctions

How might the foregoing principles be applied to create a system for scaling intermediate sanctions? In a recent survey of intermediate-sentence guidelines,[2] I sketched some suggested techniques. My suggestions assume the use of numerical sentencing guidelines, but with suitable modifications, could be carried over to narrative sentencing principles (see Selection 5.3 above).

1. The guidelines grid should contain four to six zones of discretion

The polar zones are one in which the crimes are so serious that any punishment less than imprisonment would unduly depreciate the seriousness of the offence, and a second in which the crimes are so venial that any punishment harsher than standard probation, a minor fine, or restitution would be unjust. At least two other zones should be created: one authorizing restrictive sanctions such as in-patient drug or other treatment and partial confinement, and another authorizing less restrictive sanctions such as unit (day) fines, intensive supervision, house arrest, and community service. At its upper and lower margins, each zone would "overlap" with the next, thereby giving judges authority, without departing from the guideline ranges, to choose among sanction types.

In order to maintain norms of proportionality, guideline cells in each zone could specify maximum durations or amounts for authorized sanctions, and these could vary with offence seriousness or extent of criminal history. The cells could also specify maximum aggregate penalties, including back-up sanctions.

Grids containing more than four zones could be particularly useful in setting back-up sanctions when offenders breach conditions of their sentences. Often, judges confronted by an offender breaching conditions of a non-custodial penalty believe their only choices are, in effect, to ignore the breach or confine the offender. Under a system with six zones of discretion, a judge could punish condition breaches by a Zone 2 offender by imposing sentences authorised by Zones 3 to 6. Policy statements could provide guidance to judges on the details of breach penalties and on resentencing to a higher zone's sanctions.

2. Guidelines should include dispositive presumptions

Zones of discretion, standing alone, give judges little guidance in choosing among sanctions that are authorized within the various zones. Some policy guidance should be given by way of presumptions. One possiblity would be to adopt a "least restrictive alternative" presumption and establish norms that order sanctions in their degree of restrictiveness: for example, to provide guidance regarding the relative onerousness of such measures as small flat fines, unit fines of various numbers of units, intensive probation, partial or intermittent confinement, and so forth. Judges would be directed to impose the least restrictive sanction authorized in the applicable cell, or to explain why a more restrictive sanction was appropriate in the particular case.

A second, related possibility would be to adopt a series of offender- or offence-specific presumptions. These might, for example, call for sanctions that require drug treatment in the case of drug-dependent offenders of certain types; or, in the case of offenders who are primary care or income providers for their families, call for penalties that permit the offender to continue in these roles. A dozen or so such dispositive presumptions might be adopted. Their content would vary with the jurisdiction, and their cumulative effect would be to provide guidance to judges in choosing among authorized sanctions. These dispositive presumptions would interact with the "least restrictive alternative" presumption. A presumption calling for a term of confinement for those convicted of crimes involving gratuitous infliction of violence, for example, would override the "least restrictive alternative" presumption.

3. Guidelines should authorize judges to declare and be guided by the relevant purposes at sentencing

Whether there are four, six, or more zones of discretion, judges will be left with considerable discretion to choose among generically different penalties. Whether a particular penalty is appropriate often depends upon the offender's characteristics. For crimes of comparable gravity that fall in the same cell but are different in their character, differing kinds of penalties may be appropriate. In choosing which kind of penalty to impose, the judge should have to explain his purpose *at* sentence: that is, what aim or aims he seeks in selecting the sanction he has. Thus judges—subject to the limits provided by the various grid cells—might identify the following different purposes at sentence:

(1)   For the drug-dependent burglar or drug dealer, prevention of future crimes and rehabilitation may be the most significant aims sought to be achieved. These aims might be sought through sanctions (resident or non-resident) involving compulsory drug treatment, with restitution or community service as an adjunct.

(2)   For the perpetrator of a commercial fraud, retribution and general deterrence may be the appropriate aims at sentence, and hence restitution, stigmatizing community service, and substantial fines the appropriate sanctions.

(3)   For an employed blue-collar head of family who has committed a serious assault while intoxicated, retribution and deterrence may be the primary aims, and a substantial fine plus night-time or weekend confinement (thus permitting him to continue to work and support his family) the optimal sentence.

In making these choices, the judge would be guided by the dispositive presumptions spoken of above.

4. Guidelines should establish policies and presumptions concerning categorical exceptions

The presumptions spoken of earlier are ones that apply to choice of the sanction within the applicable guideline cell. For certain categories of offences, however, penalties outside the normal cell ranges may be desirable. Consider intra-familial sex offences. Because such offences often involve psychopathology; because a prison sentence would break up the family, possibly leaving the victim guilt-ridden for having reported the offence; and because such conditions sometimes can be successfully treated, treatment and family preservation may be important enough goals to override the normally-applicable desert limits. Without categorical exceptions, however, the judge could depart from the applicable cell range only by citing suitable (ordinarily, desert-related) mitigating circumstances. If broader authority for departure is desired, it may be appropriate to create a categorical exception—stating that the lower limit of the normally-applicable cell range does not restrict the sanction that may be chosen. Such exceptions may either be permissive—in which case the judge may impose a lesser sentence; or else presumptive—in which case such a lesser sentence would ordinarily be recommended.

Together, these four suggestions may help us move toward principled guidance for the use of intermediate sanctions—guidance of a kind that may help achieve reasonable consistency, while allowing judges to take into account meaningful differences among cases.

Notes

1. Norval Morris and Michael Tonry, *Between Prison and Probation: Intermediate Punishments in a Rational Sentencing System* (1990).
2. Michael Tonry, *Intermediate Sanctions in Sentencing Guidelines* (U.S. National Institute of Justice, 1997).

Suggestions for Further Reading

1. Recent Surveys and Analyses of Intermediate Punishments

Petersilia, J., *Expanding Options for Criminal Sentencing* (1987); Bottoms, A. E., "Limiting Prison Use: The English Experience", (1987) 26 *Howard Journal of Criminal Justice* 177; Tonry, M. and Wills, R. *Intermediate Sanctions*, A Report to National Institute of Justice 1988) (unpublished manuscript, available from National Institute of Corrections, Washington, D.C.); NACRO, *The Real Alternative* (1989); Vass, A. E. *Alternatives to Prison* (1990); Byrne, J. M. Lurigio, A. and Petersilia, J. (eds.), *Smart Sentencing* (1992); Davies, M. *et al.*, *Criminal Justice* (1995); Tonry, M., *Sentencing Matters* (1995); Tonry, M., and Hamilton, K., *Intermediate Sanctions in Overcrowded Times* (1995); Ashworth, A., *Sentencing and Criminal Justice*, 2nd edn. (1995); Mair, G. "Community Penalties and the Probation Service", in M. Maguire, R. Morgan, and R. Reiner, (eds.), *Oxford Handbook of Criminology*, 2nd edn. (1997).

2. Probation

McAnany, P., Thomson, D. and Fogel, D., *Probation Reconsidered* (1984); Shaw, R., and Haines, K. (eds.), *The Criminal Justice System: A Central Role for the Probation Service* (1989); McWilliams, W., and Pease, K., "Probation Practice and an End to Punishment", (1990) 29 *Howard Journal of Criminal Justice* 14; Lurigio, A. (ed.), "Special Issue . . . Intensive Probation Supervision", (1990) 36 *Crime and Delinquency* No. 1 (3–191); Petersilia, J. and Turner, S., "An Evaluation of Intensive Supervision in California", (1992) 82 *Journal of Criminal Law and Criminology* 610; Raynor, P., Smith, D. and Vanstone, M., *Effective Probation Practice* (1994); Newburn, T., *Crime and Criminal Justice Policy* (1995); McIvor, G., *Working with Offenders* (1996); Petersilia, J., "Probation in the United States", (1997) 22 *Crime and Justice: A Review of Research* 149.

3. Community Service and Other Community Orders

Young, H., *Community Service Orders* (1979); Pease K. and McWilliams, W. (eds.), *Community Service by Order* (1980); Pease, K. "Community Service Orders", in M. Tonry and N. Morris (eds.), *Crime and Justice: An Annual Review of Research*, vol. 6 (1985); McDonald, D., *Prisons without Walls: Community Service Sentences in New York City* (1986); Tonry and Will, *Intermediate Sanctions*, above, ch. 5; Vas, A. and

Menzies, K. "The Community Service Order in England and Ontario", (1989) 29 *British Journal of Criminology* 225; McIvor, G., *Sentenced to Serve: the Operation and Impact of Community Service by Offenders* (1992); Ashworth, A., *Sentencing and Criminal Justice*, above, ch. 10; Whitfield, D., and Scott, D., *Paying Back: Twenty Years of Community Service* (1993); Mair, G., "Community Penalties and the Probation Service", above.

4. Fines and Day Fines

Friedman, M., "The West German Day-Fine System: A Possibility for the United States?" (1983) 50 *University of Chicago Law Review* 281 (1983); Hillsman, T., Sichel, L. and Mahoney, B., *Fines in Sentencing: A Study in the Use of the Fine as a Criminal Sanction* (1984); Thornstadt, H., "The Day Fine System in Sweden", (1985) *Criminal Law Review* 307; Hillsman, S. and Greene, J., "Tailoring Criminal Fines to the Financial Means of the Offender", (1988) 72 *Judicature 38*; Greene, J., "Structuring Criminal Fines", (1988) 13 *Justice System Journal* 37; Hillsman, S. "Fines and Day-Fines" in M. R. Tonry and N. Morris (eds.), *Crime and Justice: An Annual Review of Research*, vol 12 (1990); Gibson, B. *Unit Fines* (1990); Moxon, D. Sutton, M. and Hedderman, C., *Unit Fines: Experiments in Four Courts* (1990); Tonry, M. and Hamilton, K., *Intermediate Sanctions in Overcrowded Times*, above, pp. 15–55; Walker, N., and Padfield, N., *Sentencing: Law, Theory and Practice* (1966), ch. 16.

5. Home Detention and Electronic Monitoring

Lilly, R., "Tagging Reviewed", (1990) 29 *Howard Journal of Criminal Justice* 14; Mair, G., and Nee, *Electronic Monitoring* (1990); Smylka, J. O., and Selke, W. L., *Intermediate Sanctions* (1995); Tonry, M., and Hamilton, K., *Intermediate Sanctions in Overcrowded Times*, above, pp. 104–20.

6. Scaling Intermediate Punishments

Bottoms, A. E., "The Concept of Intermediate Sanctions and Its Relevance for the Probation Service", in R. Shaw and K. Haines (eds.), *The Criminal Justice System*, above; A. von Hirsch, M. Wasik, and J. Greene, "Punishments in the Community and the Principles of Desert", (1989) 20 *Rutgers Law Journal* 595; Morris, N., and Tonry, M., *Between Prison and Probation: Intermediate Punishments in a Rational Sentencing System* (1990); von Hirsch, A., "Scaling Intermediate Punishments: A Comparison of Two Models", in Byrne, J. M., Lurigio, A., and Petersilia, A., *Smart Sentencing*, above; von Hirsch, *Censure and Sanctions* (1993), ch. 7; Petersilia, J., and Deschenes, D. P., "What Punishes?—Inmates Rank the Severity of Prisons versus Intermediate Sanctions", (1994) 58(1) *Federal Probation* 3; Harlow, R. E., Darley, J. M., and

Robinson, P. H., "The Severity of Intermediate Penal Sanctions: A Psychophysical Scaling Approach for Obtaining Community Perceptions", (1995) 11 *Journal of Quantitative Criminology* 71; Spelman, W., "The Severity of Intermediate Sanctions",(1995) 32 *Journal of Research in Crime and Delinquency* 107.

7. Issues of Intrusiveness and Demeaningness

von Hirsch, A., *Censure and Sanctions*, above, ch. 9.

7

Restorative Justice

The fourth quarter of the twentieth century has seen a resurgence in restorative theories and victim-centred theories of criminal justice. In former times, victims had played a major role in criminal justice. In the tenth century many offenders, pursued by the victim, had to pay financial compensation in the form of a *bot* to the victim and a *wite* to the victim's lord. In the twelfth and thirteenth centuries the King began to assert control over criminal justice, and took over payments from the offender, subsequently replacing them with other forms of sentence.[1] While victims continued to play a primary role in the prosecution of suspected offenders until the nineteenth century, the victim's involvement in what came to be "sentencing" faded away. Recent years have seen the re-emergence of concern for victims, at a political level, among some criminal justice practitioners, and among criminal justice theorists. Approaches with somewhat different origins and emphases may be found: restorative theories are not necessarily victim-centred, and victim-centred approaches are not necessarily restorative. There is a wide variety of theories and practical approaches, and this chapter will necessarily be selective. The first step will be to give brief descriptions of two of the principal paradigms.

Two Preliminary Paradigms

One paradigm would be termed compensatory in the United Kingdom and restitutive in the USA, and its main component is to assure proper financial recompense to the victim of the crime. This recognizes the right of a victim of crime to be compensated by the offender, and the duty of the offender to assure compensation. It is an elementary instance of corrective justice. However, it does raise questions about who or what may properly be regarded as victim(s) of a crime. Some restorative writers recognize that criminal offences have a double aspect, impinging on the rights of a victim and constituting some kind of wider harm. Insofar as this is correct, it would then be necessary to ensure that the restorative approach applies not only to the direct or primary victim but also to this wider or secondary victim. It will be noticed that restorative theories with this kind of focus may not be presented as theories of punishment: their principal aim is restitution or compensation, although punishment may be a side-effect, especially in a mixed system where compensation is added to another sentence in a fairly conventional criminal justice setting.[2] The reading from Lucia Zedner (Selection 7.4) discusses this paradigm.

Another paradigm is that of conflict resolution. Each crime is regarded as the site of a conflict, and the proper response is to attempt a resolution of that conflict. This approach typically relies on mediation and other forms of dispute resolution, not upon a judicial system as conceived in modern Western states. Once again, there is the question of who the parties to the conflict are. In particular, does the wider community or the state have an interest, or is it merely the offender and the immediate victim? Insofar as the community is recognized as having an interest, this would shape the form of dispute resolution, and would ensure that it is not simply a private affair. It will be noticed, again, that theories of this kind are not theories of punishment as such: instead, they advance justifications for responding to crimes in a different, socially integrative way. The readings from Nils Christie (Selection 7.1) and from Philip Pettit and John Braithwaite (Selection 7.2) draw upon this paradigm. In the same vein, Daniel Van Ness has referred to the purpose of criminal justice as "the restoration into safe communities of victims and offenders who have resolved their conflicts".[3] In Selection 7.5 Michael Cavadino and James Dignan develop this paradigm in a slightly different way.

In addition to these two paradigms, two further tendencies in the debate should be noticed. One is the argument that victims, so long neglected by the criminal justice system, should be given a voice in proceedings. Sometimes this goes no further than allowing the victim to submit a "victim impact statement", detailing the effects of the crime on her or his life. In some jurisdictions the approach is taken further, and a victim is empowered to express an opinion on what sentence would be appropriate in the case. The implications of this kind of approach will be examined below. What is apparent at this stage is that this paradigm does not belong, necessarily, to either a restorative or a punitive system of criminal justice. It suggests that the victim's preferences ought to be relevant in sentencing, but it may not specify the direction in which those preferences should lead. They may well vary from victim to victim: some may be punitive, others non-punitive, and still others restorative in their preferences.

A further tendency is to develop welfare provision for victims of crime. Crime victims can fairly expect support after the offence, proper information about the progress of the case, support and information if the case comes to court, and proper compensation from the state if it is not forthcoming from the offender. This is not the place to assess the extent to which the system in any particular jurisdiction measures up to these legitimate expectations,[4] but the importance of this kind of welfare provision is beyond doubt. It may form part of a conventional criminal justice system or one that is orientated primarily towards restorative justice.

The Foundations of Restorative Theories

The re-emergence of restorative theories focuses attention on certain fundamental issues in criminal justice. Both the compensatory paradigm and the conflict resolution paradigm raise deeper questions about the interests relevant to criminal justice, about the place of crime prevention, and about wider community involvement in the administration of criminal justice. Each of these questions will now be discussed briefly.

First, what interests are relevant in a criminal case? It is one thing to argue that the interests of victims have been neglected in many criminal justice systems for much of the twentieth century. It is quite another thing to specify what interests of victims ought to be recognized, and what other interests ought to be recognized. It has become implicit in much modern Anglo-American legal doctrine that a criminal offence is a crime against the state: the victim's legal interest is an interest in compensation, on the corrective justice argument above, and the victim also has welfare interests in proper support, information, etc. Christie (Selection 7.1) argues that what has happened over the centuries is that the state has "stolen" the conflict from the victim (and from society). He argues that the victim's right to a central role in the proceedings should be restored. The implication is that the victim has a right to negotiate (or to be involved in the negotiation of) the resolution of the conflict, with any attendant compensation or penalties. It may be argued that many crimes do not involve a "conflict", in the sense that there may be no disputed claims and no prospect of future dealings between the parties. However, Christie adopts the "conflict" model, and he goes on to recognize that the victim's interest is not the only one: he mentions the wider community's interest, too. This suggests that each crime is a wrong against the direct victim and against the community, and that each therefore has some consequential right to participation in the criminal justice process. Pettit and Braithwaite adopt a similar approach (Selection 7.2), regarding crimes as offences both against the victim's dominion and the interest of the community in the security that helps to constitute dominion,[5] but some questions about the absence of safeguards against excessive penalties are raised by Ashworth and von Hirsch (Selection 7.3). The issue of the public interest is developed rather differently by Cavadino and Dignan (Selection 7.5). Does their "human rights" approach, with its reliance on the notion of retributive outer limits, overcome the counter-arguments in Selection 7.3 (see also Chapter 4 above)?

This readiness of modern restorative theorists to recognize the wider community's interests in crime should not, however, deflect attention from the question of the nature of the victim's interest. Is it not arguable that one key element in modern states is that the state takes over the responsibility for government and law; that it does so in order to ensure efficiency and consistency, and especially to displace vigilantism and to prevent people from "taking the law into their own hands"; that therefore the state ought to control adjudication and sentencing; but that its doing so ought not to deprive victims of their right to compensation (as happened for some centuries, and happens in some cases now)? It may be true that one of the driving forces behind modern restorativism is dissatisfaction with the "conventional" punishment paradigm, as developed in many criminal justice systems. But the question is whether what is wrong is the paradigm or the way in which it has been developed. How convincing are Christie's arguments that "conflicts" should be taken back from the state and returned to the victim and her or his community? To what extent does Pettit and Braithwaite's conception of dominion, in the context of their wider republican theory,[6] imply that the particular victim has an interest going beyond compensation and "recognition", and do they accept that it is the state's function to decide on the measure and form of "recognition, recompense and reassurance"?

Similar questions are raised when we turn to the compensatory paradigm. Whether it is a fully compensatory paradigm, in which the whole purpose of criminal justice is to ensure that victim and community are compensated for the crime,[7] or merely a process of grafting such an approach on to a "conventional" criminal justice system, a range of difficult issues arises, as Zedner recognizes (Selection 7.3). Most poignantly, if it is recognized that the victim has a right to compensation and also that the state has interests, which should be accorded priority, in cases where both cannot be satisfied? Would the answer be different in a punitive system, where the state's role is to ensure the punishment of offenders, and in a reparative system in which reparation to the community is considered important? These questions raise issues about the theoretical foundations of the interests in a criminal case, although, as Zedner shows, there are also prudential considerations in favour of greater attention to victim compensation.

To what extent are restorative theories advanced as a means of crime prevention? Christie (Selection 7.1) is careful not to justify his victim-centred approach on the basis that it would lead to reduced recidivism, but others who advocate a conflict-resolving approach sometimes make this claim, particularly for some versions of the "family group conferencing" approach to criminal justice, outlined below in this Introduction. The question is whether restorativism (howsoever defined) is an end in itself, not reliant on the achievement of rehabilitation of offenders, crime prevention or deterrence for its "success", even though these may be desirable side-effects.

The principal basis for Christie's advocacy of the conflict-resolving approach is that it can be designed so as to involve the wider community in the administration of criminal justice. This is partly because Christie is mistrustful of lawyers' heavy involvement in more traditional criminal justice systems, and partly because he believes that there are great potential advantages for increased social cohesion if ordinary people, including victims and offenders, are drawn into the resolution of criminal cases. These arguments resonate with the views of Pettit and Braithwaite, and of other restorativists who deplore the state's dominance of criminal justice on the ground that it produces distancing and alienation. Insofar as crimes take place in, and have an impact upon, the community, and almost all offenders will continue to live in or will soon return to that community, there is good pragmatic and political sense in greater community involvement in criminal justice. How strong is this argument, however, when attention is turned to the question of what counts, for these purposes, as "the community"? How local or national is the community to which reference is made, and can we be sure that dispositions which are labelled "community sentences" are consistent with the idea of "community" which inspires many restorative theories?[8]

Some Problems of Restorative Justice

We return now to the two paradigms sketched earlier, and give attention to some difficulties that may flow from those approaches.

Compensation and punishment

There is often a confusion between the two distinct concepts of punishment and compensation, and the implications that each of them has. Compensation is a form of financial restoration to the status quo, so far as possible. In principle, the greater the harm suffered, the greater the compensation due. Punishment is a form of censure, and should be influenced not only by the gravity of the harm done (or threatened) but also by the culpability of the offender. Thus, in two extreme cases, an attempted murder (e.g. by shooting) which did not actually cause harm would justify severe punishment but low compensation, whereas a death caused by gross negligence might justify a lower punishment but higher compensation.

Community restoration

This notion remains rather unclear. By what metric is it to be decided how much damage has been done to the community and how it needs to be restored? In sketching answers to this question, some writers (such as Van Ness)[9] come close to embracing a desert-based scale , taking account of harm and culpability. It is by no means clear what other metric can be used. There is also the question of what types of measure can be regarded as restorative. Monetary fines would be a clear example, but there are limitations on offenders' ability to pay and on the length of time for which it is fair to exact financial penalties. Zedner (Selection 7.4) argues that community service orders can readily be conceptualized as a form of community restoration, and Lode Walgrave takes a similar view:

> "Community has been 'victimised' by the disruption of public order and can demand compensation for it in the form of a (compensatory) service to the community. From one who jeopardised community life by a lack of respect for others and social order, community can demand a (symbolic) effort in favour of community to compensate for the harm done".[10]

The difficult question is what other restorative measures, symbolic or otherwise, might be contemplated; and whether, and in what circumstances, custodial sentences might be used. This may be regarded as a major difficulty with Pettit and Braithwaite's theory. They give prominence to the notion of "reassurance" of the community as a feature of the appropriate response to offending. While they accept (Selection 7.2) that imprisonment has been much used and yet provides only false reassurance, the parameters of their own approach remain unclear, especially because they remain vague about the upper limits of state intervention in offenders' lives. They argue that courts should take account, among other things, of "how far the offender is capable of offending again", and of "how common that offence has become in the community". Ashworth and von Hirsch (Selection 7.3) point out that the authors do not propose any clear proportionality limits on sentencing, and appear to leave open the possibility of severe incapacitative and deterrent sentences. The assertion of Pettit and Braithwaite that "what rectification requires will vary with the character and circumstances of the offender" suggests few practical constraints and, having jettisoned the punishment paradigm, their writings offer no clear rationale for upper limits on sentence severity.

Organizations as victims or offenders

Restorative theories must deal with the fact that many offences do not have individual victims or offenders. These may be offences by companies (such as pollution, health and safety violations, consumer offences), against companies (typically theft and deception), or against the government (such as damage to government property, or falsification of tax documents), or even "victimless" crimes such as drug offences and other crimes of possession. There is no reason in principle why companies should not play their part in a restorative justice system, but one would need to guard against inequalities of power in any negotiations with individual offenders.[11] As for government, it would be possible to designate certain officials as representatives of the state for the purposes of restorative justice, but that raises various questions about the policies they should follow in any negotiations. Some family group conferences are adapted to deal with victimless crimes such as drunk-driving.

Victims in the service of offenders?

Restorative theories based on the conflict-resolution paradigm depend on the willingness of victims to become involved, and some are unwilling.[12] There should be no question of compelling victims to become involved, especially since the risk of secondary victimization through the criminal process is a known phenomenon, although no doubt restorative theorists would hope that a higher proportion of victims would become involved as the community became more familiar with the new processes. Nonetheless, conflict-resolution theorists must decide what approach to take if the victim is unwilling. To allow the victim effectively to veto a restorative approach might severely handicap restorative programmes, unless most victims showed a willingness to participate. And even then, what should be done in those cases where a victim wants no involvement? Finally, there is the more general warning, insisted upon by Christie among others, that there should be clarity about whether the victim's involvement in these processes is justified insofar as it may help the victim, or as part of a reintegration process for the benefit of the wider community, or chiefly for the offender's future well-being. If victims really are being used in the service of offenders, or even of the wider community, this needs to be supported by clear justifications.

Victim services or procedural rights for victims?

Those who favour a punishment paradigm for the sentencing process might draw a distinction between a victim's right to services and a victim's procedural rights in the criminal process. As argued earlier, victims may fairly expect support when victimized, respect from the police and lawyers during questioning, accurate information about the progress of the case and any court hearing, separate waiting areas and active support at courts, and so forth. There is also a strong argument that the state should assure compensation to the victims of crime, at least in the broad category of violent crimes.[13] But giving victims the right to be consulted on decisions to prosecute, on the acceptance of a plea of guilty, or on matters of sentence, is more difficult to justify. Procedural rights need to be justified according to the purpose of the criminal justice system, and that brings in the issue of the state's responsibility and the victim's rights (discussed above in this Introduction). Victim-centred approaches to criminal justice often seem to assume, without much argument, that victims have some such entitlement. This may draw on Christie's notion that the conflict somehow belongs, in part at least, to the victim. It ignores what he and other restorative writers, such as Pettit and Braithwaite, Cavadino and Dignan, have to say about the community's interest. It also threatens to infiltrate into the criminal justice system – whether its foundations lie in the punishment paradigm or the restorative paradigm – a rogue individualism, which might make decisions depend on whether the particular victim is forgiving or vengeful. Many jurisdictions now permit a victim to submit a "victim impact statement", detailing the effect of the crime on the victim and/or victim's family. Even where such statements do not include any suggestions on sentence, there are various difficulties of principle and practice which must not be overlooked.[14] However, it can be argued that within a restorative system any "rogue individualism" could be contained by establishing some kind of guidelines for the outcome of a mediation or conference. As Cavadino and Dignan (Selection 7.5) argue, the victim could be allowed a strong voice on the quantum and type of reparation, whilst maintaining a more objective (less individualized) approach to the question of restoration of the community.

Restorative Justice in Action

Although the focus of this book is upon sentencing principles, it is appropriate to devote some attention to the practical forms of restorative justice, if only because they differ from those in "conventional" criminal justice systems. As for the first paradigm, there are few criminal justice systems that have embraced a fully compensatory approach. More commonly a compensatory approach is grafted on to a "conventional" criminal justice system, giving rise to some of the questions of priority discussed by Zedner (Selection 7.4). The conflict-resolving paradigm has given rise to a range of different initiatives, of which two might be outlined here – mediation, and Family Group Conferences. The tendency thus far has been to use such approaches chiefly (but not exclusively) for minor cases or when dealing with young offenders.

Mediation

There are between 25 and 50 mediation schemes in England and Wales, many of them focused on non-serious crimes, and many of those dealing solely or chiefly with young offenders. The format differs from scheme to scheme: some mediation schemes are used as a means of diversion from prosecution, others as alternatives after conviction and before sentence, with further variations. A mediator, often a member of the Probation Service, will bring together the offender and the victim (provided they are both willing), will allow each of them to make a statement, and will try to bring about some kind of agreement on what should be done (such as an apology, repairing of damage, etc).[15] Whether the court takes account of the outcome, in cases where the offender is prosecuted, is a matter for the court. Some English schemes have been more ambitious, with the Leeds Mediation and Reparation Project aiming at non-minor offences, and the Northamptonshire Adult Reparation Scheme aiming at adult offenders, the latter with modest successes in terms of participation and satisfaction of victims.[16] Somewhat similar, and of longer standing in North America, are the various forms of Victim Offender Reconciliation Programmes, although they may take place after the offender has been sentenced rather than before. Their chief objective is to bring about some understanding between the victim and offender.[17]

Family Group Conferences (FGC)

These were introduced in New Zealand in the 1980s, and are now the principal means of dealing with young offenders under the Children,

Young Persons and their Families Act 1989 (NZ). Although diversion from court processes is one of their functions, they differ from mediation schemes in that there are other people present. Thus a FGC would include a representative of the police, the youth justice co-ordinator, the young offender and family, and the victim and family. The procedure provides, among other things, for the victim to give his or her view of the offence. The conference should move towards the formulation of an agreed plan, response or outcome. If none can be agreed, the case will be returned to the court – although this does not necessarily mean that the court will impose a punitive, as distinct from a reparative, sentence (this is certainly true of the South Australia scheme). Of course FGCs do not satisfy all victims, but there is evidence of considerable satisfaction,[18] and they have now been introduced in some Australian jurisdictions and in some localities in Britain. Braithwaite has expressed enthusiasm about the prospect of achieving "reintegrative shaming" through this kind of gathering,[19] although it appears that most of the schemes in operation do not employ the concept of "shaming" as such.

Conclusions

Restorative theories of criminal justice have a long history and a powerful contemporary presence. Many of those who oppose the repressive tendencies in recent penal policy are bound to be interested in restorative approaches, if only as less punitive alternatives. The first two readings below (Christie, Pettit and Braithwaite) are representative of those who would go further and argue for a fuller commitment to restorative justice. The last two readings (Zedner, Cavadino and Dignan) illustrate two of the intermediate points between conventional or desert-based systems and restorative justice. Among the important questions that remain are: have they defined satisfactorily the position of the victim? What is the interest of the state, and/or the community? Are individual victims to have a role in the choice of response to an offence? In determining what response would restore the community, what are to be the parameters? If proportionality to the offence is not to be recognized as a determining factor, to what extent can incapacitative and deterrent measures be taken against offenders? Do the writings of Braithwaite and Pettit, in particular, contain sufficient safeguards against the imposition of drastic sentences?

[A.A.]

Notes

1. For discussions of the history, see S. Schafer, *Restitution to Victims of Crime* (1960), and M. Wright, *Justice for Victims and Offenders* (1996), ch. 1.
2. See L. Walgrave , "Restorative Justice for Juveniles", (1995) 34 *Howard J.C.J.* 228, at 234.
3. D. Van Ness, "New Wine and Old Wineskins: Four Challenges of Restorative Justice", (1993) 4 *Criminal Law Forum* 251.
4. See the discussion by J. Dignan and M. Cavadino, "Towards a Framework for Conceptualising and Evaluating Models of Criminal Justice from a Victim 'Perspective' " (1996) 4 *International Review of Victimology* 153.
5. See also Walgrave, above n. 2, pp. 234–5, on harm to "the fundamental values of society".
6. J. Braithwaite and P. Pettit, *Not Just Deserts: a Republican Theory of Criminal Justice* (1990).
7. See, for example, G. del Vecchio, "The Struggle against Crime", discussed by A. Ashworth, "Punishment and Compensation: Offenders, Victims and the State", (1986) 6 *Oxford J.L.S.* 86, at 92–4.
8. For an analysis of variations in the use of the term "community" in contemporary criminal justice, see N.Lacey and L.Zedner, "Discourses of Community in Criminal Justice", (1995) 22 *Journal of Law and Society* 301.
9. D. Van Ness, "New Wine and Old Wineskins: Four Challenges of Restorative Justice", (1993) 4 *Criminal Law Forum* 251; see the critique by A. Ashworth, "Some Doubts about Restorative Justice", *ibid.*, 277, and the reply by Van Ness, *ibid.*, 301.
10. Walgrave , above n. 2, p. 235.
11. Cf. J. Braithwaite and S. Mugford, "Conditions of Successful Degradation Ceremonies", (1994) 34 *B.J.Crim.* 139, esp. at 156–8.
12. For some figures from New Zealand, see A. Morris, G. Maxwell and J. Robertson, "Giving Victims a Voice: a New Zealand Experiment", (1993) 32 *Howard J.C.J.* 304.
13. European Convention on Compensation for the Victims of Crimes of Violence (1984).
14. See A. Ashworth, "Victim Impact Statements and Sentencing", [1993] *Crim.L.R.* 498.
15. See, e.g. M.Wright, "Victims, Mediation and Criminal Justice", [1995] *Crim.L.R.* 187; and the chapters by Dignan and by Marshall in A. Duff, S. Marshall, R. E. Dobash and R. P. Dobash (eds.), *Penal Theory and Practice* (1994).
16. See J. Dignan, *ibid.*
17. See M. Wright and B. Galaway (eds.), *Mediation and Criminal Justice* (1989).
18. e.g. A. Morris, G. Maxwell and J. P. Robertson, "Giving Victims a Voice: a New Zealand Experiment", (1993) 32 *Howard J.C.J.* 304; New Zealand Ministry of Justice, *Restorative Justice* (1995), esp. chs. 5 and 7.
19. J. Braithwaite, *Crime, Shame and Reintegration* (1989), as applied in J. Braithwaite and S. Mugford, "Conditions of Successful Reintegration

Ceremonies", (1994) 34 *B.J.Crim.* 139. Cf. H. Blagg, "A Just Measure of Shame?", (1997) 37 *British Journal of Criminology* 481, and J. Braithwaite, "Conferencing and Plurality: Reply to Blagg", *ibid.*, at 502.

7.1

Conflicts as Property

NILS CHRISTIE

Full participation in your own conflict presupposes elements of civil law. The key element in a criminal proceeding is that the proceeding is converted from something between the concrete parties into a conflict between one of the parties and the state. So, in a modern criminal trial, two important things have happened. First, the parties are being *represented*. Secondly, the one party that is represented by the state, namely the victim, is so thoroughly represented that she or he for most of the proceedings is pushed completely out of the arena, reduced to the triggerer-off of the whole thing. She or he is a sort of double loser; first, *vis-à-vis* the offender, but secondly and often in a more crippling manner by being denied rights to full participation in what might have been one of the more important ritual encounters in life. The victim has lost the case to the state.

Professional Thieves

As we all know, there are many honourable as well as dishonourable reasons behind this development. The honourable ones have to do with the state's need for conflict reduction and certainly also its wishes for the protection of the victim. It is rather obvious. So is also the less honourable temptation for the state, or Emperor, or whoever is in power, to use the criminal case for personal gain. Offenders might pay for their sins. Authorities have in time past shown considerable willingness, in representing the victim, to act as receivers of the money or other property from the offender. Those days are gone; the crime control system is not run for profit. And yet they are not gone. There are, in all banality, many interests at stake here, most of them related to professionalization.

From Nils Christie, "Conflicts as Property", (1977) 17 *British Journal of Criminology* 1–15. Excerpted and reprinted with permission.

Lawyers are particularly good at stealing conflicts. They are trained for it. They are trained to prevent and solve conflict. They are socialised into a sub-culture with a surprisingly high agreement concerning interpretation of norms, and regarding what sort of information can be accepted as relevant in each case. Many among us have, as laymen, experienced the sad moments of truth when our lawyers tell us that our best arguments in our fight against our neighbour are without any legal relevance whatsoever and that we for God's sake ought to keep quiet about them in court. Instead they pick out arguments we might find irrelevant or even wrong to use . . .

Conflicts become the property of lawyers. But lawyers don't hide that it is conflicts they handle. And the organizational framework of the courts underlines this point. The opposing parties, the judge, the ban against privileged communication within the court system, the lack of encouragement for specialization—specialists cannot be internally controlled—it all underlines that this is an organization for the handling of conflicts. *Treatment personnel* are in another position. They are more interested in *converting the image of the case from one of conflict into one of non-conflict* . . .

One way of reducing attention to the conflict is reduced attention given to the victim. Another is concentrated attention given to those attributes in the criminal's background which the healer is particularly trained to handle. Biological defects are perfect. So also are personality defects when they are established far back in time—far away from the recent conflict. And so are also the whole row of explanatory variables that criminology might offer. We have, in criminology, to a large extent functioned as an auxiliary science for the professionals within the crime control system. We have focused on the offender, made her or him into an object for study, manipulation and control. We have added to all those forces that have reduced the victim to a nonentity and the offender to a thing. And this critique is perhaps not only relevant for the old criminology, but also for the new criminology. While the old one explained crime from personal defects or social handicaps, the new criminology explains crime as the result of broad economic conflicts. The old criminology loses the conflicts, the new one converts them from inter-personal conflicts to class conflicts. And they are. They are class conflicts—also. But, by stressing this, the conflicts are again taken away from the directly involved parties. So, as a preliminary statement: Criminal conflicts have either become *other people's property*—primarily the property of lawyers—or it has been in other people's interests to *define conflicts away*. . . .

Conflicts as Property

Material compensation is not what I have in mind with the formulation "conflicts as property". It is the *conflict itself* that represents the most interesting property taken away, not the goods originally taken away from the victim, or given back to him. In our types of society, conflicts are more scarce than property. And they are immensely more valuable.

They are valuable in several ways. Let me start at the societal level . . . Highly industrialised societies face major problems in organizing their members in ways such that a decent quota take part in any activity at all. Segmentation according to age and sex can be seen as shrewd methods for segregation. Participation is such a scarcity that insiders create monopolies against outsiders, particularly with regard to work. In this perspective, it will easily be seen that conflicts represent a *potential for activity, for participation*. Modern criminal control systems represent one of the many cases of lost opportunities for involving citizens in tasks that are of immediate importance to them. Ours is a society of task-monopolists.

The victim is a particularly heavy loser in this situation. Not only has he suffered, lost materially or become hurt, physically or otherwise. And not only does the state take the compensation. But above all he has lost participation in his own case. It is the Crown that comes into the spotlight, not the victim. It is the Crown that describes the losses, not the victim. It is the Crown that appears in the newspaper, very seldom the victim. It is the Crown that gets a chance to talk to the offender, and neither the Crown nor the offender are particularly interested in carrying on that conversation. The prosecutor is fed-up long since. The victim would not have been. He might have been scared to death, panic-stricken, or furious. But he would not have been uninvolved. It would have been one of the important days in his life. Something that belonged to him has been taken away from that victim.

But the big loser is us—to the extent that society is us. This loss is first and foremost a loss in *opportunities for norm-clarification*. It is a loss of pedagogical possibilities. It is a loss of opportunities for a continuous discussion of what represents the law of the land. How wrong was the thief, how right was the victim? Lawyers are, as we saw, trained into agreement on what is relevant in a case. But that means a trained incapacity in letting the parties decide what *they* think is relevant. It means that it is difficult to stage what we might call a political debate in the court. When the victim is small and the offender big—in size or power—how blameworthy then is the crime? And what about the opposite case, the small thief and the big house-owner? If the offender is well educated, ought he then to suffer more or maybe less, for his sins? Or if he is black, or if he is young, or if the other party is an insurance company, or if his wife has just left him, or if his factory will break down if he has to go to jail, or if his daughter will lose her fiancé, or if he was drunk, or if he was sad, or if he was mad? There is no end to it. And maybe there ought to be none . . .

A Victim-Oriented Court

There is clearly a model of neighbourhood courts behind my reasoning. But it is one with some peculiar features, and it is only these I will discuss in what follows.

First and foremost; it is a *victim-oriented* organization. Not in its initial stage, though. The first stage will be a traditional one where it is established whether it is true that the law has been broken, and whether it was this particular person who broke it.

Then comes the second stage, which in these courts would be of the utmost importance. That would be the stage where the victim's situation was considered, where every detail regarding what had happened—legally relevant or not—was brought to the court's attention. Particularly important here would be detailed consideration regarding what could be done for him, first and foremost by the offender, secondly by the local neighbourhood, thirdly by the state. Could the harm be compensated, the window repaired, the lock replaced, the wall painted, the loss of time because the car was stolen given back through garden work or washing of the car 10 Sundays in a row? Or maybe, when this discussion started, the damage was not so important as it looked in documents written to impress insurance companies? Could physical suffering become slightly less painful by any action from the offender, during days, months or years? But, in addition, had the community exhausted all resources that might have offered help? Was it absolutely certain that the local hospital could not do anything? What about a helping hand from the janitor twice a day if the offender took over the cleaning of the basement every Saturday? None of these ideas is unknown or untried, particularly not in England. But we need an organization for the systematic application of them.

Only after this stage was passed, and it ought to take hours, maybe days, to pass it, only then would come the time for an eventual decision on punishment. Punishment, then, becomes that suffering which the judge found necessary to apply *in addition to* those unintended constructive sufferings the offender would go through in his restitutive actions *vis-à-vis* the victim. Maybe nothing could be done or nothing would be done. But neighbourhoods might find it intolerable that nothing happened. Local courts out of tune with local values are not local courts. That is just the trouble with them, seen from the liberal reformer's point of view.

A fourth stage has to be added. That is the stage for service to the offender. His general social and personal situation is by now well-known to the court. The discussion of his possibilities for restoring the victim's situation cannot be carried out without at the same time giving information about the offender's situation. This might have exposed needs for social, educational, medical or religious action—not to prevent further crime, but because needs ought to be met. Courts are public arenas, needs are made visible. But it is important that this stage comes *after* sentencing. Otherwise we get a re-emergence of the whole array of so-called "special measures"—compulsory treatments—very often only euphemisms for indeterminate imprisonment.

Through these four stages, these courts would represent a blend of elements from civil and criminal courts, but with a strong emphasis on the civil side.

A Lay-Oriented Court

The second major peculiarity with the court model I have in mind is that it will be one with an extreme degree of lay-orientation. This is essential when conflicts are seen as property that ought to be shared. It is with conflicts as with so many good things: they are in no unlimited supply. Conflicts can be cared for, protected, nurtured. But there are limits. If some are given more access in the disposal of conflicts, others are getting less. It is as simple as that.

Specialization in conflict solution is the major enemy; specialization that in due—or undue—time leads to professionalization. That is when the specialists get sufficient power to claim that they have acquired special gifts, mostly through education, gifts so powerful that it is obvious that they can only be handled by the certified craftsman.

With a clarification of the enemy, we are also able to specify the goal; let us reduce specialization and particularly our dependence on the professionals within the crime control system to the utmost.

The ideal is clear; it ought to be a court of equals representing themselves. When they are able to find a solution between themselves, no judges are needed. When they are not, the judges ought also to be their equals.

7.2

Republicanism in Sentencing: Recognition, Recompense and Reassurance

PHILIP PETTIT WITH JOHN BRAITHWAITE

In *Not Just Deserts: A Republican Theory of Criminal Justice*, we attempted to set out the overall view of the criminal justice system which a republican philosophy would support.[1] We explored the shape that a criminal justice system would assume, if it were organized so as to promote the goal of republican liberty; this goal we described as one of enjoying personal dominion. We argued that it is necessary to think comprehensively about the shape that a criminal justice system ought to take and that, in this enterprise, the republican approach serves us well. In particular, we argued that it can serve us better than any other goal-oriented approach, such as utilitarianism, and better than any approach that is built around the constraint of delivering just deserts: the constraint of meting out punishment in proportion to the gravity of the offence and the culpability of the offender . . .

In a recent response to our book, two leading retributivists, Andrew von Hirsch and Andrew Ashworth,[2] maintain that, whatever there is to be said for going comprehensive in thinking about the criminal justice system— and they express some undocumented doubts about that—the republican theory that we advanced is certainly unsatisfactory in the area of sentencing policy. They suggest that on our theory, as on other goal-oriented or consequentialist theories, the courts should pronounce sentence in the manner that best serves the society overall, even if doing so expresses an indifference to the offender's degree of guilt, or indeed the victim's level of suffering. They imply that on the republican approach, the conviction of an offender provides the courts with a licence to look to the future and try to optimize results, neglecting the nature of the offence to which the sentence is meant to be a response. "What thus remains troublesome about the authors' 'dominion' theory is its forward-looking and aggregative

From Philip Pettit with John Braithwaite, "Not Just Deserts, Even in Sentencing", (1993) 4 *Current Issues in Criminal Justice* 222–39. Excerpted and reprinted with permission.

features. These features appear to give licence to punish whenever, and to the extent that, potential victims' net gain in dominion exceeds the loss in dominion of those punished".[3]

The charge against us, then, is that whatever we say to the contrary, the logic of the republican position supports a licence-to-optimize sentencing policy. This paper is an attempt to show that that is not so, by developing in greater detail the sentencing policy implicit in the republican approach . . .

1. Republican Dominion

The main thing to say about the republican ideal of dominion is that it seeks to articulate the notion of liberty which was dominant in the republican tradition of thinking from Roman times down through the republican philosophies developed in the northern Italian republics of the late middle ages, in the course of the English Civil War, and in the development of English and American political thinking that lay behind the American revolution in the eighteenth century.[4] In that long history of thinking about liberty, as recent scholarship has emphasized, freedom was conceptualized as the social status enjoyed by someone who is not a slave and, more generally, by someone who is so protected by the law and culture of his community that he does not have to depend for the enjoyment of independent choice on the grace or favour or mercy of another. This was a tradition of thinking about liberty in which the core of liberty is the negative good of not being interfered with by others. Though the republican notion of liberty was negative in that respect, it naturally emphasized that liberty is constituted by the support against interference, and the status of being manifestly so supported, which goes with citizenship in an appropriately governed society; in a society where the rule of law obtains and power is systematically checked.

This republican notion of negative liberty was displaced in nineteenth century liberal circles by a conception of negative liberty in which the main thing is to avoid interference, not to enjoy the security and status of being protected against possible interference. The nineteenth century liberals were all involved, one way or another, in arguing the case for lifting government restraints on trade. In the course of this debate, as we see things, they invoked the language of liberty—the language of free trade—and in doing so they came to think of liberty, more and more, as the condition denied under any form of restraint, including the restraint of the law, not as the condition opposed primarily to that of the slave. Under the older, republican tradition, to be free was to enjoy a status constituted, in main part, by the protection and recognition of the law. Under the newer way of thinking, though with some reluctance and some blurring of the issues, freedom came to be represented as a condition that is compromised by any interference from others, even the sort of interference involved in the establishment of a protective law; this is a condition that is perfectly enjoyed, not in society, but in isolation from others. Republican freedom was the freedom of the city, the franchise of being incorporated and protected as well as any others against invasion; liberal freedom came to be conceptualized as the freedom of the heath, the freedom of the state of nature that is always diminished in some measure by participation in community.

Perhaps the best way to articulate the republican ideal of liberty, the ideal of dominion, as we call it, is to say that while perfect dominion requires non-interference by others, however interference is understood, it also requires two other features. First, that the non-interference be enjoyed, not just as a matter of contingent luck, but in virtue of the protection, to the highest degree standard for anyone in the society, of the law and related institutions. And second, if this needs adding, that it be salient to everyone in the society, in particular to the person enjoying it, that the non-interference involved is indeed of this resilient or secure character. Dominion is a social status, a status available in community only, which has an objective and a subjective side. Objectively, it is a condition of resilient non-interference; subjectively, it is a condition of saliently resilient non-interference . . .

It should be obvious why dominion is an attractive ideal for someone to enjoy and an appealing goal for social institutions to promote. The enjoyment of dominion means that a person can look others squarely in the eye, aware that he does not depend on their mercy or grace for living the unimpeded life. Like them, indeed equally with them, he is more or less proof or more or less secure against any ill that others wish upon him. Like them, and equally with them, this is a matter marked by common knowledge; he enjoys the socially recognized status, as well as the objectively reinforced condition of being guarded against interference. Anticipating what is essentially the liberal conception of negative liberty, Thomas Hobbes suggested that a resident of republican Lucca, protected by the law, might enjoy no more liberty than a counterpart in despotic Constantinople; if they enjoy non-interference to the same extent, albeit one enjoys it with salient resilience and the other only by good fortune, then for Hobbes they are equally free. The attraction of the ideal of dominion is that it articulates the manifest difference in the condition of these two people. They may enjoy non-interference to the same extent, but only the Lucchese enjoys freedom in the proper, republican sense of salient and resilient non-interference[5] . . .

2. Crime as the Denial of Dominion

There are two aspects to the denial of the victim's dominion involved in crime. First of all, any act of crime against an individual will involve the disregard of the dominion of that person, the flouting of his status as a citizen protected, indeed saliently protected, against interference. If someone commits a crime against a person, then his act asserts the vulnerability of the victim to his, the criminal's, will. The act of crime nullifies that status; it amounts to the claim that the status is hollow; that it is nothing in itself or that this individual is no true possessor of it.

We describe this first aspect of the evil done by a crime as the disregard of the victim's dominion. While every crime involves the disregard of dominion, many crimes will also have a second evil aspect. If they are successful—if the criminal attempt is not frustrated—then they will tend either to diminish or even perhaps to destroy the dominion of the victim. To destroy a person's dominion will be to take it away, as in kidnap or murder. To diminish someone's dominion will be to reduce the range of activities over which the dominion is exercised. For example, to take some of the person's property or to assault them physically will be to diminish their dominion: it will be to undermine certain exercises of dominion that they might have pursued . . .

So much for the evil done to the victim by an act of crime. Every crime will also tend to do an evil to the community as a whole; it will affect, not just the dominion-status of the victim, but the overall dispensation of dominion established in the society. To enjoy dominion, as we know, is to enjoy the unimpeded life with salient resilience. Every act of crime amounts to a challenge to the dominion of people in the society as a whole, it does not affect just the victim alone. This is because, with every act of crime, it becomes less clear to everyone that they really do have non-interference in a resilient manner. The best testimony to the resilience with which I enjoy the unimpeded life is the resilience with which others enjoy it. If I see that crimes are committed against others—especially when the victims of crime do not have their complaints taken seriously or redressed—then the basis for believing that I enjoy resilient non-interference is undermined. My dominion is endangered. Dominion is a good whose enjoyment by anyone is highly sensitive to evidence of its enjoyment by others. Let anyone's dominion be disregarded, let anyone's dominion be diminished or destroyed, and the dominion of others is thereby reduced in some corresponding measure. It is sometimes said, controversially, that one cannot be a just person in an unjust society. What ought not to be controversial is that one cannot enjoy dominion, one cannot enjoy the unimpeded life with the salient resilience provided by the rule of law and associated institutions, in a society where the dominion of others is systematically disregarded, diminished or destroyed . . .

3. Rectifying the Evil of Crime

If we think that every act of crime amounts in these ways to a denial of dominion, then what ought we to expect the courts to do in response to the convicted criminal? What is going to be required by way of response, in the dispensation of republican dominion? What is going to be required, if the system is to promote the enjoyment of republican dominion overall? . . .

In sentencing the convicted criminal, it appears that the courts ought to seek the *recognition* by the offender of the dominion status of the victim, *recompense* by the offender for the damage he may have done, and *reassurance* to the community of a kind that may undo the negative impact of the crime on their enjoyment of dominion . . .

Before going to a more detailed and realistic level in interpreting what the courts should do in response to convicted criminals, there is an important matter that we should mark. Dominion is unusual among goods in being such that it is possible to conceive of rectifying acts that deny it to the individual: of remedying the evil that an offence represents.[6] The damage done to the victim's dominion is undone if the offender can deliver the appropriate measure of recognition and recompense. Dominion consists in the saliently resilient enjoyment of the unimpeded life and, however unwelcome it may be, an act of interference by another does not actually deprive someone of dominion if the interferer is required to give due recognition and recompense to the victim. On the contrary, the dominion of the victim is made manifest in the imposition of that requirement: it is made clear that the victim does indeed enjoy the protected status of the full citizen. The damage done to dominion in an act of crime is not the sort of thing, then, that has to be regarded as just a sunk cost when the courts come to deal with the offender. Dominion is such that it is natural, indeed essential, for the courts to consider in the first place how to undo the damage and make the victim's dominion manifest.

The point emerging here is of the utmost importance. Although the courts are designed to promote dominion, as they ought to be under a republican regime, their first concern in sentencing is backward-looking in character: it is a concern for the rectification of the past crime, ideally by way of recognition and recompense. This point is of importance because, to return to a phrase employed earlier, it shows why a guilty verdict does not provide the republican court with a licence to optimize, where optimization is taken to be entirely a forward-looking matter. If a guilty verdict provides such a licence, it does so only in a sense in which the first element in optimization must be the rectification, so far as possible, of the damage to the victim's dominion.

What holds for the damage to the individual victim holds also for the damage done by crime, under the republican picture, to the dispensation of dominion at large. Like recognition and recompense, the notion of reassurance also has a backward-looking dimension. In seeking such measures against the offender, or such a response from him, as will reassure the community, the courts are again gauging what should be done by reference to what has been done in the past. What is sought is the restoration of the status quo in assurance: the restoration of the assurance enjoyed in the community prior to the offence. The notion of rectification, the notion of putting right a past wrong, remains firmly in place, even though the overall rationale of sentencing is to promote dominion in the society.

4. Rectification in Practice

As we look at rectification in practice, it will be useful, first, to put aside the assumption that perfect rectification is always possible: that is, to be more realistic; and second, to move from the abstract characterization of rectification, perfect or imperfect, to a more concrete description of what it is likely to involve: that is, to be more detailed. We shall take these steps in turn, looking at each stage into the requirements of recognition, recompense and reassurance.

Going more realistic

Abstractly, the recognition of the dominion of the victim by the offender would seem to require a mix of symbolic and substantial measures. Symbolically, it might involve an apology on the part of the offender for the past offence, a commitment not to offend again, and some sort of reconciliation with the victim. Substantially, it ought to involve whatever material measures are necessary to give credibility to those symbolic acts, providing an assurance of the sincerity with which they are performed. What exact mix of the symbolic and the substantial ought to be sought in practice? That will vary with different sorts of offences, depending on the relationship between offender and victim, and depending of course on the kind of offence perpetrated. The victim may not wish for reconciliation or apology; he may shy away from any exposure to the offender. The victim may be an organization that is represented by its officers; it may even be the government or the community, as in tax fraud. Or, of course, the victim may be dead, as in a case of murder, and may have to be represented by others. Again, the offender may be a hardened character in whom it is difficult to render any act of apology or reconciliation, or any commitment not to offend again, credible. With variations in these matters, there will obviously be variations in what may be thought to be required by way of securing recognition, or something close to recognition, for the victim.

Similar points apply as we begin to think more realistically, if still abstractly, about what recompense should involve. If possible, recompense would involve *restitution* to the victim of whatever it was he lost in the original act of offence. But of course restitution will not always be possible; it is likely to be possible only with crimes against property. In such a case *compensation* should be provided, if something in the way of compensation is itself possible. Compensation would involve the offender providing something to the victim to make up for the loss suffered: something different in kind, unlike the case of restitution, but considered to be at least roughly commensurable in value. But it may be that neither restitution nor compensation is possible, as in the case of murder. Here recompense would seem to require something of the kind that is traditionally describes as *reparation*. Compensation may be required for those close to, and dependent on, the victim of the offence but we would naturally look for some form of reparation to make up for the damage, the fatal damage, to the victim himself.

Finally, reassurance. Perfect reassurance would be available if the offender were removed from the community: removal from the community may be final, as in capital punishment, or temporary, as in imprisonment. But capital punishment is unlikely to appeal to republicans, because its availability would impact on the dominion of anyone who reckons— and which of us may not—that he may himself fall foul of the courts; it is liable to offend against the dispensation of dominion in the manner of the unlimited penalties discussed and rejected later in this section. And, in any case, both capital punishment and imprisonment, by the evidence of criminology, are dubious means of securing the sort of reassurance sought. Imprisonment has been the dominant means of reassurance that Western communities have pursued since the eighteenth century. But because prisons embitter offenders and introduce them to criminal values and criminal skills, they provide only a false assurance. Increasingly the falsity of the assurance given by prisons is becoming transparent to ordinary people, as the falsity of the assurance provided by capital punishment became transparent during an earlier period of European history.

What to say, then, about reassurance? We believe that the criminal justice system should take all reported crimes seriously and refrain from treating a crime lightly simply because it is a first offence or because there are so many others like it. But we think that it can do this, without responding very harshly to every offence. It will be enough for the system to be minimalist in its responses, minimalist in particular in the sentences passed by the courts, provided that the capacity is there to escalate responses progressively—ultimately to imprisonment—as an offender displays more and more intransigence about offending against others. It is the capacity to escalate responses in this way, rather than the level of response implemented in any given case, that is crucial to the promotion of community reassurance. Or so at least we believe; the claim cannot be defended in the present context.[7]

Going more detailed

So much for the more realistic but still very abstract interpretation of recognition, recompense and reassurance. The pressing question for normative criminologists is how to interpret such abstract requirements in more detailed ways. Here we can only offer some general remarks in order to indicate the direction in which specific republican proposals are likely to go.

First, some remarks about the statutory constraints which republicans are likely to want to place on the sentencing practices of the courts. We argued in *Not Just Deserts* for two general sorts of constraint. One was a constraint which would outlaw capital or corporal punishment and put in place a preference for fines and community service over imprisonment. We argued for this sort of constraint on the grounds that such punishments would interfere less with the dominion of the offenders, while promising the best that we can hope to get by way of specific and general deterrence. Second, and very importantly, we argued that the courts ought to be constrained by the statutory imposition of upper limits on the sentences that may be handed down. We argued for this constraint on the grounds that if there were no upper limits, then that would have a very negative effect on the dominion of citizens at large. It would mean that citizens at large would have to recognize that in the event of coming before a court that found them guilty of some crime, perhaps mistakenly found them so guilty, they would then be at the mercy of the courts, in particular at the mercy of individual judges and, later, prison or other authorities. This would involve a substantial breach of people's dominion generally. It would mean that there was one serious sort of eventuality under which their status would be little better than that of the slave: they would be reduced to a condition of utter vulnerability.

Von Hirsch and Ashworth counter this last argument with the following remark: "Eliminating such limits or making them easily permeable when dealing with dangerous offenders—could arguably enhance potential victims' sense of security against predatory conduct".[8] This response is misconceived. It suggests that potential victims are incapable of conceiving of themselves as potential defendants; it supposes there is a divide between victims and offenders such that measures taken against offenders are not likely to impact in any way on the status of victims. But this is a mistake. Everyone in society is a potential victim and equally everyone in society is, if not a potential offender, at least someone who may be mistakenly convicted as an offender; this danger is particularly salient for the members of some minority groups. The fact that the courts could impose a penalty of any degree of severity on a convicted offender—the fact that they could imprison him indefinitely, force him to live in servitude indefinitely to his victim, compel him to pay a substantial proportion of this income to the victim for the rest of his life—would undermine the dominion enjoyed by everyone. It would put in place the sort of vulnerability which it is the business of a republic to try to eliminate.

We have mentioned some general constraints that republicans would want to impose on the courts when it comes to what sorts of concrete sentences the courts should impose on convicted criminals. Any such constraints will leave the courts with a great deal of discretion, albeit a discretion subject to appeal and review, under a republican arrangement: the point is argued at length in *Not Just Deserts*. So how ought the courts to exercise that discretion? What particular sorts of sentences ought they to go for?

The exercise of discretion requires in every case, and in particular in the case of sentencing, a great deal of sensitivity to the particular offence in hand and general information bearing on how different initiatives are likely to work out. We think that at any time the courts ought to be directed by some general principles: ideally, by some general principles that command a high degree of assent in the community at large. But how, in general, do we think that the courts ought to behave?

Consider the issue of recognition, first of all. We think that the courts ought to look for possibilities of mediation whereby an offender might be reconciled with his victim and brought to make a commitment not to re-offend. We recognize, however, that such possibilities may not often exist. We would want the courts to explore what might be sought by way of recognition of the victim's dominion on the part of the offender in other sorts of cases. The offender ought in every case to be given the chance to understand the nature and seriousness of his offence and the opportunity to express regret and affirm a commitment not to re-offend. Failing that, the courts should seek to identify measures which, pursued against the offender, are at least likely to bring him to understand the gravity of what he has done: we are thinking here of the possibility of exposure to the results of similar offences committed by others.

Recompense will involve restitution or compensation or reparation, as we have already noted. In determining the precise form that this ought to take, we would expect the courts to take account of the circumstances of the offender. If restitution is possible, but not within the means of the offender, then it may be that extra help should be provided from a restitution fund, with the offender contributing only a part. Compensation and reparation will often be so imperfect that what matters is not the cash or service or whatever that is provided by the offender but the cost to the offender of providing it. A poor person may be able to make reparation, offering a credible token of repentance, by means of a payment that it would be derisory to impose on a rich individual or corporation. Thus we would expect the courts to be directed in such cases to take account of the wealth and status of the offender in determining what it is right to require of him by way of compensation or reparation.

Finally, reassurance. The courts should pay attention to the contrition and credibility of the offender, so far as there is reliable evidence on this matter; it would be relevant, for example, that this is a first offence and not one of a series of offences. Equally the courts should take account of how far the offender is capable of re-offending again and of how much suffering his offence may have already have caused him and his own; these are matters, after all, that impact directly on how much reassurance the community may require with the offender in question. What is required by way of reassurance about not re-offending, of course, is likely to be a function of how common that offence has become in the community. And so in certain circumstances we might expect the courts to be directed also to take account of the extent of that offence in the community at large.

These remarks are patchy and unstructured. They are meant simply to illustrate the direction in which republican theory is likely to go. What they should illustrate is that while republicans will always seek rectification of the original offence in the sentence imposed by the courts, what rectification requires—what is required by way of recognition, recompense and reassurance—will vary with the character and circumstances of the offender. Every crime will require to be rectified, and that means that the courts must attend to the gravity of the offence and the culpability of the offender. But rectification of the same type of offence may require one set of measures in this instance and another set of measures in that. Putting the matter otherwise, two sentences that represent formally equivalent attempts at rectification may differ materially—and quite dramatically—from one another.

5. Rectification Versus Retribution

The discussion so far ought to have indicated that it would be quite inappropriate to charge republican theory with supporting the licence-to-optimize policy of sentencing that may rightly be associated with more traditional consequentialist approaches. In bringing that sort of charge against republican theory, von Hirsch and Ashworth are simply not paying attention to the difference between republicanism about criminal justice and other consequentialist theories. But in conclusion to this discussion, we would like to spend a little time considering how republican theory compares with the retributivism—the just deserts theory—supported by thinkers like von Hirsch and Ashworth.

One feature in common between republican theory and retributivism is that they would each have the courts look backwards to the offence committed in determining the sentence to be imposed; they would each reject the licence-to-optimize approach, where optimizing is thought of as a forward-looking activity. But this common point leaves room for three major differences between the approaches and these differences all argue in favour of republican theory, at least by our lights.

The first difference is that whereas retributivist theory cannot go very deep in motivating the sort of response which it would have the courts display in sentencing, republican theory can provide a general and compelling motivation for the response it would seek. The retributivist will say that in passing sentence the courts ought to repay the offender for what he has done, express blame for what he has done, restore the balance that he has disturbed, or something of the kind. Why should the courts seek to do some such thing? The only answer available is that that is what it is right to seek: no crime should go unpunished, and that is an end of the matter. The republican theorist can say much more about why he would want the courts to sentence convicted offenders along the lines that he recommends. He can argue that this is the right thing for the courts to do because it is the sort of contribution required of the courts if they are to serve, as the criminal justice system in general should serve, in the promotion of dominion. There is no quick end of the matter here: the promotion of dominion serves as an independent yardstick for the appropriateness of the court's response.

A second difference between the two approaches is that whereas retributivists look in general for some way of repaying the offence, seeking a penalty that is proportional to it, republican theorists look to what is required by way of rectifying the offence. The point is not to repay in proportional coin, however the need for repayment is formulated, but to put right or to rectify. Thus, whereas the retributivist concentrates on the offence in abstraction, the republican will look to the harm done to victims and communities and will consider how best that harm may be put right in the sentence imposed on the offender. The retributivist may say in his defence that he looks to the law of tort for the rectification of the harm done to the victim and that, more generally, he looks outside the criminal justice system for how the victim may be compensated. The republican will see this defence as a mere statement of conservatism, for he will be happy to see compensation and other tort considerations involved equally in the criminal law: he will see it only as right to take compensation into account when considering matters of punishment. He will argue that a justice system which leaves it to victims to use tort law to get criminal compensation will put compensation beyond the reach of all but the very rich. If compensation comes apart from punishment in his book, that will only be because compensation will often be the appropriate response for the state to make to a victim of crime in the event of the crime not being solved.

Finally, and perhaps most importantly, there is a great difference between the predisposition of the retributivist and the republican when it comes to the question of what kind of penalty and what degree of penalty ought to be imposed. Retributivists generally look for hard treatment as the appropriate kind of response—this is often justified on grounds of deterrence—and seek proportionality between offence and punishment in how this hard treatment is delivered. "Punishment consists in (1) the imposition of hard treatment, in a manner that (2) conveys disapproval of the actor for his conduct."[9]

This means, in effect, that retributivists tend to impose upper and lower limits on the sentences which the courts may hand down. The courts are required to ignore many differences in the character and circumstances of offenders and their families; they are expected to scale the sentences to the gravity of the offence committed and the culpability of the offender, ignoring other factors. Some room may be left for taking other considerations into account but this is generally very restricted.[10]

Republican theorists have a very different approach to the matter of what kind and level of response is suitable for a given offence. Republicans will say that so far as possible every offence ought to be rectified. But, when it comes to the matter of what rectification requires—and many principles, parsimony to the fore, will govern the interpretation of what it requires—they acknowledge that that can differ widely from case to case; the point was made in the previous section. Republican theorists will want to impose upper limits, as mentioned, on the rectification which the courts may pursue. But they will not impose any lower limits, recognizing as they must, that in many cases what is sufficient for rectification may fall well below what is required on some retributivist metric of punishment.

We mentioned that we thought these three differences between retributivism and republican theory all argue in favour of the republican approach. But that claim may be challenged in regard to the third difference. For it may be said, as indeed it has been said by von Hirsch and Ashworth, that republican theory allows a sort of unfairness in the treatment of convicted offenders which retributivism would outlaw. What to say, finally, in response?

What we have to say is that at the formal level, at the level where we consider rectification as such, there is no unfairness in the treatment of convicted offenders. All are treated in the manner required for the rectification of what they have done. If there are differences of a material kind between formally equivalent sentences—if what is required for rectification here is harsher than what is required there—that is hardly something of which an offender can complain, particularly if he is guaranteed against being punished beyond a certain level. A complaint about the matter would be akin to someone complaining that because taxes are proportional—proportional, not even progressive—he, a rich man, is treated unfairly in comparison to someone who is poor: he pays the same percentage of his income but a higher absolute amount.

If the criticism of unfairness continues to be pressed, there is another consideration that we can also mention: one discussed at length in *Not Just Deserts* but ignored by von Hirsch and Ashworth, when they level the charge against us. This is that we are lucky in any actual society if we can apprehend and punish the offenders in 10 per cent of crimes. Thus a concern with the material differences between how we punish convicted offenders is not as well motivated as it might be if we were able to identify and indict most offenders. For if we vary the sentences so that not all get the upper limit of what is permitted by way of material response to crime, that may serve to reduce the sort of unfairness involved in only 10 per cent of offenders getting any punishment at all.

Notes

1. J. Braithwaite, and P. Pettit, *Not Just Deserts: a Republican Theory of Criminal Justice* (Oxford: Oxford University Press, 1990).
2. A. von Hirsch, and A. Ashworth, "Not Not Just Deserts: a Response to Braithwaite and Pettit", (1992) 12 *Oxford Journal of Legal Studies* 83–98.
3. *Ibid.*, at p. 87.
4. See Braithwaite and Pettit, above n. 1, ch.5, for an account of these developments.
5. On the Hobbesian claim, and the response of the contemporary republican figure James Harrington, see *ibid.*, p. 59.
6. Our notion of rectification is closely related to the idea of redress introduced in W. de Haan, *The Politics of Redress* (1990), at pp. 156ff. See also G. del Vecchio, *Justice: an Historical and Philosophical Essay* (1952), at pp. 210–11, for congenial remarks.
7. See I. Ayres, and J. Braithwaite, *Responsive Regulation: Transcending the Deregulation Debate* (1992). Needless to say, sanctions are only a small part of what makes for reassurance in many cases. With domestic violence, for example, shelters may be more important than imprisonment in promoting the relevant form of reassurance. See L. W. Sherman, *Policing Domestic Violence* (1992).
8. Von Hirsch and Ashworth, above n. 2, at p. 88.
9. *Ibid.*, at p. 95.
10. *Ibid.*, at p. 96.

7.3

Desert and the Three Rs

ANDREW ASHWORTH AND ANDREW VON HIRSCH

In Selection 7.2, Philip Pettit (with John Braithwaite) replied to a critical review article of ours[1] about their book *Not Just Deserts: a Republican Theory of Criminal Justice*. Pettit's reply attempts to spell out their republican theory more fully. The application of the theory to sentencing, he asserts, should be based on three main ideas—recognition, recompense and reassurance. The three Rs do not, however, reassure us.

The book by Braithwaite and Pettit relied explicitly on aggregating concerns, particularly deterrence and incapacitation. Deterrence sets the lower limit of the "decremental strategy". Incapacitation is authorized within (vaguely defined) upper limits. Now Pettit comes with (to quote Monty Python) something completely different: a purported restorative theory embodied in his three Rs. But the old aggregative stuff is there, barely concealed, in his discussion of reassurance. To reassure the community, he says, the courts may look to the likelihood of the offender's offending again, and also to the prevalence of the offence in the community. The leeway allowed for incapacitative responses is particularly noteworthy: "crucial to the promotion of community reassurance", Pettit asserts, is the power to "escalate responses" as "an offender displays more and more intransigence about offending against others". No principled restraints are provided on the extent to which penalties may thus be increased, in order to provide the requisite reassurance to the community. Within the wide discretion beneath the nebulous "upper limits" there remains considerable freedom to optimize and to increase sanctions.

In our earlier critique of *Not Just Deserts*, we argued that the Braithwaite-Pettit goal of maximizing dominion does not of itself yield adequate fairness constraints. Pettit's article does not solve that difficulty, but only makes it worse. The problem resides in the conflict between the potential victim's dominion interest and that of the potential offender. If

From A. Ashworth and A. von Hirsch, "Desert and the Three Rs", (1993) 5 *Current Issues in Criminal Justice* 3, with some textual changes.

dominion consists, as Pettit says, of not merely avoiding victimization but also being given the sense of assurance of safety, this might be best achieved by aggressive crime control strategies. The more drastic the penalties and the more ambitious their enforcement, the more confident members of the public might be that they will not be disturbed. The trouble is, of course, that such strategies may be unfair in various ways, notably in their disproportionate severity. Such responses may, among other things, threaten the dominion of offenders and potential offenders.

If such a conflict exists, how might it be resolved? If the solution resides in maximizing dominion, there remains the problem of aggregation. And since there are likely to be more victims than offenders, an aggregative solution would point to favouring potential victims through tough penal strategies.

How does Pettit deal with this conflict? He merely denies that it exists. Everyone, he says, is a potential convict as well as a potential victim. But that surely is too easy. One might suggest that citizens have a moral obligation to feel empathy with offenders, and to put themselves in offenders' shoes. But such a demand for empathy needs some moral base other than maximizing dominion. If one were to lower the standards of proof required at criminal trials, this might be regarded as threatening to citizens because it would make them fear unwarranted convictions. But suppose that standards of proof remain unchanged, and that tougher sanctions are imposed on those who are convicted—primarily on recidivists, or on sexual and violent offenders. Would ordinary citizens have any particular reason to fear such punishments? Would they see themselves as potential offenders in these categories? No: it is much more likely that they would feel their security against crime (i.e. their dominion) enhanced. Thus the emphasis on citizens' sense of security and vulnerability is worrisome. Increases in sanction severity often have few traceable preventive effects, as research on deterrence and "selective incapacitation" indicates. But even if tougher policies do not actually make citizens safer, they may make them *feel* safer. To the extent that tougher policies have this placebo effect on "fear of crime", they would be warranted under Pettit's notion of reassurance.

The other two Rs—recognition and recompense—are no less problematic. Some victims may be forgiving and others vindictive, for example. Pettit accepts that "with variations in these matters, there will obviously be variations in what may be thought to be required by way of securing recognition, or something close to recognition, for the victim". If this would allow sentences to vary according to the disposition of the individual victim, it is surely problematic. Later, however, Pettit relinquishes

victim-oriented terminology and states that courts "should seek to identify measures which, pursued against the offender, are at least likely to
bring him to understand the gravity of what he has done", for example
"exposure to the results of similar offences committed by others". This
suggests a different approach, not dependent on the disposition of the victim, although again there is no mention of limiting principles. However,
when Pettit states that "two sentences that represent formally equivalent
attempts at rectification may differ materially—and quite dramatically—
from one another", he acknowledges that parity among defendants is not
a relevant factor. Yet when we are dealing with deprivations of liberty and
restrictions on liberty imposed by the state, is it right that similarly situated offenders who commit like offences should be subjected to greatly
different sentences, simply because of the victim's disposition or because
of the court's opinion of the best route to rectification?

Similar difficulties occur with recompense. On the one hand Pettit cas-
tigates desert theorists for regarding compensation as a matter only for the
civil courts: in fact desert theorists can and do accept that criminal courts
should be able to make compensation orders in favour of victims, and they
may also go further and discuss questions of priority when desert and
compensation conflict[2]—a point neglected by Pettit in relation to recompense and reassurance. On the other hand, Pettit refers sweepingly to the
republican's contentment to "see compensation and other tort considerations involved equally in the criminal law", whilst stating elsewhere that
the amount to be paid by the offender to the victim will depend on the
offender's wealth—a consideration well-established in criminal sentencing
but unknown to the law of tort. Del Vecchio and some other restorative
theorists argue that offenders should be made to labour in order to pay
their victims in full, which has the merit of following logically from their
premises.[3] How far Pettit goes down this road remains unclear.

Another unresolved problem arising from Pettit's gesture towards
restorative theory is that the requirements of recompense and of reassurance may conflict. A sentence which achieves reassurance might preclude
the rendering of recompense, and vice versa. It is a familiar weakness of
restorative theories that they assert the need to ensure both compensation
for the victim and some form of reparation to society at large, and yet fail
to specify what the latter consists of and how it differs from punishment
according to desert, the pursuit of a deterrent strategy or whatever. In
addition to the difficulties (noted earlier) with the notion of reassurance,
nothing is said about the differing demands of recompense and reassurance. On these issues, Pettit's article does not even "illustrate the direction
in which republican theory is likely to go".

We have suggested that the mnemonic attractiveness of the three Rs is not matched by the persuasiveness of the theory on which they are based. What about their application in a practical situation? Consider two offenders, one of whom (X) commits a minor crime and the other (Y) a more serious one. Suppose, however, that Y is quick to acknowledge the wrongfulness of his action (or at least to seem to do so), has a victim willing to be reconciled, has ample funds with which to pay compensation, and appears to have a low risk of future offending. X has a defiant attitude, has a vindictive victim, has few means with which to pay compensation, and presents a poor risk of future law-abidance. All three Rs would point to a much harsher response to X than to Y—even though X's original offence was much less serious. This seems to trample on elementary notions of fairness. Not only that, but Pettit's article suggests that the court would receive little guidance on how different cases might be dealt with—everything would turn on what seems likely to provide recognition, recompense and reassurance in the particular case. The unfettered discretion and lawless sentencing of the rehabilitative era would be reintroduced, only now in the name of dominion and rectification. This would be a step backwards, not forwards.

We should add that the discussion of desert theory at the end of Pettit's article betrays an unfamiliarity with the literature on the subject. Desert theorists such as ourselves (1) do not think that punishment should "repay" the offence, (2) do not think it should or can restore a balance,[4] (3) do think it should express blame, but (4) do not merely assert this last point, but try to argue why so. Maybe our arguments are mistaken, but that is different from saying that we give none (see, e.g., Selection 4.4 above). Nor do desert theorists wish to punish the offence "in abstraction". Variations in the degree of foreseeable harmfulness and of culpability of the conduct should be taken into account.

A penal theory should provide principled and fair guidance on the ordering of criminal penalties. Desert theory, we think, provides such guidance, however, imperfectly. The dominion theory of Braithwaite and Pettit—with or without the three Rs—does not. It appears that almost any ordering of penalties might conceivably be defended as promoting dominion or achieving rectification, especially when the notion of reassurance is so open-ended, and the still vague upper limits seem unlikely to provide much restraint. Pettit refers to the upper limits as the "guarantee against being punished beyond a certain level", but far too little is said about what notion of fairness underpins the guarantee, how it can be translated into fair maxima, and why it has not been assigned a more central role. The wide discretion and vague parameters of their new notion of rectification make these enquiries all the more important.

Notes

1. A. von Hirsch, and A. Ashworth, "Not Not Just Deserts: a Response to Braithwaite and Pettit", (1992) 12 *Oxford Journal of Legal Studies* 83, reprinted in slightly revised form as ch. 3 of A. von Hirsch, *Censure and Sanctions* (Oxford: Oxford University Press, 1993).
2. See further A. Ashworth, *Sentencing and Criminal Justice*, 2nd edn. (London: Butterworths, 1995), pp. 256–61.
3. For brief discussion of the theories of Giorgio del Vecchio and others, see A. Ashworth, "Punishment and Compensation: Offenders, Victims and the State", (1986) 6 *Oxford Journal of Legal Studies* 86.
4. For discussion, see von Hirsch, above n. 1, ch. 2.

7.4

Reparation and Retribution: Are They Reconcilable?

LUCIA ZEDNER

The arguments advanced for incorporating reparative elements into the criminal justice system are for the most part pragmatic and economic ones. At the most basic level, reparative justice is supported on the grounds that it is functional for the state to secure the payment of compensation or to support other ventures which seek to repair the damage done by crime. To the extent that reparative ventures are actually perceived by victims as having desirable effects, they reduce the possibility of a disgruntled victim taking the law into his or her own hands to seek redress. In the same vein, they lessen the likelihood that the victim will become so disaffected that they themselves turn to crime. Moreover, the prospect of reparation may encourage victims to report crimes, to co-operate with the police and to appear at trial, hence increasing the efficacy of the criminal justice process. Given that the vast majority of crimes are detected only with the aid of the general public, it must be desirable for these forms of co-operation to be encouraged . . .

Reparative sentences would, it is argued, not only lessen the burden of punishment on the offender but offer the possibility for constructive, forward-looking sentencing. Making good, whether via monetary compensation or other reparative endeavour, is also applauded as having psychological advantages over traditional retributive penalties. Reparation, it is argued, relieves the offender's feelings of guilt and alienation which may precipitate further crimes. The effect is said to be restorative not only to the victim but also to the offender, increasing their sense of self-esteem and aiding reintegration.[1]

These pragmatic purposes are largely uncontroversial, such controversy as exists arising mainly from doubts about the ability of reparation to achieve them. The theoretical reorientation posed by a fully developed

From Lucia Zedner, "Reparation and Retribution: are they Reconcilable?", (1994) 57 *Modern Law Review* 228–50. Excerpted and reprinted with permission.

reparative schema is more challenging. Such a schema would demand the abandonment of culpability of the offender as the central focus of sentencing and, in its place, pay much closer attention to the issue of harm. It would reconceive crimes less as the willed contraventions of an abstract moral code enshrined in law but, more importantly, as signals of social disfunction inflicting harm on victims (and perhaps also offenders) as well as society. According to this view, criminal justice should be less preoccupied with censuring the code-breakers and focus instead on the process of restoring individual damage and repairing ruptured social bonds.[2] In place of meeting pain with the infliction of further pain, a truly reparative system would seek the holistic restoration of the community. It would necessarily also challenge the sole claim of the state to respond to crime and would instead invite (or perhaps demand) the involvement of the community in the process of restoration.

What is Reparative Justice?

"Reparation" is not synonymous with restitution, still less does it suggest a straightforward importation of civil into criminal law. Reparation should properly connote a wider set of aims. It involves more than "making good" the damage done to property, body or psyche. It must also entail recognition of the harm done to the social relationship between offender and victim, and the damage done to the victim's social rights in his or her property or person. According to Davis, reparation "should not be seen as residing solely in the offer of restitution; adequate reparation must also include some attempt to make amends for the victim's loss of the presumption of security in his or her rights".[3] This way of thinking echoes, consciously or not, the concept of "dominion" developed by Braithwaite and Pettit.[4] For dominion to be restored, what is sought is some evidence of a change in attitude, some expression of remorse that indicates that the victim's rights will be respected in the future. Achieving such a change in attitude may entail the offender agreeing to undergo training, counselling or therapy and, as such, these may all be seen as part of reparative justice. A forced apology or obligatory payment of compensation will not suffice; indeed, it may even be counterproductive in eliciting a genuine change of attitude in the offender. But is "symbolic reparation" alone sufficient? According to Braithwaite, if reparation is not to come too cheap it must be backed up by material compensation. Accepting Braithwaite's view, the distinctions made between material and non-material or symbolic reparation tend to lose significance. It would seem that in most cases for full reparation to be achieved some mixture of the two will be required. Let us examine each in turn.

The most obvious and concrete form of reparative justice is compensation. Monetary compensation recognizes the fact that crime deprives its victim of the means to pursue life choices: it seeks to recognize that deprivation and to restore access either to those means which have been denied or to comparable alternative means . . .

In practice, compensation orders are set with reference to the ability of the offender to pay and, given that the majority of offenders are of limited means, they rarely result in complete restoration. In so far as reparation also seeks to promote the reintegration of the offender, it would surely be counterproductive to heap intolerable burdens on him. Although in seeking to embrace both reintegration and restoration simultaneously, reparative justice is necessarily riven by tensions, we should not see these aims as competing or necessarily in conflict: they are rather two sides of the same coin.

Less tangible but nonetheless important is what we might call "symbolic reparation". This might be an apology made by the offender to the victim or other attempts at reconciliation. The reparation here is "symbolic" in that it does not entail the return of money or material goods. Proponents of reparative justice argue that if the apology is not merely an empty gesture but one which conveys remorse and a genuine change of attitude, then such symbolic reparation is quite as important as more tangible returns. Mediation seeks to provide a way for parties to resolve disputes without recourse to the vagaries of the courts. It aims to allow both parties to retain control over the dispute and to voice their grievances under the supervision of a mediator, whether a trained professional or lay volunteer. In theory, the mediator acts only as a conduit and ideally any resolution is reached by the mutual agreement of the two parties. In practice, the form and organization of mediation schemes vary considerably . . .

Is Reparation Compatible with Punishment?

This is not the place to enquire into the philosophical foundations of the criminal law nor to explore at length theories of punishment. It is enough to recognize that certain basic elements of the prevailing paradigm must be fulfilled if reparation is to claim a place within it. These include: first, the imposition of "pain"; second, that the sanction is invoked in response to social wrongs (crimes); and, third, that it is applied against culpable offenders. Reparative justice must satisfy each of these elements if it is to escape the tag of "conceptual cuckoo". Let us examine them in turn.

(a) Punitive quality

Perhaps the most telling objection to reparative justice is that it has no intrinsic penal character and that to enforce civil liabilities through the criminal courts is not, of itself, to punish . . .

It is questionable, however, whether a compensation order can properly be seen as no more than a civil instrument riding on the back of a criminal trial. Unlike the French device of the *partie civile*,[5] compensation in English law is fully integrated into the criminal process and has the formal status of a penalty. . .

It is significant also that compensation orders extort money which, in the vast majority of cases, offenders would not otherwise have been required to pay. First, the action for recovery is brought about without financial cost to the victim. And, secondly, the state has the coercive mechanisms to ensure that repayment is actually made. In this sense, it may be said that the compensation order inflicts "pain" which is "additional" to that which civil law would otherwise exact. These factors also help to ensure that compensation orders are perceived both by offenders and society as "real" punishment. But the danger here is that to claim compensation orders operate as a punishment may lead us to the unhappy conclusion that for the offender the compensation order is undifferentiated from the fine and has little or no reparative quality. If the goal of restoring the recipient to a position akin to that which existed prior to the offence is obscured in the offender's mind by the punitive bite of the penalty, then it is unlikely that its avowed reintegrative aspects will be effective.

The objection that compensation lacks "penal value" becomes even more difficult to maintain in light of the fact that, since 1973, it has been possible to impose compensation as the sole penalty. Stigma attaches to conviction whatever the subsequent penalty and, where compensation is ordered alone, it too is accompanied by the shaming mechanism of the guilty verdict. We might do well to separate out notions of censure and sanction. It is possible to argue that the public drama of the trial, the naming of the defendant and, in particular, the formal attribution of guilt goes a long way toward fulfilling the requirements of censure. Once the demands of reproof have thus been met, is it not excessive to demand that penal sanctions also be endowed with censuring qualities?

In respect of mediation and reparation, the issue of punitive quality becomes more complex still. Purists might argue that the offender must enter into the process voluntarily and participate willingly in seeking an outcome. To the extent that participation is coerced, the reintegrative impact of mediation may be lost. But such a view is predicated upon reaching a resolution which is fully agreed upon by both parties. If the offender is a less than willing participant who agrees only reluctantly and under pressure, then it is more likely that he or she will fail to abide by the resolution reached. How, then, should enforcement be assured? Should mediation agencies have access to the full coercive powers of the court and, if they were to do so, would there not be a danger that the reparative potential would be undermined? Proponents of reparative justice might argue that discussion about enforcement is to miss the very point of mediation—that the outcome should be freely agreed and its terms willingly met. The experience of mediation in other areas (for example, the settlement of family disputes)[6] suggests that we would do well, however, to reflect further on what should happen if offenders fail to fulfil their part of the bargain. Should offenders be brought back to court, as would happen on breach of any other community disposal, and, if so, by whom and with what consequences?

(b) Recognition of social wrong

As we have seen, the original appeal to reparative justice was made through an evocation of a nostalgic vision of a bygone community in which disputes were settled by the parties to them.[7] Present mediation practice reflects this view and tends to treat crime as a personal issue between offender and victim. Not only does mediation take the private conflict as its sole object, but its organizational context sets it apart from the public symbolic processes of criminal justice. Most schemes promote mediation as an alternative to formal procedures, as a way of diverting the offender away from public prosecution. they host discussions between the immediate parties alone with only the mediator in attendance and shield their participants from media exposure. Whilst proponents might argue that all these measures are purposively designed to ensure that the parties retain a sense of ownership over "their" dispute, such tactics tend also to overlook the wider interests at stake. They tend also to strip the process of its power to signify public disapprobation and to inflict shame upon the offender. To this extent, it is arguable that reparation, narrowly conceived, fails to recognize that it is not only the victim but also society that has been wronged by the disregard shown for its norms and the general threat posed to public dominion. Another objection is that to make reparation to identifiable victims the primary aim of criminal justice would be effectively to decriminalize the mass of "victimless" offences. The model of mediating a dispute between two parties may operate with some plausibility in respect of interpersonal crimes of violence or theft, but offers little by way of resolution to crimes such as motoring violations, vandalism or public order offences.

It is surely possible, however, to put forward a broader conception of reparative justice which recognizes that the rights infringed by crime are not those of the victim alone but are held in common socially.[8] It is this social aspect which distinguishes crime from the private harms inflicted by torts. Thus, even where there is no identifiable victim, reparation to the wider community for actual harms or public "endangerment" is owed. Is it possible also for reparative forms of justice to fulfil the public functions (both recognition of the social wrong and public shaming) demanded by infringement of the criminal law? Proponents might legitimately argue that it is misplaced to look upon compensation and mediation as the only means to reparation and that penalties such as community service orders are better placed to make reparation to the wider community. One might then ask how far, or indeed whether, the community feels itself to be "repaired" by such activities. Until there is empirical research which offers evidence as to the psychological impact of "community service" on the community it purports to serve, it is probably unwise to make assertions about its wider reparative quality. Even to propose such research raises questions about the very entity of "community" and whether it actually refers to more than the geographical location in which mediation, reparation or community service orders take place.

If reparative justice, as currently conceived, fails to respond adequately to the social wrong which has been perpetrated, is it possible to envisage modifications which would allow it better to fulfil the public purposes of punishment? One would be to open up the mediation process, either by allowing the public to observe the proceedings or by permitting the media to report on both process and outcome. This would meet the requirement that the offender's offence be publicly known and censured. The danger in using the media as instruments of censure in this way is, however, that, as Dignan has pointed out, "the kind of shaming indulged in by much of the media is highly stigmatizing and might well make the process of reintegration all the more difficult".[9] A stronger and perhaps more controllable version of public participation would be to elevate the mediator from the position of go-between in an essentially bilateral negotiation to that of a third party representing the public interest. If mediation is to respond adequately to the social wrong which has been done, then it must take due heed of the wider social purposes of the criminal trial. These include the reassertion of normative order, the re-establishment of the rights and obligations of citizens, the interpretation and development of doctrinal law and of policy, and even the elaboration and maintenance of legal ideology. One may debate how and to what ends these goals should be pursued, but a system which wholly failed to acknowledge their place would scarcely merit the label of criminal justice.

Can Reparation Comply with the Principles of Punishment?

So far we have examined the capacity of reparative justice to mirror or incorporate the chief elements of punishment. If reparative justice is to claim a full place within the penal system, then it must also accord with the principles which delimit the intrusive powers of the state. Can reparation satisfy the requirements for fairness, consistency and proportionality which currently underpin and frame our penal system? Once again, let us look at each element in turn.

(a) Fairness

A primary criticism faced by the reparative approach is that it would create a system of penalties which would have little regard to the means of the offender and so impinge differently on rich and poor. At worst it might allow the very rich to "buy" their way out of punishment by paying off their victim for harms suffered . . .

In practice, in the interests of fairness to the offender, the amount payable in compensation is often scaled down below that which is proportional to the harm done. Critics of reparation would argue that it is right that fairness to the offender should take priority over that to the victim. But a pure restitutionist approach might insist that the harm be "made good" at whatever cost is necessary. Can it be right than an offender with meagre resources suffers, in real terms, a greater punishment than the wealthy offender for whom the payment is no burden at all? Is it desirable that an impoverished offender might work for years to pay off a compensation order (perhaps to a victim whose own wealth makes the sum received negligible)? All these factors clearly do considerable damage to the idea of fairness in criminal law. Yet one might argue that this conception of justice is predicated on being fair to the offender and that an alternative version might equally well be predicated on the rights or interests of the victim and be prepared to sacrifice fairness to the offender to this end.

(b) Consistency

The attempt made by desert theory to develop a coherent, structured approach to sentencing has been applauded as a move toward certainty and consistency. For the same reason Ashworth has objected to reparative justice on the grounds that it would allow the victim to influence sentencing, as happens in the United States through the use of victim-impact and victim-opinion statements. In so doing, it would be damaging to the pursuit of consistency.[10] If victims are given the right to influence the penalty, a twofold danger arises. Both the form of the penalty (be it reparative or retributive) and its size (be it monetary value or duration) may vary according to the temperament of the victim. But are such criticisms well-grounded?

First, there is a danger of presuming that the objective calculus posited by desert theory is in practice feasible or realistic. Individual sentences will always depend in part on subjective assessments regarding the gravity of the offence made by the sentencer. Thus, while just deserts may promise consistency, it cannot guarantee it. Second, Ashworth's objection makes certain assumptions about the reparative justice model which are questionable. It is not necessarily the case that reorientating the system around "making good" must inevitably entail allowing the victim to usurp the role of the state in determining the appropriate sentence. Reparation is owed not just to the victim but to all those whose interests are threatened, and the author would agree that it is not appropriate for the victim to determine the nature or extent of reparation. The harm suffered is a social one and it is for society to determine what is necessary to effect reparation. Just as the state now makes judgments about the seriousness of the offence and the severity of punishment deserved or, indeed, about the harm done and the quantum of compensation owed, so within a reparative model the state could retain the right to determine the penalty. One might even envisage a system which imports a standardized scale for determining the seriousness of harm analogous to that suggested by von Hirsch and Jareborg in their development of a "living standard analysis" for gauging criminal harm.[11] Whereas their model is backward-looking and concerned solely with "how much harm a standard act of burglary did", a reparative schema would need to furnish criteria for assessing what would be necessary to "make good" the harms done. Within this schema, victim-impact statements might furnish necessary information about the harm inflicted and the consequent needs of the victim upon which impartial judgments might be made about the reparation required. By developing a framework for making such judgments systematically, the risk that offenders would find themselves at the whim of vindictive or overly forgiving victims is surely overcome.

Conclusion: Can Reparation and Punishment be Reconciled?

Let us close by considering some points at which reparation and retributive punishment coincide. First, both retribution and reparation are predicated upon notions of individual autonomy. Unlike rehabilitative or "treatment" orientated models of justice, both reparation and retribution presume that offenders are rational individuals able to make free moral choices for which they may be held liable. The offender may thus be legitimately called to account, whether by making good or suffering a proportionate punishment. However, both approaches are open to the objection that they ignore the structural imperatives of deprivation and disadvantage under which many offenders act. Both assume that all offenders are rational, free-willed individuals despite the disproportionate incidence of mental illness and disorder, social inadequacy and poor education among our offending population.

Secondly, it might be argued that both reparation and retribution derive their "authority" from the offence itself and impose penalties according to the seriousness of the particular crime. Unlike the utilitarian aims of general deterrence or rehabilitation which import wider notions of societal good, both retribution and reparation exclude (or nearly exclude) consideration of factors beyond the particular offence. The offender's personal history, the social or economic causes of crime or the need to prevent future offending (all of which extend the limits of intrusion by the state under deterrent or rehabilitative theories) are here deemed irrelevant. As such, both retributive and reparative justice, it is said, impose strict constraints on the intrusion of the state into the lives of offenders. This apparent congruity is not, however, as close as it first seems. The seriousness of the offence is set according to two different sets of criteria. Retribution demands punishment proportional primarily to the intent of the offender, whereas reparative justice derives its "proportionality" from the harm inflicted on the victim. Whilst intent is generally focused on outcomes, and intent and harm may thus coincide, the two may point to very different levels of gravity. If reparation and retribution were to be wholly reconciled, then it would be necessary to devise a measure which integrated intent and harm in setting offence seriousness. A greater difficulty still is that, if reparative justice is to be more than a criminal analogue to civil damages, then it should go beyond the offence itself to enquire about its wider social costs and the means to making them good.

Finally, reparation and retribution have been described by Davis as each a "species of distributive justice, the root metaphor in each case is that of justice as balance, the object being to restore the distribution of rights which existed prior to the offence".[12] Whilst one seeks to restore equilibrium by depriving the offender of his rights, the other pursues the same goal by recompensing those whose rights were injured by the crime. This redistribution of rights is analogous to Ashworth's notion of criminal justice as a "form of social accounting".[13] In respect of mitigation, for example, laudable social acts by the offender are balanced against crimes to arrive at the appropriate penalty. Ashworth suggests that this calculus is based upon rehabilitative reasoning which sees the offender's subsequent conduct as evidence of his reform. Another possible view is that mitigation is justified here on the grounds that some restoration of the legal order has been made.

These "distributive" or "accounting" metaphors go some way to describing the common ethos of retributive and reparative justice. But they rely on a very narrow conception of reparative justice as solely restitutive in intent, seeking only to return to the preceding legal order.[14] Moreover, the legitimacy of a justification based on "restoring the balance of rights" is open to question on a number of counts. First, to use the criminal justice system solely as a means of restoring the balance of rights which existed prior to the offence is to condone the reinforcement of pre-existing social inequality. Secondly, many of those activities defined as criminal and those groups identified as offenders reflect the interests and values of a socially dominant group. If reparation, with retribution, seeks to restore the values which criminalization underpins, it is likely not merely to recreate but to accentuate social inequality. Thirdly, as Davis has also argued, to demand that offenders bear the full burden of restoring the distribution of rights is to expect too much from that "unrepresentative and generally impecunious group of citizens who come to the attention of the criminal courts", both practically and as a matter of principle.[15] A powerful objection to the increased use of compensation orders, for example, is that they ignore the fact that very many offenders are in straitened financial circumstances. To impose further financial burdens upon impoverished offenders may simply be counterproductive.

In the light of these conceptual links, the concurrent re-emergence of retributive and reparative thinking is perhaps less surprising than it first appears. Ironically, however, the very points at which reparative and retributive justice coincide appear on closer inspection to be the points of greatest weakness within the reparative justice model. Its frailty is greatest in respect of its "redistributive" purposes which, while theoretically attractive, are predicated on a fictitious just society in which the only imbalance of rights is caused by crimes themselves. A truly reparative model might better recognize that much crime is not simply a cause but also the consequence of social injustice and that the victim, the community *and* the offender are probably in need of repair if criminal justice is to contribute toward a more reintegrated society.

We began with the questions "can and should" the penal system embrace both punitive and reparative goals: let us return to them by way of conclusion. From our discussion it would seem that while "making good" entails certain difficulties within a criminal justice system, reparation is quite capable of fulfilling the basic demands of punishment and, thus far, is reconcilable with retribution. The danger, however, is that the attempt to accommodate reparative justice to the rationale of punishment so perverts its underlying rationale as to strip it of much of its original appeal, not least its commitment to repairing ruptured social bonds. We are accustomed to seeing criminal justice as the repressive arm of the state, but might it not better be conceived as one end of a continuum of practices by which social order is maintained? Punishment has a very limited ability to control crime and, to the extent that it is disintegrative, it inflicts further damage on society. Given that the high profile "law and order policies" of the past decade have done little to stem spiralling crime figures, perhaps it is time to explore the integrative potential of reparative justice on its own terms.

Notes

1. J. Braithwaite, *Crime, Shame and Reintegration* (1989).
2. D. van Ness, "New Wine in Old Wineskins: Four Challenges of Restorative Justice", (1993) 4 *Criminal Law Forum*, p. 251.
3. G. Davis *et al.*, *Preliminary Study of Victim-Offender Mediation and Reparation Schemes in England and Wales* (1987), p. 7.
4. See Selection 7.2 above.
5. Or the German *Adhesionsverfahren*, though interestingly this device for attaching civil proceedings to the criminal process is rarely used: see Mueller-Dietz, "Compensation as a Criminal Penalty" in Kaiser, Kury and Albrecht (eds.), *Victims and Criminal Justice* (1992).
6. S. Roberts, "Mediation in Family Disputes", (1983) 46 *Modern L.R.* 537.
7. See Christie, Selection 7.1 above.
8. Watson, Boucherat and Davis, "Reparation for Retributivists", in M. Wright and B. Galaway (eds.), *Mediation and Criminal Justice* (1989); Pettit and Braithwaite, Selection 7.2 above.

9. J. Dignan, "Reintegration through reparation", in A. Duff, S. Marshall, R. E. Dobash and R. P. Dobash (eds.), *Penal Theory and Practice* (1994).

10. A. Ashworth, "Victim Impact Statements and Sentencing", [1993] *Crim.L.R.* 498.

11. See Selection 4.6 above.

12. G. Davis, *Making Amends: Mediation and Reparation in Criminal Justice* (1992), p. 11.

13. A. Ashworth, *Sentencing and Criminal Justice* (1992), p. 133.

14. They may also be inadequate for desert theory, which has moved away from the metaphor of "restoring the balance": see above, introduction to Chapter 4 and Selection 4.4 above.

15. Davis, above n. 12, p. 12.

7.5

Reparation, Retribution and Rights

MICHAEL CAVADINO AND JAMES DIGNAN

Never the Twain? A Strictly Proportional Composite System

It seems to us that—*pace* Ashworth (1993)—it would be possible in principle to imagine a criminal justice system in which reparation played a large part but which still adhered to a fairly strict system of proportionality. We call this imaginary system the "Strictly Proportional Composite" model. It would work as follows. There would have to be a public tariff of standard, proportionate sentences for offences of particular descriptions, so that offenders, victims and state officials would know before reaching the sentencing stage what sanctions would be imposed by a court for any offence. However, the standard sentences need not take only one form for a particular level of seriousness; for example the public tariff for an offence could posit as alternative penalties either X hours of community service or a fine of Y units, these being sanctions deemed to have equivalent "punitive bite".[1] Moreover, the public tariff could contain among its equivalent sanctions certain standard measures of reparation to individual victims. An obvious equivalence would be between a fine and a compensation order for a like sum; similarly a specified number of hours of agreed work for the victim could substitute for the same number of hours of community service, thus replacing a period of "reparation" to the community in general with a similar period of reparation directed towards the specific victim.

Either the state or a voluntary agency could provide a local reparation service. This service would be allocated the task, either prior to the prosecution decision or following conviction but before sentence,[2] of investigating the possibilities of constructing a suitable reparative measure or package of measures, whether by mediation between the victim or offender or otherwise. However, any such package would have to be of

From M. Cavadino and J. Dignan, "Reparation, Retribution and Rights", (1997) 4 *International Review of Victimology* 233 with some textual changes.

equal "punitive bite" to the standard tariff penalty or penalties for the offence. If the package were acceptable to both offender and victim, then it could be certified by either the prosecutor or sentencer as appropriately punitive and could be allowed to take effect as the penalty for the offence.[3] Some agency would have the task of monitoring whether the agreed reparation was actually carried out satisfactorily. If no reparative package could be agreed (or if no individual victim could be identified, or if the offender failed to carry out the agreed reparation), then the criminal justice system could revert to a "default setting" of strictly proportionate justice with no element of individual reparation.

This would in our opinion be an enormous improvement on the existing criminal justice system,[4] and would sin little if at all against the principle of just deserts. However, it would not be our preferred system. It can be criticized on a number of counts.

In the first place, there would be the practical drawback that offenders would have relatively little incentive to accept a reparation package if it meant that they necessarily had to suffer a "penal bite" strictly equivalent to what their penalty would be if they rejected the package. In theory, equivalent penal bites should mean that the choice between reparation and retribution was a matter of total indifference to the offender; in practice some offenders might find the proffered reparation package slightly more congenial, but others would not. Given the attractions of reparation discussed previously, this would be a sad loss all round, for victims, offenders and the wider community.

Secondly, both the exact amount and the forms of reparation that were on offer would probably in practice be fairly restricted. The amount would be restricted by the notion of penal equivalence, while the form would be confined to financial compensation and/or the performance of so many hours' work on behalf of the victim, with the exact mix of financial and non-financial reparation and the exact form of the work for the victim being perhaps the only real issues for negotiation and mediation. These kinds of reparation might attend to the *material* damage that is caused by an offence—harm to the victim's person or lost or damaged property—but they might do little to repair the emotional upset caused by an offence or to restore the moral equilibrium that has been disturbed by undermining the victim's presumption of security (Watson *et al.*, 1989). Consequently, the system would do relatively little to empower victims, to reassert their autonomy following an offence—or to encourage them to participate in the restorative process.

Thirdly, the composite model would do little more than the existing conventional approach to engender in offenders a sense of responsibility or accountability for their conduct. There would be very little incentive or scope for offenders to offer to make amends in ways that were not catered for in standard reparation packages. Reparation would most likely be offered to both offenders and victims on a more or less "take-it-or-leave-it" basis—and offenders would often leave it. This seems a missed opportunity, not only because victims might lose out, but also because encouraging offenders to consider how they might properly make amends could be a way of rekindling in *them* a sense of autonomy and empowerment that is often absent (Cantor, 1976).[5]

Fourthly, from a broader crime prevention standpoint the composite model may also be seen as a missed opportunity. It is often argued by proponents of the justice model (e.g. von Hirsch, 1993) that official censure (denunciation) in the form of deserved punishment is an appropriate response to crime. However, punishing offenders is by no means the only way of censuring wrongdoing, and there is a growing conviction in many quarters that it is not the most effective way either.

One of the attractions of reparation is that it enables denunciation to be expressed in a currency other than that of retributive-style punishments (Wright, 1991; p. 113). John Braithwaite (1989) has suggested that a more effective way of achieving this[6] would be to find ways of censuring (or "shaming") offenders in such a way as to promote their reintegration into the community of law-abiding citizens rather than alienating them from it in the way that conventional forms of punitive censure often seem to. This would not be possible under the composite model, since, as we have seen, the only forms of reparation that are on offer are effectively tied to the standard retributive tariff in much the same way as currencies were once tied to the "gold standard". If Braithwaite's approach were to be adopted, therefore, reparation would need to become a "fully convertible currency" and this would require the adoption of much more imaginative forms of reparation than those likely to occur under the composite model.[7] This would often be of benefit to both victims and offenders.

For all these reasons, we believe that there are substantial grounds for rejecting this composite model in favour of an approach that is less strait-jacketed by the demands of strict proportionality. We call this approach the "Integrated Restorative Justice" model . . .

For "Restorative Justice"

Our favoured "Integrated Restorative Justice" model is an attempt to put human rights theory into practical penal form. Elsewhere we have expressed our preference for a theory of punishment that is based on the recognition and protection of human rights (Cavadino and Dignan, 1992, pp. 52–5). There we suggested that one of the attractions of "rights theories" (of the kind propounded by Ronald Dworkin (1978) and Alan Gewirth (1978)) is that they provide the basis for a principled compromise between retributivism and reductivism,[8] one in which the principle of just deserts is one—but only one—valid principle for the distribution of punishment. Our argument may be briefly summarized as follows. The protection of the human rights of potential victims via crime reduction gives us the "general justification" for having a system of punishment; while the desirability of conveying correct moral messages about the relative wrongfulness of different actions that affect human rights argues for a general principle of proportionality in the amount of punishment imposed on individual offenders. However, this principle of proportionality need not be strict or paramount and may rightly give way at times to other aims—aims that are themselves means to the furtherance of human rights via mechanisms other than censure.

We wish now to argue further than human rights theory also provides the basis for a principled compromise between retributivism and reparation or restorative justice. (It is, however, by no means necessary to subscribe to human rights theory, let alone any particular version of it, in order to see merit in a restorative approach to criminal justice. It seems possible to conclude from a wide variety of perspectives that such an approach is capable of striking a fairer balance between the interests of victims, offenders and ordinary law-abiding citizens—who are also potential victims—than is currently achieved under the conventional model of criminal justice.)

One of the most important human rights—perhaps *the* fundamental human right—is the equal right of individuals to maximum "positive freedom",[9] by which we mean their ability to make effective choices about their lives. Rights theory allows for a person's rights (including even the right to positive freedom), to be restricted in certain circumstances, but only where the restriction is justified on the basis of another person's "competing rights" (Dworkin, 1978). Victims of crimes experience a reduction in their positive freedoms (to function free from physical or psychological pain or disability, or to choose how to use or dispose of their resources) and it is this "special harm" that entitles the victim to reparation at the hands of offenders even though *their* positive freedom will be diminished thereby. As Watson *et al.* (1989) have pointed out, the harm inflicted on a victim is never confined to physical injury and loss or damage to property but also entails emotional upset and damage to the relationship (however tenuous it might be) between that person and a fellow citizen, effects which also diminish the positive freedom of the victim. Consequently, reparation, if it is to be adequate, must attend to both the material and non-material effects of an offence. Once again this would argue for a broader notion of reparation than is recognized by either the "Conventional" model of criminal justice or the "Strictly Proportional Composite" model which we discussed earlier.

One of the most effective ways of restoring the victim's sense of autonomy—of *re-empowering* the victim—is to invite him or her to participate in determining ways in which the upset and any material loss might be made good. Indeed, it is very difficult to see how adequate reparation could be arranged without involving the victim in the deliberations.[10] (Note however that the assertion of a right for victims to participate in the offence resolution process in this way is very different from asserting the kind of right of victim allocution on the appropriate *retributive* sentence to which Ashworth is so vehemently—and in our opinion rightly— opposed.) Moreover, if victims are to be treated with *equal* concern and respect (Dworkin, 1978) then their entitlement to reparation should not be governed by the seriousness of the offence as is the case at present.[11]

Two questions still need to be addressed: firstly, to what extent should any negotiated reparation agreement between victim and offender influence, or even determine, the final outcome of the case? And secondly, what upper or lower limits (if any) should be imposed on the amount of reparation and/or other punishment which may be imposed upon the offender?

In answer to the first of these questions, we have already argued that the adoption of a rights-based approach requires the "private" element, comprising the actual harm that is inflicted on the victim, to be taken much more seriously than at present. In our view this would best be secured by asserting a *prima facie* right of victim participation in the offence resolution process in all cases, regardless of seriousness and irrespective of the nature of the offence. Further, we would agree with Watson *et al.* (1989) that where an outcome is negotiated, and reparation performed which is acceptable to both parties, this should always be taken into account, and due weight given by the court when determining sentence. We would also argue that exactly the same considerations should apply when determining whether an offender should be prosecuted in the first place.

Just how much weight is to be given to the nature and amount of any reparation that may be agreed will depend on an assessment by the prosecutor or the sentencing court of the appropriate response, taking into account the "public" and "private" elements that may be involved in an offence. In a system based on an "orderly plurality of sentencing aims" clear guidance would need to be given to these decision-makers rather than leaving it to their unstructured discretion. In the great majority of less serious offences we would take the view that these are more appropriately seen as akin to "private wrongs". Accordingly, provided that reparation is agreed and performed to the satisfaction of both parties and at least where there is no evidence of a history of similar offences, the fact that the offender has been willing to make suitable amends should normally be taken as evidence of a renewed respect for the rights of others, and in the absence of any other "public element" the case for any additional punishment in such cases would appear very weak. However, in order to safeguard the public interest (i.e. the human rights of people other than the individual victim and offender), the final say in each case would rest with the prosecutor or the court and not with the parties themselves.

In more serious cases, or in cases where the offender has unreasonably refused to make adequate amends, greater weight would need to be placed on the "public" aspect of the offence—in particular the fact that it represents a potential threat to the rights of other law-abiding citizens whose interests also need to be taken into account in determining the final outcome. Once again, however, due weight would need to be given to any reparation that might have been undertaken since this might indicate a willingness to respect other people's rights in the future. Where this is thought to be the case it should somewhat allay the concerns of potential victims, but in any event the *overall* response to the offence would still need to be proportionate (see below), and for this reason also due allowance would need to be made for any reparation before determining what additional penalty might be appropriate.

What principles should apply regarding the amount of reparation or punishment to which an offender should be liable? We have seen that the goal of empowering victims and offenders to participate actively in the offence resolution process is not compatible with the principle of strict proportionality. Nor is the preference for more flexible and innovative forms of reparation and for the development of reintegrative shaming which holds out the promise of a more constructive long-term response to crime. Nevertheless proportionality of a less strict kind still has an important rôle to play within the restorative justice model—firstly in setting the upper and lower parameters within which the overall amount of compulsory reparation and any additional punishment is to be determined; and secondly in acting as a "default setting" where informal offence resolution proves impossible or is inappropriate.

Although offenders are liable to forfeit certain of their rights (including to some extent, the right of positive freedom) because of their infringement of the rights of others, retributivists are right to insist that the response to this infringement should not be excessively severe, taking into account the moral gravity of an offence. This principle, known as the "retributive maximum" (Morris (1974), p. 75; Morris and Tonry (1990); Cavadino and Dignan (1992), pp. 54–5) prescribes an upper limit for the response to an offence, taken as a whole, and is important if the risk of "double punishment" is to be avoided. Consequently, any reparation would have to be taken into account when deciding the overall response, and may be sufficient, at least where the offence is not a serious one. The retributive maximum would also apply to the amount of reparation that an offender could be ordered to make, though offenders would be free to assume a greater obligation provided this was done voluntarily and on a fully informed basis.

At the other end of the scale it would also be desirable to insist on a "retributive minimum", at least in cases with a strong "public element". This would enable the interests of potential victims and the wider community to be safeguarded in cases where the agreed reparation is manifestly inadequate—for example, in the unlikely event of an attempted murder victim agreeing that the offender should simply be allowed to clean her windows for her. *Within these retributive limits* victims and offenders would be encouraged to agree on forms of reparation that were appropriate to their circumstances. As in the case of the "Strictly Proportional Composite" model, a state or voluntary agency could be charged with the responsibility for investigating the possibilities of devising a suitable reparation package in conjunction with the parties themselves[12] and ensuring fair play and a just outcome. Ultimately, however, final authority for determining how the case should be resolved would again rest with the prosecutor or court—there would be a "state veto"— though they would again be obliged to give due weight to any reparation already undertaken or agreed.

Finally, the principle of proportionality would also operate as a "default setting" in cases where no informal resolution proved possible, though even here its role would be to influence rather than determine the final outcome. In cases where an offender refused to make or undertake adequate reparation, for example, it might be appropriate for punishment to be increased to some extent in relation to the retribution that is imposed in order to reflect the refusal to acknowledge responsibility for putting right the private harm. Conversely, where a victim unreasonably refused an offender's sincere and genuine attempts to make adequate amends it might be appropriate to reduce the level of punishment somewhat in order to take account of the offender's willingness to respect the rights of the victim.[13] In all cases involving use of the "default setting" courts and prosecutors would be obliged to ensure that adequate and appropriate reparation was ordered where possible;[14] and then to consider what additional punishment might be required to take account of the "public element" that is involved.[15]

Such a system would allow for a very substantial injection of reparation into the criminal justice system; indeed we do not see in principle why in the long run the arrangement of reparation could not become the routine response to offending. The public interest and a duly modest version of the proportionality principle would both be safeguarded—indeed, we would say they would be safeguarded to a greater extent than they are under existing arrangements—while allowing victims, offenders and communities the benefits of reparation. The only casualty would be an over-rigid vision of strict proportionality which, as we have argued, is in any event indefensible in principle.

This does not of course mean that we are under any illusions as to whether such a scheme can easily be instantiated in the real world of penal politics. One of us has previously (Dignan, 1994) discussed the kind of "transitional strategy" required to bring such a system closer—or rather, to bring existing criminal justice systems closer to our vision. We will not rehearse these matters here; for our purpose in this article has been purely to argue that a shift towards a more reparative criminal justice system— within general retributive limits—is desirable in principle. The practical task is indeed to make it happen; but part of that task is convincing people that it should happen. Our hope is that this article contributes to that process.

Notes

1. See Robinson (1994) and also the notion of "interchangeability of punishments" developed by Morris and Tonry (1990): see Selection 6. 5 above and the introduction to Chapter 6.
2. Some existing mediation schemes also engage in post-sentence mediation between offenders and victims, with the agreement of both parties. As long as such arrangements are voluntary they do not offend against the argument here, and we would favour them. Since they cannot affect either prosecution or sentencing decisions, they are also immune to the criticisms put forward by Ashworth (1993).

3. This state oversight to ensure that the punitive level of the package was right should satisfy not only proportionality but also Ashworth's more general concerns about safeguarding the interests of the public and of potential future victims.

4. Provided that the tariff were set at an acceptable level. One danger of moving towards fixed sentences is that the overall level of punishment may rise as a result.

5. The composite model could also be unfair as between and offenders if, as is often the case, there is an element of fault on the victim's part which ought in fairness to be reflected in any settlement that is reached. This is because a retributive tariff is concerned essentially with the wrongfulness of the offender's action rather than with the victim's conduct.

6. Effective in the double sense of communicating blame in ways that are less easy for the offender to ignore, and at the same time taking positive steps to secure the offender's reinstatement as a law-abiding member of the community. It seems plausible to suppose that the first of these might often be achieved by involving victims in the process of censure while the second might be assisted by involving appropriate members of the offender's immediate social circle, who might be expected to assist in the process of reintegration.

7. Examples might include meetings or other communications between offenders and victims (possibly also involving others: see previous note) to discuss how amends might be made in a wider sense for the harm that has been caused and how reconciliation might be achieved (where victim and offender are known to one another and would desire this); to reassure the victim of the offender's acknowledgement of the harm that has been caused or to provide some explanation for it; to reassure the victim of a change of attitude on the part of the offender, backed by a commitment to seek appropriate help or counselling; or to discuss how the offender might seek to regain the trust of fellow members of the community.

8. This is the belief that punishment helps to reduce the incidence of crime, and that it is this reduction which is the justification for punishment (see Cavadino and Dignan (1992), p. 32).

9. The concept of "positive freedom" is closely akin to that of "autonomy", and is discussed more fully in Cavadino (1989) and Gould (1988).

10. This may either be done directly, by inviting the victim and offender to take part in face-to-face discussions under the guidance of a mediator, or indirectly through a form of "shuttle diplomacy" in which the mediator acts as a "go-between".

11. This tends to happen in two main ways. The more serious the offence is, the less likely it is to be considered suitable for mediation or reparation even in areas where such schemes exist, in addition to which the decision to imprison an offender may effectively preclude the award of any financial compensation to the victim. In the case of less serious offences a decision to caution an offender will also rule out any prospect of compensation for the victim in practice.

12. The "Communitarian" model of restorative justice (see Dignan and Cavadino (1996)) would aim to involve in this process members of the community who are significant to the offender and the victim (cf. above n. 6). While we also favour

such arrangements, the exact nature of the process whereby a reparation package is constructed does not affect the argument in the present article.

13. One of the practical merits of the "Integrated Restorative Justice" model is that it would in this way provide an incentive for offenders to undertake reparation for their victims as a routine response to their offending behaviour. So long as this reparation was genuinely acceptable to the victim, we are not as concerned as some have been (Watson *et al.*, 1989) about the possible motivation for undertaking this though we accept that it may have a bearing on whether any professed attitude change by the offender is genuine or not.

14. Though the kinds of reparation that an offender could be ordered to make to an individual victim (apart from financial compensation or possibly an "individual service order") would of necessity be very much more limited than those which might be freely undertaken.

15. As far as possible, we would favour this additional punishment taking forms which were "reparative" in the wider sense, such as community service.

References

Ashworth, A. (1993), "Some Doubts about Restorative Justice", 4 *Criminal Law Forum* 277–99.

Braithwaite, J. (1989), *Crime, Shame and Reintegration* (Cambridge: Cambridge University Press).

Cavadino, M. (1989), *Mental Health Law in Context* (Dartmouth).

Cantor, G. M. (1976), "An End to Punishment", 39 *The Shingle* 99–114 (Philadelphia Bar Association).

Cavadino, M., and Dignan, J. (1992), *The Penal System: an Introduction* (London: Sage).

Dignan, J. (1994), "Reintegration through Reparation: a Way Forward?", in Duff, R. A., Marshall, S., Dobash, R. E., and Dobash, R. P. (eds.), *Penal Theory and Practice* (Manchester: Manchester University Press).

Dignan, J., and Cavadino, M. (1996), "Towards a Framework for Conceptualising and Evaluating Models of Criminal Justice from a VIctim's Perspective", 4 *International Review of Victiminology* 153.

Dworkin, R. (1978), *Taking Rights Seriously* (London: Duckworth).

Gewirth, A. (1978), *Reason and Morality* (Chicago: University of Chicago Press).

Gould, C. (1988), *Rethinking Democracy* (Cambridge University Press).

Morris, N. (1974), *The Future of Imprisonment* (London: University of Chicago Press).

Morris, N., and Tonry, M. (1990), *Between Prison and Probation* (New York: Oxford University Press).

Robinson, P. H. (1994), "Desert, Crime Control, Disparity and Units of Punishment", in Duff, R. A., Marshall, S., Dobash, R. E., and Dobash, R. P. (eds.), *Penal Theory and Practice* (Manchester: Manchester University Press).

Von Hirsch, A. (1993), *Censure and Sanctions* (Oxford: Oxford University Press).

Watson, D., Boucherat, J., and Davis, G. (1989), "Reparation for Retributivists", in Wright, M., and Galaway, B. (eds.), *Mediation and Criminal Justice* (London: Sage).

Wright, M. (1991), *Justice for Victims and Offenders* (Milton Keynes: Open University Press).

Suggestions for Further Reading

1. Restorative Justice in Theory

Schafer, S., *Restitution to Victims of Crime* (1960); Barnett, R. E., "Restitution: a New Paradigm of Criminal Justice", (1977) 87 *Ethics* 279; Christie, N., "Conflicts as Property", (1977) 17 *British Journal of Criminology* 1; Braithwaite, J., *Crime, Shame and Reintegration* (1989); Braithwaite, J., and Pettit, P., *Not Just Deserts* (1990); Cragg, W., *The Practice of Punishment: Towards a Theory of Restorative Justice* (1992); von Hirsch, A., *Censure and Sanctions* (1993), ch.3; van Ness, D., "New Wine and Old Wineskins: Four Challenges of Restorative Justice", (1993) 4 *Criminal Law Forum* 251; Ashworth, A., "Some Doubts about Restorative Justice", (1993) 4 *Criminal Law Forum* 277; Zedner, L., "Reparation and Retribution: are they Reconcilable?", (1994) 57 *Modern Law Review* 228; Walgrave, L., "Restorative Justice for Juveniles", (1995) 34 *Howard Journal of Criminal Justice* 228; Wright, M., *Justice for Victims and Offenders*, 2nd edn. (1996); Walgrave, L., and Aertsen, I., "Reintegrative Shaming and Restorative Justice: Interchangeable, Complementary or Different?", (1996) 4 *European Journal on Criminal Policy and Research* 67; Dignan, J., and Cavadino, M., "Towards a Framework for Conceptualising and Evaluating Models of Criminal Justice from a Victim's Perspective", (1996) 4 *International Review of Victimology* 153.

2. Restorative Justice in Practice

Davis, G., Boucherat, J., and Watson, D., *A Preliminary Study of Victim-Offender Mediation and Reparation Schemes in England and Wales* (1987); Wright, M., and Galaway, B., *Mediation and Criminal Justice* (1989); Davis, G., *Making Amends: Mediation and Reparation in Criminal Justice* (1992); Morris, A., Maxwell, G., and Robertson, J. P., "Giving Victims a Voice: a New Zealand Experiment", (1993) 32 *Howard Journal of Criminal Justice* 304; Braithwaite, J., and Mugford, S., "Conditions of Successful Reintegration Ceremonies", (1994) 34 *British Journal of Criminology* 139; Dignan, J., "Reintegration through Reparation: a Way Forward?", in Duff, A., Marshall, S., Dobash, R. E., and Dobash, R. P. (eds.), *Penal Theory and Practice* (1994); Wright, M., "Victims, Mediation and Criminal Justice", (1995) *Criminal Law Review* 187; New Zealand Ministry of Justice, *Restorative Justice* [1995]; Galaway, B., and Hudson, J. (eds.), *Restorative Justice: International Perspectives* (1996); Marshall, T., "The Evolution of Restorative Justice in Britain", [1996] 4 *European Journal on Criminal Policy and Research* 21; Blagg, H., "A Just Measure of Shame?", (1997) 37 *British Journal of Criminology* 481; Braithwaite, J., "Conferencing and Plurality: Reply to Blagg", (1997) 37 *British Journal of Criminology* 502; Daly, K., and Immarigeon, R.,

"The Past, Present, and Future of Restorative Justice: Some Critical Reflections", (1998) 1 *Contemporary Justice Review*.

3. Victims' Needs and Rights

Shapland, J., Wilmore, J., and Duff, P., *Victims in the Criminal Justice System* (1985); Maguire, M., and Pointing, J., *Victims of Crime: a New Deal?* (1987); Joutsen, M., *The Role of the Victim of Crime in European Criminal Justice Systems* (1987); Walklate, S., *Victimology* (1989); Kaiser, G., Kury, H., and Albrecht, H.-J., (eds.), *Victims and Criminal Justice* (1991); Maguire, M., "The Needs and Rights of Victims of Crime", in M. Tonry (ed.), *Crime and Justice: a Review of Research* (1991) 14, 363; Miers, D., "The Rights and Responsibilites of Victims of Crime", (1992) 55 *Modern Law Review* 482; Ashworth, A., "Victim Impact Statements and Sentencing", (1993) *Criminal Law Review* 498; Mawby, R., and Walklate, S., *Critical Victimology* (1994); Fenwick, H., "Procedural 'Rights' of Victims of Crime: Public or Private Ordering of the Criminal Justice Process?", (1997) 60 *Modern Law Review* 317; Zedner, L., "Victims", in Maguire, M., Morgan, R., and Reiner, R. (eds.), *Oxford Handbook of Criminology*, 2nd edn. (1997).

8

External Critiques of Sentencing Theory

In many of the previous chapters we have noted and debated, both in the Introductions and through the readings, various criticisms of the sentencing theory under discussion. These criticisms have been *internal* to sentencing theory, however: that is, they have accepted the parameters of the debate, and have argued about the strength or relevance of the arguments adduced on either side. The readings in this chapter have a different focus, and that is upon criticisms of the whole enterprise of sentencing theory, at least in the "conventional" forms outlined in Chapters 1 to 4 above. The arguments are, in general, not that one of those sentencing justifications is weaker than another but that all of them—and their very frame of reference—neglect or gloss over important aspects of sentencing.

Critical punishment theory is certainly not a "school of thought", in the way that desert or deterrence theory might be represented. At most it is a movement, consisting of a variety of writers, particularly in the second half of the twentieth century, who have mounted external critiques of the justifications for punishment and sentencing—whose project is "to go beyond explication and rationalization and to interrogate the deeper political, historical and philosophical logics which underlie the power of law".[1] Yet those critiques are diverse, as one might expect, and include those who engage in "Marxist legal theory, American critical legal studies, feminist legal theory, critical race theory and postmodern jurisprudence".[2] Some of those whom we might, for convenience, describe as belonging to the "critical movement" are also advocates of restorative justice. Thus Nils Christie, whose work was discussed in Chapter 7 above (and see Selection 7.1 above), starts from an external critique of conventional sentencing theory which would fit well into this chapter. For example, he questions the dominant concept of a state-run system of criminal law and then, as we saw in Selection 7.1, he develops an approach which emphasizes the resolution of "conflicts" between individuals. Other penal abolitionists have developed slightly different theories from this point.[3] But the focus of the "critical movement" lies not upon the most desirable techniques for achieving crime prevention, justice, or social harmony, but upon the critique of conventional punishment theory, and it is on that critique that this chapter will concentrate.

Although there is considerable diversity among critical theorists, one piece of fairly common ground is the emphasis on the "failure" of sentencing. Punishment systems the world over are said to be unsuccessful, and likewise the conventional sentencing theories are doomed to fail. Punishment systems fail because they are usually judged by reference to their instrumental success in controlling crime, which is a goal they are unlikely to achieve because crime rates are affected by so many other factors. Conventional sentencing theories fail because they, too, put forward instrumental goals which are impossible of achievement.[4] This built-in tendency to fail is most apparent in deterrence theories and in rehabilitative theories, which can only expect to influence the behaviour of certain people in certain situations. On this view, the failure of general policies based on these theories is no surprise; yet when the failure of rehabilitative sentencing was proclaimed in the 1970s,[5] it was treated as a possible reason for the revival of desert theory rather than as the natural outcome of overblown expectations. However, it might equally be argued that desert theory is bound to fail—notably, in that proportionality cannot be achieved without a wide margin of contestability. This inherent source of disagreement about the criteria and overall severity levels of penal desert undermines the theory's claim to produce fairness in sentencing.[6]

One interesting side-issue of this particular debate is that many of those who stand on different sides share a commitment to penal parsimony. We saw in Chapter 4 above that many contemporary desert theorists argue for a reduction in penalty levels. Likewise, many of those in the "critical movement" wish to see lower penalty levels, some going further to embrace abolitionism. There are, however, at least two fundamental differences. One is that critical writers do not assume that the sentencing system must continue to deal with all or most offenders. And the second is that critical writers tend to give a higher priority to penal parsimony than to conceptions of "fairness"—a view which is not exclusive to critical theorists,[7] but which leads some of them to argue for policies of penalty reduction which would not satisfy ideals of fairness and equal treatment promoted by desert theorists.[8]

If one piece of common ground among critical writers is the idea that conventional sentencing theories have, as it were, an inherent tendency to fail when put into practice, another might be that the conventional theories are riven by internal contradictions. Critical theory tends to be historical in its approach, and indeed the ahistorical nature of much contemporary sentencing theory is regarded as a source of its weakness. One example of this genre is Alan Norrie's work on *Law, Ideology and Punishment* (see Selection 8.1). His argument, in brief, is that modern punishment theory, and especially desert theory, is fundamentally flawed in ways which can be found inherent in other writings from Hobbes, through Kant and Hegel, through the English idealists of one hundred years ago (such as Bradley and Green), to contemporary writers. On the one hand these writers construct their theories on the basis of individual citizens who are rational actors, and whose consent grounds the legitimacy of government. On the other hand all of the writers are forced to recognize the social reality that many citizens break the law, that such conduct is related to conditions such as poverty and deprivation, and that measures of control or prevention are called for. The contradiction, then, is that the rational individual is an abstract or ideal construction, when the reality is known to be different. On Norrie's account, this inherent tension led to the self-destruction of retributive theory at the beginning of the twentieth century, as its proponents reached the point at which they embraced the idea of an interventionist state dedicated to remedying unfortunate social realities—simultaneously undermining the idea of citizens as rational actors on whose consent the system rests. On this view, when desert came back into prominence in the 1970s, largely as a *pis aller*, its fundamental contradictions remained. However, it did and does, Norrie concedes, have a significant strength which marks it out from other sentencing theories—its insistence on the state respecting the rights of individuals, and on placing boundaries on the ways in which it uses its power over them.

Readers will be able to assess, by reference to Chapter 4 above, the persuasiveness of Norrie's criticisms of desert theory. That theory's foundations have changed considerably in modern times, even in the years since 1976 when *Doing Justice* was published.[9] Have the development and refinement of arguments concerning the elements of censure and hard treatment, in the 1990s, removed some of the contradictions? Or would Norrie argue that they have "internalised" the contradictions, by recognizing that individuals may be weak and fallible (see Selection 4.6, and perhaps 4.8, above)? Do not desert theorists wish to "have their cake and eat it", by propounding notions of proportionality based on rational actors and yet allowing mitigation grounded in social and situational pressures? Do the developing arguments about the approach to sentencing persistent offenders (see Selection 4.7 above) recognize and resolve any contradiction here? Are the arguments over the (im)possibility of just deserts in an unjust society (see Selection 4.9 above) convincing? And if, as Norrie recognizes, desert theory has strong attractions because of its insistence on the rights of all citizens, including offenders, against the state or the collectivity, might this not support efforts to develop and refine the theory?

Norrie's critique, then, is internal to sentencing theory at several points. However, his principal argument is external: that all retributive theories are doomed to fail, at an intellectual level, because of their inherent contradictions. Typically, among critical theorists, he adopts a frame of reference which includes both the historical and the social-political. This connects with what might be identified as a third piece of common ground in the "critical movement": an emphasis on the social and cultural dimensions of sentencing, and a consequent unease about what is seen as the reductionism of much (modern) sentencing theory. Thus the tendency of those theories discussed in Chapters 1 to 4 above to strive to present a unified approach, a single principle or set of principles from which the answers to other key questions can be derived, is criticized for its neglect of the social and political contexts and meanings of sentencing and state punishment. David Garland, after a detailed analysis of the writings of Durkheim, Marx, Foucault, Elias and others, in their historical and social contexts,[10] argues in favour of an approach in which the theory and social reality of punishment systems are more explicitly linked.

Garland's approach is not, of course, an indiscriminate eclecticism. His concern (see Selection 8.2) is rather to escape from the narrowness of, on the one hand, philosophical theories of punishment which are often abstracted from the social realities of sentencing systems, and, on the other hand, penological approaches which tend to focus on the effectiveness of various types of sentence in terms of prevention, rehabilitation, or some other penological goal. Each of those perspectives has its value, he argues, but only if linked with the other and located in broader conceptions of punishment as a complex social institution, serving a whole variety of (sometimes conflicting) goals. Any analysis ought to include the history of social and political institutions, including punishment, and an assessment of the way in which the contemporary sentencing system is affected by assumptions and policies relating to (for example) the economy, social affairs, health, and political realities (including the role of the media). To isolate sentencing in laboratory conditions, as it were, away from the complexities of social reality, is likely to produce an inadequate theory. Indeed, one might go further and argue that any normative theorizing is doomed to inadequacy, since it cannot hope to deal with the full range of social realities and is therefore bound to be reductive.

This kind of critique raises profound questions about social analysis. Very few of the writers discussed in Chapters 1 to 4 above could be said to ignore social realities entirely. Among deterrence theorists, Bentham and Posner might be thought to come close to this. Some adherents of rehabilitative and of incapacitative theory may be thought to have a poor sense of history in the latitude they give to the opinions of "experts" and the power of the state. Some would press the same argument against desert theorists, although Andrew von Hirsch includes in his 1993 book[11] discussion of such matters as the principled arguments against certain types of "degrading" punishment, the problem of just deserts in an unjust society, and the link between levels of penality, cultural expectations and political trends (see also Chapter 9 below, on "The Politics of Law and Disorder"). It is true that extremely few of the writers discussed in Chapters 1 to 4 above have conducted the kind of detailed historical analysis of punishment theories that is to be found in the works of Norrie and Garland. But it is equally true that extremely few of the writers who might be placed within the "critical movement" have developed their work in a normative direction. The work of deconstruction has rarely been followed by reconstruction,[12] and it could be argued that in a social and political context in which courts are imposing sentences, people are being imprisoned, fined, etc., and decisions and policies on punishment are being fashioned, a position of abstentionism is difficult to defend. If, as critical theorists argue, conventional writers on sentencing theory are strangled by their own narrowness, are not critical writers themselves left with a normative void in the face of the real social events of which, they urge, account must be taken?

This kind of over-simplification can be resisted by drawing into the discussion a further strand of critical writing, associated with authors such as Barbara Hudson and Nicola Lacey. Both of these writers might accept many of the elements of the "critical movement" described above. But, in their different ways, they have begun to develop normative theories that supply answers to some of the key issues in sentencing. Thus Hudson's writings lay emphasis on three goals relating to sentencing policy: first, recognizing the links between the penal system and wider social policy, and taking steps in fields such as employment, education, housing and leisure facilities which may alter the conditions in which much offending takes place; second, reducing levels of penality, as these wider social and preventive measures are put in place; and third, giving specific attention to the importance of non-discrimination against the poor, against ethnic minorities and against women in the sentencing system.[13] Whilst Hudson is concerned that the penal system should provide proper opportunities for the rehabilitation of offenders, rather than harsh or negative regimes, her later writings recognize the importance of the proportionality principle in sentencing (see, e.g. Selection 4.9 above).[14] Such recognition is not found, for example, in the writings of Braithwaite and Pettit (see Selection 7.2, and the Introduction to Chapter 7, above).

Nicola Lacey's emphasis is upon the development of a theory of punishment that recognizes the primacy of the community, as Selection 8.3 shows. Like Norrie, Lacey finds the chief weakness of most modern (retributive) theory in its view of the individual as abstracted from the social world, and finds the chief strength of desert theory in its respect for the rights of individuals, especially when confronted with the might of the state. Lacey's distinctive contribution lies in her development of the notion of community and of the role of the institution of punishment within it. She also gives particular emphasis to feminist arguments, on the basis that the abstract individual in liberal theory is too often assumed to be male.[15] In later writings she has sought to explore the communitarian perspective and to warn against some dangers arising from it. From these writings emerge three distinct arguments in favour of adopting a communitarian approach. The first is that it draws attention not merely to interactions between the individual and the state but also to the interactions of both with intermediate community activities—raising questions, for example, about the extent to which communities should themselves play a role in matters of law, sentencing and punishment. The second is that communitarianism insists on developing and taking seriously a number of social or collectivist concepts which do and/or ought to play a role here, and which find no place in traditional liberal theory. Among these are public safety, environmental protection, reciprocity and solidarity. The third argument is that communitarianism recognizes not only that individuals are social beings but that each of us has "a number of community attachments, articulated in terms of factors such as race, ethnicity, class, gender, age, sexuality, occupation. Thus the position of a particular individual as subject of and to the legal order is neither fixed nor stable".[16]

However, in her recent work Lacey warns against a too ready embrace of community perspectives on justice, and raises questions about how a community is to be identified and who has membership. To the extent that community processes are formalized, they may tend to create their own hierarchies, and to raise difficulties about the location of the power to shape and to enforce community standards. To the extent that informal processes are developed, they may either play into the hands of the powerful or degenerate into mob justice. To avoid dangers such as these,

> ". . . we must continue to explore the different possibilities of violent, regulatory and persuasive/rhetorical modes of social regulation, and of the reconstruction of legal and quasi-legal practices in genuinely persuasive and inclusive terms. While we may recognise that the goal of attaining justice through law is in principle impossi-

ble of achievement, it is unclear what other form a transformative legal politics could take".[17]

A.A.

Notes

1. N. Lacey (1996a), p. 131.
2. *Ibid.*, p. 132.
3. See, for example, Mathieson (1990), Hulsman (1986), Bianchi (1986).
4. See, for example, Hirst (1986), ch. 6, and Mathiesen (1990).
5. Discussed in Chapter 1 above.
6. Lacey (1988), pp. 16–27.
7. See, for example, Morris and Tonry (1990).
8. e.g. Pires (1991).
9. See Selection 4.1 above, and the introduction to Chapter 4 above.
10. See Garland (1990), and, in much briefer form, Garland (1991).
11. von Hirsch (1993).
12. See the careful discussion of the concepts of deconstruction and reconstruction by Lacey (1996a).
13. e.g. Hudson (1987), Hudson (1993), and Cook and Hudson (1993).
14. See Hudson (1995), and Selection 4.9 above.
15. She is, however, critical of some strands of feminist theory: see Frazer and Lacey (1993).
16. Lacey (1996b), p. 121.
17. Lacey (1996b) p. 135.

References

Bianchi, H. (1986), "Abolition: Assensus and Sanctuary" in H. Bianchi and R. von Swaaningen, *Abolitionism: Towards a Non-Repressive Approach to Crime.*
Cook, D., and Hudson, B. (eds.) (1993), *Racism and Criminology* (London: Sage).
Frazer, E., and Lacey, N. (1993), *The Politics of Community: A Feminist Critique of the Liberal-Communitarian Debate* (Hemel Hempstead: Harvester).
Garland, D. (1990), *Punishment and Modern Society* (Oxford: Oxford University Press).
——— (1991), "Sociological Perspectives on Punishment" in Morris, N., and Tonry, M. (eds.), *Crime and Justice*, vol. 14.
Hirst, P. Q. (1986), *Law, Socialism and Democracy* (London: Allen & Unwin).
Hudson, B. (1987), *Justice through Punishment* (Basingstoke: Macmillan).
——— (1993), *Penal Policy and Social Justice* (Basingstoke: Macmillan).

Hudson, B. (1995), "Beyond Proportionate Punishment: Difficult Cases and the 1991 Criminal Justice Act", 22 *Crime, Law and Social Change* 59.

Hulsman, L. (1986), "Critical Criminology and the Concept of Crime", 10 *Contemporary Crises* 63.

Lacey, N. (1988), *State Punishment* (London: Routledge).

——— (1996a), "Normative Reconstruction in Socio-Legal Theory", 5 *Social and Legal Studies* 131–57.

——— (1996b), "Community in Legal Theory: Idea, Ideal or Ideology", 15 *Studies in Law, Politics and Society* 105–46.

Mathieson, T. (1990), *Prison on Trial* (London: Sage).

Morris, N., and Tonry, M. (1990), *Between Prison and Probation* (New York: Oxford University Press).

Pires, A. (1991), "Ethiques et Reforme du Droit Criminel: au-dela des Philosophies de la Peine", 3 *Ethica* 47.

von Hirsch, A. (1993), *Censure and Sanctions* (Oxford: Oxford University Press).

8.1

The Limits of Legal Ideology

ALAN NORRIE

1. The Philosophical-Historical Development of the Liberal Ideal of Criminal Punishment

I want to now summarize the development of the philosophy of punishment that has led to this situation in which we find ourselves "at sea as to first principles". My starting point was Hobbes's attempt to establish political (and punitive) authority on the back of a materialist view of people and society. He retained the aim of a moral justification of state power, but his materialism could provide no basis for a normative legitimization of the sovereign and his actions. Hence the "play" on the concept of "natural law" *and* the central role that he gave to the moral-juridical moment of individual consent in the social contract. From his point of view, Habermas has stressed the significance of the former element in the Hobbesian philosophy but missed the latter. MacPherson, on the other hand, focused on the material individuality (the egoism) of Hobbesian man, and identified this crucial element as a specifically bourgeois historical discovery by Hobbes; but he missed the essential schizophrenia of *Leviathan* in which the dark, brutal egoist becomes, on fairs and holy days, an ideal juridical individual—a bright alter ego, whose presence is in no way presaged in the materialist analysis.

It is the Hobbesian dualism that gives us a starting-point into the analysis of the modern classical philosophy of punishment. *Homo juridicus*, first cousin to economic man, emerges onto the stage of philosophical history fully-fledged as the founding principle of modern state sovereignty and authority. It is his rightful consent that establishes the basic notion of *do ut des*, of the transference of a liberty amongst equal individuals which allows for the legitimate constraint of the sovereign. From the other side

From Alan Norrie, *Law, Ideology and Punishment* (Kluwer, 1991), ch. IX (footnotes reduced). Excerpted and reprinted with permission. The chapter summarizes the arguments in earlier chapters of his book.

of Hobbes's philosophy, the creation of punishment is only too necessary: men's natural willfulness from this standpoint needs a strict control through sovereign punishment. But the compatibility between the ideal theory of consent and the prosaic reality of constraint is superficial. Given his nature, what man would or could consent to his punishment; given the moral-juridical capacity, how could such an individual *need* punishment? There is a contradiction between the surface *form* of the theory and its content as a *bellum omnium contra omnes*, between the presentation of social consensus and underlying social conflict. That conflict is understood in an individualist fashion (though remember Hobbes's reflections on the "common people") but, following MacPherson, it is a conflict that is nonetheless to be understood historically, resulting from and reflecting the birth of a specifically bourgeois society founded upon competition for resources and power.

Moving to the classical statements of the modern theory of punishment in Kant and Hegel, we find that the essential components that Hobbes had set in motion, and in tension, in his philosophy are combined and recombined in highly sophisticated ways in order to attempt to resolve the contradiction between the ideal (the moral) and the real (the actual, the material). In Kant, the attempt is made to achieve a radical separation of moral form and natural content, but the hermetic sealing off of the rational and normative from the real and the practical is only achieved at the price of rendering the former incompetent either to pass judgement on the latter[1] or to mediate relations within that sphere. Thus it is that an ideal theory of punishment can have nothing to say about the justice of punishment amongst mere mortals, nor establish sound measures for that most prosaic of social facts, punishment. Furthermore, with Kant, the gap between form and content now becomes recognizable as a *social* gap, for Kant acknowledges (around the edges of his materialist understanding of human nature) the social quality of wrong-doing in a world where false incentives to action are everywhere. The gap now becomes one between juridical appearance or representation (rational individualism) and social reality (a world of incentives to individual criminality).

Hegel did most to stop the more distasteful elements of social reality from impinging upon the world of rational individuals comprehended in his philosophy. With great ingenuity, he did it in a way that appeared to incorporate reality within the rational (and vice versa). The cunning of the Hegelian method lay in its ability to lay hold upon those elements of material reality which corresponded to the ideal, while shunning those elements which contradicted it. Thus punishment and criminal justice, prosaic institutions, become emanations of the Idea on its speculative path through history and society, but are only presented in so far as they conform to the requirements of the Idea. If the rational is real *and* the real is rational, then all thoughts of social irrationality—for example of crime as a fixed and necessary social phenomenon—must and can be cast aside in the wake of reason's triumph. But it turned out that history was more cunning than Hegel and the philosopher was forced to acknowledge the turbulent and inequitable nature of "rational", bourgeois (civil) society, and thence to recognize the class basis of criminality among the poor and the rebellious. Content rebelled against the ideal form that sought to speak through it like a ventriloquist's dummy, and Hegel was anxious enough about the fate of civil society to recognize it. But the question then arose, what role was the state to play in a world where rational atomized individuals turned out to be aggressive, needy occupants of inequitable class positions? The concept of the state, in the realm of crime and punishment, had not been premised upon social, structural recalcitrance on the part of members of civil society. Hegel did not hesitate to say that if individuals did not behave as individuals should, then nor could states be expected to. The juridical form of the *Rechtsstaat also* turned out to be an appearance hiding a deeper reality as Hegel justified the death penalty for petty theft. The State became (what it always was behind the juridical form) a mechanism of social control on behalf of one class over another. Class conflict is the "worm in the bud" of the ideal penal theory of Hegel.

With Kant and Hegel, the elements within the modern classical theory of punishment receive their most sophisticated expression. Already, however, we can see the temptation for these elements to tear the theories apart. Kant agonizes over the question of social justice and Hegel subverts his own theory on the subject of the death penalty. These were theories of the bourgeois Enlightenment; that is, they were theories that expressed a *political* as well as a philosophical idealism.[2] At this stage in historical development the philosophers could still maintain a basic conviction in the value of their central terms. Later on, however, thinkers in the tradition had to recognize that the fabric of an ideal juridical individualism could not be made to stretch any further to cover the emerging crises of social development within capitalism. The effects of poverty and pauperism, of idleness and drunkenness, of exploitation and vice upon the criminality of the body politic could not be ignored or represented as a matter of pure individual choice. The English Hegelians, writing in late Victorian England, did not initially discard this notion, but they sought to hedge it around by reconceiving the state not as a *Rechtsstaat* but as a social, interventionist state, designed to cure defects in minds that could not be relied upon to follow rational tenets. In this situation, the classical theory began to fall apart. Because society and social order were no longer understood to rest upon individual consent or reason, juridical individualist ideology could no longer be the true basis for the political legitimation of social institutions. Simultaneously, the state could no longer be seen as an ideal counterpart to a society of free individuals, as a juridical *primus inter pares*. More emphasis had to be placed upon the role of the state as an institution that "knows better" and that intervenes in order to make people better citizens.

In this move, the classical relationship between form and content breaks down at the level both of the individual and of the state. With regard to the former, individuals are no longer portrayed as free, equal and rational. They are *socially* formed and, where poor, potentially inadequate. The juridical form of the responsible rational individual begins to dissolve into the social context of individual life. Similarly, the state is no longer the guarantor of individual right, administered equally. It must move amongst and against the lower classes ensuring their proper participation in social arrangements. Behind the rhetoric of welfare, the aim is reconstruction of the poor and the inadequate, regardless of their actual will in the matter. The state's form of neutrality dissolves as it intervenes in class relations. For T. H. Green, the historical developments in Victorian England necessitated a re-theorization of Hegelianism which emphasized the whole over its parts, the state over its citizens. But this tendency, to "reify the universal as against the individual", was nonetheless still "counteracted by [an] adherence to the progressive tendencies of Western rationalism"[3] with the result that the theory was not only contradictory but also profoundly unstable in its elements. Lesser philosophers within the same tradition sought to resolve the contradictions by removing one pole of the central antithesis and by moving entirely in the direction of statist, collective authority against the individual. Green had opened up this avenue, but he had baulked at progressing too far down it. Philosophers like Bradley and Bosanquet marched ahead, confident that they were armed with an idea "whose time had come". The state would deal with crime directly and ruthlessly as the whole crushed its recalcitrant parts. Thus it was that in the final phase of its development, the retributive philosophy became transformed into the opposite of what it had been. From being an expression of individual autonomy and defence of individual right, it became a principle of authoritarian state interventionism without regard to or respect for the individual. But this doctrine still retained the name "retributivism", leading to its utter discredit in an intellectual culture where fascism remained an eccentric and borderline conviction.

It is crucial to note that the downfall of retributivism at the beginning of the twentieth century was an essentially organic and dialectical playing out of the contradictions within the philosophy in the context of the developing historical realities of capitalist society. It was the increasing tension between the ideal juridical foundations of the theory and the underlying social developments, between its form and content, that led to its downfall as the concepts of the rational individual and the *Rechtsstaat* were both discarded to meet the same requirement: a more "effective" form of social control. From the late nineteenth century, the interventionist ideology of "welfarism" and social eudaemonism grew to replace the old juridical ideologies of individual responsibility and the rule of law (or at least to knock them sideways as they—temporarily, as it turned out—took centre stage). As a result, and in the context of the "organic" self-destruction of retributivism, it was hardly surprising that it should be a utilitarian theory emphasizing social intervention for the general good as part of a commitment to social amelioration in a welfare-liberal polity that should emerge as the predominant justification of punishment. Retributivism had shot its bolt; utilitarianism, it transpired, was the idea whose time had really come.

It was in this way that the intellectual framework for the familiar twentieth century debates was set. The legacy of retributivism's decline was a discursive terrain in which the elements of juridical individualism had been displaced from centre stage but had to be constantly re-asserted within a polity that remained ideologically liberal. Utilitarianism started off from the position of the need to promote the social good, but then had to incorporate into its analysis a juridical element in support of individual right so as to defend itself against the charge of authoritarianism. Similarly, utilitarianism was predominantly based upon the materialist analysis of individual conduct which had emerged with the Enlightenment and which tended to reduce individual subjectivity and responsibility to the effects of psychological and physiological processes.[4] This then had to be offset by arguments which could rescue the concept of responsibility from the reductionist context. In both situations, however, the assertion of the twin juridical values of individual right and responsibility was fundamentally weakened by the hegemonic position of the overarching utilitarian, materialist theory. Juridical individualism had to be inserted into an intellectually hostile environment. Individual rights against social intervention had to be defended within the discourse of social intervention, and individual responsibility and freedom had to be asserted within a discourse of determinism. Having ceased to be a fundamental principle of social and political theory, as it had been within the modern classical approach, juridical individualism, like an old aristocrat fallen upon hard times, had to scratch a living as best it could with second rate materials. Juridical individualism had become a secondary, technical element within an overarching materialist utilitarian theoretical context and could not regain the glorious primacy it had enjoyed in the period of revolutionary political enlightenment. Criminality had passed into the worlds of social science and social policy; juridical punishment had become an intellectually outmoded idea,[5] hanging on by little more than the theoretical skin of its teeth. The theories based upon the form of juridical individualism persisted, and the ideas continued to "go round in circles", but the circles became in the twentieth century ever-diminishing in size and intellectual scope.

2. The Return to Kant

It is in the context of the historical decline of retributive philosophy that we can understand the ambivalence and ambiguity present in the writings of those who have recently returned to Kant (or, at least, a modernized version) through the so-called justice model. This philosophical move which developed in the 1970s and early 1980s emerged as a response to increasing dissatisfaction with the utilitarian and rehabilitative consensus that had existed in the criminal and penal process. It was becoming clear that greater injustices could be perpetrated under an ideology of welfare than under the juridical ideology of punishment that welfare had supplanted. The move to a justice model, premised on Kantian principles, entailed a desire to limit the ability of the state to intervene in the lives of individuals. In von Hirsch's words, it involved "a crucial shift in perspective from a commitment to do good to a commitment to do as little mischief as possible".[6]

But why this return to retributive principles of "guilt" and "just deserts"? Had these concepts not been discredited many years earlier in the critiques of both philosophers and criminologists? How could these ideas, apparently so definitively consigned to the scrapheap, emerge as the bright and shining hope for penal reform? The key to answering this question lies in recognition of the thoroughly contradictory nature of this return to Kantian principle. For example, the criminologist, Stanley Cohen could describe the "justice model" as "the most promising possible" option for criminology to espouse, yet in the next breath, counsel extreme caution as to the dangers of such an approach. The "justice model" is in fact extremely *unjust* because it denies what criminology has known for a century, that individual criminal acts are always inherently social phenomena. The "justice model" makes us "forget that by the time many offenders get to this wonderful justice system the damage has already been done". It is obvious, says Cohen, "to anyone who has spent five minutes in a court or prison that it would be blatantly *unjust* to return—even as an intermediate tactic—to an undiluted classicism".[7]

Again, we are back in the contradiction between the *form* of criminal justice and the *content* of social relations and criminal conduct. As early proponents of the "justice model" put it, the attempt to establish "a just system of criminal justice in an unjust society is a contradiction in terms". Criminal justice is inextricably interwoven with, and largely derivative from, a broader social justice.[8]

In considering this debate one has very much the sense of a clutching at philosophical straws in the face of a recalcitrant reality. Lucien Seve's description of "a science [which] goes round in circles" is very much to the point. Consider Cohen's bewildered summing up of the development of criminology in the late seventies:

> "One upon a time it was radical to attack law; then it became 'radical' to attack psychiatry. As we now rush back to the bewildered embrace of lawyers, who always thought we were against them, we should remind ourselves just what a tyranny the literal rule of law could turn out to be."[9]

Amongst the philosophers, Murphy has come closest to confronting the contradiction between criminal and social justice, between a model of punishment based upon an abstract juridical conception of agency and the concrete determinations of conduct within social life. He concedes that "modern societies largely lack the moral right to punish"[10] and seeks to resolve the issue by hitching his Kantian theory of punishment to a Marxian analysis of social injustice. If we consider that "institutions of punishment are necessary and desirable" and we are to have the moral right to inflict it, we must first have "reconstructed society in such a way that criminals genuinely do correspond to the only model that will render punishment permissible". The paradox of this position is, as Murphy notes, that if crime is a general product of social conditions, then such a restructuring of society would entail that "crime itself and the need to punish would radically decrease if not disappear entirely".[11] Here, Murphy is only repeating a logic that we have already seen in Kant himself. If we lived in a world that had been radically restructured, why *would* we consider institutions of punishment to be "necessary and desirable"? On the other hand, without such a restructuring punishment is unjustified.

Thus the return to the justice model is a highly contradictory affair. Written from the point of view of a modern awareness of the social roots of criminality, it is impossible for proponents not to exhibit an extreme ambivalence about their project. However, it is wrong to examine the "justice model" only in its negative aspect. From one point of view, the justice model leads not to justice but to injustice. From another point of view, however, it is a means of seeking to impose limits upon the power of the state, and this is the aspect that proponents of the model have most emphasized. A system of strict punishments may be unjust, and therefore oppressive, when viewed in the context of broader, social relations. It may be (relatively) liberative when viewed as a check upon state power. It is necessary to understand both the positive and negative aspects of the justice model.

The key to these two aspects lies in the important duality within the ideology of juridical individualism . . . [the] two contradictions at the heart of legal ideology concerning the nature of the individual and the nature of the state. The first contradiction exists between the abstract individualism of the law and the concrete individuality of human beings in different social contexts, with different needs, experiences and personalities. In this context, the liberty of the abstract juridical individual appears shallow and insignificant when contrasted with the real human needs of actual human beings in particular social contexts. It is obscurantist in its ability to hide the underlying social relations which provide the actual springs of human conduct behind the "front" of the abstract responsible individual. From the point of view of a politics of human libration, abstract juridical individualism, with its shallow concepts of freedom and equality, is a barrier to the achievement of real human freedom and equality, both of which require the transformation of social relations, not a spurious respect for an abstract model of the individual. This much is implicit in the self-critique of the "justice modellers", that we have considered above. Marx expressed much the same point of view when he described the formal rights of bourgeois society as providing a "narrow horizon" beyond which a communist society should have to go.[12]

With regard to the second contradiction, however, between individual right and social power, things look quite different. Here, the juridical form entails an assertion of the rights of the individual against the interests of the state, so that from the point of view of a politics of human liberation, juridical individualism is an important positive element in this antithesis. In this context, we can see that bourgeois right's "narrow horizon" remains valid and worth defending. Better a narrow horizon than no horizon at all. The strengths and weaknesses of the "justice model" are embedded within this complex duality of juridical ideology. It is the two-sided nature of such ideology that accounts for the ambivalence of those who support the "justice model", and it is because of the complexity of the legal form that any politics which dismisses legal ideology wholesale will throw out a very important baby with some admittedly rather murky bathwater. A considered politics must take both aspects of juridical ideology into account.

3. The Ideal and the Actual

We are left with a nuanced analysis of juridical individualism which recognizes from one side the obscurantist and, in the Marxist term, fetishized character of the legal form; from the other side, the liberative and safeguarding role of individual right is also acknowledged. For this reason, no proper analysis of the legal form can either defend it wholesale or repudiate it wholesale. In the postscript to his historical analysis of the development of the bourgeois criminal law, E. P. Thompson argues that the "rule of law" is a juridical-political concept that transcends class divisions and has a quality that elevates it beyond the purely historical.[13] Yet his own analysis shows that his paean to the law is overdone, for two reasons. First, the rule of law was introduced primarily as a means of oppression of the peasantry and developing working class. The bourgeoisie sought an efficient system of law which would clearly establish very tight bonds of legality and punish illegal behaviour resolutely.[14] Often, what was regarded as illegal was what had previously been accepted by all social classes as lawful conduct and as a matter of customary right.[15] The introduction of the rule of law from the point of view of the poor and the powerless was not regarded as a good, it was a fetter and a means of protecting the property of the rich. To have fixed rules prohibiting a peasant from doing what he had previously done without hindrance was no advance from the peasant's viewpoint.

Second, the rule of law was not regarded from the ruling classes' point of view as anything to be taken too seriously when it came to the rights of the working class. When it came to developing the law, criminal law was the last area in which adherence to rational legal principle occurred or was to be expected.[26] To be sure, where it was a matter of the rights of the middle class and landowners to private property, the lawyers spoke loud and clear,[17] but when it came to the rights of those who confronted private property as a limit upon their actual freedom and social equality, things were different.[18] As Foucault expresses it in his analysis of the penal reform movement on the continent of Europe, the arguments for the rule of law and the rights of the subject, while universal in their form, had two quite distinct targets. One was against the "super-power" of the absolute sovereign, who needed to be controlled in the interests of the bourgeoisie. The other was against the "infra-power" of the masses who also needed to be controlled in the interests of the bourgeoisie.[19] The different was that in the former case, the rule of law was designed to protect the bourgeoisie from autocratic rule; in the latter case, it was designed to control the illegality of the masses. This difference in function and in content necessarily led to a difference in form, in emphasis upon the quality of legal rights to be bestowed upon the different sectors of the population. The rule of (the criminal) law was introduced as a means of more effectively controlling the illegality of the common people with the judges paying little more than lip service to the rational controls that this placed on state power.

On the other hand, there is something in what Thompson says. As time wore on, the logic of the rule of law became interwoven into the character of judicial discourse so that the judges were (and are) forced to take it seriously. This does not mean that they will always follow the dictates of its logic . . . To the extent that they do not do so, however, they are forced to cover up their actions, for the rule of law has become a part of the publicly declared legitimating ideology of the Western polity. Thus it is that the rule of law, which in the realm of criminal law began as a means of more effective social control and exploitation, came to possess an emergent, potential quality as a safeguard of the rights of all classes, including those who were exploited. Such a safeguard is never either guaranteed in itself or necessarily adequate in its terms. It must be fought for, defended and extended all the time. Nonetheless, it is an emergent and potential quality of the rule of law, of the juridical discourse of individual right.

At the same time, however, it must be reasserted that this positive aspect of the rule of law remains tied to the negative aspect: that the rule of (the criminal) law is primarily a mechanism for protecting the property of those who possess it from those who do not, and, more generally, of maintaining a level of social control over those whose position in society makes them victims at the same time as they victimize others.[20] In this context, the ideal Kantian form of criminal justice is in contradiction with the actuality of crime and criminality. Capitalist society gave birth at one and the same time to relations of social exploitation and to an ideal juridical form. They were part and parcel of the same social and economic moment in history: the birth and growth of capitalism as a market society. Hence it is that theories based upon the ideology of juridical individualism are constantly shadowed by the darker and more brutal social existence of struggle and oppression. The two go together as a hand fits in a glove.

It is the nature of crime as a product of social conflict and malaise that lurks behind the idealism of the Kantian theory of punishment, and which makes any ultimate justification of punishment in Kantian terms impossible. Analysis of the historical development of the philosophy of punishment makes it clear that the radical disjuncture between the ideal and the actual is no passing feature. It is a constant and fixed quality which necessarily undermines a principled justification of punishment in an unprincipled society. Because of this, any attempt to moralize punishment in capitalist society along the lines of individual desert is doomed to failure. Juridical form and content remain in contradiction, so that any attempts at rationalisation and legitimation can only succeed on the basis of an occlusion of the fundamental, historical relationship between the Western individualist ideology of punishment and the underlying social character of criminality and state power.

Notes

1. MacIntyre (1967), pp. 197–8; Wolff (1973), ch. 2.
2. See Ree, Ayers and Westoby (1978), ch. 3, esp. pp. 89–90.
3. Marcuse (1941), pp. 391–2.
4. Of course not every form of utilitarianism corresponds to this description. It is the predominant Benthamite form that is referred to here.
5. "Intellectually" is emphasized because it is clear that judicial ideology will continue to play a fundamental role in Western societies regardless of its justifiability. Ideas can and do retain their currency long after their deficiencies have been exposed where they continue to reflect the principles embodied in dominant social relations. While the moral narrative constructed around law has become threadbare, the need to legitimate it remains.
6. von Hirsch (1976).
7. Cohen (1979), pp. 35–41.
8. American Friends Service Committee (1971), p. 6.
9. Cohen (1979), p. 41.
10. Murphy (1979), p. 95.
11. Ibid., p. 110.
12. Marx (1961), p. 320.
13. Thompson (1977), p. 268.
14. Hay (1977); Foucault (1979), pp. 82–103. This was even more starkly the case where Western legal forms were imposed in colonial contexts: Fisch (1983).
15. Thompson (1977), pp. 240–1.
16. Ibid., pp. 208–11, 251–4.

17. Hill (1965), p. 257; Little (1969), p. 174.
18. Hay (1977); Hill (1967), pp. 113–14.
19. Foucault (1979), p. 87.
20. On the modern class distribution of processed criminality, see e.g. Braithwaite (1979); Quinney (1980); Box (1983 and 1987).

References

American Friends Service Committee (1971), *The Struggle for Justice* (New York).
Box, S. (1983), *Power, Crime and Mystification* (London).
———— (1987), *Recession, Crime and Punishment* (London).
Braithwaite, J. (1979), *Inequality, Crime and Public Policy* (London).
Cohen, S. (1979), "Guilt, Justice and Tolerance" in D. Downes and P. Rock (eds.), *Deviant Interpretations* (Oxford).
Fisch, J. (1983), *Cheap Lives and Dear Limbs* (Wiesbaden).
Foucault, M. (1979), *Discipline and Punish* (Harmondsworth).
Hay, D *et al.* (1977), *Albion's Fatal Tree* (Harmondsworth).
Hill, C. (1965), *The Intellectual Origins of the English Revolution* (Oxford).
———— (1967), *Reformation to Industrial Revolution* (London).
Little, D. (1969), *Religion, Order and the Law* (New York).
MacIntyre, A. (1967), *A Short History of Ethics* (London).
Marcuse, H. (1941), *Reason and Revolution* (London).
Marx, K. (1961), "Critique of the Gotha Programme", in K. Marx and F. Engels, *Selected Works in One Volume* (London).
Murphy, J. (1979), *Retribution, Justice and Therapy* (Dordrecht).
Quinney, R. (1980), *Class, State and Crime* (New York).
Ree, J., Ayers, M., and Westoby, A. (1978), *Philosophy and its Past* (Hassocks).
Thompson, E. P. (1977), *Whigs and Hunters* (Harmondsworth).
von Hirsch, A. (1976), *Doing Justice* (New York).
Wolff, R. P. (1973), *The Autonomy of Reason* (New York).

8.2

Sociological Perspectives on Punishment

DAVID GARLAND

I. Sociological Perspectives on Punishment

The standard ways in which we think and talk about punishment are framed not so much by sociological theory as by two rather different discursive traditions, which might best be described as the "penological" and the "philosophical" . . .

In recent years a third style of thinking about punishment has begun to develop and to offer a different framework for the analysis of penal issues. Instead of viewing punishment as a means to an end or a stock problem for moral philosophy, sociologists and historians have begun to conceptualize punishment as a social institution and to pose a series of questions that stem from this approach. In place of questions about punishment's effectiveness or its justification, these writers have been asking, "How do specific penal measures come into existence?" "What social functions does punishment perform?" "How do penal institutions relate to other institutions?" "How do they contribute to social order, or to state power, or to class domination, or to the cultural reproduction of society?" and "What are punishment's unintended social effects, its functional failures, and its wider social costs?" "Punishment" is thus understood as a cultural and historical artifact that may be centrally concerned with the control of crime but that is nevertheless shaped by an ensemble of social forces and has a significance and range of effects that reach well beyond the population of criminals. And the sociology of punishment—as I shall term this emergent tradition—has been concerned to explore the social foundations of punishment, to trace out the social implications of specific penal modes, and to uncover the structures of social action and webs of cultural meaning that give modern punishment its characteristic functions, forms, and

From David Garland, "Sociological Perspectives on Punishment", in Norval Morris and Michael Tonry (eds.), *Crime and Justice*, vol. 14 (Chicago: University of Chicago Press, 1991). Excerpted and reprinted with permission.

effects (Ignatieff (1981); Garland and Young (1983); Jacobs (1983), ch. 1; Cohen (1985), ch. 1; Hirst (1986), ch. 7; Garland (1990a)).

However, it would be quite misleading to continue to discuss the sociology of punishment as if it were a single, unified framework of thought (Garland, 1990b). On closer inspection, the sociological and historical literature on punishment displays a range of theoretical approaches, analytical perspectives, and concrete interpretations that do not necessarily add up to form a single coherent or comprehensive account. Instead, what one finds is a set of competing interpretations, each one drawing on a different model of sociological explanation, each one going at the problem in a different way and for a different purpose, and each one highlighting a different characteristic of punishment and its social role. Like much of sociology, the sociology of punishment is characterized less by a settled research agenda and agreed parameters of study than by a noisy clash of perspectives and an apparently incorrigible conflict of different interpretations and varying points of view. One response to this situation has been to adopt a particular perspective—say, a Marxist approach, or a Durkheimian one—and to develop this analysis in critical disregard of other ways of proceeding. However, it is at least arguable that such an approach is less fruitful than one that tries to bring these different theoretical perspectives into conversation with one another, seeking to synthesize their interpretative strengths, to identify analyses that are complementary rather than contradictory, and to isolate specific points of disagreement so that one can endeavour to resolve them by means of further research or theoretical reflection.

What I do in this essay is to survey the major sociological interpretations of punishment and to give some sense of the resources that social theory offers for the understanding of punishment. I set out a number of perspectives in turn, dealing first with the more established traditions associated with the work of Durkheim, Marx, and Foucault and then with the perspective suggested by the work of Norbert Elias . . .

II. A Multidimensional Approach

These four broad perspectives that have been outlined—punishment as a moralizing mechanism, a component of class rule, an exercise of power, and an enacted cultural form—cannot be simply added together to provide some kind of grand overview of punishment and penal history. The danger of such eclectcism is that, in drawing on arguments made by different theorists about "punishment and society", one can too readily assume an identity of concerns where none in fact exists and end up in an intellectual tangle of incompatible premises, ambiguous concepts, and shifting objects of study. Trying to say everything at once, one can wind up saying nothing with any clarity or conviction. Any account of punishment drawing from more than one theoretical source must therefore be careful to avoid mixing up analyses and propositions that are theoretically incompatible. But while eclecticism has these risks, there is a definite explanatory strength to be found in theoretical pluralism, by which I mean a willingness to draw on more than one interpretive perspective and to construct multidimensional accounts of the phenomenon being investigated. What I have tried to suggest in this essay is that these different interpretations might be played off against each other—and against the factual research evidence that they help generate—in such a way as to overlay them, build them up, and use each one to correct and refine the others. Proceeding from one explanatory perspective to another, it becomes clear that each one asks slightly different questions about the phenomenon of "punishment", each pursues a different aspect, reveals a different determinant, and outlines a different connection.

Sometimes, of course, different theorists do address the same issue, only to interpret it in different ways—as when Marxists and Durkheimians disagree about the role of the state or of popular sentiments in the formation of penal policy. In such cases, one needs to argue out this disagreement and resolve it in favour of the best explanation—or else develop an alternative account that improves on them both. At other times, however, theoretical disagreement may, on closer inspection, turn out to be less substantive than it at first appears. Thus, as we have already seen, where Durkheim insists that modern punishment is irrational, emotional, and punitive, Foucault appears to argue that neither punitiveness nor vengeful emotion has any place in the rationalized disciplinary strategies of modern punishment—a direct contradiction of Durkheim's view. But in fact this statement misrepresents the scope of Foucault's argument. His analysis, unlike that of Durkheim, does not cover the whole social process of punishment, from prosecution through court trial to penal disposition. Instead he focuses on the practices of prisons and the rationalities that they employ. His is primarily an account of penal administration and technology—that is to say, of one crucial aspect of the penal process, rather than the whole process from beginning to end. And precisely because his purpose is to understand the mechanisms of positive, disciplinary power— rather than to understand "punishment" as such—his work makes no attempt to discuss the extent to which emotions and moral sentiments continue to structure the context in which imprisonment is used. Thus, what appears to be a direct contradiction can be viewed as a difference of interpretive focus and theoretical concern: Foucault, who seeks to understand the rationality of modern power, puts penal institutions into the foreground of his analysis, while Durkheim, concerned to understand social morality, bases his account on the courtroom ritual and the legislation of criminal law. Seen in this way, as interpretations grounded in different aspects of a differentiated process, the question should no longer be, Which one is correct, Foucault or Durkheim? Instead, we should enquire how the different tendencies that they describe interact with one another, how these conflicts are managed, and what effects these tensions have on the modern process of punishment.

In other cases, it may be that a particular theorist successfully identifies an element of penality that seems to escape the scrutiny of other theoretical accounts—as with Foucault on power-knowledge techniques, Durkheim on the role of the onlooker, Rusche and Kirchheimer on the role of the market, or else Elias on changing sensibilities. Here again, we are reminded that "punishment" is not a unitary thing but rather a complex and differentiated process, involving discursive frameworks of authority and condemnation, ritual procedures of imposing sentences, a repertoire of penal sanctions, institutions, and agencies for their administration, and a rhetoric of symbols and images with which the process is represented to its various audiences. One is therefore led to investigate how these different elements and aspects of punishment fit together to form a complex internally differentiated whole. At the same time, this realization allows us to better understand the diversity of interpretations that has been brought to bear on "punishment" and to acknowledge the possibility that these interpretations might be in some ways complementary and mutually confirming rather than mutually exclusive.

Thus, to give another example, although they start with quite different premises, both Durkheim and the Marxist writer Douglas Hay agree that punishment works through the forms of ritual display and symbolic representation and addresses itself to an audience of onlookers as much as to the offender in the dock. Both insist that such displays can be crucial to the generation and regeneration of a society's culture and the individual's commitment, whether by shoring up the claims of authority or else by dealing with social dangers. Despite radical disagreement over the interpretation of penal symbols and the nature of the societies that they depict, both accounts confirm the operation of punishments within this wider sphere of cultural and psychic life. Similarly, the Foucauldian and Eliasian accounts begin from very different positions in their analysis of penal history—one emphasizing the importance of sensibilities, the other insisting that these are merely a gloss concealing relations of power and knowledge—but their accounts of the removal of punishment from the public sphere into the privacy of institutional enclosures, administered by specialist functionaries in technical rather than emotive terms, can be seen as dealing with two dimensions of the same historical process and, thus, as mutually illuminating and reinforcing.

The theoretical conclusion that these considerations suggest is that a pluralistic, multidimensional approach is needed if we are to understand the historical development and present-day operation of the penal complex. If there is to be a sociology of punishment—and by this I mean a set of general parameters from which specific studies can take their theoretical bearings—then it should be the kind of sociology advocated by Marcel Mauss (1967, p. 78) when he talked about the need for a synthesis and consolidation of perspectives. It should be a sociology that strives to present a rounded, completed image: a recomposition of the fragmentary views developed by more narrowly focused studies.

One can rephrase this argument as a warning against reductionism in the analysis of punishment—by which I mean the tendency to explain penality in terms of any single causal principle or functional purpose, be it "morals" or "economics", "state control" or "crime control". Instead of searching for a single explanatory principle, we need to grasp the facts of multiple causality, multiple effects, and multiple meaning. We need to realize that in the penal realm—as in all social experience—specific events or developments usually have a plurality of causes that interact to shape their final form, a plurality of effects that may be seen as functional or non-functional depending on one's criteria, and a plurality of meanings which will vary with the actors and audiences involved—though some meanings (or, for that matter, causes and effects) may be more powerful than others. The aim of analysis should always be to capture that variety of causes, effects and meanings and trace their interaction, rather than to reduce them all to a single currency.

The utility of the individual interpretive frameworks that I have discussed lies not in their creation of broad theoretical perspectives with which to view punishment—although these in themselves can sometimes change the ways in which we think about penal issues—but rather in their capacity to guide and inform more specific studies of penal practice and penal policy. For practical purposes, the kind of knowledge that is most useful is detailed, specific, local knowledge, focused on a particular problem, or institution, or policy question and informed about the specific cultural, political, and penological circumstances that apply. The best studies of this kind are nuanced, subtle, and complex; are able to see the phenomenon in all its complexity and yet at the same time clearly situate it within its social and historical context; and aim to unravel the details of its many determinants, dynamics, and consequences. Typically, works of this kind—whether historical or contemporary—tend to utilize the kind of interpretive pluralism I have been describing rather than rely entirely on one or other interpretive framework. Thus, for example, recent work by David Downes (1988) and by Zimring and Hawkins (1990) that attempts to explain differential rates of imprisonment have stressed the need to draw on a range of theoretical traditions and to construct a complex account of interacting variables and contributory factors. Similarly, the best historical studies in this field—such as those by Michael Ignatieff (1978) and by John Beattie (1986)—mobilize forms of analysis and lines of inquiry suggested by not one but several sociological perspectives and manage to bring them together in ways that do justice to the complexity of real events. As John Beattie has put it, summing up his magisterial study of penal change in early modern England:

> "Changes in punishment are almost certain not to arise from a simple, one-dimensional effect. The forms of punishment employed by a society at any one moment are shaped by a variety of interests and intentions. They arise in response to what must often be antagonistic considerations, including the framework of law, what is technically possible, what seems desirable or necessary in the light of the apparent problem of crime, what society is willing to accept and pay for. Why one method of punishment loses favour over time and gives way to another is a complex question because penal methods evolve within a larger social and cultural context that in imperceptible ways alters the limits of what is acceptable and what is not" (1986, p. 470).

Sociological theories, such as those discussed in this essay, are useful in the understanding of punishment because they alert us to the kinds of constraints and structures within which policy is developed and to the kinds of social consequences that punishment can have. They point to the interconnections that link punishment to other spheres of social life and the functional role that it occupies in the network of social institutions. They can reveal institutional dynamics, characteristics, and effects that might otherwise go unacknowledged and of which policymakers themselves may be unaware. But only empirical research can determine how these conditioning circumstances come together at a particular moment to shape a course of action or define a particular event. Theory should be a set of interpretative tools for guiding and informing empirical inquiry—not a substitute for it.

III. Punishment as a Social Institution

What I have tried to do in this essay is to suggest how the theoretical tools of sociology can be used to help us think about punishment in its various aspects. Each of the different traditions of social theory provides a specific set of tools in the form of a specially adapted conceptual vocabulary, designed to explicate a particular aspect or dimension of social life. And, as I have tried to indicate, each of these interpretative vocabularies has its uses in understanding punishment and becomes more or less useful depending on the questions asked and the characteristics being explained. Thus, in some circumstances, and for some people (e.g., those groups for whom the law is merely superior force, coercively imposed), punishment is an exercise of raw power, best understood in vocabularies such as those supplied by Foucault or Marx. Yet at other points, and for other people— perhaps in the same society and the same penal system—punishment may be an expression of moral community and collective sensibility, in which penal sanctions are an authorized response to shared values individually violated. In these circumstances, the vocabularies of power and ideology need to be tempered by the rather different concerns articulated by Elias and Durkheim. The object of theoretical work in this area should not be to create a grand synthesis of these traditions, nor to construct some kind of overarching theoretical model. Rather, it should be to investigate how we might most usefully utilize the range of perspectives and vocabularies through which punishment can be variously understood and to develop a conception of punishment that can ground this multiplicity of interpretations and show how they interrelate.

These social interpretations might thus be used to enrich our understanding of punishment, leading us to conceive of it not just as a crime-control mechanism but instead as a distinctive and rather complex social institution that, in its routine practices, somehow contrives to condense a whole web of social relations and cultural meanings. This more developed, sociological conception of punishment can, I think, have important implications for the way we think about punishment and penal policy. By making the social dimensions of punishment explicit, and by showing the kinds of internal conflicts and social consequences that penal institutions entail, the sociology of punishment provides a more adequate empirical basis for policy evaluation, philosophical reflection, or political judgment in this area. As I suggested earlier the evaluation of punishment is too readily cast in the narrow terms of instrumental utility. We are too prone to think of punishment as a simple means to a simple end—usually that of crime control—and to treat all other aspects of the institution as minor considerations. So, for instance, imprisonment, or probation, or rehabilitative policies, or even capital punishment, are all too frequently approached as if the major question to be answered concerned their technical efficacy as instruments of crime control. Their evaluation thus turns primarily on measures of recidivism, or deterrence, and on correlative crime rates rather than on judgments of their total worth as social practices. But, as each of these sociological perspectives makes clear, we can hardly begin to understand penal institutions if we insist on treating them as instrumentalities, geared to a single penological purpose—so the tendency to evaluate them in these terms seems misguided and unproductive.

Thus, to conclude with an illustration, we might consider the ways in which the institution of imprisonment tends to be evaluated in contemporary discussions. As every critical report reminds us, this institution signally fails to achieve the ends of crime control that, it is assumed, form its basic raison d'être (for a summary, see Mathiesen (1990). Most prisoners are not reformed, new generations of criminals go undeterred, national crime rates are not forced into decline, so that by all these criteria the prison is deemed an inefficient instrument (though, it should be noted, not much more inefficient than many of its alternatives). This margin of failure—it is not suggested that prison has *no* success—is such that the prison and its present high frequency of use present a serious puzzle for social commentators and penal reformers alike. Theorists such as Foucault assume that the prison's failures must, in some covert sense, be "useful for power". Historians such as Lawrence Stone (1987, p. 10) assume it is a "vestigial institution" that has somehow outlived its usefulness. Liberal criminologists throw up their hands in despair at the "irrationality" of policy and urge governments to pay attention to penological research findings and the failures that these imply. But, in an important sense, this argument is misconceived, and the "puzzle" of imprisonment arises only because of the too-narrow starting points from which these analyses begin.

Neither the prison, nor any other penal institution, rests solely on its ability to achieve such instrumental ends. Despite recurring hopes and the exaggerated claims of some reformers, the simple fact is that no method of punishment has ever achieved high rates of reform or of crime control—and no method ever will. All punishments regularly "fail" in this respect because, as Emile Durkheim (1973, chs. 10 and 11) and others have pointed out, it is only the mainstream processes of socialization (internalized morality and a sense of duty, the informal inducements and rewards of conformity, the practical and cultural networks of mutual expectation and interdependence, etc.) that are able to promote proper conduct on a consistent and regular basis. Punishment, so far as "control" is concerned, is merely a coercive backup to these more reliable social mechanisms, a backup that is often unable to do anything more than manage those who slip through these networks of normal control and integration. Punishment is fated never to "succeed" to any great degree because the conditions that do most to induce conformity—or to promote crime and deviance—lie outside the jurisdiction of penal institutions.

It will always be open to critics of the prison to point to its failures of crime control and use these as an argument for reform. But it seems altogether inappropriate for a sociologist or a historian to take these same arguments and draw from them the conclusion that the prison is a penological failure that owes its existence to some covert political strategy or else to the dead hand of history. Like all complex institutions, the prison simultaneously pursues a number of objectives and is kept in place by a range of forces. Crime control—in the sense of reforming offenders and reducing crime rates—is certainly one of these objectives but by no means the only one. As we have seen, the prison also serves as an effective means of incapacitation, securely excluding offenders from society, sometimes for very long periods, and containing those individuals who prove too troublesome for other institutions or communities. Unlike lesser penalties, it does not require much in the way of co-operation from the offender, so that it can deal with recalcitrant individuals, by force if necessary. In the absence of the generalized use of capital punishment, forced exile, or transportation, the prison thus forms the ultimate penalty for most modern penal systems, providing a compelling and forceful sanction of last resort. Most important, the prison provides a way of punishing people— of subjecting them to hard treatment, inflicting pain, doing them harm— that is largely compatible with modern sensibilities and conventional restraints on open, physical violence. In an era when corporal punishment has become uncivilized, and open violence unconscionable, the prison supplies a subtle, situational form of violence against the person that enables retribution to be inflicted in a way that is sufficiently discreet and "deniable" to be culturally acceptable to most of the population. Despite occasional suggestions that imprisonment is becoming too lenient—a view that is rarely shared by informed sources—it is widely accepted that the prison succeeds very well in imposing real hardship, serious deprivation, and personal suffering on most offenders who are sent there.

In terms of penological objectives then, the prison supports a range of them and is "functional" or "successful" with respect to some, less so with respect to others. Nor is there any need to argue that the prison's "failures" are somehow "useful"—as Foucault and others do. The fact that prison frequently reinforces criminality and helps produce recidivists is not a "useful" consequence desired by the authorities or part of some covert "strategy". It is a tolerated cost of pursuing other objectives such as retribution, incapacitation, and exclusion and is accepted in the same reluctant way that governments absorb the high financial costs entailed in the frequent use of imprisonment. So long as such costs appear to the authorities—and to the public—to be outweighed by the desirability of imprisoning offenders (and this desire has become an established element within public beliefs, institutional frameworks, and social traditions), then the prison remains a "functional" institution—and neither a puzzle nor an anachronism.

Consequently—and this is my point—if one wishes to understand and evaluate the prison as an institution—and the same arguments apply to the fine, probation, the death penalty, and the rest—it does little good to do so on a single plane or in relation to a single value. Instead, one must think of it as a complex institution and evaluate it accordingly, recognizing the range of its penal and social functions and the nature of its social support. Nor does this mean that one must abandon a critical approach because the prison is less irrational than it at first seems. One can challenge the institution by showing that the control of troublesome individuals can be undertaken in more humane and positive settings, that exclusion is anyway an unacceptable goal in a caring society, or that many prisoners are no real danger to the public and could, under certain conditions, be tolerated in the community. One could endeavour to expose the real psychological violence that exists behind the scenes of even the best prisons and argue that such violence is as retrograde and uncivilized in its way as the corporal and capital punishments that the prison replaced. Equally, one could challenge the cost of prison as a means of expressing punitive sentiments and exacting retribution against offenders and show ways in which funds and resources could be put to better use—for instance in compensating victims, in crime-prevention schemes, or in basic educational and social provision. In effect, the more one's understanding of an institution begins to capture its nuances and complexities—and its positive effects together with its negative ones—the more thoroughgoing, informed, and incisive will be the critique that one can mount.

Thinking of punishment as a social institution should change not only our mode of understanding penality but also our normative thinking about it. It should lead us to judge punishment according to a wider range of criteria and to bring to bear the kinds of demands and expectations that we customarily apply to social institutions. To say this is not to suggest that there is some universal normative approach that we always adopt toward social institutions—different institutions have distinctive functions and characteristics and give rise to diverse forms of evaluation. But nevertheless, when we think of "the family" or "the law", "the government" or "the economy", and subject them to normative judgment, we do so in ways that are considerably more complex than our thinking about punishment tends to be. In none of these cases do we think it proper to judge these institutions according to purely instrumental criteria, nor do we suppose that they should serve a single end or affect only a particular sector of the population. Instead, they are all commonly viewed as if they were "total social facts" (Mauss, 1967), the character of which is in some way constitutive of society's identity and character.

Perhaps the best example of this is the kind of thinking that emerges whenever a democratic society deliberately undertakes to reform its major social institutions by means of a written constitution. People do not ask of such a constitution merely that it should "work" with some degree of efficiency—although that is itself crucial. They also demand that its moral, political, economic, and cultural significance be considered and that these wider ramifications be made to conform, as far as is possible, to deeply held conceptions of what kind of people they are, how they wish to be governed, and what kind of society they wish to create. The implication of the sociological perspectives considered here is that punishment should be considered in the same kind of way and in the same kind of depth as other social institutions. We need an enriched form of penological thinking that considers penality as an institution through which society defines and expresses itself at the same time and through the same means that it exercises power over deviants (for an elaboration and development of this project, see Garland (1990a)).

To think of punishment in this way is to question the narrow, instrumental self-description that modern penal institutions generally adopt (and which technical penology tends to repeat) and instead to suggest more socially conscious and morally charged perceptions of penal affairs. By demonstrating the deeply social nature of legal punishment, and revealing the values and commitments that are embodied within its practices, the sociology by punishment tends to undermine any attempt to compartmentalize "the penal question" or to deal with it in a purely administrative way. By showing how penal issues pull together many diverse currents of political and cultural life, such an approach helps to reconstitute a more comprehensive social awareness and to counter the tendency of modern institutions to fragment consciousness and narrow perception. It gives a sense of the sociality of punishment—of the extended significance and depth of stored-up meanings that exist beneath the surface of this complex institution.

References

Beattie, J. M. (1984), "Violence and Society in Early Modern England", in Doob, A. and Greenspan, E. (eds.), *Perspectives in Criminal Law* (Aurora, Ont.: Canada Law Book).

——— (1986), *Crime and the Courts in England, 1660–1800* (Princeton: N.J.: Princeton University Press).

Cohen, S. (1985), *Visions of Social Control* (Oxford: Polity).

Downes, D. (1988), *Contrasts in Tolerance: Post-war Penal Policy in the Netherlands and England and Wales* (Oxford: Oxford University Press).

Durkheim, E. (1933), *The Division of Labor in Society*, translated by G. Simpson (New York: Free Press), (originally published 1893, Paris: Alcan).

——— (1973), *Moral Education: A Study in the Theory and Application of the Sociology of Education*, translated by E. K. Wilson and H. Schnurer (New York: Free Press), (originally published 1925, Paris: Alcan).

——— (1983), "The Evolution of Punishment", in Lukes, S. and Scull, A. (eds.), *Durkheim and the Law* (Oxford: Martin Robertson).

Elias, N. (1978), *The History of Manners: The Civilising Process*, vol. 1 (Oxford: Basil Blackwell), (originally published 1939, Basel: Hans Zum Falken).

——— (1982), *State Formation and Civilization: The Civilising Process*, vol. 2 (Oxford: Basil Blackwell), (originally published 1939, Basel: Hans Zum Falken).

Foucault, M. (1977), *Discipline and Punish: The Birth of the Prison*, translated by Alan Sheridan (London: Penguin).

——— (1978), *I, Pierre Riviere* (Harmondsworth: Penguin).

——— (1980), "Prison Talk", in Gordon, C. (ed.), *Power/Knowledge: Selected Interviews and Other Writings, 1972–77* (New York: Pantheon).

——— (1990), "The Dangerous Individual", in Kritzman, L. D. (ed.), *Politics, Philosophy, Culture: Interviews and Other Writings, 1977–1984* (New York: Routledge).

Garland, D. (1990a), *Punishment and Modern Society: A Study in Social Theory* (Oxford and Chicago: Oxford University Press and University of Chicago Press).

——— (1990b), "Frameworks of Inquiry in the Sociology of Punishment" 41 *British Journal of Sociology* 1–16.

Garland, D., and Young, P. (1983), "Towards a Social Analysis of Penality", in Garland, D. and Young, P. (eds.), *The Power to Punish* (London: Gower).

Hay, D. (1975), "Property, Authority, and the Criminal Law", in Hay, D., Linebaugh, P. and Thompson, E. P. (eds.), *Albion's Fatal Tree: Crime and Society in Eighteenth-Century England* (Harmondsworth: Penguin).

Hirst, P. Q. (1986), *Law, Socialism and Democracy* (London: Allen & Unwin).

Ignatieff, M. (1978), *A Just Measure of Pain: The Penitentiary and the Industrial Revolution* (London: Macmillan).

—— (1981), "State, Civil Society, and Total Institutions: A Critique of Recent Social Histories of Punishment", in Tonry, M. and Morris, N. (eds.), *Crime and Justice: An Annual Review of Research*, vol. 3 (Chicago: University of Chicago Press).

Jacobs, J. B. (1983), *New Perspectives on Prisons and Imprisonment* (Ithaca, NY).

Mathiesen, T. (1990), *Prison on Trial* (London: Sage).

Mauss, M. (1967), *The Gift: Forms and Functions of Exchange in Archaic Societies*, translated by Ian Cunnison (New York: Norton), (originally published in (1923–41) 1 *L'annee sociologique* 30–186).

Rusche, G., and Kirchheimer, O. (1968), *Punishment and Social Structure* (New York: Russell & Russell), (originally published 1939, New York: Columbia University Press).

Stone, L. (1979), *The Family, Sex and Marriage in England, 1500–1800* (Harmondsworth: Penguin).

—— (1987), *The Past and the Present Revisited* (London: Routledge & Kegan Paul).

Zimring, F. E., and Hawkins, G. (1990), *The Scale of Imprisonment* (Chicago: University of Chicago Press).

8.3

Punishment and Community

NICOLA LACEY

The Ideal of Community

The starting point for our reconstruction of normative arguments about punishment, then, must be a particular vision of political society, and in this context I shall sketch a conception which is in certain important respects different from the traditional liberal ideal. The definition of a community, and of the distinction between a community and a society or indeed any other group of associated persons, can be developed in many different ways, most obviously in terms of size, extent of shared goals, or degree of common values and conceptions of the good.[1] A religious order, for example, is often cited as the central case of a community: relatively small, homogeneous and organized around a shared conception of value. A political grouping such as a state, on the other hand, might well be seen as a central instance of a society: an association of persons for certain limited purposes, identified by a lower threshold of common goals and values, creating a framework within which diverse forms of life, including the formation of communities and other groups devoted to particular ends, can develop and flourish. In developing my own account of community, I shall not be much concerned with this often-used distinction between society and community, although all of the features which I have mentioned so far will be important in sketching the conception. The idea is rather to develop, in the light of the assumption of the primacy of the social, a conception of what a political society such as our own might ideally become, particularly in terms of the relations between, and what unites and identifies, its members.

In the first place, any community must be identified by the existence of a certain threshold of shared goals and values. It is, of course, clear that

From Nicola Lacey, *State Punishment: Political Principles and Community Values* (London: Routledge, 1988), ch. 9. Excerpted and reprinted with permission. Footnotes reduced.

the nature and extent of these shared goals an values will vary enormously from community to community, depending on cultural, economic and material factors. In some communities, the (from our perspective) relatively minimal goal of survival might almost exhaust the public culture; in orders, a wide array of shared ends and indeed conceptions of the good acknowledged as legitimate will be publicly endorsed. Nor is this variety a matter of open choice—it will be constrained, and sometimes even determined, by prevailing material conditions. But within these constraints, it is clear that the setting of the threshold—the extent of commitment to common values or shared goals, and the ambit left open for human diversity, will be to some extent a question open for political decision. Thus a question arises as to the proper means to be adopted in a community for the making of social choices, and we must advert, albeit briefly, to this fundamental matter. It is important, however, to avoid setting up yet more false dilemmas: it will sometimes be the case that a fuller adoption of common goals and values will straightforwardly detract from the amount of freedom individuals or groups have to pursue different goals and forms of life—but this is not necessarily the case. For often, a common commitment to the pursuit of shared goals will actually enhance the possibility of the development of different forms of life.[2] For example, a public commitment to providing a certain level of goods and services in the context of health, education and welfare, or facilities or subsidies for the arts and sports, will increase the opportunity for diversity and development at the personal level. Once again, we should be suspicious of the collective/individual, public/private dichotomies which our thinking has inherited from classical liberal thought.

How, then, would common decision-making be accomplished in an ideal community? If we acknowledge that human beings and human nature are essentially socially developed, we must also acknowledge that the process is circular or continuous. Just as human beings go through a process of socialization, so too they react to and have some capacity to act upon their social environment, which thus develops incrementally over time. The nature of this process is beyond the scope of this inquiry, but even this brief allusion gives rise to certain rather obvious conclusions about appropriate methods of social decision. It points in the direction of some democratic conception in which citizens have the fullest possible opportunity to shape their own community and take on part of the collective responsibility for its maintenance and development. On the face of it, what seems to be indicated is some form of participatory rather than merely representative democracy,[3] through which people not only participate in decision-making, but are also shaped and made aware, their identity with the community reinforced, by the experience of participation itself. Here, I would argue, lies an important key to understanding the ideal of community—one less often discussed at least in the modern tradition than are common values, but of at least equal significance. This feature lies in a commitment to, the adoption of responsibility for, the community of which one is a member. This commitment, realized ideally through participation in the process of government and administration, can be seen as the ultimate expression of the vision of humans as primarily social beings: if community is essential to human existence, commitment to community is a more "natural" or appropriate assumption or ideal than is the liberal vision of persons as rational, calculating and self-interested. This is not to say, of course, that self-interest is not a feature of human motivation; but it is at least to admit that self-interest, even when a dominant motivation, has need of social means and framework for both its development and effective pursuit to a greater extent than is often acknowledged in liberal theory.

It is often objected to the vision of genuinely participatory democracy and to the ideal of human beings as committed to community, that in the context of large, heterogeneous political societies, the former is impractical, the latter unrealistic. This is not the place for any full exploration of the effects of numbers on human attachment or alienation; suffice it to say that it does not seem appropriate to give up the ideal without exploring much more fully than do most objectors the possibility of overcoming this problem—as indeed several political theorists have begun to do.[4] The possibility of decentralized, participatory local government united by a federal or partially centralized state run on representative lines is just one of the more obvious options. Moreover, it seems on the face of it possible that, linking the two features, the experience of participation in community decision-making would actually foster and enhance the sense of community and social responsibility which I have argued is a natural corollary to human beings' primarily social nature.

Thus the notion of community which I shall be employing in developing a theory of punishment is that of a group of human beings, each participating directly, and also possibly indirectly by electing representatives, in the development of their group framework, policies and norms, bound by a sense of commitment to the maintenance of the community, through acknowledgment of its importance for themselves and others and united thus by a second-level commitment to the values and goals adopted through the process of public decision on democratic principles. In such a community, members could maintain a sense of themselves, whilst acknowledging, creatively, their interdependence. This conception of community represents an idealized version of the notion of a group developed by Honoré[5] . . .

The Functions of Punishment

We are now ready to turn to an exploration of what the salient aims of punishment would be in the community we have envisaged. We do not have to assume, of course, that the forms which punishment would take in such a society would necessarily be the same as those practised in our society: . . . we need only envisage a social response to breaches of the criminal law which imposes what are generally regarded as disadvantages within that society, in order for the problem of justification to arise. What reasons can be adduced, within the political values of community, for this disadvantaging social response: by what means can the prima facie wrong of punishment contribute to the welfare and autonomy of members of a community? By stating the problem in this way, it will be clear that by "functions" I am comprehending not only goals in the sense of tangible effects to be sought, such as general deterrence, but also the values which the practice seeks to foster and promote—its legitimate purposes in a more general sense. Thus one aim of a punishment may be to deter a harmful form of behaviour, but it is also part of its function to underline and support the social judgment that that form of behaviour is indeed harmful and wrong—to reinforce, in other words, the "moral analogy" which I have argued constitutes an important part of the social meaning of criminal as opposed to civil law. This breadth of perspective will in fact be crucial to the main thrust of my argument . . .

At the crudest level, the contemporaneous setting up of the threat of punishment (which seems, in the absence of unrealistic assumptions about the possibility of shams, to presuppose the actual infliction of punishments in the case of at least a significant number of detected offences)[6] is justified simply by its necessity as a means of making the standards of the criminal law *real*: as a way of stating that the meeting of those standards is a matter of duty or obligation, from community's legal point of view, rather than merely a matter of exhortation or aspiration.[7] From the point of view of the law of the community, . . . the standards of the criminal law become non-optional—and the very idea of non-optionality seems to presuppose some kind of consequence on breach. In some cases mere formal conviction may be sufficient to preserve the reality and efficacy of the standards of the criminal law; but, at the systemic level, it seems necessary to have in reserve some stronger marker of the reality of the law's prescription, and penal sanctions constitute the most obvious candidate for such a role. This is not a question of righting the wrong done in the compensatory sense of making good the loss to the particular victim (although this kind of response may also be called for). Nor is it exclusively a matter of deterrence, individual or general. It has principally to do with a collective need to underpin, recognize and maintain the internalized commitments of many members of society to the content of the standards of the criminal law and to acknowledge the importance of those commitments to the existence and identity of the community. If, in general, the norms of the system can be breached with impunity, why should any member of the community put her faith in and give her allegiance to the community as guardian of the framework of common values within which citizens can develop their lives?[8] If the criminal law is indeed one of the planks of survival of the community, yet can be broken at will, why should citizens continue to observe it themselves, or not attempt to form an alternative community in which framework values are taken seriously and enforced? If no social response enforcing central values is forthcoming, why have a community at all?

Flowing from this general argument from necessity at the systemic level is a cluster of specific aims and goods which can and should be fostered by the existence of institutions of punishment. Beginning with the most general factors, it seems likely that inflictions and threats of punishment, although not occasions for celebration, could in this context have beneficial side-effects in terms of restoring social cohesion which may be threatened or disturbed by certain sorts of offending which present clear threats to fundamental social values, and in reaffirming the social values endorsed by the political process and entrenched in the criminal law. By the same token, the public process of conviction affords an opportunity for reassessing the criminal law itself, and especially when a particular kind of offence becomes prevalent, or a conviction seems counter-intuitive, the process may prompt a rethinking of the substantive law, if the political structure is appropriately sensitive. Such possibilities can, of course, be allowed for by institutions such as the absolute discharge in English law, which registers a technical conviction but acknowledges that it raises an unforeseen defect in the law by removing the normal consequences from that conviction, punishment included. These factors stress the importance of maintaining a practice of punishment which is, in so far as is possible, public and open. Linked to these general side-benefits is the educative function which a criminal process can have, through the affirmation of social values fostered by the denunciation of the behaviour involved in the offence, that denunciation being implicit and also often explicit in the process of conviction and sentence.

Moving on to a plane of greater specificity, we come to the more familiar goals encompassed by the utilitarian theories of punishment, perhaps more directly apposite to the rationale of individual punishments than the general functions already mentioned. Hard though the attainment of such objectives may be (their assessment presents further problems of its own)[9] a certain level of general deterrence through the threat of punishment, and individual deterrence through its experience, might realistically be hoped for, although in the ideal community it might well be hoped that more "internal" motivations having to do with the affirmation of the values embedded in the law, or at least recognition of their importance to others and to the community itself, would suffice for the great majority of the population.[10] Furthermore, there is the (albeit very modest) contribution which can be made to the level of social security by the practice of punishment, not only by way of deterrence, but also, in the case of some forms of punishment, through the incapacitation of the offender for a certain period of time. Related to social protection, but also closely linked to the need to demonstrate that the norms of the criminal law are "for real", is the need to forestall, or at least to minimize, any resort to private vengeance or self-help, which might cause disproportionate suffering and indeed involve excessive costs, whilst undermining the stability of and respect for the community's legal system as a whole. Again linked to these aims is that of appeasing and satisfying the grievance-desires of victims, not only so as to reduce their suffering and forestall self-help, but also to demonstrate that the community takes seriously the harm done to the victim and takes upon itself the responsibility for upholding the standards breached, which it hopes to vindicate through the process of conviction and punishment. I leave until last, because I take it to be an indirect side-effect rather than a central aim of punishment, the opportunity which it may give to the offender to reflect and resolve to reform; in so far as this could be said to be a direct aim of punishment, it seems to be an aspect of the reaffirmation of collective values, in which it is possible for the offender to participate from a special point of view. The value attached to autonomy, however, is such as to dictate that this aim be pursued no further than in the giving of an opportunity: "coerced cure" would be ruled out. I shall have more to say on this when considering the forms which punishment might take in the ideal community.

It is thus, I would argue, a combination of, and the interdependence between, the symbolic meaning of punishment, the values it seeks to enforce and uphold, and its practical effects which constitutes, in Hart's terms,[11] its general justifying aim. The concept of the functions of punishment which I have defended thus goes beyond his utilitarian conception in important respects. It is because of the meaning and significance which punishment would have for the citizens of a community that it can hope to have the practical consequences which we have explored. Conversely, without any hope of those real, countervailing benefits, punishment as a merely symbolic social response, without any practical enforcing aspect, would become the pointless, empty moral alchemy which I argued to be the implication of a pure retributivism. In a sense, this conception forges the retributive and utilitarian aspects of punishment, (although doubtless neither a utilitarian nor a retributivist would see it in quite that light!). For although at the core of my account is what I shall call the argument from necessity, that necessity itself flows to at least some extent from the potency of intuitions which are most obviously and centrally acknowledged in the traditional retributive theories. The idea of punishment as a significant and necessary symbol of the assertion of the community's own entitlement to enforce, to respond severely to breaches of its democratically determined central values, may be difficult to explicate purely in terms of rational judgments about how particular social goals may be pursued. It does, however, form a central part of our moral thinking. The community conception reflects, whilst it restrains in a morally acceptable way, the role of punishment in our emotional and affective lives. But I do not accept the retributivist claim that a *purely* symbolic system of punishments, an institution which had no beneficial effects, could be justified. It is the combination of its social meaning and its actual consequences which provides the strongest argument for preserving the threat of punishment at the centre of political life in the community.

But my solution, unlike Hart's mixed theory and weak retributivist arguments, is not dependent on the *separation* of distinct questions— although I acknowledge the special significance and complexity of distributive issues, which I shall deal with in the next section. The conception of punishment which I have described, like its counterpart conception of the criminal law, is neither backward-looking nor forward-looking in a purely instrumental sense: it is rather *functional*. In other words, my conception emphasizes the significance which punishment has for the citizens of a community, the place which it occupies in the development and cohesion of the community, rather than simply tangible goals such as deterrence or a particular desirable endstate. By conceiving the functions of the criminal process in both direct and indirect, in both general and specific terms, and by broadening the conception of its aims beyond any utilitarian vision of goals in the sense of tangible states of affairs, I hope to have developed a conception of the nature of punishment which is sufficiently complex to generate the sorts of limitations on the practice which we generally think to be necessary from within the conception itself, rather than by appeal to any independent principles. Thus whilst my theory resembles the mixed theories both in its pluralism and in many common aims, it differs in terms of the structure of the argument which it employs. The significance of this difference will be explored in the course of the discussion of the distributive aspect of the community conception.

The Distribution of Punishments

On this conception of punishment, justified ultimately by its contribution to the welfare and autonomy of members of a community, principally through its necessity as a central plank in the maintenance of the community itself and the stability of the relations within it, the question naturally arises as to who should be punished, and this question in turn raises in a stark form the issue of the relationship between the two principal political values: autonomy and welfare. Are the dictates of autonomy, realized principally in the context of punishment as a requirement of responsibility, to act as absolute side constraints on the pursuit of the general justifying aims of punishment as they do in Hart's theory? Should we, conversely, merely accommodate autonomy as one aspect of human welfare? Or must we forge, as I suggested in the last section, a middle way through these extremes?

It is important to emphasize, at the outset, the place of the value of autonomy within our conception of the aims or functions of punishment, both directly, for example through its contribution to social protection and thus the autonomy of potential victims of crime, and indirectly, through its support of the community which is committed to maintaining and fostering the value of autonomy. Thus the question concerning the need for trade-offs which the issue of punishment raises does not relate only to trade-offs between the core values of welfare and autonomy, allowing the realm of each value to be confined within one particular question (welfare with general justifying aim, autonomy with distribution, in Hart's scheme). Because the two basic values relate to the questions *both* of the functions of punishment *and* of its proper distribution, the potential need to make trade-offs turns out to be much broader, the issue more fragmented: trade-offs will have to be made in order to answer the allegedly separate questions which Hart identifies, as well, of course, as in considering the relative and potentially conflicting claims to autonomy and welfare of different persons and groups of persons. For example, decisions about whether to include a particular form of behaviour within the ambit of the criminal law, and what function criminal regulation should fulfil, already require balancing judgments which proceed from a plurality of values. However, these problems are not acute in the way suggested by the traditional mixed theories because, as we have seen, the realization of the two values is interdependent and not always a matter of opposition or competition. But it is crucial to see that these problems arise *not only* at the stage of distribution, but also in the specification of the aims and functions of punishment. It is not a question of punishment aiming to promote welfare but limited by a principle of autonomy in distribution: the pluralist picture emerges with respect to both function and distribution. Thus, as R. A. Duff has convincingly argued, we should expect to find *internal*, logical relations between the "general justifying aim" of punishment and the principles on which it is to be distributed.[12] Although, as Hart has shown, the two questions can usefully be separated as an expositional device in bringing out different aspects of the problem of justification, the device can be misleading if used so as to suggest a discontinuity of justifying arguments—hence the difficulty . . . in relating the two parts of Hart's theory to one another.[13] Problems of both aim and distribution are equally a part, in a manner of speaking, of the meaning of punishment.

In the community which I have envisaged, which endorses a pluralist conception of political value, citizens would demand that their political practices acknowledge and accord a special weight to human autonomy over and above its direct or indirect contribution to welfare. This is not to say that they would never be prepared to make trade-offs between welfare and autonomy, nor to make the mistake of assuming that the demands of autonomy and welfare are always in competition or that autonomy is something which one either has or has not: there can clearly be degrees of autonomy and in the general run of things we value our remaining autonomy more as we suffer further encroachments upon it. I am not going to defend autonomy as a side constraint upon the pursuit of the aims of punishment, as a principle with a rigid lexicographical priority such as Rawls' principle of liberty.[14] It seems to me quite clear that the threshold at which human beings would be willing to trade off some measure of their sense of their own power, freedom or diversity for other goods will vary between people and will depend in an important way (as Rawls acknowledges to a limited extent)[15] on material social conditions and the nature of the other goods in question. Thus I do not suggest any fixed or precise solution to the ordering of the two general political principles in the context of criminal justice, but would refer again to the conception of a consistent pluralism[16] in which a conscientious effort is made to balance the pursuit of, and to recognize the discrete value of the goods in question, endorsing them consistently across different persons and spheres of political life whilst, of course, recognizing relevant differences between the various spheres. Notwithstanding the attractions of a formal scheme of priorities or conflation of different values into a common currency, the determinacy which such devices offer simply seems to be inconsistent with a genuine commitment to a plurality of values and an adequate appreciation of the complexity of moral problems.

Bearing in mind this background structure of political value, and our conception of the legitimate functions of punishment, it is not difficult to see why punishment in a community would be restricted to those who had been judged to have actually perpetrated criminal acts—the "actus reus" requirement of the criminal law. Any other solution would unjustifiably violate important aspects of the very values which the general functions seek to realize, not only because, for example, the preventive detention of a person who has not committed an offence would be likely to harm her welfare in a specially grave way, but also because it would directly violate, to the extent of denying, that person's autonomy by acting towards her for reasons which are irrelevant to and unsubstantiated by any unambiguous and interest-threatening expression of her own disposition towards the criminal law. Any practice of punishment which sanctioned such a victimization would thereby sacrifice its claim to be acting in the interests of the welfare and autonomy of each member of the community by legitimating penal responses which evinced no respect for and accorded no weight to autonomy. This is not to say, of course, that it is never justifiable for the criminal law to step in before any tangible interest has been "harmed"; it may do so when a citizen's behaviour produces a clear and immediate threat to fundamental interests (as in the case of inchoate offences such as attempt, incitement or conspiracy); but this must be a matter for political decision about the content of the substantive law, and not as an exercise of residual punitive power exercised without proper political safeguards. As I have argued, this conception of punishment must be taken to generate limitations not only on proper ends but also on the means to be employed in reaching them.

The proper meaning of punishment within a community, then, has to do with its response to actions which are hostile to and express rejection of fundamental community values . . .: that is, actions which violate the fundamental interests upheld and protected by the criminal law. To punish those who have exhibited no such hostility would be to fly directly in the face of those values themselves, and to join the same moral category of wrongful action as offending against the criminal law. By emphasizing the place of protection of autonomy within the functions of punishment, we can see how an adequate distributive principle can actually flow from, rather than merely act as a limit upon, the justifying aim itself. But this is only possible if we keep at the forefront of the argument the underlying general political values of the community and the place which punishment occupies in the structure of political value. It is also to acknowledge the existence of intrinsic values, or at least to modify one's conception of consequentialism so as to include such goals as securing or maintaining respect for values, thus arguably undermining the status of consequentialism as a distinctive form of moral reasoning[17] . . .

There is, however, another problem of distribution . . . of great practical significance. I am referring to what I shall label the problem of uniformity of application: should each and every dispositionally responsible offender be detected, convicted and punished? This raises many questions, not all of which can be tackled here, and several of which could only be answered in a concrete political context. How many resources should be devoted to the detection of crime, and what proportion of suspected offenders should be arrested and prosecuted? What should the shape and nature of the trial process be; how high should we set the burden of proof, and how many resources should be devoted to the development of elaborate procedural safeguards?[18] It is often assumed in liberal (particularly retributive) theory that the actual incompleteness of application in most systems raises grave problems of injustice because of the principle that like cases must be treated alike. However, it seems that on the community conception of punishment, mere incompleteness of application does not raise an intractable problem of fairness, although unevenness in the sense of a skewed distribution of enforcement on irrelevant lines such as class, race or outward appearance certainly does so.[19] On the community conception, so long as the antecedent chances of detection and conviction are roughly equal for similar kinds of offenders, it is consistent with a concern to foster equally the welfare and autonomy of all that the community should determine a certain level of enforcement (at the points of detection, prosecution and procedural legislation) for certain bands of offences, as a conscientious political decision in the light of available resources, other social goals and priorities, respect for the autonomy and welfare of different groups, and judgments about the relative likelihood of efficacy of criminal enforcement as opposed to other social responses. There will generally be a threshold below which non-enforcement will risk a loss of credibility of that particular norm or even the system as a whole, but the threshold will depend on the type of offence. Particularly with some kinds of offence, it may be more efficacious to put social resources into the development of preventive devices such as environmental design than to spend them on the expensive business of criminal enforcement. There may also be occasions when resources within the system need to be specially diverted to particular offences or indeed particular localities, where the prevalence of a certain kind of offending is such that a public response to it has become a social priority, thus creating a relevant difference between that instance of the offence and its occurrence at a different place or time. Moreover, as well as such distributive decisions *within* the criminal process, important political decisions have to be made about the total resources to be devoted to criminal justice as opposed to other social concerns such as health and education. Once again, we witness the continuity of problems of distributive justice and efficacy in the community, and the impossibility of insulating criminal justice as a political issue. Once we locate punishment within its proper political context, we see that the issue of uniformity of application is not so intractable as it seems; each responsible offender of any particular type runs a certain risk of punishment: beyond this, the proper threshold of even-handed, non-universal application is a matter for social and political decision from the community's point of view. Within our political conception, although the impact of the *threat* of punishment must be equal or not disproportionately different for different offenders, the impact of *enforcement* may be unequal. For the offender, this is an instance of the inevitable influence of "moral" luck.[20]

The Form of Punishments

It remains to make some relatively brief observations about what form punishment might take in such a community, given its central justifying functions and related principles of distribution. Perhaps the main point to be made here is that, on our conception of punishment, in which a central function is its reaffirmation of social values, punishments might well be expected to be, at least to a greater extent than is now the case, of a formal or symbolic nature. This would mean not only an emphasis on the symbolic or denunciatory element implicit in all punishments, but the use in some cases of a *purely* symbolic penalty in the form, for example, of a formal statement of conviction and denunciation handed down by the judge and perhaps publicised more systematically than is currently the practice. An element of denunciation and disapproval would be an important feature in such punishments, and it might often be the case that the disadvantages meted out could be both moderate and symbolic, supplemented by adequate practices of social compensation for the victims of crime. However, it may often be the case that, in order to fulfil its important function of fostering the central values of community and supporting the community itself, it will be necessary to punish more severely in order to satisfy strong grievance-desires on the part of victims, to prevent resort to self-help, to underline a social judgment of behaviour as especially injurious, or to emphasize a generally deterrent threat in the case of a particularly advantageous form of offending, which form an immediate aim of particular punishments.

What place would a principle of "proportionality", supported by retributivists and acknowledged by several exponents of mixed theories, have in setting the scale of punishments? It is clear that proportionality to socially acknowledged gravity could serve a useful function in underlining community values, but the symbolic element in punishment will probably detract from the tendency towards a rigid hierarchy of punishments according to gravity of offences. And the central functions of punishment will dictate that the scale be modified in order to accommodate goals such as deterrence, incapacitation and prevention of resort to self-help. Indeed, it seems very likely, not least on the basis of the empirical evidence . . . , that such goals could be pursued optimally by means of a penalty scale of much more moderate severity than those used in our current system, and in particular that, at least for first offenders, a system organized around the values I have defended would be willing to employ purely or principally symbolic measures. However, this conception would not rule out the use of severely incapacitating methods such as incarceration in secure but humane conditions for persistent and serious offenders who pose grave threats to the fundamental framework of the community or the most important interests of its members. Indeed, the logic of my argument might well suggest that the proper punishment for such offenders would be exclusion from the community, at least on certain conditions. Whether or not this constitutes a feasible and humane option will depend on many factors; in the present world, it is hard to envisage exile as a real moral possibility. If such conditions continue to prevail, internal incarceration in humane conditions seems the best alternative. Ultimately, the shape of and moral limitations upon the scale of punishments will be to a significant extent socially conditioned: what my conception of criminal justice dictates is that the scale must accord with a conscientious attempt to meet and balance the welfare and autonomy not only of victims and potential victims, but also of offenders and potential offenders. The principle of residual autonomy must be preserved, for no punishment must be so severe as to reflect a complete absence of respect for or denial of the offender's autonomy—or indeed for her welfare. Also implicit in this conception is a principle of humane economy; the commission of an offence does not deprive an offender of her civil rights. She, like other citizens, may be treated, within the limits of overriding political values, in a way which advances central community ends. She has behaved in such a way as to put herself in a relevantly different position from other citizens, which renders her liable to be punished according to the substantive argument which we have examined, for the good of the community of which she is a member— but the justification runs only to the extent that is absolutely necessary to the fulfilment of legitimate functions of the criminal law.

Notes

1. For discussions of the notion of community in the context of political philosophy, see Sandel (1982), pp. 59–65, 96–103, 147–83; Walzer (1983), pp. 31–94, 227–42; and Dworkin (1986), pp. 164–71, 206–24, 400–10.
2. Raz (1986), chs. 10, 14, 15.
3. See Barber (1984), pp. 117–311.
4. *Ibid.*
5. Honore (1973), p. 1.
6. Quinn (1985).
7. Gross (1979), pp. 375–412.
8. Finnis (1980), pp. 260–4.
9. See Lacey (1988), ch. 2, and Hood and Sparks (1970), pp. 171–92.
10. See Duff (1986), ch. 9.
11. Hart (1968), pp. 8–11.
12. Duff (1986), pp. 151–64, 233–5.
13. Hart (1968), ch. 1, and Lacey (1988), pp. 49–53.
14. Rawls (1971), pp. 40–5, 243–51, 541–8.
15. *Ibid.*, pp. 152, 247–78, 542–3.
16. See Lacey (1988), ch. 5, esp. pp. 117–18; Barry (1965), pp. 4–8, 35–8, 94–6, 286–91.
17. Raz (1986), pp. 267–71.
18. For an illuminating discussion of the significance of procedural safeguards, see Duff (1986), chs. 1 and 4.
19. See Lacey (1988), ch. 5, esp. pp. 113–17.
20. Nagel (1979), p. 24; Williams (1981), pp. 20–39.

References

Barber, B. (1984), *Strong Democracy* (Berkeley: University of California Press).
Barry, B. (1965), *Political Argument* (London: Routledge).

408 *External Critiques of Sentencing Theory*

Duff, R. A. (1986), *Trials and Punishments* (Cambridge: Cambridge University Press).

Dworkin, R. (1986), *Law's Empire* (London: Fontana).

Finnis, J. M. (1980), *Natural Law and Natural Rights* (Oxford: Oxford University Press).

Gross, H. (1979), *A Theory of Criminal Justice* (New York: Oxford University Press).

Hart, H. L. A. (1968), *Punishment and Responsibility* (Oxford: Oxford University Press).

Honore, A. M. (1973), "Groups, Laws and Obedience", in A. W. B. Simpson (ed.), *Oxford Essays in Jurisprudence: Second Series* (Oxford: Oxford University Press).

Hood, R., and Sparks, R. (1970), *Key Issues in Criminology* (London: Weidenfeld & Nicolson).

Lacey, N. (1988), *State Punishment* (London: Routledge).

Nagel, T. (1979), "Moral Luck", in his *Mortal Questions* (Cambridge: Cambridge University Press).

Quinn, W. (1985), "The Right to Threaten and the Right to Punish", 14 *Philosophy and Public Affairs* 327.

Rawls, J. (1971), *A Theory of Justice* (New York: Oxford University Press).

Raz, J. (1986), *The Morality of Freedom* (Oxford: Oxford University Press).

Sandel, M. (1982), *Liberalism and the Limits of Justice* (Cambridge: Cambridge University Press).

Walzer, M. (1983), *Spheres of Justice* (Oxford: Blackwell).

Williams, B. (1981), *Moral Luck* (Cambridge: Cambridge University Press).

Suggestions for Further Reading

1. External Critiques of Punishment Theory

Rusche, G., and Kirchheimer, O., *Punishment and Social Structure* (1939; reprinted 1968); Hay, D., "Property and Authority", in Hay, D. *et al.*, *Albion's Fatal Tree* (1975); Christie, N., "Conflicts and Property", (1977) 17 *British Journal of Criminology* 1; Thompson, E. P., *Whigs and Hunters* (1977); Foucault, M., *Discipline and Punish* (1977); Christie, N., *Limits to Pain* (1981); Garland, D., and Young, P., *The Power to Punish* (1983); Hirst, P. Q., *Law, Socialism and Democracy* (1986), ch. 6; Box, S., *Recession, Crime and Punishment* (1987); Garland, D., *Punishment and Modern Society* (1990); Mathiesen, T., *Prison on Trial* (1990); Abel, R., "The Failure of Punishment as Social Control", (1991) 25 *Israel Law Review* 740; Garland, D., "Sociological Perspectives on Punishment", in Morris, N., and Tonry, M., *Crime and Justice* (1991); Garland, D., "The Limits of the Sovereign State", (1996) 36 *British Journal of Criminology* 445.

2. Critical Punishment Theory

Bianchi, H., and van Swaaningen, R., (eds.), *Abolitionism: Towards a Non-Repressive Approach to Crime* (1986); Hudson, B., *Justice through Punishment* (1987); Lacey, N., *State Punishment* (1988); de Haan, W., *The Politics of Redress: Crime, Punishment and Abolition* (1990); Norrie, A., *Law, Ideology and Punishment* (1991); Hulsman, L., "The Abolitionist Case: Alternative Crime Policies", (1991) 25 *Israel Law Review* 681; Cohen, S., "Alternatives to Punishment: the Abolitionist Case", (1991) 25 *Israel Law Review* 729; Black, S., "Individualism at an Impasse", (1991) 12 *Canadian Journal of Philosophy* 347; Hudson, B., *Penal Policy and Social Justice* (1993); Norrie, A., *Crime, Reason and History* (1993), ch. 10.

9

"Law and Order"

No discussion of sentencing can be complete without looking at the phenomenon of "law and order". Recent decades have witnessed the advocacy and adoption of increasingly drastic penal measures. In the USA, this trend has gone furthest—with the enactment of tough mandatory prison sentences, the required elimination of educational and other programmes in prison, and even (in some Southern states) the revival of chain gangs and striped uniforms for convicts. The trend has not gone so far in Western Europe, but a sharpening of the tone of debate is plainly visible in many countries.

In today's "law and order" politics, two elements are apparent. First, appeals are being made for much more stringent penal policies: criminals are to be treated with exemplary severity. In the USA, this has gone to remarkable lengths—as is apparent in California's "Three Strikes and You're Out" legislation, enacted in 1994. That state's Three Strikes measure calls for the imposition of prison terms of at least 25 years' imprisonment (and up to life) upon conviction of certain felonies. The first two "strikes" need not actually be violent—a burglary conviction will do. The third "strike" may be any felony, including many commonplace property offences.[1] In a much publicized recent case, a person with two prior burglary convictions was given a virtual life sentence upon his subsequent conviction of an offence involving the snatching a slice of pizza from a child. Such sanctions are plainly out of all proportion to the gravity of the defendant's conduct, but only the harshest measures are said to suffice. Michael Howard, Britain's Home Secretary for the period 1993–97, secured the enactment of his own lesser version of Three Strikes: giving lengthy prison sentences (ones traditionally reserved for crimes of violence) to offenders convicted for the third time of burglary and drug offences. His Labour Government successor, Jack Straw, has put a portion of these measures into effect.[2]

A second element in the politics of law and order is the explicit appeal to fear. Much tougher penal policies are said to be necessary because crime represents a threat of such extraordinary magnitude. Such appeals are typified by the slogan which the Swedish Conservative Party put on Stockholm's buses in the 1991 election campaign: "They [the criminals] should sit inside so that you can go outside". The suggestion is that the streets of Stockholm had been taken over by marauders who had to be removed before decent Swedes could venture outside their homes again.

Criminal justice policy-making has always involved a certain amount of posturing. Vigorous steps against crime were urged during elections— often followed, however, by adoption of more pragmatic policies. What is different about "law and order" in the 1980s and 1990s is the stridency of the appeals to fear; the greater harshness of the measures proposed; and the willingness actually to adopt such measures. Three Strikes was not just a campaign slogan but actually became law.

Any Substantive Penal Aims?

Traditionally, penal measures have been conceived of and debated in terms of certain substantive purposes. There have been two main traditions. One is that of Jeremy Bentham, according to which penal measures should aim chiefly at reducing the rate of crime—through their rehabilitative, incapacitative or deterrent effects (see Chapters 1 to 3 above). This tradition has diverse manifestations, with some of its adherents urging mild measures, and others urging more stringent policies. (An example of the latter is the "selective incapacitation" strategy of targeting supposed high-risk offenders for lengthy prison terms, urged by the American criminologist James Q. Wilson and some of his colleagues during the mid-1980s (see Selections 3.6 and 3.7 above).) Another tradition (said to go back to Kant, although his observations on punishment were actually quite obscure) holds that concerns about justice should be paramount, and that sanctions should be designed fairly to reflect the degree of reprehensibleness of the criminal conduct (see Chapter 4 above). Although some critics have asserted that this latter approach supports severe measures, most of its advocates have supported significant reductions in sanction levels.[3] Different as these traditions are, they share an emphasis on substantive aims: some penological objective is to be promoted through punishment, whether it be less crime, more justice, or a combination of these. The emphasis on substantive aims makes penal measures debatable on their merits. For example, Wilson's "selective incapacitation"—extensively debated in the mid-1980s—lost considerable credibility when further research suggested that the likely crime-prevention benefits were more modest than originally projected.[4]

Disturbingly, "law and order", modern style, shows little concern for any of these substantive objectives. It is certainly unconcerned with justice or proportionality; indeed, a central theme is the imposition of sanctions having little relation to the gravity of the conduct. California's Three Strikes is a dramatic example: two routine burglaries and a third conviction for a lesser offence suffices for lifetime or near-lifetime imprisonment.

Is crime prevention the aim? "Law and order" rhetoric often employs the language of crime prevention: recidivists, drug offenders, or whomever are to be locked up for lengthy periods to "get them off the streets". Nevertheless, such measures do not seem to be designed seriously as ways of improving the incapacitative effectiveness of the sentence. Incapacitation depends on restraining an offender during the most active phase of his criminal career. Three Strikes imposes its lengthiest prison terms late in that career, when the offender has already accumulated a substantial record of convictions; and those prison terms are likely to extend for many years beyond the likely termination of his criminal career.[5] In England, Michael Howard introduced "boot camps" for young offenders—that is, detention in camp-style facilities employing tough "military" discipline. The proposal was made at a time when boot camps had already been tried extensively in the USA, and repeated research evaluations had reported disappointing results.[6]

The unprogrammatic character of such measures is confirmed by the lack of interest in research. Whereas the "selective incapacitation" proposals of the mid-80s were accompanied by elaborate efforts to estimate crime-reduction effects (see Selection 3.6 above), no comparable efforts were made by the proponents of the various versions of Three Strikes when these measures were introduced. The 1996 UK Government White Paper proposing mandatory prison sentences for third-time burglars and drug dealers was notable for its absence of argument or supporting data.[7]

"Law and Order" and Resentment

If "law and order" politics is thus deficient in substantive penal aims, what is its purpose? It seems largely concerned with fostering and exploiting public resentment of crime and criminals.[8] Implicit in "law and order" appeals—indeed, often explicit in them—is the notion of the targeted group (say, criminals) as creatures wholly different from ourselves. The persons to be dealt with—repeat offenders, drug dealers or whomever—are characterized as being vicious and debased creatures. The perpetrator of the "third strike" is seen as a predator at worst and a parasite at best, which is what supposedly makes it appropriate to put him in prison for very long periods.

In "law and order" politics' most virulent form, this stance on offenders is coupled with similar postures aimed at other unpopular groups: the politics of resentment may have criminals as only one of its targets. It seems no accident that Three Strikes in California was adopted at the same time as a measure denying access to schooling and medical care for the children of illegal immigrants;[9] criminal recidivists and illegal entrants from Mexico were treated as two subspecies of undesirables. Likewise, it is not surprising that former British Home Secretary Michael Howard during his term in office not only advocated much increased criminal sentences, but also a crackdown on asylum-seekers and gypsies.[10]

If "law and order" measures lack apparent substantive goals of justice or crime prevention, and cater mostly to resentment, are their advocates being irrational? They are not. The strategies have an instrumental function, but it is not primarily a substantive one: it is concerned, instead, with the acquisition of power. Exploiting popular resentment is a way— and sometimes, unhappily, an effective way—of garnering political support.[11]

Modern society provides fertile ground for such appeals. Crime is a highly visible (and frightening) social phenomenon, made all the more so by the manner in which it is reported in the media. Modern life also has multifold frustrations that do not relate directly to crime, but rather to the general bleakness of existence for so many people; crime serves as an apt symbol for these manifold ills. Today's societies also include a variety of groups (including criminals but not limited just to them) that frighten and exasperate the ordinary citizen. Appeals to resentment can tap these various sources of ill-feeling.

"Law and order" politics, however, is no mere response to popular animus, much as some politicians might wish to characterize it that way. A recent study of public attitudes about crime in the USA suggests the extent to which those attitudes have been shaped by the media's and politicians' characterizations of crime and criminals.[12] An examination of British public attitudes, based on the British Crime Survey, has found that the British public greatly overestimates the prevalence of violent crime, and much underestimates actual sentence levels imposed by the courts.[13] The images which the media and "law and order" politics have been supplying of extraordinary rates of predatory crime and of "soft" judges seems to have contributed to such misconceptions.

Examples of the political use of "law and order" appeals are numerous. In the late 1980s, then President George Bush used his "War on Drugs" as a means of demonstrating that he was made of sterner fibre than his detractors had suggested. California's Governor Pete Wilson made the Three Strikes law (plus the measure aimed at illegal immigrants) the centrepiece of his strategy for re-election as that state's chief executive, and later of his campaign for the 1996 Republican presidential nomination.[14] Michael Howard announced his various crime initiatives not from Whitehall but (in the most strident terms) at Blackpool, during annual Conservative Party conferences; "law and order" became one of the few unifying themes for an increasingly divided party.[15]

Beyond the purely instrumental aim of exploiting popular resentments to gain or retain power, "law and order" politics can have a base in ideology. Populist politics, at least in some of its versions, contains a strong element of the purge mentality. Sharp distinctions are drawn between ordinary, respectable persons and various "undesirables" who supposedly threaten the physical and moral health of the community. Against those undesirables, it is said to be necessary to proceed with utmost ferocity. The purge, the inner war, is seen as not merely dealing with supposed threats, but also as reviving the vigour and moral health of the community. Such sentiments were most clearly apparent in European right-wing movements of the 1930s, but they remain present also in some contemporary political ideologies.[16] To see conceptions of the targeted groups as different and inferior, it is necessary merely to peruse the writings of, say, Charles Murray—with his claims about an "underclass" comprised of persons of low intelligence and low self-control.[17]

Unfortunately, "law and order" politics is not restricted to rightist political ideologies. Once introduced into political discourse, the phenomenon has a tendency to spread. In the late 1990s, for example, several European parties of the moderate left have espoused and pressed for the adoption of surprisingly repressive penal policies. At least in part, the strategy seems to be one seeking protection from vulnerability to attacks for being "soft" on crime, by showing toughness on penal issues.

This means that use of appeals to resentment in criminal policy is not a simple matter of right versus left political philosophies. Some Conservative governments—notably Mrs Thatcher's Conservatives during the late 1980s,[18] and Helmut Kohl's German Conservatives during the 1980s and early 1990s—were quite pragmatic in their criminal-justice policies, as have been some social-democratic governments such as Sweden's. Other social democrats have been willing to resort to "law and order" appeals, as is true not only of British Labour during the 1997 election,[19] but also of some German social-democratic politicians in the late 1990s.[20] In the USA, both Republicans and Democrats invoke "law and order".

Do "law and order" politics derive from influence of a penal-industrial complex, as Nils Christie has suggested?[21] I think not—or at least, not primarily. Private prisons are a growing business, and the large companies owning them have considerable financial incentives to press for more extensive use of imprisonment. Some police officials have also been vocal in urging tough penal policies, as have recently certain prison guards' unions (for example, in California). Other officials, however, have expressed different views: correctional chiefs and prison governors in many West European countries, for example, have been notably unenthusiastic about raising punishment levels—in part because of the prison crowding and resulting management problems to which this would lead.[22] More fundamentally, however, efforts to lobby for tougher penalties require an underlying political dynamic: if "law and order" appeals were to lose their perceived vote-getting potential, the entrepreneurs of private prisons and their lobbyists would lose much of their influence.

"Law and Order" as Symbolism: Communicating What?

In a critical essay about the mandatory sentences being enacted in various parts of the USA, Michael Tonry speaks of them as being mainly "symbolic" measures[23]—but then, symbolic of what? As earlier selections in this book suggest, the communicative character of punishment is receiving increasing attention (see Selection 4.3 and 4.4 above). Can "law and order" be seen as a species of communicative punishment?

If the aim is communicative, it is communication of a particular kind: namely, the expression of social approbrium.[24] Repeat burglars or drug offenders are to be given lengthy prison sentences as a way of giving expression to the contempt with which such persons and their conduct are to be regarded. On this view, it would not be necessary (as preventionists hold) to try to make the penalty optimally effective; nor (as desert theorists wish) to make the penalty commensurate in its severity with the gravity of the crime. The sole concern, instead, is with the audience: with publicly expressing strong animus against crime and criminals. If imprisonment (or imprisonment for long terms) does this expressive job best, so be it.

On the desert-oriented version of penal communication discussed in Chapter 4 above, the censure is visited upon the offender, perceived as a person capable of moral agency. Certain conduct is deemed reprehensible; and the sanction is supposed to convey the requisite measure of blame for that conduct. However, the actor should only receive as much censure as comports with the degree of reprehensibleness of his conduct. And since the blame is being conveyed through the medium of penal deprivation, the severity of that treatment should fairly reflect the gravity of his criminal conduct and not more: hence the requirements of proportionality (see more fully, Selection 4.4 above).

On the "law and order" version, however, the convicted offender is excluded from the moral universe of discourse, and is made to serve merely as the object of and conduit for public messages of denunciation. If tougher sanctions express that message best, they are deemed preferable—and the offender is allowed no standing to claim that the sanction overstates the blame due to him. Such a perspective is ethically problematic, because it treats the offender as little more than an object, and provides no principled grounds for limitation. If the aim is to devise sanctions that register resentment of criminals in visible and dramatic form, there could be no reason for rejecting sanctions (however harsh these might be) that provide the best drama.

Collateral Crime-Prevention Effects?

Even if "law and order" measures do not really aim at crime prevention, might they have collateral preventative effects anyway? Granting that lifetime imprisonment of third-time burglars makes little sense as an incapacitant, might not such a measure "work" nonetheless—for example, as an *in terrorem* deterrent?

Some penologists have recently asserted that the extraordinary increase in imprisonment levels associated with American "law and order" policies has helped bring about a significant decline in crime rates.[25] The evidence they bring forward is actually quite weak: changes in the severity of punishment in England and the USA in the past decade and a half have not even been strongly correlated with crime rates.[26] But even if such claims could be sustained better empirically, problems remain.

The most obvious problem is ethical: should (say) burglars be dealt with through such seemingly unjust measures as the imposition of near-life-imprisonment for a third offence? Another problem is that "law and order" measures disregard social and human costs. In the selective-incapacitation debate of the 1980s, much attention was given to the impact of incapacitative policies on prison populations (see Selections 3.6 and 3.7 above). Proponents of selective incapacitation argued that this approach was preferable to across-the-board imprisonment policies, in that they called for less extensive use of prison resources; critics of selective incapacitation, in turn, questioned proponents' claims of saved space. With "law and order" measures, however, costs tend to be disregarded. California's Three Strikes measures may have devastating long-run impacts not only on the processing of criminal cases, but also on the state resources available for other social ends, such as higher education.[27] Such concerns, however, seem to have been accorded little weight when the proposal was adopted.

If "law and order" measures chiefly serve symbolic rather than substantive ends, moreover, they are not likely to be abandoned by their proponents were their impact on crime to prove disappointing. In the mid-1980s, England introduced more demanding regimes for short sentences of detention for juveniles, as a "short, sharp shock"; but subsequently ended the policy when studies suggested that it had little measurable effect. But "law and order" policies, mobilized as they are through appeals to resentment, are not apt to be given up if the policies fail to reduce crime —indeed, that may just trigger more appeals to resentment. (The American advocates of mandatory sentences, for example, did not admit failure when various empirical studies of these measures suggested that their impact on crime rates was marginal.[27]) As a result, claims that "law and order" measures "work" to prevent crime seem to be just window dressing—a way of providing respectability for policies driven by other concerns.

Dealing with "Law-and-Order" Politics

How should penologists respond to the "law and order" phenomenon? I have only a few, quite tentative suggestions. First, the phenomenon needs to be recognized for what it is—for otherwise, certain current developments in criminal policy become incomprehensible. Recent policy-making on sentencing issues in a number of American jurisdictions, for example, have been crucially influenced by "law and order" politics: this is true, for example, of much of the sentencing policies of states such as Texas, California and New York; of American drug policies during the 1980s and 1990s; and of sentencing policies for Federal offences, including these embodied in the guidelines of the U.S. Sentencing Commission.[29] Efforts to attribute these policies to traditional penology—whether to crime-prevention theories or to desert theories and to the guidelines movement[30]—simply will mislead. It is necessary to understand that such policies are primarily designed to stimulate and exploit resentment at crime and criminals, not to promote this or that penological objective.

Secondly, penal reformers need to take the potential impact of "law and order" politics into account. A reform which seems sensible on its merits may backfire in a jurisdiction that is strongly affected or potentially affected. Consider the device of sentencing guidelines, discussed in Chapter 5 above. Guidelines have operated reasonably well in a number of American states such as Minnesota and Oregon, where they have had a modicum of success in keeping prison populations from rising too quickly.[31] But the guideline device is not suitable everywhere. The U.S. Sentencing Commission, the body empowered to write sentencing guidelines for federal crimes, was established in the mid-1980s, at a time when Congress had shown a willingness to legislate very large penalty increases, and when the Reagan Administration's Justice Department was committed to an unambiguous "law and order" stance. Not surprisingly, that stance was reflected in the appointments to the Commission, and in the character of the guidelines that body issued.[32]

Thirdly, while it is easy enough to recognize the importance of "law and order" politics in general, it is much more difficult to assess its potential force in a particular jurisdiction. In 1991, England reformed its sentencing law to give considerably more prominence to the principle of proportionality, and to encourage more parsimonious use of imprisonment. The measure passed under a Conservative Government, with considerable support from opposition parties. England, at the time, seemed blessedly free from American-style posturing on penal policies, and few observers expected any great change in the political environment of criminal justice. Two years later, however, there was a dramatic *volte-face*, with both major parties competing about who could appear to be the toughest on penal questions.[33] It would have required considerable political discernment to have forecasted this change.

Certain general factors might help account for variations in the degree of politicization of crime issues in different countries. One factor is, of course, levels of popular resentment—which depend not only on crime rates but on the way in which crime is dealt with in the media, and on the degree of social and political polarization within a country. Another factor may be variations in popular "sensibility", in Norbert Elias' meaning of the term.[34] "Law and order" politics involves a willingness to impose drastic deprivations on members of the targeted groups—and that willingness may vary in different political cultures. Yet another factor is the influence of elites. Denunciation of elites has often been fashionable, but (in Europe, at least) it has largely been certain elites—criminologists, senior correctional officials, and in some places judges and prosecutors— that have led efforts in recent decades to scale punishments down; such groups may be essential for resisting escalation of punishment today.[35] The more strongly populist a country's criminal justice politics are, the greater the potential influence of law and order. Factors such as these may explain, at least to some extent, why some American states have been more susceptible than (say) continental West European countries.

However, in law and order politics (as I have mentioned above) politicians tend to lead rather than follow public opinion. It is not easy to assess the factors which, at different times, induce political parties to resort to these kind of appeals. Sometimes, this has a base in ideology: a party which emphasizes the purge mentality and which generally stresses the need for a crackdown on "undesirables" is likely to urge a draconian penal policy: it is hardly surprising that rightist politicians such as France's Jean-Marie Le Pen or Austria's Jorg Haider favour such measures. In other instances, however, the embrace of such policies may be tactical: they may be adopted by a social democratic party, if it is fearful of attacks from the right and if it lacks a tradition of strong civil-liberties concerns.

More reflection and research about the "law and order" phenomenon is urgently required. We need to understand better why this kind of penal politics has flourished in the present historical situation, and what social and political factors tend to foster or impede it.[36] We need to distinguish the "law and order" phenomenon from other subspecies of symbolic criminal-justice politics. One such subspecies seems to be a certain mixture of nostalgia and notions of "instilling discipline", represented by measures such as curfews for young teenagers. The children involved are not necessarily characterized as vermin or targeted for drastic sanctions; the idea, rather, seems to be the instillation of a certain "benevolent" discipline: those young people should be made to toe the line and be kept off the streets, as they were in the "Good Old Days". While this latter perspective has its own troublesome aspects, they are different ones.

The real difficulty of responding to "law and order" appeals is that its proponents seldom allow themselves to be drawn into a debate on the merits. How can one argue with a politician who urges escalation of prison sentences because "prison works", if his real criterion for working is so little concerned with the effectiveness or fairness of such measures, and so much concerned with using these measures to mobilize public resentment? Presenting evidence on the ineffectiveness, unfairness, or costliness of such policies is only a start. What is also needed is to lay bare the character of the policies as primarily directed to resentment; and to mobilize the sources of resistance to such policies as exist in the jurisdiction.

Were "law and order" politics to recede, what kind of sentencing policy would remain? One cannot confidently say. While greater attention would be paid to matters of substance, these (as suggested above) are themselves contestable. It would still be necessary to decide upon the relative emphasis to be given to crime-preventative and to desert-oriented approaches. Debates would continue about whether greater or less rigour in punishment could achieve the desired aims best. Hopefully, however, the various penological aims would be taken seriously, as would evidence and argument about how they may best be achieved. Meanwhile, penologists (however they might disagree on rationale and preferred sentencing strategies) should understand that "law and order" appeals are of a different character, and should unite in seeking to resist these appeals. It is a misunderstanding to try to characterize "Three Strikes" as a misguided application of retributivism or crime-prevention; it is neither of these, but rather a way of trying to mobilize fear and loathing.

Notes

1. A description of the legislation and a discussion of its potential impact is set forth in Peter W. Greenwood, *et al.*, *Three Strikes and You're Out: Estimated Benefits and Costs of California's New Mandatory-Sentence Law* (RAND Corporation, 1994).

2. Howard's Crime (Sentences) Act 1997 prescribes a minimum sentence of three years for third burglary offences, and seven years for third drug offences. The legislation, in accord with British practice, was to take effect only when and to the extent that the minister involved (in this case, the Home Secretary) filed with Parliament an instrument of implementation. The Conservative Government fell shortly after passage of the law in the spring of 1997, not permitting Mr. Howard to implement it. His Labour Government successor, Mr. Straw, has put the mandatory minimum for third-time drug dealers into effect, albeit not the mandatory minimum for burglary.

3. See Selection 4.4 above; see also Andrew von Hirsch, *Censure and Sanctions* (1993), ch. 10; Andrew Ashworth, *Sentencing and Criminal Justice*, 2nd edn. (1995), ch. 9.

4. See Selection 3.7 above; see also Franklin Zimring and Gordon Hawkins, *Incapacitation* (1995), pp. 25–38.

5. See Selection 3.7 above and Greenwood, *et al.*, above n. 1.

6. Those research evaluations are summarized, and the relevant citations provided, in Doris Layton MacKenzie, "Boot Camps: A National Assessment", 5(4) *Overcrowded Times* 1, 14–18 (August 1994).

7. The White Paper preceding the Crime (Sentences) Act 1997 (see n. 2 above) asserts that the proposed mandatory sentences would reduce crime rates for the affected crimes by 20 per cent, and utilizes that claimed effect in estimating the measure's impact on prison populations. However, the 20 per cent figure

was pulled from the air: Howard's successor, in reply to a Parliamentary question, has conceded that the figure was not derived from any actual empirical estimates.

8. For more on resentment and penal policies, see Andrew von Hirsch, "The Future of the Proportionate Sentence", in Thomas Blomberg and Stanley Cohen (eds.), *Punishment and Social Control: Essays in Honor of Sheldon Messinger* (1995), pp. 123–43 and especially pp. 131–4.

9. This measure, Proposition 187, was also passed in 1994 by popular initiative. Its provision on medical care denies non-emergency care to such children.

10. For discussion of Howard's measures against gypsies, which became law as part of the Criminal Justice and Public Order Act of 1994, see Sue Campbell, "Gypsies: Criminalisation of A Way of Life?" [1995] *Criminal Law Review* 28.

11. Svend Ranulf, *Moral Indignation and Middle Class Morality* (1938).

12. Katherine Beckett, *Making Crime Pay: Law and Order in Contemporary American Politics* (1997).

13. Michael Hough and Julian Roberts, *Attitudes to Punishment: Findings from the British Crime Survey* (Home Office Research Study No. 179, 1998).

14. His campaign for the American Republican Presidential nomination ultimately did not succeed, but during late 1994 and early 1995, he was spoken of as a serious candidate—largely on the the basis of the political credibility established through such measures.

15. Speech of Hon. Michael Howard to the 100th Conservative Party Conference at Blackpool, 6 October 1993.

16. Stephen J. Lee, *The European Dictatorships 1918–1945* (1987); Hans-Georg Betz, *Radical Right-Wing Populism in Western Europe* (1994).

17. See, e.g., Charles Murray, *The Emerging English Underclass* (London: Institute for Economic Affairs, 1990); Charles Murray and Richard Herrenstein, *The Bell Curve: Intelligence and Class Structure in American Life* (1994).

18. This was the period when Mrs Thatcher's Government developed the legislation that later (under the early days of her successor) became the Criminal Justice Act 1991, which made proportionality the primary criterion of sentence and sought to reduce reliance on imprisonment. For discussion of the 1991 Act, see Ashworth, n. 3 above, and Selection 5.2.

19. The 1997 Labour campaign featured the slogan, "Tough on crime and tough on the causes of crime", but the emphasis was definitely on tough crime policies. In office, the Labour Government's early steps have been in the direction of stringent crime policies—including the partial implementation of Michael Howard's mandatory minimum sentences (see n. 2 above), and the sponsorship in its Crime and Disorder Bill of sweeping and very severe measures aimed at disruptive neighbours (for a description and critique of this latter scheme, see Ashworth, A., Gardner, J. *et al.*, "Neighbouring on the Oppressive" (1998) 16 *Criminal Justice* 7. At the time of this writing (January 1998), however, it is still too early to make any confident characterization of the main thrust of Labour's crime policies. An important indication will be the Government's stance on the use of imprisonment, and the character of the reasons given for that stance.

20. In a nationally-significant election in the city-state of Hamburg in mid-1997, the

chief executive and social-democratic candidate, Henning Voscherau, made "internal security" his main theme. Contrary to expectation, he lost.

21. Nils Christie, *Crime Control as Industry* (1993).

22. See more fully my review of Christie, "The Logic of Prison Growth", (1994) 57 *Modern Law Review* 476, particularly pp. 476–7.

23. Michael Tonry, *Sentencing Matters* (1995), ch. 5.

24. Dan M. Kahan develops this kind of denunciatory conception in a recent essay. The emphasis on punishment as public drama is present in his account, as is the rejection of desert constraints. He does state a preference for "shameful" non-custodial punishments, but only because he feels these could be given sufficient dramatic content. But the logic of his position would support "law and order" initiatives that include much-increased use of imprisonment, provided merely that one were to assume that Kahan's suggested alternatives would provide insufficient drama, compared with the expressiveness of long prison sentences. While such a conception might seem to derive from Durkheimian conceptions of punishment as promoting social solidarity, its crucial difference is that it is not just describing a latent social function of punishment but asserting that criminal sanctions *ought* to serve this function. See, Dan M. Kahan, "What Do Alternative Sanctions Mean?" (1996) 63 *University of Chicago Law Review* 591.

25. See, e.g., Charles Murray, *Does Prison Work?* (Institute of Economic Affairs, 1997).

26. It is likelihood of conviction, rather than severity of punishment, that correlates significantly with crime rates in the USA and England. There is also little evidence as to how much the public was aware of changes in sentence levels in the two countries, and such awareness is essential for sentencing to work; for the issue of public awareness, see Hough and Roberts, n. 13 above. The possible deterrent effects of recent changes in sentencing policy is examined in some depth in Andrew von Hirsch, A. E. Bottoms, *et al.*, *Criminal Deterence and Penal Policy: A Literature Review of Recent Research* (forthcoming 1998).

27. See Greenwood *et al.*, above n. 1.

28. See Tonry, above n. 23, ch. 2.

29. Thus in an analysis of the U.S. Sentencing Commission's guidelines, Anthony Doob suggests that the Commission's principal aim was substantially to raise penalty levels rather than to implement any identifiable set of principles. See Anthony Doob, "The United States Sentencing Commission Guidelines", in C. M. V. Clarkson and R. M. Morgan (eds.), *The Politics of Sentencing Reform* (1995).

30. For claims that the sentencing-guidelines movement led to large punishment increases in the USA, see David Rothman, "More of the Same: American Criminal Justice Policies in the 1990s", in T. G. Blomberg and S. Cohen (eds.), *Punishment and Social Control: Essays in Honor of Sheldon L. Messinger* (1995); for a reply, emphasizing the influence of "law and order" politics, see Andrew von Hirsch, "The Future of the Proportionate Sentence" in the same volume, particularly pp. 133–4.

31. Tonry, above n. 23, ch. 2.

32. See Doob, above n. 29.

33. For the Criminal Justice Act 1991, see n. 18 above. For an account of the *volte face* in 1993, see Lord Windlesham, *Responses to Crime: Legislating With the Tide* (1996), chs. 1–4.
34. See David Garland's discussion of Elias' notion of "sensibility" in his *Punishment and Modern Society* (1990), ch. 10.
35. Von Hirsch, above n. 22.
36. For two interesting theoretical perspectives, see A.E. Bottoms, "The Philosophy and Politics of Sentencing", in Clarkson and Morgan (eds.), *The Politics of Sentencing Reform*, n. 29 above; David Garland, "The Limits of the Sovereign State", (1996) 36 *British Journal of Criminology* 445.

Suggestions for Further Reading

Ranulf, S., *Moral Indignation and Middle Class Psychology* (1938); Cohen, S., *Folk Devils and Moral Panics* (1972, repr. 1987); Hall, S. *et al.*, *Policing the Crisis* (1978); Hall, S., "Drifting into a Law and Order Society" (1980), republished in J. Muncie, E. McLaughlin, and M. Langan (eds.), *Criminological Perspectives: A Reader* (1996); Garland, D., *Punishment and Modern Society* (1990), ch. 10; Murray, C., *The Emerging British Underclass* (1990); Scheingold, S., *The Politics of Street Crime* (1991); Christie, N., *Crime Control as Industry* (1993); von Hirsch, A., "The Logic of Prison Growth", (1994) 57 *Modern Law Review* 476; Simon, J., *Poor Discipline* (1993); Cohen, S., "Social Control and the Politics of Reconstruction", in D. Nelken (ed.), *The Futures of Criminology* (1994); Murray, C. and Herrenstein, R., *The Bell Curve* (1994); Rothman, D., "More of the Same: American Criminal Justice Policies in the 1990s",in T. G. Blomberg and S. Cohen (eds.), *Punishment and Social Control* (1995); von Hirsch, A., "The Future of the Proportionate Sentence," in the same volume; Bottoms, A. E., "The Philosophy and Politics of Punishment and Sentencing" in C. M. V. Clarkson and R. M. Morgan (eds.),*The Politics of Sentencing Reform* (1995); Doob, A., "The United States Sentencing Commission Guidelines", in the same volume; Tonry, M. *Malign Neglect* (1995); Tonry, M., *Sentencing Matters* (1996), ch. 5; Kahan, D. M., "What Do Alternative Sanctions Mean?" (1996) 63 *University of Chicago Law Review* 591; Garland, D., "The Limits of the Sovereign State", (1996) 36 *British Journal of Criminology* 445; Windlesham, D., *Responses to Crime*, vol. 3 (1996); Cohen, C., "Crime and Politics: Spot the Difference", (1996) 47 *British Journal of Sociology* 1; Murray, C., *Does Prison Work?* (1997); Beckett, K., *Making Crime Pay: Law and Order in Contemporary American Politics* (1997); Morgan, R. and Downes, D., "Dumping the 'Hostages to Fortune'—The Politics of Law and Order in Post-War Britain" in Maguire, M., Morgan, R., and Reiner, R., *The Oxford Handbook of Criminology*, 2nd edn. (1997); Hough, M., and Roberts, J. V., *Attitudes to Punishment: Findings from the British Crime Survey* (Home Office Research Study No. 179, 1998).

Index